£15-95

C000178052

Elements of Export
Marketing and Management

BOOKS BY THE SAME AUTHOR:

(1984) *Dictionary of Commercial Terms and Abbreviations*, 1st edn, (6000 entries), Witherby and Co. Ltd, London.

(1985) *Elements of Export Practice*, 2nd edn, Chapman & Hall, London.

(1986) *Dictionary of Shipping/International Trade Terms and Abbreviations* (9000 entries), Witherby and Co. Ltd, London.

(1986) *Elements of Port Operation and Management*, 1st edn, Chapman & Hall, London.

(1988) *Economics of Shipping Practice and Management*, 2nd edn, Chapman & Hall, London.

(1988) *Dictionary of English–Arabic Shipping/International Trade/Commercial Terms and Abbreviations*, (4400 entries), 1st edn, Witherby and Co. Ltd, London.

(1989) *Import/Export Documentation*, 1st edn, Chapman & Hall, London.

(1989) *Dictionary of Multilingual Commercial/International Trade/Shipping Terms in English/French/German/Spanish* (13 000 entries), 1st edn, Witherby and Co. Ltd, London.

(1989) *Elements of Shipping*, 6th edn, Chapman & Hall, London.

Elements of Export Marketing and Management

Second edition

Alan E. Branch
F.C.I.T., F.I.Ex.

Shipping Executive/Lecturer/Chief Examiner
Shipping and Export Practice/Shipping and Export Consultant

CHAPMAN & HALL
London · New York · Tokyo · Melbourne · Madras

UK	Chapman & Hall, 2–6 Boundary Row, London SE1 8HN
USA	Chapman & Hall, 29 West 35th Street, New York NY10001
JAPAN	Chapman & Hall Japan, Thomson Publishing Japan, Hirakawacho Nemoto Building, 7F, 1–7–11 Hirakawa-cho, Chiyoda-ku, Tokyo 102
AUSTRALIA	Chapman & Hall Australia, Thomas Nelson Australia, 102 Dodds Street, South Melbourne, Victoria 3205
INDIA	Chapman & Hall India, R. Seshadri, 32 Second Main Road, CIT East, Madras 600 035

First edition 1984
Second edition 1990
Reprinted 1991

© 1984, 1990 Alan E. Branch

Typeset in 10 on 12 pt Bembo by Photoprint, 9–11 Alexandra Lane, Torquay, Devon
Printed in Great Britain by T.J. Press (Padstow) Ltd, Padstow, Cornwall

ISBN 0 412 35540 X

British Library Cataloguing in Publication Data

Branch, Alan E. (Alan Edward) 1933–
Elements of export marketing and management. –
2nd. ed.
1. Great Britain. Exporting. Marketing
I. Title
658.8'48'0941

ISBN 0–412–35540–X

Library of Congress Cataloging in Publication Data

Elements of export marketing and management /
Alan E. Branch. – 2nd ed.
p.   cm.
Includes bibliographical references (p.).
ISBN 0–412–35540–X
1. Export marketing. 2. Export marketing –
Management. I. Title.
HF1416.B73   1990
658.8'48–dc20   89–27715
CIP

To Duncan and Malcolm

Contents

Acknowledgements

Association of British Chambers of Commerce
British International Freight Association
British Overseas Trade Board
British Shippers Council
British Standards Institution
British Telecom International
Central Office of Information
Foremecon Services Ltd
German Chamber of Industry and Commerce
HM Customs and Excise
International Chamber of Commerce
Institute of Export
Lloyds Bank PLC
London Chamber of Commerce and Industry
Midland Bank PLC
Nielsen Marketing Trends
Research Solutions Ltd
Road Haulage Association
Simpler Trade Procedures Board
Swiss Bank Corporation

Preface to the second edition

It is appropriate that the second edition of this established book – sold in over 150 countries and regarded by many as the standard work on the subject – should be published at a time of international trade expansion and change. This edition reflects such change, and has been enlarged to meet the new opportunities and techniques found in the process of export marketing and management.

The book continues to provide a practical overall understanding of the techniques of export marketing, and also to help the exporters, large or small, to develop and expand their overseas market(s) profitably. Overall, the book reflects the author's 30 years' experience in the industry, both in the manufacturing and consultancy fields including International Donor Agencies. The increasingly important role of export management is also covered with special attention being given to guidelines and checklists. It stresses particularly the need to be completely professional and totally committed to overseas trade and thereby develop viable markets and customer loyalty in a competitive environment.

The book is ideal, not only for students preparing for export marketing examinations, but also for persons employed in export marketing/shipping offices. In short it is an *aide-mémoire* to those engaged in export marketing and is regarded by many as the Export Executive's handbook. Every Export Company should have a copy in their reference library. Readers who wish to know more about the distribution and processing of export orders, transport modes, freight rates and export documentation should study the companion volume *Elements of Export Practice* (see Appendix A).

The opportunity has been taken to widen the scope of the book, with new chapters being introduced concerned with the 1992 Single Market Entity (Chapter 13) and export marketing strategy (Chapter 14). In addition, a number of existing chapters have been expanded in the areas of export selling/negotiation, market research, licensing, pricing strategy, joint ventures, overseas business visits and market selection.

Such enrichment in the Second edition should further the book's popularity in institutes, colleges and universities throughout the world. The book will be useful for students taking International Trade/Marketing/Business/

Distribution examinations at degree/diploma level. It will be particularly ideal for examinations conducted by the Institute of Export Part I and II, Institute of Marketing diploma and certificate, British International Freight Association, Institute of Transport Administration, Chartered Institute of Transport, Business Technical and Education Council and British Council.

The book is ideally suited not only for university and polytechnic courses in the United Kingdom, but also for courses in Hong Kong, Nigeria, Australia, Malaysia, Jamaica, the USA, the Middle East and Third World countries. It will be ideal for students or Export Executives taking a short export marketing course.

The subject is treated in a practical way, providing the reader with an overall understanding of export marketing practice on a cost-effective basis, in a competitive environment. Emphasis is placed on complete professionalism and commitment together with the strategies and techniques to identify and develop profitable overseas markets. Attention is also given to the market entry option and the servicing and Management of the overseas market.

I am greatly indebted to the various organizations listed in the acknowledgements for the assistance they have so enthusiastically given me. The fact that the list is much enlarged reflects a wide interest in the book, and its further enrichment therefrom.

Finally, I would particularly like to acknowledge with grateful thanks the generous secretarial help from Mr and Mrs Splarn, my friend Maurice Hicks with proof-reading, and, as always, my dear wife Kathleen for her forbearance, encouragement and help in this task, especially with proof-reading.

A. E. B.

Senior Lecturer
Course Director – International Trade,
19 The Ridings   Basingstoke College of Technology
Emmer Green   Worting Road
Reading   Basingstoke

Foreword

The United Kingdom's prosperity depends increasingly on success in overseas trading. Those selling to buyers outside the United Kingdom face fierce competition. There is every reason to suppose that this picture will hold for the foreseeable future. If international trade is to make its maximum contribution to the well being of this country, it needs to be conducted with ever growing efficiency so as to yield an increasing share of the profits which are the life blood of industry and commerce. This demands professionalism. Those engaged in international trade at every level need to be as well trained and educated as possible.

Against this background I welcome Mr Branch's achievement in producing this book on the *Elements of Export Marketing and Management* to set alongside his successful *Elements of Export Practice*. The Institute is always happy when one of its Fellows contributes to export education, and I commend this work as a very useful addition.

THE EARL OF LIMERICK KBE
President of the Institute of Export

1 Introduction and the export marketing office

1.1 INTRODUCTION

Export marketing is the process of identifying, or anticipating, and satisfying a customer overseas. It is a management function and is undertaken, usually with the motivation of profit, by the seller. Essentially it is a communication function involving various stages in its execution until the export sale is completed.

It is also a partnership between the exporter and importer, each of whom derives benefit from the transaction. Hence it is up to the exporter to foster such relationships as will enable the importer to develop a business strategy always to buy the exporter's goods and not those from another source.

Export marketing involves many ingredients established through market research, embracing identifying the market and its characteristics/profile and volume, existing and potential; consumer needs; competition; import regulations; the promotion/advertising/selling of the product, and how best this can be done, by enquiring of the market entry options and their constraints and opportunities, both short and long term; the pricing of the product/service, which requires consideration of exchange rates, level of competition, product/distribution cost and mark up/profit level; product specification, reflecting overseas consumer needs and local trading regulations/requirements; and the overseas visit and negotiation of the sales contract embracing terms of sale, i.e. FOB, CIF, method of payment, distribution arrangements/options, delivery dates, and so on. Overall, this can best be described as the transfer of the marketing mix from manufacturing and selling a product in the home market to the overseas market(s). Marketing mix involves product specification, place of sale, price and promotion (see section 14.4). A fundamental point is the need to supply the overseas consumer with a product to accord with their taste/fashion/specification/design/price and reflect local trading regulations. Hence the exporter is likely to require his home market-designed product to be modified to meet the overseas territory needs/regulations which is an additional expense to the seller and accordingly may be reflected in the price. This introduces the next consideration, that of endeavouring to sell in those markets with similar or identical market tastes to the exporter's home market to lessen product cost modification and increase market volume potential. Conversely, if the home market volume is small, it is likely that the strategy will be to develop a product specification which commands the highest volume base, involving maybe six overseas territories, and thereby giving less importance to the home market needs. This is called market selection, and involves the development of the market cluster concept by selling in territories contiguous to each other with the added benefit of lower distribution cost.

Overall, the foregoing requires the export company to devise a strategy, and this will be contained in the company's three- to five-year business plan. Areas of consideration involve adequacy and sources of finance – payments arising from overseas trade take longer than those from the home market and usually involve more risk; adequacy of product, its product life, its competitiveness in price, specification and technology in the overseas territory, and modification cost; production resources within the company to cope with the additional volume; personnel resources embracing executives to research design, sell, market the product and artisans in the factory to produce it; evaluation of current markets served and reconciliation of overseas territory needs having regard to longer lead time from production to the consumer coupled with variation of seasonal needs; and the political/competitive situation in existing markets served and those the exporter is considering entering. Above all, it involves an effective market and cost analysis to determine the level of investment return and its reconciliation with market trends, opportunities and competition. This involves company strategy, as explained in section 14.

Export marketing is basically targeted towards the needs of the user/importer, who is anticipating the following with regard to the product or service offered:

1 a price which is regarded as reasonable;
2 built-in acceptability in terms of its quality, durability, performance and so on;
3 availability at the right time and place through the adequacy of the distribution arrangements;
4 honest and accurate information on what is being offered, together with all the necessary advice, where appropriate, on operation, care and maintenance including safety factors.

In regard to the intermediate customer such as the export house agent, retailer, or distributor, clients are looking not only for items (1) to (4) involving the product/service, but also the following requirements:
5 trade margins, discounts and credit policies which provide them with an adequate return for their role in sharing risk and arranging distribution;

6 reliability of the supplier on delivery promises and the maintenance of quality standards;
7 reasonable policies with regard to stipulated size of orders and an adequate market opportunity to liquidate their own investment in such order quantities (through territorial franchises etc.);
8 where appropriate, assistance with stock turn-over through advertising support and assistance with trade exhibitions, the provision of sales promotional material, retail display material, etc.;
9 suitable support in arranging an adequate level of after-sales service and an effective system for dealing with complaints.

Overall, one must bear in mind that the importance of each item will vary by circumstances. Moreover, one must acknowledge that export marketing involves obtaining sales from a required volume, at an adequate rate of flow per time period, at an acceptable level of cost in a competitive environment. It also involves different cultures, languages and local trading regulations.

Export marketing is a growth market and is an exciting and stimulating environment in which to work. It is demanding and requires total commitment to be successful. Above all, one must be completely professional and ideally have entrepreneurial and diplomatic qualities.

Given below are the benefits which accrue to the company selling overseas.

1 It generates additional income and profits.
2 It enables higher production volumes to be attained, thereby lowering unit costs and permitting the company to become more competitive.
3 It permits the company to operate/sell in a variety of markets each with a different profile and market risk/opportunity. Hence, such versatility enables the exporter to cushion more effectively any decline in one market as it is countered by an increase in another. This places the company in a stronger position in the market place with less risk of liquidation and better able to counter competition in any one market. Single market producers are very vulnerable in the market in which they operate, as they are compelled to meet any variation of market demand in order to remain competitive and sustain their market share. They are also more vulnerable to imported competition which may have more experience in other markets and greater strength of financial base to counter any price war. The latter criterion assumes one is operating in a free market with no local controls to protect the home producer, as obtained in COMECON and centrally-controlled markets.
4 The export company has a higher market profile compared with the single market producer. It tends to attract higher calibre management teams at all levels, reflecting the more challenging work environment and usually

higher salary level. The export marketing/sales executive has a far more stimulating/challenging job than his colleague developing the home market.
5 It generates substantial income to the visible exports account which in turn develops a high value and stable currency and, by bringing additional income to the country, generates jobs, higher earnings, improved living standards and better community facilities in terms of the country's infrastructure.
6 Export-led growth economies tend to generate less inflation risk and be more stable. The more a company produces for overseas markets, the lower the unit cost, which in turn requires more personnel and financial resources devoted to product research and development. This is set to become an ever more important area as companies become more competitive and base their sales and marketing penetration performance on technology and price competitiveness, including non-price areas such as warranties, after sales service, reliable delivery dates and so on.
7 Export growth companies tend to foster specialization by having volume markets. An example is the Japanese motor-cycle industry which, through its global marketing, has developed such specialization in the motor-cycle industry that a single-market producer could not complete either on price or advanced technology due to lack of finance, experienced engineering personnel and robotized production techniques.

There is no doubt that an increasing number of single-market producers must enter/develop overseas markets to become more competitive, lower unit cost, generate adequate funds for research and development, as otherwise, without government protection, the company will decline through import penetration of more competitively priced goods of superior quality, specification and more consumer-orientated in terms of their market needs.

1.2   ROLE OF THE EXPORT OFFICE

A successful exporting operation requires effective organization designed to enlarge the market share of the company. Above all, it must be profitable and well-paid personnel of a high calibre are instrumental in attaining this objective.

This portion of the chapter will consider the function of the export office with particular emphasis on the marketing role. It is essential, however, that the marketing and shipping departments work very closely together to ensure efficiency and customer satisfaction. If the importer is dissatisfied, because of poor distribution arrangements, the company is placing the prospect of repeat orders at risk.

The size of the company, the nature of its products, the profile of the overseas markets, and the scale of its export business are the main factors which influence the nature of an export organization. Moreover, company structure and organization, and how the export role can best be incorporated into it, must be taken into account. In broad terms, the industrial company has three functions – production, finance and sales. In addition, there are subsidiary activities which contribute significantly to the running of the company, including personnel, administration, research and development, training and purchasing.

The export department has two main functions: marketing and shipping. The marketing office is responsible for market research, sales, pricing enquiries, quotations, recording and checking orders, promotion and research, whilst the shipping department deals with transportation, distribution, documentation, packaging and costings for distribution. There must be close liaison at all times with the accounts department, particularly on credit control, costings, exchange rates and financial documentation/information and the production department to monitor the progress of the export order and ensure that the delivery date is met. The shipping office must ensure that the export order processes run smoothly from start to finish, with customer satisfaction and company profit in mind. Hence, all the aspects of an export operation are interlinked, with clearly defined functions and responsibilities of either a horizontal or a vertical export department organization and efficient, well-trained staff. Many export offices are computer-operated and provide computerized management data and documentation (see *Elements of Export Practice*, pages 316–21).

1.3   ORGANIZATION AND RESPONSIBILITIES

A small export department may consist of export manager, shipping clerk, word processor operator and accounts clerk. At first, the department may be engaged merely in shipping orders secured by the sales organization but, as the export trade develops, the department will enlarge and have its own sales organization – it will become a self-contained department. The overall aim of the export department is to collect sufficient data to enable them to quote, promptly and accurately, a competitive CIF or other delivery term price, for transporting any consignment to any important trading centre of the world. This involves an evaluation of the most suitable method of despatch and requires knowledge of rates, services, routes, transit times, terminal charges, insurance, packing, documentation, etc.

The export department must study the needs of different markets, their trends and likely future developments, and possible methods of increasing overseas sales. This involves the scrutiny of overseas agents, distributors' reports and adequate publicity through overseas journals/trade publications and local press. In addition, close liaison must be maintained with trade associations, donor agencies and relevant government departments on opportunities for market development. Overseas representatives must be kept informed of all developments at home (including manufacturing and

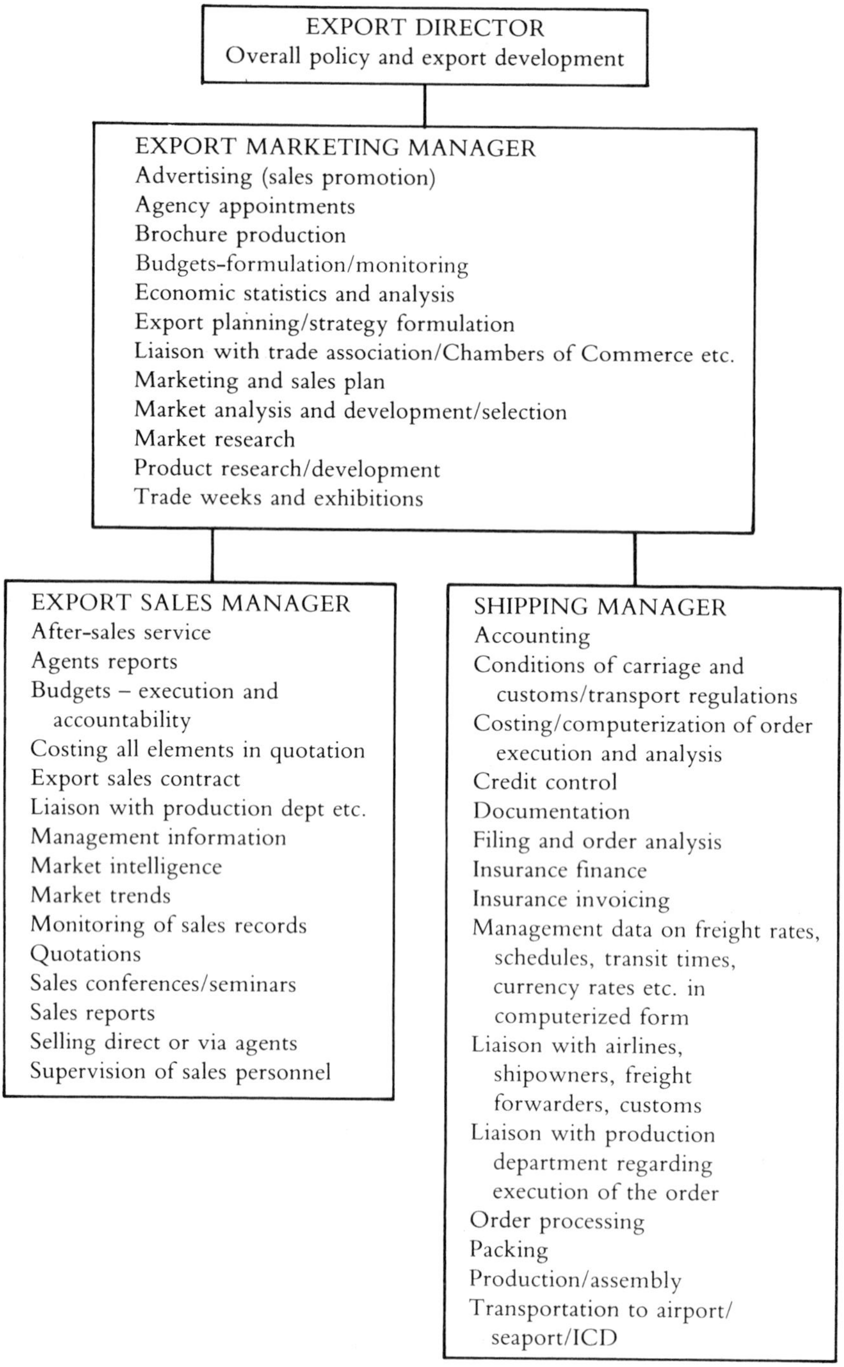

```
┌─────────────────────────────────────────┐
│           EXPORT DIRECTOR                 │
│   Overall policy and export development   │
└─────────────────────────────────────────┘
```

EXPORT MARKETING MANAGER
Advertising (sales promotion)
Agency appointments
Brochure production
Budgets-formulation/monitoring
Economic statistics and analysis
Export planning/strategy formulation
Liaison with trade association/Chambers of Commerce etc.
Marketing and sales plan
Market analysis and development/selection
Market research
Product research/development
Trade weeks and exhibitions

EXPORT SALES MANAGER
After-sales service
Agents reports
Budgets – execution and
  accountability
Costing all elements in quotation
Export sales contract
Liaison with production dept etc.
Management information
Market intelligence
Market trends
Monitoring of sales records
Quotations
Sales conferences/seminars
Sales reports
Selling direct or via agents
Supervision of sales personnel

SHIPPING MANAGER
Accounting
Conditions of carriage and
  customs/transport regulations
Costing/computerization of order
  execution and analysis
Credit control
Documentation
Filing and order analysis
Insurance finance
Insurance invoicing
Management data on freight rates,
  schedules, transit times,
  currency rates etc. in
  computerized form
Liaison with airlines,
  shipowners, freight
  forwarders, customs
Liaison with production
  department regarding
  execution of the order
Order processing
Packing
Production/assembly
Transportation to airport/
  seaport/ICD

Figure 1.1 Export office organization.

technical aspects of the commodity, distribution methods and any new products in the range) to enable them to keep their customers informed and thereby aid market development. Reports indicating shortcomings in any aspect of the operation should be acted upon quickly by the Exporter to retain market confidence.

The export department not only has the task of obtaining and executing the export orders, but also of ensuring payment is received without undue delay, in accord with the terms of sale in the export contract. Enforcement of rights in foreign courts of law is often a troublesome business and tends to create a bad public image for the company. It is prudent, therefore, to liaise closely with and/or use the export services provided by International banks and the Export Credits Guarantee Department on financial matters.

In larger export-orientated companies, a greater degree of specialization is essential, which usually means appointing an export marketing manager, an export sales manager and a shipping manager, each with defined responsibilities under the control of an export director who would be a board member (see Figure 1.1 for example).

1.3.1   The export director (or marketing director)

The export director is a board director. His sole task may be overseas marketing, selling and related elements or, in the smaller company, he may deal with both the home and overseas markets. The latter arrangement is not ideal, as conflicting interests may arise.

Ideally the occupant of this position should be a person of wide experience with wise judgement, a good business acumen, dynamic, with a vision for opportunity, and knowledge of several languages. He should know the products he is exporting, and their overseas markets. Above all, the director should be energetic and tenacious in his endeavours and have a high profit motive. The ability to identify and develop new markets is an important part of the work. A fault of many companies which are fairly new to the overseas business is the enthusiasm to sell in many countries. It is usually better to start in a few countries first (maybe three to five, possibly in the same region or trading area) rather than to spread out thinly around the world, when resources within the export office may be stretched. Consolidation within a few countries in the early stages usually aids efficiency and profitability, and customer satisfaction. Market strategy and planning, plus regular visits to overseas markets, are important features of the job. Moreover, the export director should have an intimate knowledge of the product – its strengths and weaknesses – in a competitive environment, and should be innovative in product development/promotion. Market analyses, which should be based especially on market and volume potential, general profitability and the market acceptance/demand of the product, should help in selecting the markets. The director must work very closely with the export marketing manager, and the shipping manager is often directly responsible to him.

1.3.2   The export marketing manager

The export marketing manager has overall executive control of the department, usually under the export director. He controls and co-ordinates the activities of the export sales manager and shipping manager (in smaller companies he may fulfil all three roles). Ideally, all marketing personnel involved in marketing development, marketing analysis, marketing and selling should be able to speak the language of the host's/buyer's country, and should know the market intimately, including its infrastructure, and should have spent at least six months in the overseas territory.

The export marketing manager is responsible for formulating the marketing and sales plan in consultation with the export sales manager: this is ultimately approved by the export director. Budgets are treated in a similar manner. Advertising and general sales promotion, including participation in any trade exhibitions overseas, is an important part of the job. This is likely to involve liaison with the British Overseas Trade Board and Chambers of Commerce/trade associations. The appointment of advertising agents is the responsibility of the export marketing manager.

Market analysis, market research and compilation of economic statistical analysis is a specialized area; in a larger company a market research officer may be appointed. Much reliance is placed nowadays on obtaining such data from the British Overseas Trade Board (BOTB) and Central Office of Information (COI). Again, the appointment of overseas agents and distributors is usually a task for the export marketing manager.

It cannot be stressed too strongly that the roles of the export director, export marketing manager and export sales manager overlap. The allocation of responsibility shown in Figure 1.1 should not be regarded as firm, as it may vary from company to company. The export marketing manager travels extensively, and needs to be multi-lingual, possess a good business acumen, and needs to have a good product and overseas market knowledge. In some companies, the export director and export marketing manager share the overseas markets, with the director, for example, taking Europe and Asia, and the manager the Americas and the Middle and Far East. Again, much depends on the spread of the markets and the individual company's structure. The task could, indeed, be split three ways: director/marketing manager/sales manager.

1.3.3   The export sales manager

The export sales manager is responsible generally to, and works closely with, the export marketing manager. His main task is to generate business through his sales force. He would, ideally, be multi-lingual and, like his sales personnel, have a good knowledge of the company products. A significant part of the job is studying market trends, market intelligence and sales personnel and agency reports. He keeps the export marketing manager closely informed to aid advertising policy development, product development and market expansion. Regular meetings should be held to discuss strategy and market development, particularly when entering new markets. The adequacy of existing selling and promotional techniques should be constantly appraised against budget performance.

The department is responsible for costing, supplying quotations and drawing up the export sales contracts. When the quotation has been accepted and the export sales contract issued, the task of supplying and despatching the goods is given to the shipping manager: usually a works order or some other authority is given. The export sales manager's staff must check the details of the export sales contract closely before it is issued. Close liaison should be maintained with the production department regarding costing, supply dates, etc. The after-sales work is another important area, especially in the interest of warranties, customer goodwill and market development. It is particularly important in the engineering field and with consumer goods.

This department organizes sales conferences, which are held to launch a new product or develop existing markets. A sales conference must be planned carefully and executed professionally.

The appointment of sales personnel usually falls within the responsibility of the sales manager and the marketing manager. Again, personnel of high calibre with professional qualifications are required. They should ideally have a good product knowledge, wide experience, be multi-lingual, have a good business acumen and preferably a good knowledge of the overseas market. In many companies involving goods of high technology, it is usual for the person to have a technical qualification. Personnel joining the company should be given a period of training, both 'in house' and externally. It is worth emphasizing the need to ensure that salesmen understand fully the mechanics of processing the export order, especially obligations to each party of cargo delivery terms, financial arrangements and insurance provision. Further considerations are the after-sales service and the needs of existing customers; any problems must be resolved quickly to maintain goodwill.

The export sales manager's task is usually completed when the export order is obtained and ultimately passed to the shipping department for issuing to the factory or, in the case of a merchant, to the manufacturer. It involves the following stages:

1 Receiving the enquiry, ascertaining its feasibility, calculating the price and preparing the quotation.

2 Ascertaining the despatch date by the specified mode of transport.
3 Obtaining the sanction of the credit controller and approval of the quotation before it is sent to the customer.
4 Ensuring the quotation is sent to the customer and following it up; initiating investigations into orders presumed to be lost.
5 Receiving the order from the customer and checking it against the quotation. Where the order is received without earlier quotation, much of items 1–3 has to be done at this time.
6 Obtaining the production controller's sanction and priority rating, and the credit controller's permission (if applicable).
7 Acknowledging the order and informing the local agent of the order (if necessary).
8 Arranging for the preparation and issue of the works order.
9 Informing the records or statistics department of the details of the order. This will enable the preparation of returns for ECGD (Export Credits Guarantee Department).
10 Confirming date of despatch to clients, agents or distributors and notifying any unavoidable changes.
11 Progress chasing.
12 Handing over the order to the shipping department where the delivery procedure is arranged.

Overall, the export sales office function is to deal with enquiries and orders up to the point of order confirmation/issue of works order, leaving the shipping office to process all the distribution/transportation arrangements. Ths involves documentation provision, packing, insurance, liaising with the production department, reservation of cargo space and payment of the goods by the importer. It is an important function of the shipping manager to ensure that the goods reach their destination market by the specified date, otherwise serious problems arise and customer confidence is impaired.

1.3.4   The shipping manager

The shipping manager's task is to fulfil the terms of the export sales contract, i.e. to supply and despatch the goods. It may be organized on a vertical or horizontal basis (see section 1.4). Close liaison must be maintained with the export sales manager. Both the shipping manager and export sales manager should have access to Fax/telex facilities.

The export shipping manager is informed of any orders booked, usually via a works order, and later receives definite notice from the works/ manufacturer when the goods are nearing completion: this is achieved through continuous liaison between the production department and the shipping manager's office, and involves the following stages:

1 Linking with export sales, checking that the order complies with import/export controls and establishing, from letters of credit, details of items relevant to the ultimate forwarding arrangements.
2 Deciding on the method of transportation (if not already specified).
3 Issuing instructions for packing and marking (if not already given).
4 Chartering or booking shipping space (or other form of transport).
5 Pre-entering at customs (if necessary).
6 Issuing instructions to works, transport office and freight forwarders.
7 Drawing up all the necessary documents and later collecting, collating and cross-checking all documents after shipment.
8 Passing documents to the accounts department for collection of payment.

Overall, the export shipping function normally commences when the works order is issued and takes over fully when the goods ordered have been produced and are ready for despatch. It is a section where a sense of urgency is essential. The manager is responsible for obtaining shipping or air freight space and negotiating freight rates.

An important part of the shipping manager's job is to obtain favourable rates for international transit, whether via sea, air, rail or road, and also insurance premiums when goods are sold under CIF terms. This entails regular negotiation with airlines, shipowners, road hauliers, freight forwarders, consolidators, underwriters and insurance companies to obtain the best deals. The prudent exporter opts for a quality transport service which is reliable and which involves a competitive rate which is unlikely to be the cheapest in the market.

1.4 SHIPPING OFFICE ORGANIZATION

The two main forms of shipping manager office organization, the vertical and horizontal (Figure 1.2) are under overall control of the export marketing manager. The vertical type streamlines and simplifies the documentation. Personnel are selected on the basis of their expertise in transportation, insurance, packing, etc. and, in total, efficiency in all the stages through which the export order passes must be high. The main disadvantage of this system is that staff are limited to a specific area of activity, which can result in disinterest in the total operation, leading to frustration.

The horizontal structure, however, produces total involvement and expertise in a group of markets and thus identification with the progress of the markets. The personnel will probably handle several aspects of the subgroup's activities, thus avoiding boredom. However, this system could produce unnecessary rivalry and overlap. In many export offices, both vertical and horizontal systems are in operation, with, for example, the horizontal being applied in European and North American markets, and the vertical in the rest of the world.

Vertical organization

Export marketing manager controlling departments dealing with individual aspects as follows:

1. Credit control
2. Order processing
3. Production/assembly
4. Packing
5. Transportation and insurance   } for all markets
6. Invoicing
7. Documentation
8. Filing and records
9. Finance/accounting/costing

Horizontal organization

Export marketing manager controlling sections, each dealing with all aspects for one market, as follows:

Group market 1	Group market 2	Group market 3	Group market 4	Group market 5	Group market 6
USA	EC	Africa	Middle East	Comecon	South America
Canada	EFTA				

Figure 1.2 Vertical and horizontal organization of shipping office usually involving a computerized operation of processing the order.

It cannot be stressed too strongly the sales personnel must have a good understanding of the basic function of the export shipping office and the principles of processing the export order within the terms of the export contract/invoice, otherwise serious problems could arise, with profitability and customer confidence being seriously eroded. More detail on this subject may be obtained from *Elements of Export Practice* (see Appendix A).

1.5 SALES OFFICE ORGANIZATION

Basically there are three types of sales office, as found in Figure 1.3.

Product orientated

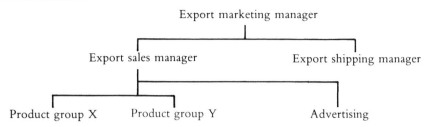

Customer orientated

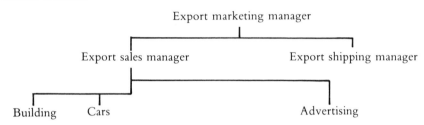

Market group

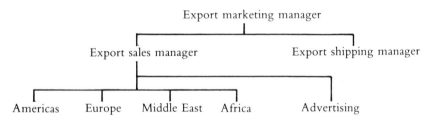

Figure 1.3 Sales office organization.

1.5.1 Product orientated organization

This type tends to be suitable where products are technically complex, or the number of products in the range is vast, or where the products are completely unrelated. It is ideal for the company who feel that product knowledge is vital in the interest of providing good customer service and market development. Medical equipment, electronics, bathroom fittings and machinery are examples of the type of goods which might benefit from this system. Conversely, it can inflate cost as various representatives will call on the same customer; this could also irritate the customer.

In an era when technical selling is becoming more important, this type of sales organization is more common. In a competitive overseas market the client requires to be convinced of the advantageous technical features of the product compared with others in the field, and the technically qualified salesman is usually the most likely to succeed in this. Further questions regarding after-sales service, technical durability and any 'in house' technical training about servicing or maintenance can arise in the sales negotiation. In fact, a good technical salesman can virtually develop a consultancy relationship with the importer which aids further development of the market. It is ideal for a wide range of capital-type goods where after-sales service and the provision of spares are important considerations.

The main criticism of this type of organization is that it can prove expensive when only one client has to be visited in one country, whereas with a market group organization several customers can be visited. The solution is to build up a clientele on a country basis and thereby enable one visit to embrace several clients.

1.5.2   Customer orientated organization

Under this system each representative specializes in a class of customer, thereby gaining expert knowledge of the industry concerned – its technology, decision patterns, etc. – which can vary by country. It enables the salesman to get to know the needs of specific customers and thereby develop a better relationship with the clients. Conversely, it does encourage duplication of journeys when more than one representative visits the same area to see different types of companies; consequently it tends to be used by the larger companies. Overall this type of organization tends to be the most popular, but its success has a high dependence on the calibre of the sales personnel.

1.5.3   Market group or area based organization

This involves allocating the salesmen to a specific area in the world and is equivalent to the horizontal system in the shipping office. It results in a clear definition of responsibility and interest in that area, which tends to lead to the cultivation of local business and personal ties. Travelling expenses are kept to a reasonable level. This system works satisfactorily when the area is not too large and where the products and customers are not too varied. Drawbacks arise when the company's products become very diverse, especially in technical terms. If such a situation emerges it will tend to involve a second visit by someone more technically qualified. This tends to inflate the cost of sales calls and creates a poor image of the company in the eyes of the importer. If such a situation occurs regularly it may prove worthwhile examining alternative ways of selling the product, such as through an agent.

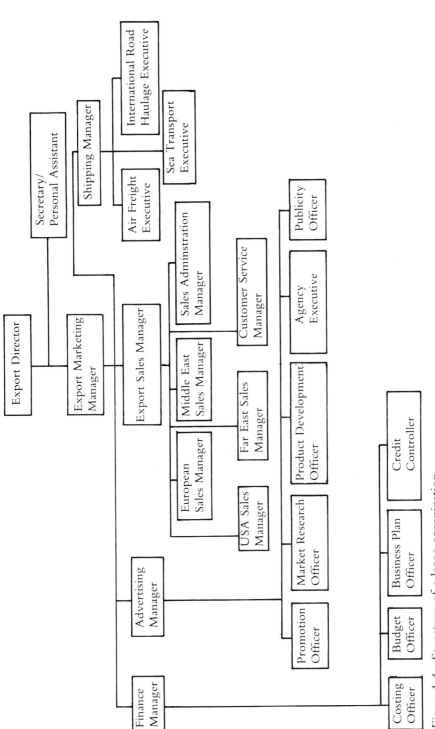

Figure 1.4 Structure of a large organization.

As indicated previously, the structure of the organization depends on the sales volume/potential nature of the product/service, and the environment in which the company operates. An example of a large organization is found in Figure 1.4. The nature of the job specification and the number of posts will vary by individual companies.

1.6 FACTORS INFLUENCING THE ORGANIZATION AND STRUCTURE OF THE EXPORT MARKETING OFFICE

It is important that the export marketing and sales organization are well structured to meet the company's market needs and opportunities overseas. The following points are particularly relevant:

1 The products marketed overseas.
2 The nature of the business.
3 The method of selling. One has the choice of relying on the direct sell with the salesman visiting the client; the agent promoting and selling the product with the aid of the company salesman; or the distributor, again with the guidance of the company salesman. Various other combinations exist, such as a mixture of the foregoing with the agent promoting the product in one country and relying on the direct sell in another region.
4 The degree of profitability.
5 Any involvement with other companies relative to the marketing, promotion and distribution of the product. An increasing number of companies are tending to operate on a consortium basis to reduce promotion cost and deploy their limited sales resources more effectively. Alternatively, some companies work on a 'piggy-back' basis, i.e. they work in collaboration with another exporter.
6 The extent of the export marketing office responsibilities within the company, and the degree of reliance on other departments within the company. For example, does the export marketing manager have resources within his own organization to handle and develop market research and advertising programmes, or does he rely on a market research officer and advertising officer, each available to all sectors of the company business? The latter situation results in the export marketing manager losing control of the actual assignments, but has the advantage of using personnel familiar with the company product and policy (although they may not always appreciate the ramifications of the overseas market). Such a policy may prove cheaper than engaging an outside agency for market research or advertising.
7 The extent to which computers can reduce the workload and streamline the work. Maintenance of records and accounting can be undertaken by a computer which may be available to all departments within the company.
8 Personnel resources within the company, and their calibre. It cannot be

too strongly stressed that the company should have sufficient professional, qualified executives.

Experience suggests that the more influence or control the export marketing office has over the salient parts of the export marketing business, the more successful the business will be. Much depends on the scale of the business, its likely potential and the level of profitability. It is better to have a few personnel, well paid and of high calibre who rely on 'in house' departments, rather than many personnel of mediocre quality. Furthermore, in many companies, there exists more scope for the expansion of export markets compared to that of the home base. This is adequate justification for the provision of a well organized and resourced export sales office to develop these markets professionally and profitably.

To conclude, the export office, under the export director, should not be subservient to other departments but should remain completely independent and responsible directly to the managing director. Too many manufacturing companies regretfully operate on the basis of giving preference to the home market needs following production disruption, rather than complying with the export order programme. This places the export orders at risk, due to the subsequent late delivery of orders to the importers.

1.7   EXPORT POLICY AND RECORDS

The proportion of a manufacturer's output to be exported is influenced by many factors. The chief concern of a company will be to combine stability with the highest possible financial return. In many industries, this is achieved through a good balance of home and export markets, but much depends upon the product and the profile of the overseas market in which it is to feature. This is important where:

1 Exports may rely on the continued existence of one or two foreign markets, which may be cut off, for example, by changes in import licensing laws of the countries concerned.
2 Demand abroad may be seasonal for goods which require a constant market to make them pay.
3 Overseas enthusiasm for a product may depend on the fact that it is in use in the UK.

Some businesses virtually exist for export, with no significant home market. In such a situation, it is prudent where possible to have the export markets based in several countries to lessen the impact of any change of export demand in any one of the countries.

Export marketing research is an important function and involves a fact-finding enquiry on which marketing policy is based. It is dealt with more fully in Chapter 3, but it is appropriate to deal with its functions within the context of the export department:

1 Statistical. This involves the determination of the total existing market – the quantity bought, the price range, the market shares of competitors, market trends and the location. Additionally, it should indicate by comparison with the company's past trading record in the area, whether the total market is expanding or otherwise. Extensive use would be made of reports from agents, distributors, etc. and other available sources.

2 Economic. There must be evaluation of the product market potential and its acceptable market price, bearing in mind competition. In addition, patterns of new investment, purchasing power per capita and gross domestic product must be taken into account.

3 Social. This indicates the market attitude towards the products and their adequacy in terms of design, durability, fashion, technical specification, etc. Agent's reports and market research techniques such as questionnaires and interviews will provide these data.

4 Psychological. The enquiry must find out the factors which motivate the consumer to buy the product, evaluate measures to further its market growth and assess the ways in which the market is adversely influenced by competition and substitutes.

5 Political attitudes are playing an increasing role in international trade today and this must be considered in market research analysis.

6 Demographic. An analysis of population movements/changes (for example, is the market serving a young or ageing population?). A young population enables the supplier to have a comparatively longer loyalty period than would an ageing population: likewise with the differing family-unit size and diverse socio–economic classes. Such factors will differ extensively by country and culture.

It is important that close liaison should be maintained with trade associations, Chambers of Commerce, Central Offices of Information, banks and other sources which provide reliable data on market developments, trends and attitudes. In larger export companies a qualified market research officer is often employed.

The results of research in the export market can be correlated with parallel activities on the home market so that an overall marketing policy may be formulated. However, the divergence of treatment called for by home and overseas markets makes a fusion of the export department with the home marketing organization, under a general marketing manager, most unwise.

With regard to accounting, there is no fundamental difference between the methods adopted in an export company and those in any other concern. However, certain accounts (sales and cash returns, for example) should be subdivided into those for home and export markets.

A firm engaged solely in export business does so either (a) as an export merchant exporting its own goods to buyers overseas; (b) as commission agent for foreign importers; or (c) as an export agent undertaking the export business of manufacturers in a variety of industries. Freight forwarders do not engage in the trade of goods, but undertake the transportation arrangements, sometimes including a packing service.

In the case of a manufacturer, it is usual for the export department to keep separate accounts. When an order is received from an overseas buyer, the goods will be subsequently invoiced giving details of the sale price. Where appropriate, further records will be maintained of charges such as insurance, freight and packing. The usual method of charging out export orders is to use serially numbered invoice sets with the order having a works order number. These give instructions to the finished stores department on advising and charging the customer. An alternative method is to issue warehouse instructions and process them through the various offices. The former is the most up-to-date method and is often computerized.

If the exporter does not manufacture his own products, he either buys the goods for export or exports on behalf of a manufacturer. An exporter who has bought the goods may concentrate solely on the overseas trade or he may be a general wholesaler maintaining an export department. In the latter case, the accountancy of the export department will be similar to that in a manufacturing concern, the sole difference being that instead of producing merchandise for home and overseas markets, the business merely purchases the goods, in bulk or break bulk, as the case may be.

2 *Market analysis*

2.1 OBJECTIVES OF MARKET ANALYSIS

An exporter must have a good knowledge of the market in order to exploit it to his most profitable advantage. This requires thorough market analysis not only prior to entering the market, to determine its prospects, but also as a continuous assessment to keep pace with its trends and opportunities.

Prior to considering the various elements involved in market analysis, we will establish its objectives:

1 To identify suitable markets with a view to their profitable development both short-term and long-term.

2 To aid profitability of the company. The ultimate objective of selling in a market must be profit, although this may not always be attained in the short term. In general terms, the larger the exporter's market share in a particular country or region, the lower the unit cost. For sustained profitability the volume of business must be economic in production, distribution and marketing terms.

3 To keep in touch with market development and opportunities. This can be achieved through regular market reports produced by the exporter's agent and through other sources including the press, journals and trade associations.

4 To produce a trend of market developments and aid long-term market sales prospects. This helps to plan production and develop sales strategy within the market. For example, if another competitor is planning to enter the market next year, additional advertising can be provided.

5 To aid preparation of more meaningful market reports. These are often produced by agents and obviously the more data available, including information on market share, market trends, size of the market, profile of the market, etc., the better.

6 To aid production, in terms of design and specification, of more competitive commodities. The more information one has about one's competitors, especially of future plans and market reaction to a product, the greater the ability of the exporter to produce a more competitive product in terms of price, durability, specification, packaging, image, etc.

7 To produce more effective management information. The decision-making process is facilitated by current and relevant statistical data.
8 To keep in touch with technical trends. This involves both pending legislation on future product specification codes, and technical product development by competitors.
9 To identify new product developments. This aspect would emerge through regular market reports and continuous vigilance by agents.

2.2   MARKET STRUCTURE

Knowledge of the composition, profile, or structure of an overseas market enables an exporter to plan the promotion and development of a product in a particular market. The following are the salient questions which must be answered when determining market structure:

1 Who are the main domestic suppliers to the market? Answering this involves determining the reasons why each company is successful or otherwise, i.e. its strengths and weaknesses. Details of their promotion techniques and general distribution and retailing arrangements should be sought of competing companies.
2 Which countries are the main source of imports? Again details of the manufacturers involved should be sought, together with their techniques in promotion, distribution and retailing. The strengths and weaknesses of the product should be evaluated. If possible an attempt should be made to ascertain the future intentions of both export and domestic manufacturers within the market place with regard to such areas as product improvement and new models.
3 Which importing firms are the most important? Do they have an increasing or diminishing share of the market? What is their position in the market?
4 What is the export performance of main competitors? Information should be sought on whether they have any particular advantage in the market place, such as preferential import tariffs due to the manufacturer operating within a free trading area.
5 Which are the competitor's main markets? Do they operate within a particular region or concentrate on a particular specialized market.
6 What are the geographical variations in the market?
7 What are the seasonal/cyclical variations in the market and can they be extended through skilful promotional techniques and/or market pricing? The seasonal/cyclical variation tends to push up unit cost, and an attempt to extend the retail selling period could aid the general competitiveness of the product by spreading the cost over a longer period.
8 What factors, current or in the longer term, favour the emergence of new competition? In a depressed economy starved of capital, an exporter may be able to enter a market through superior design and technology of his

product, possibly at a lower price. Alternatively, existing domestic producers may not be able to meet the home market demand and an exporter can fill the gap through a competitive product without any consumer resistance, such as reluctance to buy foreign goods.

9 What factors are likely to lead to the reduction of competition? This may emerge through the competitor lacking capital to fund new technology, the presence of too many competitors in the market to support the domestic market on a profitable basis, or the absence of good management in domestic producers which results in deteriorating levels of profitability.

10 Which are the main user-industries?

11 Which are the subsidiary user-industries?

12 Is in-feeding significant in the user industries? (In-feeding involves the exporter developing his success as a result of another exporter's success in the market).

13 Do reciprocal trading practices exist? If so, is it more difficult to break into a market?

14 Do any of the companies' main or secondary user-industries receive any government grants/subsidies, or benefit from home market protectionist policies? Such policies make it difficult for an exporter to break into such markets.

2.3 MARKET SHARE

Market share is an important consideration in a general market analysis, but the paramount concern, long term, must always be the degree of profitability each market share commands. The long-term motive for entering the market must remain one of profit attainment unless compelling commercial reasons dictate otherwise. The following questions are relevant:

1 What share of the market does the firm command? This requires very careful evaluation and includes factors such as socio-economic class and the nature of the product within the supplier's range. For example, a motor manufacturer would expect the models at the more expensive end of the range to be bought by clients in the AB group.

2 What is the prospect of adapting the home market product to suit tastes and any relevant regulations overseas? For example, in many countries the safety regulations of car specification are stringent. The possibility of future legislation must be investigated.

3 What are the market shares of the main competitors and is there likely to be much change in the foreseeable future: if so, for what reason? What is their position in the market place and extent of their resources, especially financial, to combat a price war?

4 What is the firm's share of the market when analysed in terms of industry, size of company, general credibility and geographical location?

5 What are the main competitors' shares of the market when analysed in the same terms?

6 What share of the market is held by imported products, and is there likely to be any significant change in the long-term future?

7 To what extent – if any – is the present market share influenced by tariffs, import restrictions and currency controls? Does the government impose a policy directly through tariff barriers or quota systems, or indirectly through complex import documentation procedures or stringent construction and safety regulations on imported products? In other words, is there a home industry protectionist policy?

8 What factors support the market share of the imported product?

9 What percentage, in volume terms, is from old and new customers, and how does this correlate with the demographical analysis?

10 How concentrated or dispersed are sales?

11 Is the existing distribution system affecting the market share, and can this influence be changed to the benefit of the exporter? Effective distribution can reduce unit cost, which in turn gives the exporter a price advantage.

2.4 MARKET TRENDS

Market trends fulfil an important part of market analysis as they point the way to future development. Particular attention should be given to the economic and political circumstances and background under which the trends emerged and to whether any significant changes have occurred during the period of the market trend analysis. The following questions are relevant:

1 How does the market size compare with that of ten and five years, and twelve months ago? Such an analysis should reveal growth, stagnation or decline or a combination of such features throughout the analysis period. The exporter must enquire into the reasons for the trend. If, for example, there is no growth, there might be an opportunity for the exporter to reverse such a trend through lower unit cost, improved specifications and a more competitively priced product.

2 How does the product demand differ from that of ten and five years, and twelve months ago? Such an analysis must be reconciled with economic and technical development. It could be that a demographic change, for example an ageing population, will generate less demand for cars.

3 What are the trends in shifting demands over the last ten and five years, and twelve months? Again, the trend indicated must be viewed against the circumstances influencing the analysis period, and the likely situation in the future.

4 In what ways are market changes likely to manifest themselves? This may be through an improved product range, better technology leading to lower unit cost and therefore lower retail pricing, better quality products and extended warranty, improved distribution and marketing arrangements, and differing economic and political circumstances.

5 What changes are occurring in the user-industries which are likely to induce a change in demand?

6 Likewise, what changes are occurring in the non–user-industries which are likely to induce a change in demand.

7 What changes are occurring in the firm's products and processes which are likely to induce a change in demand? These may be improved product design, new models, or an entirely new range of advanced technology superior to any known competitor. Particular attention should be given to social attitudes towards any new product, and much could be gained from test marketing. Some markets are very receptive to advanced technology, for example westernized markets. Other markets, particularly in less developed countries, do not have the technical know-how to cope with the latest generation of new technology without adequate training and education.

8 What changes are occurring in the local economy which are likely to affect demand for the firm's products? These embrace both internal and external economic factors including: export/import trends; retail/wholesale prices; consumers' expenditure; balance of payments and invisible exports; levels of exchange rates and trends; employment and income per head; industrial investment and profit; personal savings and taxation levels, both direct and indirect; industrial dividends and rates of corporate taxation; industrial production; population trends; interest rates; credit restrictions; hire purchase debt; days lost through industrial disputes; government attitude on imports. It will be appreciated that the significance of the foregoing items varies by individual country, for example through a change in government or external pressures such as the escalating price of world oil.

9 What trends are likely to attract new entrants into the industry in the future? These may involve future legislation introducing a new code of practice for a particular construction industry, change in fashion, new technology in food processing and distribution, etc.

10 What trends are likely to reduce the numbers of competitors in the future? These could include lack of investment to keep pace with technology and thereby remain competitive, or the population changing from using a long-established product to a new one resulting from modern technology, as in the change from black and white to colour television sets.

11 Are changes in materials or production methods likely to reduce the need or desire for the product?

It will be appreciated that many markets have serious debt problems, for a variety of reasons. Conversely, the newly industrialized countries (NIC), such as South Korea, have achieved dramatic results in their export performance, and provide good opportunities for exporters. Readers are urged to study the country's analysis and its market profile (see sections 2.6/2.7) to determine which countries might be ideal for their company market penetration.

The major international banks produce market reports on many major trading countries and, together with the British Overseas Trade Board, through the Overseas Diplomatic Service Posts, can provide the exporter with the answers to many of these questions.

2.5 SIZE OF THE MARKET

Market size is a major factor for the potential exporter to consider when deciding in which markets to promote his product(s). The following questions must be answered:

1 What is the size of the total market for the product? These data can be obtained from official government statistics or those produced by trade associations or Chambers of Commerce or their equivalent. The British Overseas Trade Information Service (BOTIS) can usually help to provide such information.

2 How durable is the market? Is it subject to any adverse policies, especially towards the importer, which could reduce the market size significantly? For example a country may be developing industrially with a view to having a home-based industry and relying progressively less on imported products. This may even be a governmental policy.

3 What is the domestic consumption by value or volume? Volume figures are more useful than value figures when the time comes to produce comparisons of one year with another, and/or to produce some market consumption trend. This also applies to item (4).

4 What proportion of the market, by value and/or volume, is met from imported sources? Such data may be difficult to obtain on a regional basis and might have to be gathered on a national scale. It is important that the figures are reasonably current: five years ago the situation might have been totally different. Similar remarks apply to item (5).

5 What are the main export markets from (i) domestic production and (ii) re-exported imports? Again, it might be difficult to obtain precise data.

6 What factors limit the size of the total market? These will tend to vary by country and could embrace government restrictions, depressed economic conditions, import controls, inadequate production resources through lack of modern technology, shortage of raw materials or absence of skilled labour. Another significant factor could be non-availability of capital to fund modern industrial production plant, resulting in a limited production market at high unit cost, which in turn depresses the demand for such a product.

7 What are the sizes of the various market strata? Such an analysis considers geographical region; the number of users; the type of industry; the type, quality, design or price of product; and the kind of distributor.

8 What is the size of the total market for a substitute product? This can prove difficult to estimate, but market research can help in producing such data. It is important not to take too optimistic a view of market potential without sound statistical evidence.

9 What are the export possibilities? This involves very careful, professional evaluation. Reliable data must be sought and consumer research and test marketing ideally should be carried out.

The size of the market requires careful consideration when evaluating market selection and market clusters (see section 14.2). The important aspect is the number of likely buyers and their income, purchasing power, socio–economic class and the country's gross domestic product (GDP). A good comparison is the study of the market profiles of India and West Germany. Further points to be borne in mind are whether the market is relatively near or distant and whether it has a good infrastructure.

In summary, the ideal market should be relatively large, receptive to overseas trade and without any severe political constraints. Advice should be sought from the British Overseas Trade Information Service or the Export Marketing Research Scheme, which both operate under the aegis of the BOTB.

2.6   MARKET REPORTS

Selecting the right export market or markets is essential for successful trade overseas. It requires prolonged and careful evaluation. This depends on obtaining the right information and advice from the outset. Market reports are simply a commentary on a particular market in a specified country, region, or trading community. Alternatively, the report may be less broadly based and deal with a specified commodity in a particular country or range of countries. Let us examine five examples of such market reports:

1 The Export Market Information Centre (see Appendix E) provides access to the information of overseas markets. It is run by the Department of Trade and Industry, and provides the following data:

   (a) British Overseas Trade Information Service, a database for infor-
       mation on: products and markets; overseas agents, distributors and
       importers; export opportunities; promotional events; and for an
       index of other published market information.
   (b) Worldwide statistics, which are available showing patterns of trade,
       production, prices, employment and transport.
   (c) Market Research Reports, a selection of which, including overseas
       market reports, supplements the statistics collection.
   (d) Directories, both overseas trade and telephone directories.
   (e) Mail order catalogues, ideal for checking consumer goods.
   (f) Development plans, including economic plans for selected countries,
       available on loan.

(g) Other on-line databases, a search service through commercial on-line databases can be accessed.

2 Specialist market knowledge can be obtained from the Department of Trade and Industry specialist market knowledge regional office or the country telephone desk on the BOTB, London. Data are obtained from the Diplomatic Service Post Overseas and information is available on: product suitability in a particular market; local competition; advice on marketing methods; test marketing a product to gain local response in a particular market; product/service promotion in the overseas territory.

3 The Department of Trade and Industry Export Marketing Research Scheme (EMRS) helps UK firms undertake marketing research by providing financial assistance and independent professional export marketing advice. It provides specific professional guidance on whether specific market surveys are needed, advice on how to get them under way, and offers financial support, often in the form of grants, for market research studies undertaken overseas. The scheme embraces professional consultants and the exporter's own staff, setting up the exporter's own market research facility, purchasing published marketing research data, and research commissioned by a trade association and management consultancy.

4 The final example is found in the 'trade briefs' produced by international banks. These are documents which feature trading information for UK exporters, especially the economic, financial and trade aspects for a particular country or region.

A typical market report, in a particular country and involving a specified commodity, would cover the following items:

1 The remit, which will detail the broad extent of the report, particularly any constraints found in the enquiries made leading up to its composition. For example, statistical data of a most detailed nature may not be available because of the diversity of the producers of a certain type of product.

2 The extent of the market, which is likely to cover the brief history of the market development, the method of funding such development, the main companies (including any subsequent takeovers or liquidation), the growth of the market up to the present day, the degree of overseas competition, the actual market volume and consumption per capita and an impression of the market sensitivity throughout this period – for example, did the home producers succeed because of the near monopoly of one producer/distributor, or did living standards rise, making more cash available to spend on luxury goods?

3 Industry and competition, an important part of the report which will deal with the current structure of the industry and the degree of competition within it both from home and overseas, including alternative products. For example, the butter market today is very vulnerable to the margarine

substitute for a variety of reasons. Details should be given, if available from a market survey, of the strengths and weaknesses of the established product in the market place. This will help the potential importer to decide how best his product can enter the market place successfully, especially in terms of quality, general specification, price, after-sales service, etc. Details of any other UK exporter currently in the market would be recorded, together with an appraisal of his success. Furthermore, mention would be made of any UK companies or other exporters who had withdrawn from the market in recent years, and the reasons for them so doing. The present market may be dominated by two market leaders and the report may recommend that any attempt to penetrate such a market would result in a price war, with severe losses being incurred by the exporter and little prospect of any long-term viability. Alternatively, a major car manufacturer anxious to penetrate a new market may find that an existing, long-established, home-based car manufacturer is in the process of rationalizing or reducing his agency network to reduce cost. This would result in such agents looking for fresh business, providing the potential car exporter with a ready-made agency network. This would greatly facilitate a market launch.

4 The structure of the market, which would deal with many items but especially the distribution, consumption and import/export aspects. In the case of a food product the retailing outlet may be revealed as almost exclusively super- or hyper-markets, or the traditional grocery store. Alternatively, it could be a combination of the two with the super- and hyper-market rapidly taking an increasing market share of a particular foodstuff. Again, the market may be very diverse and ripe for a new initiative to modernize distribution and retailing techniques for a new, imported brand. Such a development could involve substantial capital investment coupled with strong advertising to convince the market place of the consumer benefits of the new imported product and a modernized distribution system.

This portion of the report is likely to contain very comprehensive statistical data, possibly extending over a ten-year period to show trends. If possible, the statistical data should be analysed with reference to the main producers/suppliers, consumption per capita and significant details of any change in the market delivery during this period. For example, the market entry of new suppliers/distributors/retailers and any price cutting resulting therefrom should be considered. This would stimulate market growth, making the volume of sales suitable for modern distribution and retailing techniques, and thereby lowering the unit cost.

Statistical data should reveal the sales results of other UK exporters selling similar products in the same and other countries. If relevant, the product range should be analysed.

5 Legislation, which embraces a number of areas including import regu-lations, codes of retail practice, advertising codes and the technical specifications required of imported goods. Details of technical specification can be obtained from Technical Help for Exporters (THE) whose role is explained in section 10.12.

6 The conclusion to the report should contain some form of recommendation and, ideally, a plan of action. It should give an indication of future trends in the market, and may suggest market research to establish consumer attitudes or factors determining consumer choice. An appraisal of possible future economic trends is likely to feature in the conclusion as are any expected political developments which are relevant.

Having now established the content of a market report, let us detail the factors to bear in mind when writing it:

1 It should be lucid in its presentation, with a logical and well thought-out synopsis as suggested in the preceding list.

2 It should contain an index with acknowledgements to sources of information used and the number of respondents and response rate.

3 It should be factually correct and unbiased in its presentation. Areas of doubt, where information is scanty or non-existent, should be mentioned rather than omitted from the report.

4 Regard must be given to the terms of reference and ambiguous information must not be used. Particular attention should be given to the timescale of the report relative to its completion date and the need to use reliable and unbiased information.

5 Results from desk research or questionnaires from field research must be processed and tabulated.

6 The report should contain a summary of recommendations and, where appropriate, any financial evaluation together with the basis on which the financial data have been compiled.

7 Particular emphasis should be given to future trends and the basis of their formulation.

8 Finally, the report should be as candid as possible so as not to mislead the exporter. An interim report prior to final report can prove useful.

2.7 MARKETING INFRASTRUCTURE

In our study of market analysis it is appropriate to consider the term 'marketing infrastructure' and its application. In broad terms the marketing infrastructure of a particular country is the sum total of the facilities and services available for marketing. This would include the following items:

1 Geographical, cultural, economic and political factors of a country.

2 The media and marketing support services that are available, such as statistical data, market research agencies and advertising agencies.

3 The trading and distribution systems in the country, particularly those for related and competitive products.

2.7.1 An illustration of infrastructure

Let us examine the following four examples to draw comparisons of the marketing infrastructure.

(a) *Country A* This is a poor, densely-populated country with low levels of literacy, and is plagued by the caste system and religious prejudices. There are a number of heavy industries but both industry and agriculture are labour intensive. Newspapers and magazines have relatively small circulations in towns and cities, and in the rural areas they are almost non-existent. Radio and cinema are the important media for the majority of the population.

One can conclude from such an analysis that the income per capita is low, and the export market is more likely to be in the industrial area rather than in consumer goods. Product promotion would be through radio, cinema and poster sites.

(b) *Country B* This is a compact, wealthy country with well-established banking and commercial services and light industries. It is tri-lingual and has French, German and Italian local newspapers, national magazines, trade magazines, television, radio and cinema and good local and international advertising agencies with reliable support services providing statistical data. Overall, this is a market receptive to imported products, but likely to require quality products at competitive prices linked with good after-sales service.

(c) *Country C* This is a highly developed, industrialized country with one language and good transport system by road and rail, and a limited domestic air service. Good international air and sea transport services are available for the development of trade and tourism. Advertising media include local and national newspapers, television, radio, cinema, outdoor advertising, direct mail and so on. Quality advertising and research agencies, printing facilities and film producers are available. There is extensive government and trade statistical data. Again this is a market receptive to imported products, but likely to require quality products at competitive prices linked with good after-sales service.

(d) *Country D* This is a wealthy country, rich in raw materials. As far as the economy is concerned it is bilingual (English and Afrikaans) and is in the process of becoming industrialized. The country is subject to political pressures from the outside world and the white population has high living standards. Newspapers are available in the larger cities and towns where good supportive services exist. The cinema, television and radio are available for advertising. This market is very receptive to imported consumer goods, but carries some political risk.

2.8   COMPUTERIZATION

Our study of Export Marketing and Management would not be complete without consideration of the role of computers.

During the past ten years the application of computers has been very extensive in management and in many companies today, executives have a personal computer giving access to a wide range of data to aid the decision-making process. Some of the areas in which the computer can be applied in Export Marketing are listed below:

1 Process all export documentation involving preparation of invoice, and derivative documents such as packing list, single administrative document, Bill of Lading, CMR consignment note, insurance certificate, Air Waybill, Sea Waybill, proforma invoice and so on.

2 Maintain daily record of exchange rate levels and calculate tariffs.

3 Process cargo reservation arrangements through direct on-line computer access to major carriers such as P & O Containers operative through DISH (see *Elements of Shipping*, pages 428 and 433).

4 Maintain customer porfolio by product and country and relative sales performance.

5 Provide sales and marketing budget by country, product, sales executive/ agent or other criteria. Similarly, the expenditure budget can be recorded detailing sales cost such as advertising, distribution, agents commission and other cost elements. The spread sheet techniques can be used.

6 Maintain country portfolio in the areas of market size, market share, economic factors and analysis of competitors.

7 Constituents of product cost and pricing by market. This will reveal the profit levels/mark-up by market.

8 Develop on-line computer access with freight forwarders, international banks, etc. involving the development of the EDI (see pages 428 and 433 of *Elements of Shipping*).

9 Maintain records of available distribution services and the schedules and rates involving air, road and sea transport.

10 Develop CAD/CAM in product design and manufacturing techniques.

11 Develop credit control.

12 Provide a wide range of letters to be despatched to existing and new clients i.e. new product, price increase, etc.

The advantages of computer technology to the Export Marketer can be listed as follows:

1 It provides a whole range of readily available management information which is error-free, subject to the data input being correct.

2 It reduces laborious clerical work prone to error.

3 It enables the company to have a higher market profile.

4 It aids planning that is so essential in the Export business.

5 The company becomes more competitive and able to respond quickly to export order enquiries and various changes in the market.

6 It is available 24 hours per day.

7 It is ideal for desk research and enables a whole range of exercises to be undertaken quickly and accurately.

8 It allows for company growth without incurring additional cost to handle the business. This is subject to computer capacity and emphasizes the need to make provision for expansion when considering the computer investment options.

The above is just a broad overview of the computer application relative to the Export Marketer. It is very desirable that the computer is a corporate-one within the company and has access to the other business sectors/ divisions such as production, cost accounting, home market and so on within the company.

2.8.1 Benefits from computerization

(a) *Processing the export order*   Many companies, both for home and overseas markets, have a computerized ordering system. This gives full details of: the order specification; method of payment; terms of credit (if any); general reference or number; quantity; detailed specification of the commodity; time scale of production; exchange rate; how order was secured, i.e. by an agent or through an advert; time scale of supply; packaging specification; distribution arrangements; name of buyer or agent; any special features relative to the order; after-sales service provision; works order number; details of any penalty clause regarding late delivery; insurance provision (if any) in distribution arrangements; the department to which any queries should be addressed. It is important that the marketing and sales departments ensure that maximum, meaningful market analysis details are obtained from such a computerized operation. Such analysis can enable a realistic market and customer profile to be built up to aid further promotion of the product and develop new markets. It can be related to an advertising campaign, new launch of product in another country and overall profitability of the products in their respective market.

(b) *Documentation*   The transmission and design of shipping documentation has changed dramatically in recent years and SITPRO (see pages 317–21 of *Elements of Export Practice*) have been very much to the fore in the development of technology involving electronic data processing (EDP) techniques. This applies to all areas of international documentation involving invoices, consignment notes, customs documents, etc. It greatly facilitates customs clearance and payment and settlement arrangements. Moreover, it lessens the risk of errors as the documents are aligned so that data can be transferred easily between documents (these forms are so arranged that items of information common to all forms appear in the same relative positions on each form). Again, such data can have a market analysis role because distribution and payment arrangements can be related to commodity type.

(c) *Stock control*   Many companies keep a computerized record of stock control throughput to measure the period that the various commodities are held in the factory warehouse pending order and distribution. If the manufacturer has, for example, three months' stock on hand, management may consider the stocks excessive both in capital value and supply period terms. Accordingly, measures are taken to reduce the production levels to diminish the stockpile. Sales forecasts, which are compiled partly from computerized stock control data of earlier years, can help in stock control. They can, for example, show seasonal trends, and production targets can be altered accordingly to plan the optimum use of available resources. Overall it should improve profitability levels.

(d) *Billing of customers*   Many firms now bill their customers on a periodic basis with the aid of a computer. The international consignment is a more complex operation but nevertheless it is feasible and practised by many exporters. Again such data can prove useful in establishing customer information by country or region in terms of financial payment as it builds up a case history on each client.

2.8.2   Access to information

To conclude our brief review of computerization, it is desirable that data are available on a regular computer print-out, and that this is used in a meaningful way to build up as much relevant information about the market and customer profile as possible. The usefulness and relevance of the data supply should be reviewed regularly to determine whether any other information could be added, or any redundant information removed.

2.9   ELECTRONIC DATA INTERCHANGE (EDI)

The Electronic Data Interchange system has been in operation for many years in the banking network and, as we progress into the 1990s, it will become more established in freight forwarding/shipping/Customs. It is already established by Customs in the Direct Trader Input System (see *Elements of Export Practice*, pages 147–8) and more recently the DISH and SHIPNET systems (see *Elements of Shipping*, pages 428–33) linking shippers, freight forwarders and shipping lines. In the early 1990s the CHIEF system (*Elements of Shipping*, pages 97–9) will be introduced by HM Customs. Ultimately the aim is to have a network linking deep-sea, short-sea, and surface, air freight, banking, finance, insurance, customs, port authorities, and airports in one overall network.

The system operates on the basis that the shipper will key in his message into his own computer, which will convert the data into the required format for transmission into the EDI network. At this stage the message will be sorted and held in a temporary mail box on the EDI central computer until such time as its recipient is ready to receive it and have it processed automatically into a format ready for reading. Overall, the process takes seconds. The benefits are extensive, including the elimination of the double-entry of data, especially by the recipient, thus saving time and money, and a reduction in the error risk.

The system has much application in the area of transmission of marketing data.

3 *Export market research and survey*

3.1 INTRODUCTION

Market Research has been defined as the systematic gathering, recording and analysing of data relating to problems in the marketing of goods and services.

Export market research is a study of a given market abroad to determine the needs of that market and the methods by which the products can best be supplied. The enquirer starts with a certain product or group of products prescribed in his terms of reference by the exporter, and then gathers the facts, interprets them to form reasoned conclusions, but does not implement the decisions based on such conclusions: this is the exporter's decision. Its ultimate aim is to provide information to improve the marketing perform-ance of existing products or services, as well as producing data upon which the development of future products and services can be based, usually in a competitive environment and on a profitable basis to the supplier/exporter.

As we progress through the 1990s, market research will become increas-ingly important for a variety of reasons including:

1 The increasing level of competition within the market place.
2 The need to determine the market profile.
3 The reluctance of many companies to embark on any new market development without any professional advice from the proposed country of import.
4 The high cost of launching a product overseas and the need to ensure the most effective marketing and sales plan is produced.
5 The need to ensure the product is of the most acceptable design compatible with price and consumer needs.
6 The need to devise a cost-effective distribution system and after-sales service.
7 The need to ensure the most effective advertising through an analysis of the sales research results by various media, i.e. television, national press, commercial radio, mailing, etc.

8 The need to avoid the hit and miss management tactics whereby decisions are taken without researching the market, consumer or advertising profile.

The total market in any given product over a prescribed period is equivalent to the total sales realized in a defined geographical area, usually a region or country. Export research is concerned with a wide range of products and often tends to be less directed towards the point of retail sale. It concerns itself mainly with the chain of distribution, and covers consumers' semi-durable goods (radios, domestic appliances, cars, etc.) and capital goods (for example, building materials, machinery), as well as consumer goods.

One cannot stress too strongly the need to use current market research data that are reliable and totally relevant to the product. If the exporter is in doubt or has limited funds available for market research, it is sensible to take advice from the local Chamber of Commerce, trade association, or EMRS (see section 2.6), rather than take short cuts.

3.1.1   Reasons for conducting research

Export Market Research may be required for a number of reasons, as given below:

(a) *Tactical*   This involves what tactics to adopt in the market place in a competitive environment. It may cover pricing and the adoption of discounts, promotion using below-the-belt tactics; or distribution using a centralized rather than regional system.

(b) *Data Bank*   This involves the data required to facilitate the decision-making process. It is usually desk research, and involves the monitoring of: economic statistics; trade regulations; import regulations; exchange control; competitors' activities and so on.

(c) *Strategic*   Strategy (see section 14.3) is an important area in Export Marketing Management. It involves the provision of adequate market profile data, to determine whether or not to enter a market or cluster of markets. Usually it embraces both desk and field research and can prove a lengthy task where major investment decisions are involved. It covers both short- and long-term strategies, and is likely to produce a number of options such as the use of agents rather than distributors.

In all three situations the market research is likely to be 'on going' to enable trends to be produced and to monitor company performance in the market place reflecting the implications of the decision making process. For example, any variation of the pricing policy through discounted sales relative to sales volumes realized.

3.1.2 Peculiarities in export markets

For a manufacturer or merchant seeking markets overseas, there are numerous factors which arise that are not encountered in the home market. An examination of such features now follows.

(a) *Distance*   International distribution arrangements involve such features as customs, cargo insurance, extensive documentation and specialized packing. Additionally, international transport distribution costs tend to form a much higher proportion of the total product cost involved, up to 15–20%, reflecting the greater distances involved compared with the home market, inland transport arrangements. Market research and operational research can help to determine the most ideal distribution method. Moreover, the more distant the market, the more costly in time and money it is to service. This involves both the sales visits and the general communication process. Market research will help determine the ideal market entry option and its cost-effectiveness.

(b) *Time*   Generally, overseas consignments tend to have a longer transit time than ones for the home market, so the production department must plan accordingly to ensure the goods arrive at their destination on schedule.

(c) *Language*   Complications can arise from having to use foreign languages in labelling changes, packaging, special publicity and so on. In countries where more than one language is used, market research may be able to resolve the additional marketing problems which arise. It can be very useful to establish what competitors do to overcome any such problems. It can also give rise, in many instances, to difficulties in the market research process itself, since the most important part of the research must be carried out through discussions with the residents of the country. Problems can emerge in the use of brand names and slogans which, while acceptable in the home market, may be offensive, for example, for religious reasons, in the overseas territory. It is advisable that all publicity material be compiled by the overseas territory advertising agency. This should include the product's packaging.

(d) *Race and religion*   In many overseas countries, differences of race and religion have to be borne in mind in relation to the goods themselves, their presentation to the buying public, and the approach to publicity. It is important to secure the advantages of presentation in a favourable light by using predominantly those colours which are traditionally and emotionally associated with happiness and goodwill.

(e) *Local preferences*   Quite apart from racial and religious preferences, local idiosyncrasies must be discovered in order to set up the most fruitful approach to the market. For example, the Australians are influenced in their outlook by US sales methods which, in practice, means a higher outlay in publicity than, for example, in Ireland or a Scandinavian country. Moreover, some countries are best approached by radio rather than by newspaper publicity. Similarly, in some places the cinema slide is regarded as part of the entertainment whilst in others it is practically ignored. So far as the products are concerned, and their trade marks and packaging, some things are to be avoided and others exploited. For example, the average hen egg in Egypt is very small, so egg cups must be smaller than the UK standard size. Similarly, in France coffee is the national drink, and tea is rarely provided other than for tourists on request.

(f) *Environmental factors*   Export market research must embrace the study of the climate. For example, the sweet manufacturer would not market some of his products in a very hot, humid climate as the sweets would reach the buyer in rather a sticky mess. Climatic conditions are best examined alongside such matters as distances from ports and airports, types of communication, gradients, location of population, etc.

Environmental factors and the country's infrastructure are very important aspects to bear in mind in evaluating and researching a market. Less developed countries tend to have a poor infrastructure. This has a profound effect on distribution to and from the seaport or airport. Moreover, such countries may rely on feeder services as the larger vessels are physically unable to be accommodated at the seaport and the markets cannot support such regular services offering high capacity tonnage. In consequence the distribution tends to be slow and the containerized cargo is stuffed and discharged at the seaport and its environs, as the road network will not accommodate the container being conveyed inland to the agricultural regions. Accordingly, the goods are road-borne to and from the container yard. The situation is less serious in countries with good rail networks to and from their seaports. Undoubtedly the situation will improve as the National five/ten-year rolling economic plans of such countries unfold, but it is an inhibiting factor in a country's development. A good example is Thailand.

(g) *Business practices and credit worthiness*   This embraces enquiry into the code of legal practice regarding the conduct of business in the overseas country. For example, it would include the giving and implementation of guarantees and warranties connected with the suitability of the goods and performance for a certain period after sale. Additionally, one would establish that the importer administered his business in an honest and fair way without a taint of corruption. In many markets the goods cannot be imported until they have been examined and an approval certificate issued.

(h) *Scope of market research*   The extent and area of the market research must be determined. It may cover one country or simply an area or region within a country. Cost and remit terms will play a large part in reaching the decision. None of the foregoing items can be taken for granted in any market abroad. Research undertaken to establish the characteristics of the market is not easy to undertake and to bring to a successful outcome; the scale of the market research undertaken is influenced by the exporter's budget and his estimate of the market potential. Care should be exercised in establishing the scale and extent of the research to ensure that it is not too ambitious, nor that the data produced be so scanty as to be meaningless. Guidance should be sought from the market research agency conducting the research in the overseas territory.

To be effective, the market research must be well planned and well executed, and it must have a defined objective. It is advisable to spend some time reflecting on the terms of the remit to ensure that it meets the requirements for production of the desired research results. Ideally, it is desirable to undertake a pilot survey of the assignment to eradicate any unforeseen problems which may emerge. Ultimately, this also ensures that a more meaningful report is produced. A further point to bear in mind is that the scope of research can vary by individual country. Pilot exercises tend to reduce the risk of misgivings and avoid a simple market research exercise being transformed into an enquiry of its inadequacies.

In some circumstances, it may be preferable to undertake multi-market research, that is, to conduct market research within several countries simultaneously with the same objective in view. This is complex and can be difficult to administer, particularly when several languages are involved and the countries differ in their local idiosyncrasies.

Effective market research is best undertaken by engaging a market research agency in the overseas territory. Care should be exercised in its choice and the local embassy's Commercial Attaché can usually give guidance. A visit to the territory is essential to discuss the matter and evaluate options and decide on strategy. Such field research would only be undertaken when the desk research has established a *prima facie* market potential for the exporter's product and service.

There are four basic aspects of market research.

1 Social aspects:

   (a) the market preference in terms of colour, habits, foibles;
   (b) product design in the light of handling and general use.

2 Statistical aspects:

   (a) an analysis of buying habits in terms of consumer profile, at what price and at what place which may include factual information showing where the manufacturer stands in relation to competition

and overall position in the market and an analysis of the strengths
and weaknesses of the products in the market place;

(b) an analysis, over a specified period, of whether the total market
demand is rising or falling, which will enable the exporter to
determine the effect on his market share.

3 Psychological aspect:

(a) a comprehension of the reasoning behind the public preferences and
habits; this may suggest certain religious or political motivation in
customer choice which may prejudice them against some imported
products;

(b) an analysis of the market reaction to any possible product improvement devised to overcome the weaknesses or prejudices detected
from earlier research;

(c) an analysis of the most cost-effective distribution system and promotion techniques; the latter could involve special advertising campaigns and test marketing.

4 Economic aspects. Consumer analysis relative to income group, class,
age group, sex and particularly price acceptability. For example, some
consumer groups may prefer the cheaper, less powerful car whilst others
who have a much higher income and are status conscious may prefer the
more expensive and faster car range.

It will be appreciated that some of the research will produce data of a
qualitative nature and some will give quantitative results. The qualitative
data will enable the market to be measured in terms of product preference
such as durability, specification, etc, whilst the quantitative analysis is
found in the product demand and associated consumer profile by age,
salary, class, sex, etc.

Market research results must always be viewed against the terms of the
remit and the circumstances under which the research is conducted. The
date when the research is undertaken is particularly relevant as the information can become quickly out of date. Moreover, one must bear in mind
there is always a lead-time for the product launch, and developments and
the implications of this time-scale must be carefully evaluated by the export
company when deciding what action to take on the market research report
recommendations. Also details of number of respondents and response/
sampling criteria.

3.2 CONSTITUENTS OF MARKET RESEARCH (see Figure 3.1)

There are ten main areas to be covered by market research where the
export market is concerned:

1 The actual market constitution and features are surveyed as a prelude to

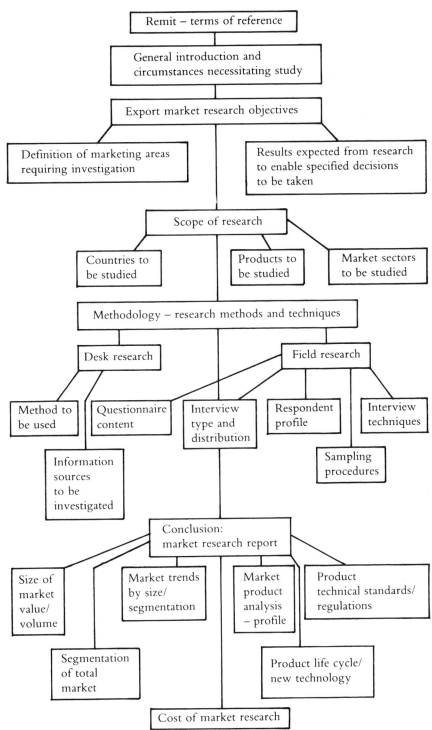

Figure 3.1 Constituents of an export marketing research proposal.

deciding whether to launch a particular product, including an enquiry into the market profile and consumer habits through a questionnaire. Test marketing may be carried out, where consumers are encouraged to answer questions on the product. Alternatively, a survey may be conducted whereby the respondents answer a postal questionnaire or are interviewed by researchers. For example, a manufacturer may provide samples of a brand of perfume so that consumer reaction and the potential market can be assessed from the results of a survey, before the product is launched. It is worth engaging a professional market research agency in the importer's country to undertake the task.

2 Sales research usually involves a thorough examination of existing and past selling techniques. It will be conducted on the basis of country, region, type of retail outlet, or other convenient parameter. Such a survey would highlight the strengths and weaknesses of the system, particularly its cost-effectiveness (cost of selling per unit, for example). It could indicate the need to change the distribution arrangements from the direct sale to one through an agency distribution whereby the latter shares promotional cost.

In many instances, there will be considerable interaction between the product and the outlet through which it is sold. New products and those of technical complexity require the back-up of a competent sales person who can explain the product's use and benefits and educate the consumer/user. Additionally, there may be after-sales responsibilities to take account of, for example, terms of repair and maintenance, including spares. The company may also wish to compare their level of sales with those of their competitors, as well as comparing the performance of individual sales persons or particular outlets through which the product is distributed. Discrepancies revealed by research can be explained and remedial measures taken to improve the firm's competitive position in terms of market share and profitability. Sales research can also be used to devise sales forecast.

3 Consumer and dealer research involves primarily the following two points:

(a) The situation where all the companies dealing in the same product range achieve their targets in the type of consumer they attract, price level and volume.

(b) The reasons why the consumer chooses one product in preference to another, including any data forthcoming on whether consumer behaviour is affected by a change in packaging, price variation or quality. Sales research deals only with the output of a particular company. Consumer and dealer research involves all firms operating in the market, with specific reference to product competition at the time the research is being conducted for a client. Sometimes the information can be obtained from published data, but more frequently separate research must be undertaken for each assignment. This may be market analysis involving the factual examination of a market where sales are achieved, or behavioural research concerning the factors which underlie a product sale.

(c) Consumer research involves evaluating the ultimate user of the product or service and has three prime divisions:

   i. Consumer goods such as food, clothing, footwear and confectionery which have a rapid turnover and are subject to continuous change in regard to taste, fashion, etc.

   ii. Consumer durable goods such as TV, kitchen furniture, cars, etc. A product subject to change in fashion, design, technology, etc.

   iii. Consumer services embracing hotels, restaurants, leisure, finance, insurance, and so on. This involves a labour intensive area in some of the items such as hotels, restaurants, leisure, etc. As in item (i), it has a strong loyal clientele market potential.

4 Advertising research analyses of various advertising media and their effectiveness. For example, does the market response of the sales from one newspaper advertisement generate double the quantity compared with its competitor, and how do the rates for advertising compare (i.e. what is the cost per unit sale)? This information will help determine future advertising strategy in the most cost effective way practicable. Overall, it is a question of ensuring the media chosen and the advertising campaign strategies used have maximum coverage and impact on the target audience. A system of test marketing can be used to assess the effectiveness of the campaign and the media involving press, magazines, television, radio, etc., and adjustments made to improve their appeal and market penetration.

5 Promotion research involves evaluating/researching the effectiveness of the company promotion plan. Again, the tendency is to test market the promotional plan on the target market to ensure it will be effective. The promotional mix may include: exhibitions; merchandizing and point-of-sale material involving brochures; consumer and trade advertising (above the line and below the line: see section 4.15); special offers; couponing; sponsors; free samples; public relations campaigns; and so on. The scale of the research undertaken in each element of the promotional mix will vary by circumstances and significance in the overall marketing promotion strategy.

6 Packaging and packing research represent an integral part of the product offering. It is an area where adequate research is essential to formulate the appropriate package design and specification. This is likely to involve test transits for the packing of the consignment to ensure it arrives in a quality, undamaged condition, and test marketing to ensure the packaging is acceptable to the consumer and, for consumer products, is achieving the desired sales results at the point-of-sale environment.

Overall packaging and packing research should strive to establish the following data:

(a) whether it is necessary to devise any special outer packs to withstand rough handling during transit;

(b) whether, because of tropical conditions, to avoid certain printing processes in the preparation of packaging/merchandizing material;

(c) the need to take any special precautions relative to the transit such as arises with dangerous classified cargo;

(d) given any significant cultural and religious factors in the market place which colours, symbols, etc. should be avoided;

(e) the size(s) of the packages, which will be influenced by: average size of family; incidence of the newer forms of retailing such as hyper-markets, discount houses, etc.; frequency of shopping trips; per capita income; cultural aspects of the market; demographic factors; and so on;

(f) legal requirements such as those affecting product design, description of the products, product marking/labelling and statutory declarations such as the nature of the ingredients and their quantity;

(g) the transport modes used.

The aspects should not be regarded as exhaustive but each product requires to be individually evaluated.

7 Product research scrutinizes the development, design packaging, branding and testing of the products. Acceptance of the packaging, colour and general satisfaction of the product are also relevant.

This is an important area of research and should be undertaken continuously especially for many classes of fast-moving consumer goods (f.m.c.g.) such as foodstuffs. In the latter situation the packaging and effectiveness of the point-of-sale environment are dominant factors. Skilful adjustments to the brand image and packaging can conspicuously improve the product's visual appeal and sales performance.

Another area of continuous research analysis is to carry out comparisons of the exporter's products with those of the competitor. This involves the need to establish the strengths and weaknesses of the products in the market place as perceived by the user/consumer. The results could differ by country or region, and will reflect local culture and taste and the varying degrees of competition. Technology, price and consumer behaviour will play their part in determining the factors favouring a particular product by the consumer. A further consideration will be the product life cycle (p.l.c.) and impact of taste/design and selling environment including packaging. Emphasis should also be given to non-price items such as warranty after sales service and so on.

Product research involves product development to satisfy the needs of the consumer/user. This embraces the total product including: the product itself; accessories; any installation service; a user guarantee, provision of adequate after-sales service and the ready availability of spares and replacement parts; any operating manual; and a package and brand name. All these factors represent successful overseas marketing, as the user is entitled to trouble-free, continuous use of the product despite the considerable distance from the exporter's premises. Adequate after-sales service may be costly and difficult to arrange in foreign markets, but it cannot be neglected. Moreover, it must be borne in mind that for an adequate total product, the producer is entitled to ask a reasonable price (see also section 14.3).

8 Distribution research concerns testing the adequacy of the transport arrangements of the consignment and its related elements. This includes conducting test transits to establish areas where delays occur and the convenience of service to the importer. The introduction of a particular brand may warrant research into the agent, consumer and advertising areas. All could be undertaken skilfully through a well thought-out questionnaire.

Distribution research requires continuous monitoring correlated to sales volume and what the competitors are doing. As the market changes with improvement in sales performance and market penetration into other regions/areas, it calls for a radical review of the system currently in use. It may result in moving from the LCL (less than container load) to the FCL (full container load) consignment with a revised warehouse/distribution network. Opportunity may exist to operate in a piggyback situation with another exporter despatching compatible products. The results of any research will establish the pattern, the strengths and the weaknesses of the existing distribution network, and point the way to improvement. Quicker transits with improved quality service can lower unit distribution cost and improve sales. It tends to be a neglected area by some exporters and should assume a higher profile in determining export marketing strategy.

9 Distribution channels research. This involves the research to define and evaluate alternative channels of distribution – current and emerging – as a basis for advising on optional channel strategy and on tactical requirements for selecting, motivating and supporting third party outlets serving an overseas market.

Examples are given below:

(a) Characterization of distribution channel alternatives available to sup-pliers embracing market focus, skills and capabilities and geographical coverage.
(b) Evaluation of change in the relative importance/role/volumes of individual channel types.
(c) Identification of channel support needs and channel/supplier terms and conditions.
(d) Investigation of supplier selection procedures and policies.
(e) Assessment of supplier image and awareness.
(f) Distribution channel analysis.

10 Information technology research. This is an area of increasing activity and embraces computers, electronic data interchange and communication.

Given below are examples of such overseas research:

(a) International strategy for product development and marketing in the area of decision support software and applications development tools.
(b) An on-going company image tracking research programme covering all the company's target markets, opinion influences, and channels of distribution.
(c) A multi-project research programme to assist a company to identify and exploit opportunities in applications-based integrated value and data systems.
(d) A study of the profile opportunities available to a potential operator in the catalogue-based mail order channel for computer and related accessories and consumables.
(e) An awareness and image study for a major datacomms manufacturer.
(f) A market study for micro to main frame communications over a five-year period in specific hardware environments.
(g) A market place study for large-scale systems integration consultancy and project management services.
(h) Research to fine tune a planned advertising campaign for new digital PABX (private telephone exchange).
(i) Research to list the reactions of key distributors to a new package of distribution management controls.
(j) A study of the potential market for PCs (personal computers) in association with the evaluation of third party networks.
(k) An overseas market evaluation for third party maintenance services involving in-depth study of end-user requirements and intentions.

To conclude, it will be appreciated there is some overlap in the ten areas of export market research discussed. However, the important aspect is to ensure the enquiry raises the relevant questions so that the research data can be analysed to produce the information management is seeking to aid the decision-making process. Market research should be applied both to consumer and industrial products and cover all aspects of the marketing mix.

3.3   PROCESSING THE MARKET RESEARCH SURVEY

It is appropriate, prior to processing the various types of market research, to examine in broad terms the essential steps in the conduct of a market research survey.

1 The first point to consider is the area or commodity in which the survey is to be conducted. Much will depend on company policy but it is desirable to give attention to the following aspects:

(a) Amount of money available to conduct the survey.

(b) The type of research and resources available both in-house and in the overseas territory.

(c) The time scale from the time the agreement is obtained to start the project until the report is published.

(d) The likely benefits to be derived from the survey.

(e) The market potential available and the possible degree of profitability to the company in the event of the exporter entering the overseas market. Generally the larger the market the bigger the profits which will flow, although in the early years, when a foothold is being established, the margins could be small or even produce a small loss.

(f) The ease or difficulty which is likely to be experienced in the penetration of such a market.

(g) The urgency of the assignment.

(h) The long-term cost to the company of entering the overseas market. This will involve: adjustment of production schedules to meet larger output demands; the investment in plant to fulfil such production expansion needs; and the need to redesign the product to take account of overseas market fashions and/or technical specification. Furthermore, the company will need to feature the project in the business plan. Usually, the business plan will contain a commitment on the part of the company to develop existing overseas markets, or enter new markets. This will be subject to the market research findings, which will advise as to whether or not the overseas market development will take place.

(i) The appointment of agents and/or distributors to retail the product in the overseas market. Other market entry options may exist, and one of these may be chosen (see section 6.1).

All the foregoing factors require reconciliation and the significance of each will vary by company. In broad terms it is better to concentrate on one commodity or commodity range, in one country or region. The wider the product range, and the greater the number of countries, the less likely the survey is to be successful due to the varying circumstances described earlier in the chapter (see section 3.1.1).

2 The second aspect is the terms of the remit. This requires careful evaluation and discussion with other personnel within the company including those in export marketing, production, finance and research and development.

3 The type of survey and the method. This may involve desk research, postal questionnaire, field interviews, etc., carried out by an overseas market research agency, the merchant, or the market research personnel employed by the manufacturing company. All these options are examined in greater depth in section 3.4.

4 When the decision has been taken to conduct the survey in a prescribed

manner, those entrusted with the task must be given a brief, which is agreed upon by both parties after extensive discussions. It may well be the staff of a market research agency who receive the remit terms and a broad outline of the way the exercise is to be carried out. For the purpose of this exercise we will assume that a market research agency is conducting the survey through questionnaires which can be completed by the respondent with little or no assistance from the agent's personnel who distribute them, and be returned by post. In the discussions with the exporter, the overseas market research agency may have suggested improvements to the manner of conducting the survey, especially with regard to the content of the questionnaire and the scale of the exercise. Such discussions, which continue from the time the agency has been approached, enable them to get to know more about the product. This is particularly valuable as the agent is likely to be located in the country in which the survey is to be conducted. An area of amendment is the terminology of the questionnaire to ensure that it is fully understood, completely impartial, and does not cause offence.

It is possible that several agents would be approached to conduct the survey and separate tenders and proposals would be received. In some cases the exporter may narrow the field down to two agents; after informal discussions and examining some of their work for other companies, the final selection will be made. Alternatively, the two major advertising agents in contention for the account may each do a presentation of their ideas/ proposals before a final decision is taken. The BOTB and COI can usually help in finding suitable market research agents in various countries. It is essential that the exporter visits the overseas territory and is present at all negotiations and discussions.

5 The fifth aspect is the question of whether a test survey should be carried out. They have the advantage of determining the feasibility of the questionnaire and the likely market response. If the questionnaire proves inadequate in certain areas, e.g. if it is too long, ambiguously worded or produces biased answers, the opportunity is available to correct the situation. The important thing to bear in mind is that the survey should produce the data from which a meaningful, creditable report, completely relevant to the remit, can be produced. Test surveys tend to increase the cost and extend the time-scale of the project, but have the benefit usually of producing a more meaningful and comprehensive report.

6 Prior to launching the test survey and when actually undertaking the survey, adequate briefing must be given to all concerned to ensure the objective exists and is achieved. This involves particularly those conducting the survey and those editing the completed questionnaire, especially if a computer is to be used to process the data, as is likely nowadays. At such briefing meetings the agency would invite the exporter to deal with any queries which may arise and supplement the agent's presentation of the project.

The agent will prepare a brief which is likely to fall into two parts. The first part will prescribe the way the survey is to be conducted and its objectives, whilst the second part will describe the method/code to be adopted in editing the questionnaires prior to them being processed through the computer. This may involve two groups of personnel, or one group which is to undertake both the field and editing work. The brief will contain the following salient features:

(a) *Field work*
   i. A general introduction giving details of the object of the survey and how the data should be sought from the respondent in a completely unbiased way.
   ii. A brief commentary on each question found in the questionnaire detailing the thinking behind the inclusion of each question and the information sought; if necessary, definitions of any of the terms found in the questionnaire will be given. Such data will enable the research assistant to deal adequately with any queries arising from the content of the questionnaire.
   iii. Emphasis of the complete confidentiality of the survey insofar as the respondent is concerned.
   iv. Instructions on the distribution of the questionnaire. This may involve: distributing to people at random in the street on a specified day or time in a particular area or to a certain age group; distributing to householders in a particular area as detailed in the brief; selecting names at random from the telephone directory to receive such a questionnaire on the basis of a pre-determined criterion; using a mailing list and undertaking a random sample selection, e.g. every tenth name; or distributing the questionnaire at a railway or bus station, for example. Such arrangements must be carefully thought out to ensure the respondents are interested in such a survey because it is relevant to their needs or interests. It is, for example, no use distributing a questionnaire to determine public attitudes towards a new brand of baby food on an estate which is largely composed of old people.
   v. The timescale of the project, indicating the date of the survey.
   vi. The details of general administration, embracing travel arrangements, payment to researchers, emergency or contingency plans in the event of sickness, instructions on spoiled questionnaires, letters of authority to conduct survey or other forms of identification, etc.

One must bear in mind that circumstances will vary by survey. The more detailed the briefing instructions, the better and more meaningful will be the results. On the other hand one must ensure the investigator is given the opportunity to use his/her initiative in the conduct of the survey.

(b) *Editing*

   i. The editing instructions for each question. These will include details of any codes, lettering or number codes related to the respondent's answers.

  ii. Instructions relative to spoiled questionnaires.

 iii. Methods of sorting of the questionnaire, if appropriate. For example, in a large survey where 100 000 questionnaires were returned, it might be decided to edit only 10 per cent of them in a prescribed manner. Similarly, questionnaires distributed in different areas may be identified by different colours. The questionnaire would be sorted and processed accordingly.

7 On completion of the field survey and the editing of the questionnaire the data are processed through the computer. The research agency must decide if there is to be any cross-matching between questions. For example, the questionnaire may contain ten questions and it may be necessary to cross-match numbers two and seven to give an analysis by age group and sex of the respondents' reaction to the product. If the product is a car, the younger age group may prefer the sporting, speedier model, and the middle age group might place more emphasis on comfort and design. Such data will aid advertising strategy, particularly the type of journals, magazines or newspapers in which to promote the product. Generally, the greater the cross-matching of such questions (which can involve up to three questions) the more comprehensive and sophisticated the ultimate analysis.

8 Finally, the research agency must produce the report on the market survey results. It should be written in a lucid style and give the following information:

(a) Terms of reference.

(b) Commentary on the survey and how it was conducted.

(c) Any problems experienced during the survey or regarding editing of questionnaires.

(d) Full analysis of all the results, both in commentary and statistical terms.

(e) Response rate of the questionnaires distributed.

(f) Summary of conclusions and recommendations.

(g) Appendices containing statistical tabulations and any acknowledgements.

It is very important that the report is processed quickly by the export company. If possible, brief details of the findings should be given before the final report is provided. The task of taking action on the report contents is the responsibility of the export director, marketing manager or export sales manager, depending on the structure of the company. The following points require early attention:

1 The formulation of a plan of action, with a time scale for putting into effect the recommendations made in the report which are approved by the export company.
2 Assessment of the cost to execute the plan. This will involve costs of production, distribution and promotion. It may involve the appointment of agents and/or distributors and an advertising agency to promote the product. Overall, it will embrace the method of funding and additional company resource needs in terms of personnel and production. Adequate planning is essential.
3 The provision of monitoring arrangements to assess progress of the plan so that any necessary remedial measures may be taken. For example, if a car manufacturer is about to enter a new market following completion of the market research report, it will involve the appointment of a distributor/retail network. In such circumstances the car manufacturer could decide to set up its own company. This would control all the import, distribution and promotion aspects and maintain close liaison with all the retail outlets.

All the data emerging from the survey, especially the computerized data, should be the property of the exporter, so that subsequent surveys can be undertaken by the exporter when circumstances warrant them.

The BOTB has now devised a scheme to help and encourage UK firms to undertake marketing research overseas as an essential part of their export effort. It is basically a free, professional advisory service and is available to exporters and potential exporters whose goods or services are produced in the UK.

Financial support can be obtained for export market research, and in certain cases for subsequent management consultancy services, as listed below:

1 For commissioning professional market research consultants to undertake market research overseas.
2 For employment of professional management consultants to advise on setting up, or reorganizing, a firm's export department, where this has been one of the principal recommendations in an export market research study carried out by professional consultants with financial assistance from the Department of Trade and Industry.
3 For market research studies carried out overseas by a suitably qualified and experienced researcher on a firm's own staff, provided the research is of a standard equal to that of a professional market research consultant or agency.
4 For setting up a new export market research department, plus certain overseas travel costs, and a per diem allowance for time spent by one newly appointed and suitably qualified researcher on overseas market research projects during the department's first year of operation.

5 Purchase of multi-client studies and other published market research (excluding directories, up-dating subscriptions and market overviews).

Details of the scheme, including its constraints, criteria and method of application are available direct from the Export Market Information Centre (see Appendix E).

3.4 TYPES OF MARKET RESEARCH

Various methods of conducting market research exist and the final choice depends particularly on the nature of the product and the money available to conduct the assignment correlated to the estimated potential income from the overseas territory. The latter will be much determined by the potential market share of the product to be researched.

Data can be classified as either primary or secondary. Primary data are original data and have to be gathered in the market place. This involves interviewing people or respondents completing questionnaires. A market survey may reveal that it is better to appoint a wholesaler as sole distributor rather than for the exporter or manufacturer to maintain his own distribution organization in a particular area, as customers are scattered and transport difficult. Such an arrangement, with a smaller sales force, would be less expensive, as the sales personnel would merely serve the wholesaler and not the larger retail market involving smaller orders per outlet. Overall, primary data are expensive to obtain but have the advantage that they are reliable and relevant.

Secondary data may be either from a published source, or produced internally within the export company. Published information may be from a government source, trade association, Chamber of Commerce, etc. Such data are usually reliable but it is important to establish precisely the statistical parameters employed to avoid misinterpretation in any research analysis report. It is often not possible to obtain relevant secondary data directly, but if the information is collated with care and judgement, the conclusions drawn can be a very useful guide to framing company policy in the export field. The major benefit is that it is inexpensive and readily available, usually on a continuous basis.

Internal secondary data found in a company would consist of sales data embracing: product specification, geographical areas, types of retail outlet, product pricing and time interval between orders (the last is especially important for products with seasonal sales). Such items, although not particularly useful individually, are valid for comparative purposes on a continuing basis. They enable trends to be produced and monthly or yearly figures to be compared. Export sales invoices are a useful data analysis.

We will now examine the various types of market research available.

3.4.1 Desk research

This inexpensive technique, sometimes termed 'armchair research', simply involves an evaluation of public/trade/official statistics and reports and surveys. It enables the exporter to screen all possible markets, eliminate those offering little or no prospect, and list the remainder in order of their potential. It is also relatively quick, and ideal for monitoring market trends. The more important sources of these data are detailed below:

1 The major banks produce booklets on trade prospects in various countries. Additionally, some of them produce quarterly bulletins through their economic and commercial departments dealing with economic trends, fiscal policy and world trade prospects. All such publications are usually free.

2 *The Times, The Guardian* and the *Financial Times* from time to time produce surveys on various countries which highlight trade prospects, particularly for the UK exporter.

3 The Economic Intelligence Unit (EIU) produces reports on various industries/countries and long-term developments.

4 The various trade associations produce useful reports on their commodities and on opportunities for the exporter.

5 The EEC and OECD (particularly the former) produce numerous reports on trade prospect and related subjects.

6 The Department of Trade and Industry weekly journal, *British Business*, contains much statistical data and overseas trade news.

7 The Confederation of British Industry (CBI) produce a monthly report on overseas markets.

8 The major, UK-based Chambers of Commerce and Industry produce monthly journals on overseas markets and related matters. Moreover, UK Chambers of Commerce are situated in many countries overseas to encourage trade, and have available data on trade prospects.

9 The Central Statistical Office regularly produces extensive statistical data on international trade.

10 The Central Office of Information (COI) circulates details of UK achievements overseas and gives data on UK products available for overseas importers.

11 A computerized Export Intelligence Service (EIS) is also operated under the aegis of the Department of Trade and Industry and details overseas contracts available for which the UK exporter can tender (see section 10.2).

12 *The Economist* produces a great deal of useful statistical data on international trade.

13 Numerous Anglo–foreign Chambers of Commerce produce regular bulletins on trade prospects for their members including statistical data. These include, for example, Anglo–Israel Chamber of Commerce, Arab–British Chamber of Commerce, Belgo–Luxembourg Chamber of Commerce

for Great Britain, Canada–United Kingdom Chamber of Commerce and Italian Chamber of Commerce for Great Britain. Full details of their addresses are found in Appendix E.

In addition, the exporter can, if he so wishes, ask the Department of Trade and Industry Marketing Research Scheme (see Appendix E) to undertake a survey of a particular commodity or country. Advice can also be sought from the local Chamber of Commerce, or from banks. Full use should be made of available 'in house' data including sales invoice analysis, agents' reports, etc.

3.4.2 Field research

This is the process of conducting research in the market place involving face-to-face interviewing, postal questionnaires, telephone interviewing, the overseas trade mission, and personal visits. Basically, it is the market survey conducted with a specified remit to determine the market profile and product/service specification acceptance/opportunities as fully explained in section 3.3. It is an expensive process and can be useful when the initial desk research has identified a market potential for a product which needs to be more closely evaluated/researched. Field research needs to be both carefully planned and closely supervised/monitored.

Problems arise as a result of linguistic, cultural, economic, political and geographical factors. Some countries, particularly those of Westernized economies, offer the same facilities for sophisticated research as does the UK. Other countries, such as those in the Third World, do not. In many developing countries market research facilities are very rudimentary. The culture tends to make interviews difficult to obtain, particularly so, on occasion, with female respondents. Linguistic difficulties can hinder the gathering of objective information. The geographical spread of the population might make representative sampling difficult, and sometimes impossible. In Eastern Bloc territories field research is very difficult to undertake due to the political situation. Accordingly, research data both from the Eastern Bloc and developing countries is sought through desk research involving official statistics and through trade associations. Such data have a doubtful credibility factor at times. By contrast, Westernized economies like West Germany and France have facilities for *ad hoc* and continuous consumer research, advertising research, industrial marketing research, packaging research, product testing, attitude and behavioural research, and so on.

(a) *Overseas trade mission* The Department of Trade and Industry encourages official overseas trade missions which run, for example, a 'British Week' in Utrecht. This helps the businessman in two ways. First, it enables him to meet the local government officials and businessmen to ascertain at first hand the opportunities available, together with any constraints. Secondly, it is a means of obtaining actual business by taking exhibition space. Overall, it enables the exporter to gain first-hand knowledge of the market place and display the product, with samples and brochures to the buyer. This technique is being used more and more often, and many small exporters have started their overseas markets in this way. The local Chamber of Commerce can help, and the Department of Trade and Industry can provide financial assistance to UK businessmen to visit overseas markets on trade missions. Such trips are, however, relatively inexpensive when compared with the benefits derived.

(b) *The personal visit*   This technique is not always recommended as an ill-planned visiting programme overseas can produce indifferent results with which to appraise market potential (see section 11.2). A much better assignment is a visit to a trade fair or exhibition, which can provide a useful insight into the overseas market to establish product market potential. Much export business is secured by skilful entrepreneurs visiting overseas markets themselves, defining or identifying the market and then exploiting it. Details of such trade fairs are available from BOTB and local Chambers of Commerce.

(c) *The market research or field survey assignment*   This can be carried out in the following four ways:

First, it can be undertaken by the merchant. Advantages of this method include relative secrecy (only the merchant and the manufacturer know research is proceeding); speed of execution and report presentation; ease of collaboration between the two parties; and, if the merchant has a resident agent or branch manager in the territory, time and money can be saved in investigating that part of the market. A major disadvantage is the absence of any market research skill or technical knowledge of the product; leading to a sales outlook biased towards the producer. Ultimately such an exercise could result in friction between manufacturer and merchant.

Generally only the larger companies can undertake such a task successfully as they tend to have adequate qualified personnel. However, the staff must be well versed in international marketing techniques, have complete objectivity towards the survey and be unbiased in their approach to drawing their conclusions.

Secondly, the director or senior executive of the manufacturing company may be given the task of conducting the survey and submitting the report. In some large companies, market research staff are employed full-time. In others, the export manager or export sales manager is entrusted with the task. Advantages of this technique include: confidentiality of survey and report content (only the manufacturer is aware of such facts); speed of compilation, execution and report presentation; and, finally, convenience, particularly in keeping the costs of the assignment to a minimum and avoiding consultancy fees. However, absence of adequate market research skill in the overseas product market is again a problem, and there is a possibility of producing a biased report. In addition, when the report is published, it may be treated with suspicion as it is not produced by an independent source.

Thirdly, an independent organization may be engaged to render a specialized service for the market research exercise. Several benefits would be gained from this:

1 Modern research techniques would be employed.
2 Experienced, professional personnel would operate directly with the manufacturer and be completely unbiased towards their enquiries and conclusions.
3 In operating outside the umbrella of an advertising agency, the researchers would have no 'in-house' disadvantage from producing an unfavourable report as they would not be trying to secure the advertising account.

Disadvantages emerging from the independent organization include the following, but these can obviously vary by circumstance:

1 Lack of interests is common between the research organization and the company, other than outside the immediate research enquiry.
2 Sometimes there may exist complete lack of absorption of the client's problem, resulting in failure to devise the most effective questionnaire.
3 There is the risk that the independent organization may be stereotyped in its approach to the research task and use a technique it applied to an earlier client's similar problem. This could result in previous research for another sponsor being 're-hashed'. Each research project must be approached with an open, objective mind to ensure that the best results are achieved with no preconceived ideas or conclusions.
4 An independent organization is rarely able to handle all enquiries, so that a second organization would be brought in. Such a situation would not arise in using an advertising agency, who would get to know the market well.
5 The manufacturer tends not to engage an independent organization until the problem reaches a proportion to justify the expenditure and time. Day to day minor points for discussion are rarely raised between the manufacturer and an independent organization, as they are with an advertising agency research department.

One may conclude that the independent research organization has a role to play in international market research but it has limitations which must not be discounted.

Finally, an advertising agency's own market research unit may be employed. Often the manufacturer who engages an advertising agency tends to form a long association with a continuing mutual interest. This encourages a good relationship between the two parties with beneficial results, particularly in understanding the technical specifications and potential of any products manufactured.

Advantages of engaging an advertising agency to undertake market research include:

1 A reasonable, competitive cost.
2 A high degree of professionalism and diversity, as the agency is likely to be experienced with more aspects of research than any one of its clients and thereby able to apply expertise to any one aspect.
3 Good liaison between the research and advertising staff within the advertising agency.
4 Good degree of objectivity towards the project. The agency is well aware of the client's sales results and the researchers would risk their credibility by supplying biased data.
5 The advertising agency offers an integrated service, involving research, marketing, media planning, creative marketing, etc. This aids the production of an effective, co-ordinated marketing and sales plan, backed up by good research.

The prime disadvantages are the length of time sometimes taken to produce the final report and the risk that the agency has ulterior motives in justifying promotion of their advertising turnover. This is not to be seriously considered in respect of any reputable agency or a progressive exporter.

3.5   THE QUESTIONNAIRE

Market research is undertaken usually on a question-and-answer basis by a well-thought-out questionnaire. The questions must be explicit, inoffensive, and unambiguous, Generally the 'yes' or 'no' or pre-choice type of answer produce the best results. Politically loaded questions should be avoided. Overall, the 'yes' or 'no' technique tends to aid classification of answers and thereby enables a more meaningful report to be produced. Moreover, it is desirable that the questionnaire be tested in the field to eliminate any problems in its content which later could prove costly. Above all, the questionnaire should be so formed to produce all the relevant data required of the market research remit while maintaining confidentiality for the respondent during processing.

The compilation of a questionnaire is a skilful task and requires much thought and discussion with personnel involved in the execution of the survey. When a market research/advertising agency is conducting the survey, the manufacturer should have the opportunity to comment on it and ideally the questionnaire should be subject to a test sample to determine its effectiveness and general market response. Above all, the questionnaire terms should be relevant to the remit and must take account of the computer processing needs.

The following points should be borne in mind when drafting the questionnaire:

1 All the questions must be in a logical sequence to enable the informants' thoughts to develop easily as the questionnaire proceeds. Hence, in a product questionnaire enquiry, all the questions on usage should emerge in the early part of the document, and be followed by opinions on package, shape, size, price, etc. In broad terms, the easiest questions should come in the early part of the questionnaire, whilst the more personal matters which may cause embarrassment, or items requiring some thought, should be towards the end of the document. At this stage, the respondent's interest is fully engaged and such questions are less likely to be ignored or answered in a biased manner.

2 Establish a starting point that will ensure that the factor under review is of concern to the respondent. For example, an enquiry on a brand of cigarette must first establish that the respondent is a smoker otherwise the remaining questions are of little consequence.

3 Ambiguous questions must be avoided. To permit precise answers, questions must be specific and easily understood by the informant in the manner intended by the researcher.

4 Third party questions should be used with discretion, and rather sparingly. The question should be of the type which can be answered from the informant's own experience.

5 All irrelevant questions should be avoided as they break the continuity of thought and tend to kill the informant's interest in the enquiry. They also irritate the respondent.

6 Questions should be devised in an impartial manner and not show any bias or prejudice as regards religion, politics, colour, or any other pre-conceived ideas.

7 All 'leading' questions should be avoided because they lead to incorrect information.

8 'Repeat' questions should be omitted unless there are compelling reasons for their inclusion. For example, to ask respondents first their age group and later their date of birth can cause irritation.

9 Endeavour to keep postal questionnaires relatively brief, ideally not exceeding more than ten questions. The questionnaire interview is usually a much longer, 'in-depth' enquiry.

10 The questions should be inoffensive, and should not stray into sensitive areas.

11 At all times ensure that the questionnaire is so framed that the answers required by the remit are produced, and editing and data analysis is relatively straightforward. Avoid open-ended questions such as 'how far do you live from the nearest supermarket?' Ideally, this question should group the distances as, for example, up to 1 kilometre, 1–5 kilometres, 5–10 kilometres, so that the respondent can tick the appropriate group.

Overall there are three types of questions:

1 Dichotomous. This type of question simply requires a 'yes' or 'no' answer. It can be extended to include a 'don't know' or 'no preference' response.
2 The multi-choice question gives several possible answers to reflect varying shades of opinion and choice. For example, one can enquire what type of coffee they prefer which may be classified as black, white (with cream), black with lemon, etc.
3 The open question leaves the respondents to say what they wish. This tends to produce a very wide range of answers and can prove difficult to classify. It is a type of question best avoided unless there are compelling reasons for its inclusion.

The methods of market research can be detailed as follows:

3.5.1   Personal interview from a questionnaire

This involves engaging trained personnel to conduct field interviews. It is costly but reliable. Moreover, a greater number of questions can be asked to produce an 'in depth' interview. Such a survey usually involves fewer questionnaires being completed but produces a good response rate, with genuine answers. The person responding to a field interview tends to give more truthful answers than with a self-administered questionnaire. It can be associated with product sampling.

The following salient points emerge in personal interviews from a questionnaire:

1 The interview is controlled. Hence if the informant does not quite understand the points at issue the investigator can explain them. Moreover, the investigators can ensure that only relevant data are recorded in the answers.
2 The sample of informants is more easily controlled. Investigators choose their interviewees in accord with the instructions given by the person controlling the market research exercise. In so doing, the non-response element can be recorded together with the reason for not participating in the survey.
3 The professional investigator can quickly detect when exaggerated or false information is being given and take remedial measures when necessary.
4 It is particularly advantageous when surveys of a technical nature are being undertaken and detailed technical queries can be dealt with by the investigator thereby ensuring that a more meaningful questionnaire is completed.

5 The personal interview is usually easy to supervise and check, this substantially improves the quality of the survey.

6 The investigator can be flexible in his choice of informants and it may be in a restaurant, at the factory gates, in the supermarket, etc. Moreover, such variability of location can be applied throughout the survey to obtain the best cross-section of respondents.

7 Such a quality survey tends to be expensive per questionnaire completed compared with the shorter, self-administered postal questionnaire.

8 If the survey is conducted on the basis of interviewing specified households, it can be a problem to determine a mutually convenient time. This can prove expensive when the investigator is obliged to make several visits to conform with individual households.

9 Personal interviews can prove embarrassing to both parties, and tact, professionalism and experience are required of the investigator in such circumstances.

10 The investigator may find it difficult to contact the informants, particularly if they work shifts or are away from home on business from time to time. This all inflates the cost of the enquiry per questionnaire completed.

To summarize, the personal interview is usually more meaningful and reliable in the data obtained, but due to the high cost of such a survey the number of questionnaires completed tends to be small when compared to the postal questionnaire technique. Hence, special attention needs to be given in the selection of likely respondents to ensure that the best use is made of the investigator's time and that the number of respondents who refuse to participate is kept as low as possible.

3.5.2   The self-administered questionnaire

This may be despatched to the recipient by post, or picked up at the local retail outlet or other prescribed place. In some cases, it could accompany a product to establish the characteristics of the buying market and what motivated the purchase. This could help in preparing promotions in other areas. The self-administered questionnaire tends to contain no more than ten main questions. Longer questionnaires tend to discourage the person from completing it and thereby produce a poor response rate. The questionnaire is usually returned by post. The cost of obtaining this data on each completed questionnaire is modest compared with the field interview but the response rate tends to be low.

The planning of such field interviews and questionnaire distribution is important. It is desirable that a good cross-section of the populace be obtained relevant to the survey remit terms, and that techniques such as random sampling be adopted in the household selected, rather than a complete blanket coverage in one area which may produce indifferent results. For example, a survey on mopeds is best directed toward the age group 16–45 years, and not amongst old age pensioners.

The completed questionnaires received are edited and processed, usually through a computer to provide a presentation of statistical data in aggregate terms. This forms the basic data on which the report is written. It must be decided whether all the questionnaires are to be processed or merely a random selection of them. A report promptly produced following the survey is essential as material quickly becomes out-of-date.

3.5.3   The organized group discussion

In such circumstances, up to 15 people led by a chairman discuss the merits of a particular product. For example, a new car may have been on the market for some 15 months, and the manufacturer may wish to determine, in an overseas country, the market attitude towards its design, general competitiveness, comfort, reliability, maintenance cost, availability of spares, price competitiveness, etc. Participants in the group must, of course, have some experience of the product and it is usual for them to be all of the same social class or group. Moreover, each participant would be paid a modest fee and a psychologist would be present to help the discussion form meaningful conclusions. Overall, such a method determines attitudes towards, and trends of, a particular product in a specified market. The discussion usually lasts for up to 30 minutes, or longer if required, and is taped throughout. It is later analysed by the research company for compilation of the report.

3.5.4   Syndicated research

Another market research technique is syndicated market research, where several companies/manufacturers participate in the exercise, each bearing a proportion of the cost. For example, several manufacturers of washing machines may wish to find out more about the market in which they are selling/competing in a specified country. Alternatively, this method may involve several unrelated products and companies such as cars, televisions, kitchen furniture, household utensils, etc. Factors under investigation may include price, design, reliability, after-sales service and advertising response, with individual manufacturers providing particular but not common questions to form a composite questionnaire. Each company would receive only the data from the questions it put forward. Overall, it helps to reduce the cost of market research, but the data are not necessarily confidential, as they may be shared with others who may be competitors.

3.5.5   Proprietary research

This technique involves one client in total confidentiality, and the study findings are exclusive to the client company. This is the prime difference to syndicated research. It is the highest-priced method of agency research.

3.5.6 Omnibus surveys

These are conducted on a regular basis by market research organizations, with the client companies purchasing questions to be used in the survey.

3.6 SAMPLING

It will be appreciated that the cost of a market research survey can be considerable and to contain cost whilst at the same time ensuring that the data obtained are meaningful and representative, sampling techniques are used. Two basic types of sampling techniques exist, namely random and quota. With the former the informant is preselected whilst with the latter the informant is chosen by the investigator from pre-determined criteria.

Random sampling gives every person in the selection unit an equal chance of being chosen as, for example, when counterfoils giving the names of all purchasers of tickets are mixed in a sweepstake drum. Such a technique requires all the informants to be identified at the outset, and is completely unbiased. Disadvantages arise because it is not always possible to obtain the complete list of informants and the randomly selected informants tend to be rather scattered with the result of increasing the investigator's cost. The latter arises particularly in a random selection based on the voters lists where household calls tend to be very diverse in their location, and formulation of the visit plan is rather time-consuming. Moreover, there is always the risk the informants may be away and a second call may be necessary. This can prove expensive in areas which are sparsely populated. This technique is not usually employed in commercial research but is more commonly used in government or institutional enquiries.

Another example of a random sampling technique is the random selection of towns or cities. This technique permits the area selected to be broken down into areas of age, sex or occupation of informants before the random selection of names and addresses begins. For example, towns might be selected randomly, then parliamentary wards within them and finally polling districts within these wards. At this stage the names and addresses of the informants to be interviewed can be taken from the voters lists. In this way the addresses would fall in fairly convenient clusters in different parts of each town, thus reducing the main interviewing cost. There is one major disadvantage however; if the random selection hits an abnormal polling district, the results will be distorted. For example a survey on baby foods in a town primarily of people not of child-bearing age would be of little value. Such a situation demonstrates the importance of selecting districts with a homogeneous profile of people.

The most frequently used basis for commercial surveys is quota sampling, usually known as stratified sampling. Existing data are evaluated and broken down into their constituent parts. On completion the sample is then composed of its constituents in similar proportions. For example, where a voters list of 30 000 persons is being used and a 10 per cent quota sample is required, the investigator would take numbers 10, 20, 30, 40, 50, 60, 70, 80, 90 and 100 in the first hundred batch and subsequent hundreds until the 30 000th voter is reached at which stage the 10 per cent sample is attained. Such a technique ensures a consistent sample.

Another method is used sometimes for household products, where families throughout a specified country or region are involved. The families could be grouped as follows:

1 A proportion of families in the conurbation areas.
2 A proportion of families in urban and rural areas.
3 A proportion of families in each social (income) group.
4 Households, classified according to age of housewife.
5 Households, classified according to occupation of chief wage earner.
6 In industrial enquiries, firms classified by number of employees or turnover.

In such an example a schedule of interviews would be prepared from each of these groups and dealt with in the order shown. Hence the first breakdown would define how many calls were to be made in each selected area. Calls to the conurbation, urban and rural areas would be divided among the investigators allocated to each area, who would be instructed to spread their calls according to the relevant income group, occupation, or age. Investigators would interview suitable informants wherever they were available with the rigid strata breakdowns in mind.

One advantage of the quota sampling system is speed of operation, because the investigator is free to go where interviews can most readily be obtained. Moreover, there is no necessity for calling back or for a complicated substitution system, if the informants are not available on the first call. Furthermore, the foregoing system is much less expensive than random sampling as there is no necessity for prepared lists. Disadvantages include the possibility of investigator bias as certain localities may be avoided unless the investigator is instructed to visit them; similarly there may be informant bias, as casual interviewing means meeting only those persons who happen to be at home at the time of the investigator's call; bias from the poor spacing of calls could emerge as investigators tend to take the easiest option and interview the nearest houses in each street, or several houses close together; and finally there may be a lack of precise information on which to calculate the quotas. Overall, many of the disadvantages can be overcome through briefing the investigators well and supervising them properly.

It is evident that such strata classification based on particular characteristics can be used for the construction of random and/or quota samples. Few samples are suitable only for one or the other. The overriding criteria are to ensure that the cost of the survey is reasonable and that money is not wasted in obtaining irrelevant, biased or inadequate data. It must be recognized that some element of statistical regularity must be preserved in order to ensure that the sample is properly representative of the population.

3.7 COMPARISON OF CONSUMER AND INDUSTRIAL RESEARCH

Consumer and industrial research involve differing techniques and it is important we analyse their varying features. Table 3.1 reveals such features.

Table 3.1   A comparison between consumer and industrial research

Consumer	*Industrial*
Distribution	
Transit times longer and more diverse due to the involvement of distributors/ middlemen. It may be a groupage or full-load consignment. Distribution and infrastructure well established.	Usually direct from buyer to seller. Generally the cargo is a full-load or bulk shipment.
Products	
Quicker buying cycle. Effect of economic changes can be predicted from past experience. Short manufacturing cycle, short term forecasts. Repeat purchases in many cases. Product specification closely geared to consumer needs through market research.	Long term buying pattern and cycle. Effect of economic changes more difficult to predict. Long manufacturing cycle, long term forecasts. One-off purchases. Product specification closely geared to developments in high technology.
Buyer behaviour	
Amateur because he or she cannot have expert knowledge of all goods and professionalism in buying tactics. Irrational or sometimes unpredictable behaviour. Consumer always involved in buying decision. Subject to family and social influences. No reciprocal trade. Buyer loyalty tends to be fragmented other than in brand image goods Limited direct buyer/seller relationship in areas of equipment servicing/	Professional. Can call in experts. Natural or usually fairly predictable behaviour. Buyer can be 'rubber stamp'. The decision point is often elsewhere. Subject to company influences. Reciprocal buying/selling may take place. Buyer loyalty tends to be strong, reflecting close liaison between buyer and seller, often established through many years servicing, spares supply and product replacement.

Table 3.1   continued

Consumer	Industrial
replacement; usually undertaken by distributor/agent.	Strong relationship between buyer/ seller over the life of a product in areas of equipment servicing/replacement; can be undertaken by distributor/agent.

Demand

Direct. Ask user.	Often derived, e.g. demand for nylon-making machinery derived from demand for tights, shirts, etc.
Multitude of buyers.	
Demand can be switched, e.g. from cars to fridges.	Ask ultimate market.
Demand is geographically spread and difficult to locate.	Buyer dominance or fewer buyers. Cannot substitute easily.
Demand responds elastically to price changes.	Demand tends to be concentrated, location easier. Inelastic demand prevails, due to technical considerations.

Marketing

Promotion reliance on mass media such as newspaper, radio, TV, posters.	Promotion reliance on technical journals, trade exhibitions.
Selling – through distributors, retailers – pricing: market orientated.	Tendency to be individually negotiated involving sales engineer and financial package which could involve group of companies, with much emphasis on reliability, productivity, performance, spares, training of technicians.
Marketing – tends to be concentrated on an individual market/region basis with established distribution infrastructure.	
Marketing sales – high volume.	
Marketing – large 'in house' export marketing and shipping departments.	Marketing – tends to be fragmented over wider network of markets.
Product much lower price than industrial price and specification usually standard throughout individual markets.	Marketing – sales: small volume. Marketing – small 'in house' export marketing and shipping departments usually sales engineer orientated.
Does not feature extensively in five year Government economic plans or donor agencies.	Product much higher price than consumer product and often designed to meet specific needs. Features prominently in five year Government economic plans and donor agencies and subject to the tendering process.

Again it must be stressed that circumstances vary by individual export contracts; the foregoing must be treated as guidelines. Overall, it must be borne in mind that industrial market research involves smaller samples and longer and less-structured interviews.

3.8   CONSTRAINTS OF THE MARKET RESEARCH SURVEY

It will be readily appreciated that severe limitations do exist in conducting market research, and these are detailed below:

1 Time: a research project takes time to complete and consequently, by the time action is taken on the data, the market might have changed. This can be critical for industrial goods, but for many consumer goods it is sufficiently important for continuous research to be carried out to monitor changing trends. To lessen the cost of continuous research, one can rely more on desk research or conduct limited field research in a selected area of relevance to the manufacturer's own market. Additional research data may be available from trade associations or the COI and good use should be made of agents' reports and the export sales executive's market intelligence reports following visits to overseas territories and attendance at trade exhibitions.

2 Commercial risk: the market research exercise can never eliminate risk, it can only reduce it. Management must apply its judgement at some stage because research merely collects information and does not formulate decisions. The researcher and/or client must draw their own conclusions on survey data analysis.

3 Accuracy of data: whilst with random samples there are statistical techniques for testing accuracy, these do not apply to quota samples. Even with random samples, statistical techniques cannot detect certain types of error such as those due to poor quality interviewing.

4 Predictions: these can never be completely accurate because people can only state beliefs or intentions at any point in time and a subsequent change in circumstances can change their beliefs. This may be due to a political, economic, or social situation, for example.

5 Cost: market research, especially in the field, can be expensive. Such an exercise should be carefully costed before any commitment is made and the benefit likely to be derived therefrom should be carefully evaluated.

6 Personnel: the quality of the survey is largely determined by the calibre of the staff involved in conducting it at all levels. Personnel working in the field distributing questionnaires, conducting interviews must be properly supervised and completely committed to the assignment and its objectives. Poorly conducted interviews, wrongly distributed questionnaires and falsely completed questionnaires can produce indifferent results and consequent abortive expenditure.

7 Techniques used to purchase the product: personnel involved in the formulation and conduct of the survey must be fully conversant with the techniques in the market which relate to the buying, distribution, promotion and retailing of the product. The experienced advertising agent also conducting market research is often in a most favourable position to undertake such a task, whilst the independent research organization may not be so well situated.

8 Buyer dominance: many companies and industries are dominated by a relatively small number of large buyers. This should be reflected in the formulation of the market research plan.

It will be appreciated that the importance of the foregoing will vary by individual survey.

3.9 CONCLUSION

Market research is an important area in export marketing. It is a very specialized subject and, to obtain the best results, professional personnel of experience must be engaged to conduct it. Moreover, it is an area where money can be ill-spent without proper preparation of a well thought-out survey with clear objectives and a disciplined time scale.

It often happens that when the market research has been undertaken, the survey report, or programme of implementation as a result of the report's recommendations, is delayed for some practical reason. The important point to bear in mind is that market situations, especially profile, competition and legislation can change quickly and market research data can become out-of-date. Hence, there is a need to set the recommendations of the report into motion quickly to ensure that maximum benefit is derived. A continuous market research programme, with varying degrees of scale year by year, is also beneficial in this respect.

Finally the exporter may be interested to obtain and study the booklet issued by the International Chamber of Commerce entitled *International Codes of Advertising Practice*. It deals with International Chamber of Commerce (ICC No. 432B) marketing codes on advertising, market research, and sales promotion plus the rules of the ICC Council on Marketing Practice which apply to codes at international level.

4 Export promotion

Export promotion comprises all those activities undertaken by an exporter, by direct or indirect methods with a view to persuading general buyers (the public) or specific buyers to purchase the exporter's products or services in preference to other products, or services offered by other companies, either locally or from overseas.

Essentially, it is a communication exercise conveying a specific message to the consumer/end user. It may arise in one of the following situations:

1 Supporting the sale of existing products or services in an established market overseas.
2 Promoting the sale of a new product or service in an established market abroad.
3 Entering the market through the promotion of products or services which are entirely new to the market.
4 Informing and educating users and dealers about the exporter's organization, its objectives in the market, and seeking to influence attitudes favourably towards the exporter.

Before examining the basic principles relating to advertising we will consider a number of the factors influencing type of promotion, media choice, and the merits of various types of media presentation.

4.1 FACTORS DETERMINING TYPE OF PROMOTION

The export sales manager will feature in his sales and marketing plan the techniques to be used in the promotion of the products. In so doing he may use a combination of such techniques according to the individual country and other factors involved. This will also involve the media plan which details the advertising programme and budget for the product. Details of the factors involved in such an evaluation are given below:

1 Availability of monies for such a promotion. If it is a product launch it is likely to have a larger budget when compared with an established product, and possible ways of reducing the advertising budget must be explored. See items (17) and (18).

2 The degree of competition, both short- and long-term. Usually, the greater the degree of competition, the higher the budget allocation per forecasted product sale. Moreover, imported products generally tend to attract more advertising expenditure than the product for the home-based market.

3 The type of product involved, and its retail price. Up to 6% of the retail price can be expended on promotion, but the usual figure is 1–2%.

4 The method of sale. This may be through a group sale arrangement, a consortium or an agent. The distributor or agent often share the promotion cost with the exporter equally.

5 The type of market. In a highly industrialized country more sophisticated promotion techniques can be used compared with countries of lower educational standard, where there is more reliance on radio communication and illustrated poster sites.

6 The cost of the promotion annually/per enquiry/per order/per salesman/by media, etc.

7 An important factor, requiring detailed consideration, is the result of market research showing how the product can best be promoted from the general attitudes towards it.

8 The resources available within the company to handle the promotion and their adequacy and cost.

9 The type of sales organization that will be required for the territory (e.g. own salesman, distributor, agent, trading company or joint venture).

10 Whether the product is geared to a seasonal or all-the-year-round market.

11 The size of the market and the market share expected to be gained from the promotion.

12 The demographical and topographical features of the region(s).

13 The sizes of the various market strata by geographical region; size of user; industry; type, quality, design or price of product; and type of distributor.

14 How the market compares with one, five or ten years ago. Does any trend emerge which will influence the promotion format?

15 Any political constraints which may cause adverse market response. This may include racial or religious factors or the restrictions on certain terms or slogans imposed by any national advertising code.

16 The advertising agency recommendation in the overseas market.

17 Opportunities to promote the product through an overseas trade fair, inwards or outwards mission developed in consultation with the BOTB, Chamber of Commerce, or trade association. Other UK exporters would participate in the scheme.

18 Advertising/promotion guidance may be available from the appropriate Chamber of Commerce based in the exporter's country and representing

the buyer's country. An example is the Anglo–Dutch Chamber of Commerce based in London.
19 The timescale of the media plan.

The most important factors are the type of product involved, the cost of promotion and its potential profitable market. Another dominant feature is the level of competition the product will encounter. Successful promotion could involve more than one medium such as an advertising feature in the national papers coupled with television coverage in high density areas of population which offer good potential market response. It is advisable to give adequate thought to the type of promotion and thereby ensure that the money is spent with maximum benefit. Test marketing can prove useful in gauging market response.

4.2   ADVERTISING PRINCIPLES

Advertising may be defined as the purchase and use of space in a newspaper, magazine or outdoor locations, or of time on radio or television, by an identified sponsor such as the exporter for the promotion of goods or services. By contrast, sales promotion complements the advertising activity through personal selling and publicity especially in the areas of user interest, point of sale activity and dealer effectiveness.

The exporter conducting an overseas advertising campaign has four basic options as detailed below:

1 Through the overseas associates or subsidiaries of the firm's UK advertising agency.
2 Utilizing the firm's UK advertising agency working either direct with overseas media or through the UK representatives of those media.
3 The exporter working direct with foreign advertising agencies.
4 In a small or underdeveloped market, and usually only at the first stage, through the exporter's sales agent or distributor.

The criteria for the selection of one of these methods is as follows:

1 The number and geographical spread of the overseas markets in which the advertiser wishes to operate.
2 The size of the advertising campaign funding available.
3 The degree of sophistication required in media choice and creativity.
4 The presence or absence of the exporter's own manufacturing sales organization(s) in the market(s) overseas.

A business of modest size might have an advertising department comprising an advertising manager and possibly two assistants. Its work may be in sales promotion – dealing with catalogues, illustrated literature and occasional modest advertising activity in the trade and public press, with possible attendance at trade fairs and exhibitions. A larger, home-based company will have a correspondingly bigger advertising department, with an advertising budget running into tens of thousands of pounds. In an international firm, this figure could exceed one million pounds. It is likely that a company running a million-pound campaign would engage the specialized services of an advertising agency.

Factors influencing the merits of engaging an advertising agency and its selection include: the scale of promotion; the resources available in the exporter's company to devise an effective advertising programme; the experience of the agency with the product or similar products; the extent of television and press advertising in the promotion programme (advertising agencies usually can obtain substantial discounts in advertising rates); the general creditability of the agency; the product and market/consumer profile and the outcome of any relevant market research studies; whether the product is a new launch or a further development of an existing product range; and the acceptability of the agency's proposal for the media programme.

A favourable aspect of using an advertising agency is the possibility of obtaining reasonable rates for some services through sharing the services with the many other clients of the agency; for example, the employment of film companies for television advertising. Alternatively, the exporter can seek advice from the Overseas Press & Media Association, or the Institute of Practitioners in Advertising (see Appendix E for addresses).

The exporter may need to advertise in two ways: initially, in overseas trade papers and journals to find potential agents or distributors (the Department of Trade and Industry can help provide a suitable agent); and later, in the media of the overseas market to attract the customers.

The Department of Trade and Industry's service of identifying a suitable agent in the overseas market works through the Diplomatic Service Posts. It will require from the exporter the product specification details, trade literature and prices, and other relevant data. The Diplomatic Service Post report will short-list a number of suitable agents and identify their trading interest, capabilities, scope of activities, other agencies held, territory they can usually cover effectively, warehousing and distribution facilities, salesforce, technical 'know-how' and after-sales support. When the report is received by the exporter, it is usual for the exporter to visit the market and choose the agent. The local Diplomatic Service can assist in the selection process. In compiling relevant literature it is important to bear in mind that the language used must be that of the country which will import the goods. Similar remarks apply to packaging and other promotional material. Every language has its own idioms and colloquialisms and it would be very risky to put what is acceptable in the UK market into the list of an overseas advertising campaign without consulting experts. In many cases it is essential to keep the 'copy' (text matter) to a minimum in consumer advertising, putting the message over primarily by illustration.

The basic principle of all advertising in newspapers and periodicals is that it should be aimed specifically at the section of the community or type of clientele which buys or could be persuaded to buy the product. This involves three elements:

1 Market research must show the manufacturer quite clearly the social class (i.e. A1, B2, D, etc.) within which he can expect to sell his goods.
2 The exporter must establish – ideally at the market research stage – what periodicals and papers are read by the class defined in (1), and place his advertising accordingly.
3 The advertising copy must be appropriate to the merchandise and to the class of potential purchaser.

Finally, we must bear in mind whether the exporter wants quality advertising targetted at a specific consumer profile, or quantity advertising, involving a much larger audience, as seen on TV.

4.3   MEDIA PRESENTATION

There are four basic factors to consider in the selection of the medium type: characteristics, atmosphere, quantitative coverage and cost.

The characteristics are the qualities that the medium makes available to the product/service and its message. This includes: size of advertisement(s); facilities for colour, sound, movement and demonstration of the product; length of life of the advertisement; facilities for its repetition; support it provides for selling; impact of the medium on groups other than users, and its overall effectiveness relative to the culture.

The atmosphere derives partly from the medium itself and partly from the state of mind of the reader, viewer or listener at the time of advertisement exposure. Some newspapers have a dignified and authoritative editorial atmosphere and consequently are important for advertising to the business community. Some media such as the cinema have a youthful, light-hearted, 'escapist' atmosphere and are useful for products, and also service industries such as banks and building societies, which target the young adult market. Hence each media provides an atmosphere which can assist or be detrimental to the advertiser's message.

Quantitative coverage involves the analysis of the market profile. Market research will help to establish demographical, socio–economic classification, geographical distribution, size of firm, and other appropriate classification. Basically it is the process of matching media coverage to these user characteristics.

The cost of the media plan must be reconciled to the budget and the period of the campaign.

We will now examine the types of media available and their characteristics.

4.3.1   Press advertising

This very popular method of promotion may involve national or local newspapers, consumer or trade magazines and technical journals. Newspapers are daily or weekly, based on a national or local coverage. Additionally there are the free circulation papers which may come out weekly or monthly and feature primarily the advertisements which pay for the paper, with limited news coverage. They will carry features describing the product promoted in the advertisements displayed in the free newspaper. Magazines usually appeal to specific groups in the community, for example to women, motorists or gardeners. Technical publications are usually very specialized and are primarily directed at the trader (in catering, building or nursing, for example). They may appear weekly, monthly or quarterly.

Each newspaper or magazine has a specialized market and this should be taken into consideration, together with its circulation, to determine whether it is suitable for promoting the product. The advertising agency can give guidance on this matter. Moreover, the exporter must establish whether the publication has any political or religious allegiance, and, if so, whether this is compatible with the product and the manufacturer's promotion. One must be conscious of the risk of a negative response. For example, when promoting a product aimed at the less literate section of the community, pictorial presentations are more likely to produce the desired impact.

Another principle of good advertising, though harder to carry out in practice when advertising overseas than in the home market, is to 'key' whenever possible. A keyed advertisement is one where the public's taste is whetted to the extent that they will fill in a coupon asking for further details or a brochure. This could be linked to a special promotional offer giving a discounted price to readers of that particular newspaper or journal. The identical coupon appears in a number of newspapers or journals simultaneously, and a small code number or initial establishes from which paper the respondent took his coupon. This determines the readership response rate to the coupon promotion from each newspaper, which proves useful in subsequent promotions. The results can be grouped to establish the type of periodical on which to concentrate in future campaigns. Usually, the manufacturer finds such a task too onerous and relies on the distributor to compile the data.

It is important to ensure the correct timing of the advertising programme. For example, in an agricultural community people have little time for reading newspapers at harvest time and rarely get beyond the headlines.

However, after harvest, they have both money to spend and time to read, at which stage the advertising campaign should come on stream. Market research and/or a good distributor or agent can give adequate guidance. A further point to bear in mind is that repeated presentation tends to produce better results than isolated advertising. Conversely, to saturate the market with an extensive advertising campaign is extremely costly and of doubtful benefit when viewed against a more modest campaign.

A feature of a press advertising campaign is each paper usually has a readership factor of above one, and for journals and weekend editions it may be four or five. Hence the advertisement has a life of several days in some media and enables the reader to evaluate the message in depth. Likewise it permits the exporter to insert extensive copy material to persuade the reader of the product/service qualities and thereby secure a sale. By contrast, with TV and radio, the message has no life other than the time it is transmitted. The viewer or listener merely sees the video or listens to the audio transmission. Its impact is felt at the time of the transmission and it has no recall life in the sense the viewer/listener has no second opportunity of receiving the message other than through a repeat transmission. In consequence the advertising copy for TV and the press differ, but one may still complement the other.

To conclude our brief examination of advertising principles, one must consider each situation on its merits and have regard to the points made in the media plan on pages 77–83. It is vital to follow the guidance of market research results and the advertising agency, and to take general advice from the market itself. A basic requisite is always to use current data and to have regard for any possible future developments which may be significant (the agent should be well informed in this respect).

4.3.2   Television commercial

Many products are ideal for visual promotion on television, but it must be remembered that not all countries permit commercial advertising through this medium. However, television is a growth market in many countries, and has yet to reach its full potential in many more; where established, it has a captive audience in the home, regardless of age, religion, sex or class. Television can employ the audio message with sound effects, visual effects, animation, colour and a musical background, possibly even its own 'jingle'. It is usual to engage an advertising agency to produce a suitable television advertising campaign as they can obtain concessionary terms from film companies to produce the commercial, and discounts from the television companies. The commercial is usually based in '30 second spots', but other rates apply for 7, 15 and 45 seconds. The rates depend on the time of day or programme and, obviously, the likely viewing audience. It is essential that the commercial is well thought-out and professionally produced. Prime time is peak viewing time and commands the highest rates.

4.3.3   Radio commercial

This method is ideal for products which are easy to describe and do not have a strong visual impact. Moreover, in under-developed countries it is often the only means of communication, particularly when illiteracy is common. A radio commercial is very much cheaper than a television commercial, both in terms of programme production cost and transmission time. Commercial radio can be either a local or national network (as indeed can television, especially in industrial countries) and is a growth market which does not appear to be affected adversely by the availability of television advertising. The spoken word is a powerful, personally-directed approach; with the wide use of battery operated sets from pocket size upwards, the radio reaches areas where the press does not. It has increasing appeal as an advertising medium for the mass-produced consumer goods and semi-durable products. Advertising rates vary according to the country, time of day and duration on the air.

4.3.4   Cinema

Slide or film presentation in the cinema is becoming more popular, particularly with local promotions. It is most effective when the dialogue is limited to avoid problems with language barriers and thereby gain wider international appeal. Although the film cost may be high, its cost can be adequately recouped if it is shown in several countries. One must not discount the fact that there are still many countries where the cinema remains a great attraction such as the Indian sub-continent, the USSR, etc.

An increasing number of short advertising films are produced locally, where advertising is usually limited to consumer goods. Industrial films (16 mm) produced in the UK can be shown to selected audiences such as technical associations and education authorities. Television advertisements tend to vie with those in the national newspapers whilst cinema advertisements compete with those in local newspapers. Television has the advantage of giving the impact of a 'live' medium.

The use of cinemas for advertising purposes in overseas markets can prove very effective, but local tastes and standards are very varied and the advertiser must investigate the medium thoroughly before using it. Usually the British commercial representative such as the Embassy or High Commission can help in this respect.

There are two basic techniques which can be directed at a cinema audience:

1 Cinema slides to make single announcements, usually during the film intervals and whilst the audience lights are on.
2 Short films similar to television commercials present a moving picture and attract more attention than slides. Moreover, the audience usually sits

through them and regards the 'filmlet' as part of the total performance it has paid to see. An increasing number of UK and US manufacturers have produced 16 mm films for cinema and commercial television abroad. Sometimes the film is despatched overseas with two audio (magnetic) strips: one strip carrying the English text and the other one blank for the local language to be added on the spot before the film is circulated to the cinemas.

Overall the cinema is a medium which can produce encouraging promotion results at relatively low cost.

4.3.5   Poster advertising

Sites for poster displays are diverse. They can be situated on hoardings, vehicles or passenger terminals at train and coach stations or airports, for example. A more recent development is the illuminated poster display or pictogram in shopping centres of main shopping streets. Posters deteriorate rapidly and are used only for subjects requiring short-term publicity, but are ideal for many consumer products. Metal signs can be used to advertise such commodities as petrol, oil, tyres, bicycles, cigarettes and cars. Local Government licences may be required to display posters and signs in public places.

Poster design and artwork must be undertaken professionally. The following points are particularly relevant:

1 It is usually unwise to use posters originally produced for use in the UK, as their design is unsuited to the overseas markets; they are costly to despatch; climatic conditions may cause the poster to deteriorate if the material cannot withstand excessive sunlight, high degrees of humidity, etc.
2 The exporter should ideally despatch a selection of suggested designs and arrange for the distributor or agent to have them produced and/or distributed.
3 The display sites require careful selection and general reference to the scheme, including budget provision, will be made in the media plan. Again, site selection should be entrusted to the agent or distributor. The timing of the display sites should obviously coincide with the launch of the product; poster displays or hoardings tend to form part of an overall advertising plan and supplement television or press advertising. The site for display tends to be hired for any time up to one year, so the poster has a much longer life than a newspaper advertisement. The more popular sites such as passenger terminals or busy railway stations have to be booked up months in advance. Here, daily audiences could exceed 200 000 passengers. An inspectorate usually exists to check regularly on poster site displays.
4 A more recent development is the display showcase depicting the client's product. This is found especially at airport passenger terminals or large railway stations. It is an ideal display unit for a wide variety of merchandise

and has the advantages that the actual product can be shown on the display unit and the product display can be changed throughout the rental period to maintain public interest in the promotion. Also the video is now in use in some countries.

Many exporters fail to realize the potential of the poster display, but it is a facility worthy of careful consideration. Moreover, the cost of such a promotion can usually be shared equally with the agent or distributor.

4.4 MEDIA PLAN

In an era when more and more money is being spent on press and television advertising, it is most important that a media or campaign plan (Figure 4.1) is devised so that it reaches the right people for the product. A major media plan is usually produced by the advertising agency in consultation with the advertising or publicity department of the promoter. It is essential that it is launched to coincide with the availability of the product in the retail outlets, and this could involve a lead-time of up to twelve months from the time the plan is first discussed. Ideally all concerned with the promotion should attend a briefing to discuss objectives and strategy.

Media planning is determined by three basic points: what should be said, where should it be said, and how should it be said?

The merits of using a standardized message in a number of countries such as throughout the European Community will raise the question in each of those countries whether a common brand identity, market segmentation strategy, advertising theme and creative theme need be adopted. This strategy would permit of local variations to ensure that any particular linguistic, legal and social considerations are met. It would apply to the user population and whether identical marketing techniques of communication arise such as in the UK, the USA, Sweden, Switzerland and West Germany would prove effective. Moreover, are the buying motives/information needs the same for most markets, as they are with a complex technical product bought by industrial users? It would include data on price, durability, productivity/performance/output, after-sales service warranty and so on. This type of promotional standardization will reduce cost in such ancillaries as blocks, artwork and film production.

We will now examine the factors relevant to the compilation of the media plan:

1 The objectives of the media plan must be clearly defined and all personnel associated with the formulation and execution of the plan must be aware of them. It may involve, for example, television putting across the main message/theme and local press advertising giving details of the retail outlets and relevant 'back up' information.

2 The media plan should be costed against the market potential and be

closely in accord with the budget predictions. Advertising agencies are usually able to obtain discounts for television press advertising.

3 The plan should specify separately the television and press advertising programme. The advertising agency should be foremost in producing the format of the advertising programme, in consultation with the client. Full use should be made of any research material and statistical data on market or customer profile and any commercial intelligence data relating to the product which are available. It is often sensible to test market the advertising material to gauge the response to it. This also gives the sales personnel an opportunity to comment on the programme. It is important that the media should not offend any section of the population; remember that what is acceptable in one country may be offensive in another.

4 The media schedule should be cleared with the supply department to ensure that merchandise is available in the shops and other retail outlets. Ideally, all sales personnel and retail outlets should have details of the advertising programme so that they can inform their staff. The promoter may have special leaflets available to market the product and window displays to catch the customer's eye. Some local retailers may fund their own advertising material to support the product. Alternatively a joint scheme with the supplier could be undertaken, as described earlier (see section 3.5.4, page 61).

5 Attention should be given to regional variations in climate; if a particular region has a high rainfall level, it is unlikely to have a heavy demand for sunwear.

6 Once the media plan has been launched it should be reviewed at regular intervals, when any necessary alterations can be made in the content of the advertising programme and/or the dates when the television commercial or press adverts appear.

7 It is often the practice to run a market research survey concurrently with the advertising programme, to establish its effectiveness. This is usually on a small scale and enables the promoters to make adjustment to any subsequent plan. For example, the programme may have been launched too late in the year or resulted in shortages of the product. The latter could be due to a supply problem or a poor estimation of demand.

8 In correcting future media plans, opportunity should be taken to discuss the survey results with sales personnel and retail outlets.

9 Any advertising code of practice operative in the importer's country must be taken into account.

10 Consideration should be given to the strengths and weaknesses of existing promotions by competitors.

11 Above all, the cost of the plan must be related both to the short-term and long-term market potential of the product (see Table 4.1).

Given below is a broad analysis of a number of countries' breakdown of advertising expenditure by principal media in 1984 and 1986.

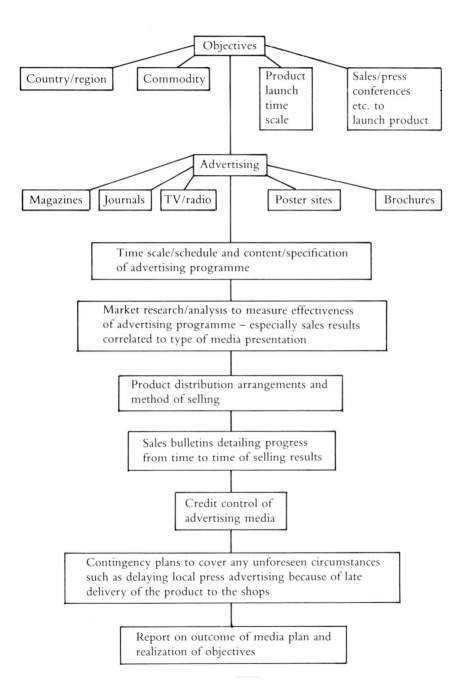

Figure 4.1 Media or campaign plan.

Table 4.1   Advertising expenditure analysis by media of selected countries 1984 and 1986 (expressed as percentage)

Country	Local currency	Total advertising expenditure millions		Total as % of GNP		Newspapers		Magazines	
		1984	1986	1984	1986	1984	1986	1984	1986
Austria	OS gross	6,380	7,512	0.5	0.5	37.3	34.7	14.9	17.2
Australia	$ gross	2,965	3,543	1.6	1.8	30.8	40.1	15.4	5.1
Belgium	FB gross	16,830	20,120	0.3	0.3	26.9	24.2	43.2	41.8
Brazil	CZ gross	8,016,150	17,760,400	0.8	0.7	32.5	24.3	10.9	13.1
Canada	CDN net	5,761	6,670	1.33	1.35	30.0	29.0	7.3	7.2
Switzerland	FS net	3,197	3,786	1.41	1.48	38.3	39.1	14.1	6.1
Colombia	CPes gross	43,478	60,576	1.2	0.9	14.0	18.0	5.0	6.0
W. Germany	DM net	15,084	16,486	0.9	0.8	39.8	38.1	17.8	16.6
Denmark	DKr gross	6,404	9,000	1.24	1.34	40.2	DNA	3.3	DNA
Spain	Pta gross	257,000	417,000	1.0	1.3	25.5	25.3	12.8	12.7
France	FF gross	36,500	44,800	0.94	0.99	22.5	23.5	33.5	34.5
G. Britain	£ gross	4,059	5,117	1.45	1.58	43.0	41.7	6.7	5.9
Greece	Dr gross	13,558	23,526	0.4 (GDP)	0.2 (GDP)	18.3	18.7	22.6	23.8
Italy	LIR gross	5,055	7,898	0.8	0.9	15.6	14.1	21.5	20.0
Ireland	IR£ net	87	116	0.7	DNA	33.5	31.0	10.2	12.0
Japan	Yen 000 net	2,916	3,051	0.99	0.92	29.0	28.8	6.4	6.9
Mexico	MPes gross	92,717	356,277	0.32	0.37	8.4	8.8	3.2	2.8
Norway	NKr net	5,300	8,890	1.2	1.7	47.5	42.7	7.5	3.3
Netherlands	NLG gross	5,809	7,128	1.46	1.66	31.7	28.5	6.1	6.3
Portugal	Esc gross	6,911	13,450	0.26	0.32	30.0	28.0	DNA	DNA
Argentina	$A net	51.2	841.3	1.1	1.2	28.6	28.0	3.7	3.4
Taiwan	NT$ gross	19,700	22,858	0.78	0.83	41.0	40.0	5.9	6.7
S. Korea	WON gross	683,354	818,539	1.06	0.98	37.8	36.7	3.5	4.2
Sweden	SKr gross	3,794	5,521	0.48	0.48	81.0	71.6	13.6	11.9
Finland	FIM gross	4,911	5,911	1.60	1.65	62.8	63.8	10.4	9.1
USA	$ net	87,820	103,140	2.4	2.4	26.9	26.4	5.6	5.2

4.5   SALES PROMOTION

The package is the container or wrapping in which the merchandise is presented to the consumer. In many countries stringent regulations exist regarding description of the goods and, for perishable goods, the final date of sale. To reduce cost, many multinational companies print the merchandise contents and, where relevant, any consumer instructions in more than one language. In other markets the goods are despatched in bulk and packaging is done locally, as this method is cheaper in the circumstances.

Country	Trade press		Television		Radio		Cinema		Outdoor transport		Miscellaneous including direct mail	
	1984	1986	1984	1986	1984	1986	1984	1986	1984	1986	1984	1986
Austria	DNA	DNA	27.5	28.6	12.2	12.4	DNA	DNA	8.1	7.1	DNA	DNA
Australia	2.0	2.9	34.5	34.2	9.2	9.0	1.4	1.5	6.7	7.3	DNA	DNA
Belgium	DNA	DNA	14.8	15.8	1.1	2.1	1.0	1.6	13.0	14.4	DNA	DNA
Brazil	DNA	DNA	48.0	54.3	8.6	8.3	DNA	DNA	DNA	DNA	DNA	DNA
Canada	DNA	DNA	16.8	16.6	9.5	9.1	DNA	DNA	6.8	7.3	29.6	30.8
Switzerland	DNA	6.3	4.4	4.6	0.5	1.0	0.5	0.6	6.1	6.6	36.1	35.7
Colombia	DNA	DNA	56.0	54.0	25.0	22.0	DNA	DNA	DNA	DNA	DNA	DNA
W. Germany	8.2	8.9	9.0	9.1	3.5	3.5	0.8	0.8	3.0	3.1	17.9	19.9
Denmark	6.6	DNA	DNA	DNA	DNA	DNA	0.6	DNA	1.6	DNA	47.7	DNA
Spain	DNA	DNA	24.7	24.1	9.7	9.8	0.9	0.6	3.1	3.5	23.3	24.0
France	DNA	DNA	17.5	19.0	9.0	8.5	2.0	1.5	15.5	13.0	DNA	DNA
G. Britain	13.3	13.7	30.7	32.7	2.1	1.8	0.5	0.4	3.7	3.8	DNA	DNA
Greece	DNA	DNA	47.2	49.2	6.5	6.4	DNA	DNA	5.4	6.9	DNA	DNA
Italy	DNA	DNA	61.5	61.8	1.4	1.6	DNA	DNA	DNA	2.5	DNA	DNA
Ireland	DNA	DNA	35.6	37.0	11.8	11.0	1.1	DNA	7.8	9.0	DNA	DNA
Japan	DNA	2.2	35.4	35.3	5.1	5.2	DNA	DNA	*21.6	*21.7	2.5	DNA
Mexico	1.3	1.5	69.7	69.0	13.3	13.7	1.5	1.2	2.6	3.0	DNA	DNA
Norway	8.5	5.1	DNA	DNA	DNA	DNA	2.8	0.6	3.0	1.1	*30.7	*47.2
Netherlands	5.6	4.7	5.3	5.9	1.1	1.2	0.3	0.2	5.6	6.1	*44.3	*47.1
Portugal	DNA	DNA	52.0	58.0	18.0	14.0	DNA	DNA	DNA	DNA	DNA	DNA
Argentina	0.3	0.3	28.3	30.6	11.6	10.1	2.0	2.5	6.8	8.2	*18.7	*16.9
Taiwan	DNA	DNA	30.0	33.9	7.9	6.5	DNA	DNA	DNA	DNA	*15.2	*12.9
S. Korea	DNA	DNA	37.1	36.5	6.3	5.4	DNA	DNA	*13.1	DNA	2.2	DNA
Sweden	DNA	5.9	DNA	DNA	DNA	DNA	0.9	0.7	4.5	4.4	DNA	5.5
Finland	DNA	DNA	10.6	9.8	0.0	0.7	0.2	0.1	1.5	1.5	*14.6	*15.0
USA	2.8	2.3	22.6	22.7	6.6	6.8	DNA	DNA	1.0	1.0	*34.5	*35.6

* Includes direct mail
Source: Nielsen Marketing Trends

The art of designing the package and its practical application are known collectively as packaging. The following are the salient considerations in choice of packaging from the sales promotion standpoint:

1 Each package must be so designed as to have a good 'eye appeal', while ensuring it is adequately robust and a convenient shape and size for both the distributor and consumer. Inadequate and flimsy packaging will produce an adverse reaction from the retailers and consumers.

2 Selection of materials is very important. The prime consideration is that the package must be strong enough to withstand transit and handling, but its choice must also have regard to climate conditions of the countries of destination, such as humidity or excessive sunlight. Today, with containerization, packaging costs tend to be reduced in international distribution, as the container itself is a major form of protection to the goods and the merchandise is only handled when the goods leave the container unit.

3 The size and configuration of the package require very careful evaluation. The optimum package size must be sought, particularly with regard to distribution arrangements; the larger the package, the more expensive the freight charges. Furthermore, skilful use of the container cubic capacity will ensure that maximum use is made of the space available and that no broken stowage results. Container stowage requires special attention in the export office and related departments and readers are recommended to study pages 94–8 of *Elements of Export Practice*. Although attractive from an aesthetic point of view, a novel package shape can make counter or window display difficult, and encourages broken stowage in the container.

4 Colours selected for the package must be appropriate for the product. Bright colours have a strong market appeal, but are not always suitable. Market research will aid in making the choice of colour compatible with customer profile. In some countries certain colours have different symbolic meanings or associations, especially in politics and religion. In this case it is better to avoid the colours in question.

5 Ideally the name display should be very prominent. Many multinational companies have developed their own and very effective brand name/ symbol/logo, which is easily recognizable and generates much good will in the market place. Through skilful design and shrewd market development these symbols can suggest to the consumer a certain range of products, which aids marketing. More companies should give attention to their brand name symbol or logo and research its effectiveness from time to time. An illiterate market will obviously respond better to a pictorial design than to a brand name symbol with wording.

6 The description and instructions for use must be brief but explicit, containing all essential details. An increasing tendency is to have multilingual instructions inserted in the package. If the exporter elects to have such details on the package itself, care must be taken to ensure such information is placed in a position in the package where it will not be damaged on opening. One must also bear in mind that legislation can vary by country as regards merchandise description – as with the *Trade Descriptions Act* in the UK. Similar remarks apply to advertising and general promotional material including brochures and posters. Moreover, a slogan appropriate in one country might cause offence in other countries and may require modification.

7 Promotional awareness, involving the provision of a package with strong

visual appeal, must be a key factor in package design: successful manufacturers usually engage their export and publicity departments to do the task.
Often the advertising agency is consulted and any market research conclusions
are noted.

8 Cost is an important element in packaging. Advice on various packaging
specifications can be obtained from such organizations as the Packaging
Industry Research Association (PIRA) (see pages 349–50 of *Elements of
Export Practice*). Ideally, a cost-effectiveness study should be undertaken for
the product involved.

To conclude our examination of the sales promotion role of the package,
it cannot be stressed too strongly the need for the exporter to give it
adequate attention using all the relevant resources available such as export
departments, publicity officer, market research and advertising agencies.
The advertising agency is likely to contact local consumer associations,
whilst the agent or distributor is preoccupied with other trade aspects. The
cost of packaging must be given proper consideration in terms of the
expense of producing and transporting the package. Overall such features
must be reviewed against market impacts; if, through spending a little more
on general presentation, sales are increased, such cost could well prove
worthwhile.

Test marketing is very worthwhile. Not only will it gauge consumer
reaction to the product packaging, but also its durability in transit. The
latter may suggest some internal strutting and/or buffering within the
package. Exporters should keep up to date on new packaging techniques
developed within the industry.

4.6 AFTER-SALES SERVICE

Failure to provide a reliable after-sales service will seriously damage the
performance of the product and the company image in the overseas market
place. Where the products require after-sales service, the agency contract is
likely to contain a clause binding the agent to provide the necessary service
and to carry a stock of spares; the same clause may require the agent to
implement the maker's guarantee, or this point may be mentioned separately.
The principal (manufacturer) undertakes to provide the agent with lists of
spare parts and maintenance or service manuals for such products in order
that the agent may carry out his part of the contract. If the product is a
fairly simple device, service may not involve many complications. The
manufacturer may even supply a pre-arranged stock of many parts which
he knows from experience are likely to fail. The spares are despatched with
the appliances. To save administrative costs and complicated accounting
procedures the spares are often despatched to the consumer free of charge.

In the case of more complicated delicate appliances the manufacturer sends, with the spares list, the recommendations regarding the quantities the agent should hold, but he leaves the agent to order what he requires. The agent may be able to obtain some of the components on the spares list in his own country more quickly and cheaply than from the exporter, e.g. standard electrical components and car accessories such as sparking plugs, batteries and tyres.

The procedure for charging for spares varies. With some appliances the manufacturer may know from experience that it is best to charge the agent and to leave claims arising from the implementation of the guarantee for subsequent settlement – the amount involved being off-set against the account for later shipments of the products. Other principals supply spares to their agents on a consignment account basis leaving the agent to pay any expenses and/or import duties involved. With regard to the settlement of a claim for failure of parts in use, evidence would be required that failure comes under the guarantee. Accordingly the agent's claim would be set against the consignment account with any incidental costs debited to him.

The nature and extent of the after-sales service provided by the agent varies according to market conditions and what has been laid down in the agreement between the principal and the agent. Thus, in a large and sophisticated market, one of the reasons that a particular agent is chosen may be that he has a service depot or repair shop under his own control – well equipped with test gear, tools, etc., employing reliable and experienced engineers and with a well proven work flow system. Conversely in a small market, especially in a backward country, the agent might not be justified in running a service organization of his own because it would be under-employed and therefore uneconomic. More and more principals are now insisting that their agents undertake their own service operations, particularly with more sophisticated products (Customer Services).

4.7 PRODUCT SUPPORT PROVISION

Product support data basically consists of technical information about a technical product; this is provided by the vendor for users, distributors and servicing engineers. It is an area which today has become essential in the product promotion package; great skill must be exercised in its composition and, above all, it must be kept up-to-date. Accordingly, distributors and service engineers must be informed through the issue of regular amendments to the operating and maintenance manual. The information must be written clearly in the native language of the country.

Given below is a list of the various technical manuals and other media available. It is usual to quote all measurements in metric units:

1 Technical specification. To define the parameters and technical features of the product. To specify the various types or models available.

2 Operator instruction cards. To provide convenient operating instructions for use with the product. On small appliances these replace item (3) below. Both items (1) and (2) are required for the more sophisticated products.

3 Operating manuals. To enable the product to be installed and commissioned. To provide operating instructions including fault diagnosis (if permitted), safety procedures and instructions for obtaining technical assistance.

4 Maintenance manuals. To provide complete technical descriptions, fault diagnosis, repair and overhaul, and routine maintenance procedures. These manuals to be distributed to service personnel.

5 Maintenance instruction cards. To be used by service engineers working on the product. On small appliances these replace item (4). Both items (4) and (5) are supplied for sophisticated products. Maintenance instruction cards can also form part of a scheduled servicing system as detailed under (7).

6 Container. To contain technical documentation, particularly in the environment of maintenance department.

7 List of spare parts. To be distributed to dealers, agents and service centres. These must be fully illustrated. On small appliances they would feature in items (3) and (4).

8 Wall diagrams. To be displayed in workshops and to be used during training of personnel.

9 Films. To be used for training personnel.

10 Video cassettes. To be used for training. Video cassettes are a popular training resource for servicing/maintenance instruction; this is especially useful when the video is colour.

11 Training manuals. If a qualified instructor is available, item (3) can be used as a training manual. Training manuals are often written in programmed format. Individual engineers may operate a self-taught project using items (8), (10) and (11).

12 Plant register cards.

13 Work instruction cards.

14 Cost cards.

15 Work specifications.

16 Work schedules.

To provide a basis for planned maintenance or scheduled servicing. When supplied with industrial products, such as machine tools, these become part of the planned maintenance system in the factory. It is usual, in many markets, for such data to be computerized.

An important feature of after-sales service is the provision of adequate training for servicing and maintenance personnel. This must be planned in consultation with the agent or distributor. It usually involves the provision of specified technical testing and maintenance equipment in the agent's workshop. This is an area that the technical sales engineer must develop prior to the product being launched into the market place.

As we progress through the 1990s an increasing number of overseas territories will have much of the foregoing data computerized. This applies not only to developed countries but also developing markets and newly industrialized countries. It covers particularly items (5), (6), (7), (12), (13), (14), (15) and (16). Long-term, an increasing number of major importers will be able to obtain technical data from the exporter's database by satellite communication. It will result in a new era of international communication (see section 2.9).

4.8   FACTORS DETERMINING PRODUCT DESIGN

Product design is an important factor in market acceptance of a product. The following points are relevant:

1 It is common practice to initiate market research into the most acceptable design for the product.

2 Test marketing is designed to establish customer reaction to a particular product design.

3 The type and perceived value of the product by the buyer/end user will influence its design.

4 Extensive legislation exists in many countries regarding the product specification, particularly concerning its technical and safety aspects which obviously will influence product design. Further details from Technical Help for Exporters (THE; see section 10.12).

5 Colour is a decisive factor in product design and particular attention should be given to religious beliefs and fashion trends (the latter will be revealed in any market research survey).

6 The method of retailing. In a shop, display units with an attractive design at the point of sale can stimulate sales very significantly.

7 Packaging and distribution. The former involving general handling of the item and the latter stowage of the commodity for example in a container. Study also Chapter 6 of *Elements of Export Practice* and reports prepared by PIRA.

8 The level of competition. A product analysis is often beneficial to determine the strengths and weaknesses of the product alongside its competitors in the market place. Improved design can help overcome some of the inadequacies of the commodity.

9 Price is a dominant factor in customer choice, and one must bear in mind the cost factor in the product design. Generally, the more sophisticated the product, the higher the percentage of the product cost can be allocated to design factors.

4.9   PRODUCT LIFE CYCLE

Product life cycle can be conveniently defined as the viable life of the product/service in a competitive market place: it may be months or years. This will vary by numerous factors including the nature of the competition, consumer behaviour, legislation, market volume, fashion, taste, demographic factors, brand name, development of substitutes (such as margarine for butter), consumer spending power, technology, culture, price, packaging, distribution and so on. The significance of each item will vary by country and especially the environment in which the product/service is marketed.

The strategy applied to the product life cycle is especially important to the larger company for the following reasons:

1 It is desirable that a company has a product range which maximizes levels of profitability and sustains/maintains an adequate, profitable market share.
2 The product(s) are competitive and provide an adequate return on capital and resources.
3 The level of profitability is sufficient to sustain an adequate programme of research and development. Such products are screened and test-marketed against a background of continuous market research. The emerging products will displace progressively the existing products.
4 The timing of the individual product replacement will vary by market. It is desirable that the product replacement programme is not bunched but formulated on a rolling programme basis consistent with the market environment and the existing product performance.
5 The replacement product is always sensitive to a market acceptance risk. Moreover, to the company it represents an investment in the future and involves product development cost, new production plant, product launch advertising, maybe new or modified channels of distribution and physical distribution. It also involves an adequate number of high calibre personnel at all levels. Usually the company tends to introduce the replacement product first in the home market and subsequently progressively in its overseas markets. This can result in the continuing production of the old and new products for a short period which can prove costly. It is lessened with the larger company who have production plant overseas and thereby switch to the new product following the home market's successful launch. It must be stressed that not all companies introduce their new product first in the home market, but elect to launch it in an overseas market with local production resources under a joint venture. This trend could increase in particular overseas markets.

It cannot be stressed too strongly that a company which fails to adopt a product replacement programme long term is likely to go out of business.

Figure 4.2 features the product's life cycle in all its five phases plus a replacement product. The five phases include introduction development, growth, maturity, saturation and decline. A commentary on each follows.

4.9.1 Introduction/development

This involves the conception of the product and its development and

PRODUCT LIFE CYCLE

Introduction/Development	Growth	Maturity	Saturation	Decline
Advertising – strong	Advertising – Less Strong	Advertising – New Initiatives	Advertising – Further Initiatives	Advertising – Low
Cash Flow – negative	Cash Flow – Positive	Especially Customer Loyalty/ Replacement Sales/Improved Product Specification	Cash Flow – Positive/ Maximum	Cash Flow – Decline
Competition – Low	Competition – Increasing	Cash Flow – Positive/ Under Pressure	Competition – Fierce	Competition – Decline
Consumer Loyalty – Low	Marketing Infrastructure – Further Improve	Competition – Increasing	Consumer Loyalty – High	Consumer Loyalty – Decline
Launch – Evaluate	Market Research – Continuous	Consumer Loyalty – Further Increasing	Marketing Infrastructure – Continuous Review	Marketing Infrastructure – Decline
Marketing Infrastructure – Develop/Review	Price – Under Pressure	Market Infrastructure – Further Improve	Marketing Research – Continuous	Market Research – Decline
Market Research – Evaluate	Product – Modification and Range Development	Market Research – Continuous	Price – Under Severe Pressure	Price – Discount
Price – High	Production – Rising	Price – Under Pressure	Product – Further Modification and Extension of Range	Product – Obsolescence
Product Awareness Developing	Profit – Low Level	Product – Modification and Range Development	Production – Peak	Production – Decline
Production – Modest	Sales – Rising	Production – Rising	Profit – Maximum	Profit – Break Even
Profit – Nil		Profit – Improving	Sales – Peak	Sales – Decline
Sales – Low		Sales – Rising		
Test Marketing				
Stage One	Stage Two	Stage Three	Stage Four	Stage Five

Figure 4.2 Product life cycle analysis.

launch. It may be a car or a pharmaceutical product, both involving expensive research and development costs coupled with continuous screening. It embraces test marketing and the plant investment. Sales will be modest; costs high with a negative cash flow situation; competition will be modest and consumers new to the product/service; the price will be pitched at a high level with a basic core product/service; advertising will be high at the product launch stage to generate product awareness, and finally it will be a testing period for the product and the infrastructure supporting its launch, including its distribution. The emphasis on each of the areas will vary by market and, if it was launched on the home market, the process of transferring the marketing mix will apply. This will involve restructuring the product, price and promotion constituents to meet the consumer profile perceptions.

4.9.2   Growth

This represents the period when the product/service enters its high production stage to meet increasing sales levels and thereby results in lower unit production cost which in turn can permit lower price levels if the competition so dictates. Many such factors in regard to price, and production level will reflect company marketing strategy and whether they wish to restrict supply to sustain price or allow the market penetration to be fulfilled through effective marketing and adequacy of product availability. At this stage an improved product may be introduced to reflect market research findings and increased competition.

4.9.3   Maturity

The maturity stage acknowledges the product is still growing in sales volume terms, albeit at a slower rate, but reaching its peak. Profitability is at a high level but under pressure, and customer loyalty is in course of continuous development with replacement sales becoming more significant especially in the area of promotion strategy. Competition is becoming more fierce.

4.9.4   Saturation

This is the stage when the product/service reaches its peak sales and maximum level of profitability. The customer profile for a consumer product will be a mass market and the company image, which could feature a brand image, reaches a peak. The level of advertising will tend to decline as the product passes from the saturation to the declining sector situation. Competition will be at its peak and special emphasis will be given to develop a marketing initiative with which to sustain product awareness, competitiveness and any product improvements since its launch. It is desirable that the saturation period should remain as long as possible to sustain profitability and new marketing initiatives taken when advantageous.

4.9.5   Decline

This is the period when the market is tending to reject the product/service due to its obsolescence, inadequate specification through new technology, fashion, tastes and so on. Production levels, cash flow, and advertising levels will be at a low ebb. Profitability will be at break-even level or in a loss situation. Competition will be in decline, with replacement products in their product launch stage, a situation which the company should be adopting.

The importance of the product life-cycle strategy cannot be overstressed.

4.10   PRODUCT DEVELOPMENT

Policy on product development has become one of the most crucial areas in determining the success or failure of an enterprise. Technological advancement, new methods in industry and rapid changes in the patterns of consumer behaviour have resulted in some products becoming obsolete at a faster rate than ever before. The overall purpose is to ensure that the product mix (the ingredients of the marketable product) is composed of those elements which optimize the profitability of resources in relation to the opportunities of the market place. This will undoubtedly vary by individual market and therefore each market performance must be carefully monitored and not too many markets with varying features should be tackled at any one time. In order to maintain the appropriate mix over time, it is necessary to introduce new products, modify existing ones and eliminate obsolete ones.

The life-cycle of the product and degree of profitability therefore must be evaluated. This will depend greatly on the market in which the product is retailed and the measures taken to promote it. Product development is usually processed through market research (see section 3.2.7) and other marketing/consumer report aids such as the agent's report. Details of the likely areas to examine in any market research are:

1 The acceptability of the product in a particular form.
2 The attractiveness and suitability of the package. In most consumer markets involving the point-of-sale technique at the retail outlet, it is desirable that the packaging be reviewed/changed every two or three years to reflect market trends in an overseas territory, increase sales and prolong product life.
3 The competitiveness of the price, taking into account any inherent qualities of the product over its competitors, e.g. superior technology, durability, etc.

4 The effectiveness of the selling method(s).
5 The patterns of distribution.
6 The possible effect of sales promotion.
7 The impact and effectiveness of advertising.
8 The necessity for, and profitable benefits from, other forms of publicity such as trade fairs and exhibitions.
9 The desirable size of a public relations exercise.

The conclusions from market research analysis will also involve the manufacturer in an assessment of the overall viability of the product(s) and whether it needs to be replaced. The following points are relevant:

1 Resources available within the manufacturing company to develop the products, especially the technical expertise.
2 The market profile, especially the consumer profile. This information is obtained from market research analysis and any market reports produced by the agent or distributor.
3 The direct cost of producing the new product or a modified one, in relation to the potential sales volume and the time scale or lead time.
4 Investment in new plant and appointment of any new agents or distributors.
5 Time scale of overall project. A critical path analysis would prove useful in obtaining such data.
6 The assessment of the product potential in the market place, through market research analysis and other techniques.
7 Distribution costs. An assessment should be made by the export shipping office.
8 Any likely import restrictions which could emerge during the life-cycle of the product(s) in the overseas territory.
9 Any constraints or regulations on product design, particularly technical and safety aspects. THE can help in this regard (see section 10.12).
10 Trends in the exchange rate in the overseas territory. This is an area where the banks can give guidance; also the Central Office of Information (COI) through their diplomatic posts. Additional information can be sought on the general economic and political stability of the overseas market.

In devising the strategy for the overseas product policy, the following points are relevant:

1 The marketing philosophy requires that new products and modifications of existing products must be related to the company's planning for an adequate return on investment.
2 The anticipated revenues from existing products and markets must be related to the projected growth of sales/profits.
3 The company must develop new or modified products so as to correct any shortfall in profit objectives.

4 Product policy must be related to the company resources available in terms of capital, personnel, production, etc. It must be borne in mind there is a lengthy 'payback' period.

5 New products development must be operated on a stable basis of existing products.

Basically, product development in overseas markets usually entails modification to existing products. Ideally the producer should endeavour to retain the core specification of the product to lessen the scale of modifications involved and investment required. The paramount consideration, however, is the need to ensure that the product is acceptable to the consumer and that it will generate sufficient sales to produce an adequate return on investment. A dominant factor will be the nature of the competitor's products. These factors will be determined through market research (see section 3.2.7) which may reveal that the product needs to be completely redesigned to meet the needs of the overseas market. This course must be followed if the supplier wishes to be successful in market penetration, and would be adopted, subject to the venture being profitable and the market sustainable in both the short and long term. It may involve a joint venture or overseas subsidiary development. The following points are relevant:

1 Product modification is likely to entail some of the following: differences in voltage supply; changes in design features, colours, pack sizes; variation arising from geographical or climatic conditions; differences in the level of technical skill of operatives; differing legal requirements entailing health, safety, labelling, etc; taxation and political considerations requiring the use of locally made components; economic considerations related to the consumer purchasing power such as a cheaper version for developing countries; the cultural considerations affecting the use of foodstuffs and so on. A major concern arising in some countries is the need to obtain an approval certificate, with all its ramifications of product modification which is required before the goods may enter the country and be retailed in the overseas territory. The THE can assist in this area.

2 Pricing policy requires the most careful consideration, and major factors include competition and product specification correlated to the acceptable market price. It is important to bear in mind that a quality product requires the appropriate pricing structure and not a low price. Another factor is the degree of profitability and the 'mark up' required. Pricing and costing strategy are dealt with in sections 6.2 and 6.3, and market forecast in section 7.4.

3 Packaging and packing charges will reflect climatic, geographical, economic and cultural considerations. This will embrace point-of-sale packaging, colour, size and language. Packing dimensions and effectiveness in stowage and protection are distribution considerations; skilful stowage of the 20-

or 40-feet containers can increase the quantity shipped and thereby lower unit distribution costs. The container shipowner can help in this regard. Overall the packaging must strike a balance between suitability to the market and preservation of the brand/company identity, reputation and standing.

4 Promotional strategy involves many aspects, and the exporter is best guided by engaging an advertising agency in the overseas territory.

Market research will point the way to the strategy to be followed, coupled with an analysis of what the competition is doing. It may involve the following situations:

1 In regard to a product launch in an overseas territory, it may prove necessary to provide extensive consumer education and heavy initial expenditure on the investment budget due to the scale of the modifications to the core of the product. Market research helps to reduce risk in new product development and to guide the successful launch of new products into the market place. Typical situations include the following:

(a) Opportunity analysis profiling – market study to assess potential for new product concept prior to commitment of development resources.
(b) User needs analysis – identification of new product concepts from evaluation of actual and latent user needs not satisfied by existing products.
(c) Product 'test and tune' – use of research to test reaction of market to product prototypes in order to identify scope/need for modification and assess preferences *vis à vis* competitor's products.
(d) Market entry options strategy – advice on targets, segments, distribution channels, pricing, support and promotion/selling activities.

2 Any advertising message must take account of the market level of literacy to ensure it is adaptable and conveys clearly the desired product image to the market.

3 Items (1) and (2) apply equally to the introduction of new products and to established products in foreign markets. Promotional strategy must feature in the market place distinctive features of the products or service, clearly align it with the wants and needs of the market, and clearly differentiate it from the competition.

Two major points arise in regard to product policy/strategy. First, whether and to what extent a standardized product or product range can be sold worldwide, and secondly whether and to what extent the marketing communications policy can also be standardized.

A number of products can be sold without modification and this includes photographic equipment, drinks, both alcoholic and non-alcoholic. This usually involves an internationally known brand name which is used to identify a standardized product, and local manufacturers licensed to supply the product under the multinational brand name.

To develop the product and marketing strategy, one must interpret the market research data and information obtained on the attitudes and requirements of end users, specifiers, distributive intermediaries into action-orientated recommendations to meet corporate, financial and marketing goals. Examples are given below:

1 Strategies to revive flagging performance of existing products in existing markets.
2 Strategies to increase sales/profitability by identifying and exploiting new/profitable applications and end-user segments.
3 Strategies to enter new overseas markets.
4 Strategies to build/protect sales by developing/modifying product range involving eliminating declining/unprofitable products, introducing new products to fill market gaps, and exploiting profitable segments.

An example of product development, the fashion market involving ladies' dresses, is given below:

1 The retailer will examine their existing range of dresses based on: sales performance by size and style and product; an analysis report identifying future trends and needs particularly those reaching the near end of their product life cycle.
2 The retailer will examine the market size within the context of replacement products and their viability, and the overall company policy.
3 As part of an on-going liaison between exporter/importer, the retailer discusses with the export manufacturer the nature of the dresses required, and the potential volume and time-scale, together with provisional price levels.
4 Both design teams (exporter and importer) produce a joint selection of designs and subsequently decide on those acceptable. Full cognisance is taken of the retailer's interpretation through market research and retailing staff of the consumer needs.
5 A modest supply for retail sale of the dresses selected is provided by the exporter for sale at maybe four out of the twenty retailer outlets in the overseas market to determine consumer reaction over a period varying from one to two weeks.
6 Consumer reaction is assessed and, if favourable, substantial quantities are ordered.

Significant aspects emerging from the foregoing are given below:

1 Demand must be adequate to sustain the product so that it reaches the required profit.
2 Market research must be adequate and continuous.

3 Any new product must be compatible with the company's experience and resources, including definition of market and consumer profile.

4 New products should be compatible with the existing product range.

5 Adequate financial resources should be allocated to the development of new products. As the product progresses from the emergence of an idea to commercial development, the cost rises with no income initially. It is essential to have well defined procedures to ensure rigorous control over how far along the sequence any given product is allowed to proceed.

6 Adequate management time must be allocated to the development of new products. This involves, for example in a fashion house store, management staff at all levels allocating time to discuss the existing product range, market trends, and suggestions and requirements for the future. It is essential this feedback reaches the appropriate department to help in the decision-making process. The exporters on their regular visits should be part of such discussions.

Product development is a continuous assignment and requires the fullest possible liaison between manufacturer and agent/end user to ensure that market needs are met and profitability is developed to the full.

4.11 OVERSEAS LICENSING

Selling information usually involves a contractual arrangement whereby a manufacturer or other commercial organization sells full details of a specific process to another organization for an agreed sum, provided that the process is executed only within a stipulated area. Occasionally the area stated will be couched in general terms but will expressly exclude certain nominated areas.

A company normally disposes of rights or expertise as a means of raising capital which can be used in the further development of the business. Since it is usually impossible for one manufacturer to cover personally the whole international area of demand, he would do well to sell mainly to those areas in which he does not intend to operate, or where he is prevented from operating. For example, if a manufacturer wishes to produce goods by a special process but is prevented from operating in a certain area because he is a foreigner to that country, he may sell the process and the right to execute it within that area to a national of that country whose registration of process and right to manufacture would be granted.

In a broad sense, the sale of 'know-how' could include the many consultancy and service functions that are a feature of modern business. The analysis and solution of the business problem has become the subject of much specialization and one finds the areas of marketing, advertising, market research, management selection, organization and methods, work study, insurance and many aspects of finance efficiently covered by the activities of a growing number of specialist consultants.

It is usually far better to market products in overseas territories than to license the patents and/or the production know-how. However, licensing can often be the only way of entering a particular market, or staying in a market when the government takes action to control imports. For example:

1 The foreign government may decide to build up its own industries by imposing import quotas, duties or tariffs to make direct imports uneconomic.
2 The product specification for the local market, including its packaging, might make it more economical to produce locally.
3 Product research may determine new specifications, ideal for limited areas, which it may be better and more economical to produce locally.
4 Shipping costs for small and comparatively low-value or bulky and heavy products could make the final selling price uncompetitive; it would be better to produce them locally.
5 Insufficient capital to enter local markets with its own subsidiary or joint-venture corporation.
6 Import restrictions which limit market development through traditional export marketing.
7 A product with a short shelf-life is such that the normal shipping periods to the market would result in the product having an insufficient balance of shelf-life remaining for effective distribution and marketing.
8 Products which are too delicate to withstand the rigours of shipment over long distances and several transport modes.
9 Where a product is not exclusive but necessarily forms part of another complementary product or process.
10 The need to link with a company with effective distribution channels serving the same potential users.
11 Where one party controls access to essential know-how, ingredients or raw materials needed in the licensed product.

A company may seek to license the production or use of a product, copyright work, process, business format or trademark which a licensee might accept either has a use or value on its own, or would have if incorporated into another product. Technology, know-how, or a business format may all be very suitable for licensing, but whatever you wish to license needs to be exclusive to you and not in the public domain otherwise the foreign party will see no need to buy a licence. If a product or process is protected by a patent, a potential licensee will only feel a need to enter a licensing arrangement if he cannot circumvent the patent readily. For that reason some companies prefer not to patent know-how and technology, where eligible for patent protection, with the awareness that patent registration only aids competitors' research, or that the new process or product really has a finite life span.

A licensee must see a licence as giving him tangible benefits, such as:

1 Measurable cost savings (e.g., better yields, lower energy usage, less other inputs, better quality control, less maintenance).
2 Acquiring internationally-recognized brand names, enhancing existing sales or reputation.
3 Acquiring a new product which complements existing products or would sell through existing outlets.
4 Inclusion of new technology in existing or new products giving additional marketing strength and tangible product advantages over competitors.

Adoption of a licence should give the licensee tangible gross profit benefits through extra sales and/or increased earnings.

A licenser can sell a licence for a fixed period and a fixed once-only fee, or, more usually, seek a smaller initial 'disclosure' fee and an on-going royalty directly related to production or sales values or volumes. Alternatively, the rights could be sold without time limit, but that is more likely to be the case if the licenser believes his licensed product has only a limited life span before obsolescence catches up.

Licences can also be granted on an inter-company basis between associated companies and parent corporations. This may be a way of clearly demonstrating ownership rights, or of increasing the level of funds that can be repatriated from foreign markets (but foreign royalties often attract a certain level of tax before remittance). Where a product formulation is being licensed a manufacturer may further be able to protect his formula by agreeing as part of the licensing agreement that a base ingredient mix will be supplied to the licensee. In such a case the licenser may choose to recover his royalties in the form of a mark up on the price of the base mix, which will generally be used as a fixed proportion of the final product.

The licenser will need to establish that the product or process being licensed can or will comply with all foreign market applicable rules and regulations, such as those relating to labelling, packaging, health and safety and ingredient usage or composition. All trademarks and patents should be clearly registered in the licenser's name, who can then grant the licences to associate companies or independent licensees.

Overseas licensing can pose many problems and disadvantages as detailed below:

1 Competition from the licensee – when the licensing agreement finally expires, the licenser may find he has established a competitor in his own former licensee.
2 Market exploitation – the licensee, even if he reaches an agreed minimum turnover, may not fully exploit the market, leaving it open to the entry of competitors. He may inevitably lose control of the marketing operation.
3 Revenue – licence fees are normally a small percentage of turnover and

will often compare unfavourably with what might be obtained from the licensee's own manufacturing operation.

4 Product quality – quality control of the product is difficult – and the product could be sold under the licensee's own brand name.

5 Government – governments often impose conditions on remittances of royalties or on component supply.

6 Disagreements with licensee – arguments will arise however carefully the licensing arrangement is drafted. A disaffected licensee can be a serious problem.

There are both short- and long-term benefits of licensing. In the short term there will be: initial down payments and subsequent royalties on production; export of materials and components not available locally; and export of plant, machinery and spare parts, and possibly service and maintenance agreements. In the long term there will be the accumulation of local knowledge (which may be useful in other territories) in the areas of commercial intelligence and market research, and new uses and development of the product. Successful co-operation between manufacturer and licenser could also lead to capital investment by the licenser and to the formation of an associate or a subsidiary company: this could be anticipated and covered in the agreement.

Larger companies might create a licensing team incorporating marketing, legal, financial and technical personnel. Smaller companies with limited resources may only be able to develop through a single individual, but can take advantage of assistance from government departments concerned with promoting trade and investment, and also use the services of outside specialist consultants in identifying and developing opportunities.

A licensing agreement is an important step for a company to take and it should not be taken lightly. A competent legal adviser should be employed from the outset; he would have the help of the licensing adviser(s) who would be familiar with the legislation of both countries. Great care must be taken not to reveal any detailed information during the preliminary discussions. Among the points that should be covered in a licensing agreement are:

1 Legality in both countries.
2 The parties and their responsibilities.
3 The products, trade marks, patents, 'know-how', improvements.
4 Territories, and exports to other countries.
5 Finance: royalties, payments and methods of payment, currency.
6 Transfer of information; methods, staff and training.
7 Patents: usage, quality control, infringement, exclusion, patent laws.
8 Cross licences and grant back.
9 Audit and control.
10 Performance based on minimum sales or royalties.

11 Procedures for settling disputes, such as an arbitration clause.
12 Applicable laws by which agreement will be enforced.
13 Investment obligations to plant and machinery.
14 Restriction clause limiting licensee to compete with similar products or markets.
15 Secrecy clause.
16 Product development.
17 Product pricing and supply.
18 Insurance cover.
19 Training.
20 Sub-licensing.
21 Assignment clause.
22 Duration of licence and provision for termination.

The selection of a licensee requires careful evaluation and the following points are relevant.

1 With a specific process for treating a raw material, ingredient or waste product, identify producers or users of the ingredient or raw material, or generators of the waste item.
2 If a raw material involved is only produced or sold through certain private or government agencies, then enter discussions with those agencies to establish which of their customers might have applications.
3 For mass market items, seek to identify which companies presently produce similar products, or who distributes to the end user.
4 If production requires certain ingredients, seek out producers of those ingredients to establish if they have an interest in expanding to supply end uses of the ingredient or raw material.
5 If a product is in a very specific market category, such as an automobile component, consider approaches to the producers of such items who might benefit from a range extension.
6 If the product must be a component or integral part of another product, logically you should approach current producers of the other product who might find technical or earnings benefit by incorporating your item.

The criteria for appointing the licensee should have regard to the following:

1 Member of a Trading Association.
2 Qualifications/calibre of Directors and Senior Managers.
3 Last three years' annual published accounts.
4 Experience of the type of business in which you are interested.
5 Current product range and product volumes.
6 Outcome/conclusions of any market research exercise undertaken to find suitable licensee.
7 Production and distribution facilities.

8 Market share and marketing capabilities.
9 Any association with a legal dispute/fraud.
10 Date company formed and experience/contacts in the market.
11 Degree to which licensee projects modern outlook and encourages staff training and adoption of modern techniques, e.g. computers.
12 Legal constraints in licensee appointment – local conditions.
13 Relationship with other organizations.
14 General competitiveness.
15 Any major shareholdings.

Licensing is particularly evident in Eastern Bloc countries and can only be achieved by outright flat payments. Moreover it is often advantageous in other countries to purchase foreign patents and 'know-how' for use in both home and overseas markets. Cross-licensing can also be undertaken with foreign manufacturers with appropriate market agreements. Further advice on licensing arrangements is available from The Department of Trade and Industry, trade associations, Chamber of Commerce and Export Credit Guarantee Department (ECGD).

Licensing products is a growth market. It may be the only option to enter the market and thereby constrain a competitor. It requires to be entered into with caution and to have adequate control and auditing of performance, quality, and market monitoring. Regular visits are desirable and the need to build up good relationships with the licensee is paramount. The most effective way of encouraging a continuing interest on the part of the licensee is to ensure that he always has something to gain from it.

4.12   COMPLETE MANUFACTURE OVERSEAS

The growth of nationalism, the desire for self-sufficiency in a number of developing industrial countries, coupled with the desire of many large companies to become international, has led to complete manufacture being planned, on a short- or long-term basis to take place overseas. This trend is particularly evident in Central and South America, the Middle East, Far East and North Africa. The OPEC (Organization of Petroleum Exporting Countries) cartel has driven up oil prices to very high levels and with the increased revenues the member countries are surging ahead with ambitious industrialization programmes. For the international company which is able to exploit these trends, there are a number of advantages:

1 Local manufacture may be the only way of staying in the market and getting inside the tariff and quota barriers.
2 There will be more overall market penetration than that which could be imported formally, not only in the host country but also in adjacent territories, subject to there being no political or ethnic barriers as mentioned previously with 'locally assembled products'.

3 The company will supply the manufacturing equipment either direct through a supplier or on a commission basis. There will be an installation agreement, training agreement and service and maintenance fees until such time as the local staff are able to manage independently.

4 Local manufacture can lead to increased exports rather than reduced levels. For example the establishment of a local manufacturing base can lead to increased exports to that country. The product mix changes, and the exports of traditional products (which are to be produced locally) will be replaced by more sophisticated and more profitable ones.

5 The new manufacturing projects will acquire expertise of their own: the use of indigenous raw materials, product specification and development to suit local tastes, and marketing techniques, can benefit the group as a whole.

6 Research and development costs for the products to be manufactured in the new country may have already been amortized. The products would be welcomed, the parent company's goodwill would be enhanced, and as mentioned in point (4), other imported goods from the company would have an easier entry.

Again advice can be sought from the BOTB on such developments, which are becoming more common.

4.13   JOINT VENTURES

An increasing number of companies are now developing their overseas markets through a joint venture. It provides greater cover over sales and distribution; develops local manufacturing, packaging and assembly; provides control over cost and production quality, and enhances market penetration, growth and customer loyalty.

Basically, a joint venture is the process of two trading companies from different countries – at least one of them being local – forming an agreement and company to manufacture/produce goods on a joint basis. Both parties have an investment commitment, the extent of each party varying by circumstances. The scale of the shareholding may vary from 10% to 90% but generally is around 25% to 75%. In many developing countries, governments stipulate a minimum national holding in a joint venture of 60%, which constitutes a majority local shareholding. In such circumstances the host country would have the majority of the directors, on the basis for example of four to the host country and three to the exporter. Examples of joint ventures may be found in Table 4.2.

Each joint venture varies by circumstances but does involve a transfer in technology to the host country, with the new company manufacturing the product under the latest technology, creating local employment, developing an industrial base in the host country; providing the opportunity to serve both the local and neighbouring markets crossing international frontiers,

Table 4.2   Examples of joint ventures

Host country (and relative financial contribution as percentage)	Overseas country (and relative financial contribution as percentage)	Product/service
Taiwan (50)	USA (50)	Aircraft construction
Austria (50)	West Germany (50)	Publishing
France (51)	West Germany (49)	Paint production
Spain (51)	UK (49)	Credit card domestic banking
Sweden/Switzerland (80)	USA (20)	Power transmission and distribution equipment
Turkey (51)	UK (49)	Military radio equipment
USA (50)	Netherlands (50)	Preprinted circuit boards
USA (51)	Japan (49)	Optical fibres
France (50)	USA (50)	Multi-terrain cars
USSR (50)	Finland (50)	Dairy packaging and food service disposables
Australia (50)	USA (50)	Heavy minerals production unit

and finally provide the exporter with a market entry which would not otherwise exist. In broad terms the joint venture is formed for one of the following reasons:

1 To enter an overseas market which was partially or completely prohibited in direct market entry terms. This may be through a quota system, import licences, or 100% import tariffs.

2 To increase and develop market penetration in the host country and develop markets in neighbouring territories.

3 To develop more competitively priced goods taking advantage of cheap local labour and eliminating expensive physical distribution and channels of distribution cost.

4 To develop the product in a volume sales market on a consumer-led product development basis.

5 To counter more effectively competition in the host country.

6 To take advantage of local investment grants and tax concessions in the host country together with cheaper raw materials and component parts.

7 The exporter home manufacturing base is working to capacity and new plant locations are being examined.

8 To enter a market which is a member of a regional or free trade market thereby providing access to member states on a most favourable basis, often free of import tariff and other controls. This includes ASEAN, EC, CARICOM and EFTA.

9 To develop favourably the host country balance of trade situation and reduce the level of imports.

Overall the advantages/disadvantages of a joint venture can be detailed as below:

1 It yields a higher investment return and affords more control when compared with a licensing agreement. Likewise the exporter can exercise more control over production, quality control, marketing, and the management decision-making process. Furthermore it provides more feedback on market intelligence, which aids market development and intelligence.

2 It develops more international expertise on the part of the exporter, and this extends to all the areas of management and marketing, including culture and diplomacy.

3 It involves a high capital involvement/commitment which is usually not available to the smaller export company.

4 It enables both parties to merge any technology, particularly the latest generation, which may enhance market volume sales.

5 It requires the exporter to provide adequate management measures which may prove too difficult to obtain having regard to the nature of the business and culture of the host country. Aspects involved include language, professional qualifications and experience. The larger exporter with more resources and a wide market base may have such personnel available in the company, but the smaller company may have to recruit such personnel.

6 The larger the investment, the greater the risk in broad terms. Such investment is always prone to the political situation obtaining in the host country, and the risk of nationalization. Advice should be sought from trade associations, Overseas Consulates/Embassies, banks and personal visits. It also extends to repatriation of profits/funds and any embargo or discriminatory taxes. This aspect involves transfer pricing. This presents the joint venture company with the opportunity to manipulate/adjust the transfer price to further the goods/aims of the entity. One method is to charge high prices for components, materials and services exported from the subsidiary to the home market. This enables the company to understate the profits of its overseas interests which thus attracts lower rates of local taxation.

7 Problems can emerge on the product specification quality and range. The host country may insist the product is geared exclusively to their needs and have no regard to neighbouring territories' requirements. Usually such problems are quickly resolved when the export potential is established.

Finally, it is appropriate to consider the salient factors before embarking on a joint venture which are detailed below:

1 Research thoroughly the host country company. This includes finance, personnel, production and the company's profile. It is desirable that this is compatible with the export company's profile.
2 Establish how the foreign subsidiary is going to raise the capital, and under what terms, especially as regards any imposed constraints. Also, examine the shareholding composition, and any allocation, and under what terms, to holding companies.
3 The degree of the host government involvement and under what terms, especially in the area of capital construction, land availability, management structure, time scale, taxation, product and plant specification, technology, repatriation of funds, expatriate employment terms, raw materials, component supply sources, and so on.

Long term, joint venture projects are likely to become increasingly common especially in countries like China, the sub-Continent, the Far East, the Middle East, Central Africa and South America. Such markets are keen to develop an industrial base, reduce the level of imported manufactured goods and export the joint venture products to neighbouring territories.

4.14   MERGERS AND ACQUISITIONS

An increasing number of companies are today developing their customer base on an increased production volume and extended diversified complementary product range basis through merging with another company or buying/acquiring it. This exploits the economies of scale and strengthens the company in marketing and capital resources terms. It is a strategy which an increasing number of exporters are pursuing.

The following points are relevant:

1 It pools/rationalizes the company resources in all its areas and provides the opportunity to develop the economies of scale. Overall, the company becomes more competitive through lower unit cost, more competitive pricing, and greater market dominance through increased market share and a larger number of markets.
2 It raises capital and thereby enables the new enlarged company to have greater financial resources for investment needs, opportunities, and competitive strategies. The new company can be restructured financially.
3 The larger, merged company has a stronger competitive base. This extends to commercial/retail outlets and could embrace a diversified or related part of the business. For example, a company specializing in garden furniture could merge with a company manufacturing greenhouses, thereby enlarging the customer portfolio and market penetration. One may be

based in the UK, and the other in Holland.

4 Marketing is decisive in a manufacturing company today. It is more cost-effective through a larger company than a smaller one.

5 The larger company has a bigger market share. This tends to increase its dominance in the market place, especially in cash flow and influence on prices, development, and innovation. It also increases the market value of the business. The area of research and development is especially important as individual products fall for renewal as their product life cycle terminates. The larger company has more and better calibre financial and technical personnel to formulate the product life cycle replacement strategy and develop innovative policies.

6 The larger company has both bigger customer- and revenue-bases, thereby providing more stability for the company. This is a competitive advantage as it can prove more cost-effective to serve through higher turnover income accounts. Moreover, the larger company has more influence in the market and resources to develop it. This is especially important in export marketing where the buyer is becoming increasingly selective of the profile of the export company and tends to favour the larger company rather than the smaller company with limited resources and lower potential in the areas of research and development. Much does, of course, depend on the product and the overseas territory concerned.

7 As mentioned under item (1), the larger company can realize economies of scale, especially in the areas of organizational structure, and gain buying power in terms of obtaining raw materials, components and so on at more competitive rates. Furthermore, the marketing team can be rationalized and develop a more strategic and effective role in the development of the business including: product development; increased market share and volume; more cost-effective physical distribution and channels of distribution; and market penetration involving developing new markets.

8 It aids diversification of business activity. This is an important area in company strategy especially in fashionable products/services. Moreover, a company marketing two products of unrelated specification can experience a decline in one and growth in another.

9 The larger company has a wider international base. It enables the new company to retain its advantageous negotiating position with its national government, trading association, etc. in terms of investment, market exposure, development grants, and so on.

10 The larger company, through acquisition or merger, obtains new market entry options. It involves new territories and an enlarged customer portfolio.

11 It aids the development of a corporate strategy. This tends to emerge through a quality directorate and management, which are more usually found in the larger company.

12 The multi-national merger or acquisition has strong advantages in terms of negotiation and influence with governments, trade associations and so on.

The exporter embarking on a merger or acquisition must process it through a merchant bank who specializes in this area. Special attention needs to be given to the company's valuation and financial structure, its financial performance, its product range, its customer portfolio and overall compatibility with the exporter company. Its overseas activities and agreements should be closely examined to determine the scale of obligations and penalty clauses in the event of any rationalization in the channel of distribution in a particular country. Legal advice should be sought.

4.15   BELOW THE LINE PROMOTIONS

A below the line promotion is one where the expenditure does not go into paid advertising media. The line is drawn through the production budget to separate what is spent on media advertising from what it costs for the other kinds of promotion such as coupons, self-liquidating offers, bargain packages, gifts, sampling, and merchandising and display. Adequate pre-planning of the promotion is required.

We will now examine each of these retail promotion methods, which are becoming increasingly popular. In all cases regard must be given to the local trading regulations and, ideally, one must reconcile such a promotion with the programme of competitors to ensure the maximum impact is made and the market share improved.

4.15.1   Coupons

The use of coupons in sales promotion is very common in the consumer goods trade. It involves passing direct to the consumer a coupon of a certain value to enable him to obtain a price reduction on a product upon presentation of the coupon to the retailer. The manufacturer (or his distributor in the market) reimburses the retailer for the price difference and may pay him a fee for handling the redemption of the coupons. Additional sales are secured because the coupon acts as an incentive to consumers to sample the product, and retailers are encouraged to stock in greater quantities and to give more space and attention to sales display in anticipation of a higher turnover.

Apart from the cost of printing the coupons, there are two other basic cost elements, those of distribution and redemption. Distribution may be accomplished by postal or hand delivery; the latter is becoming more popular as postal charges rise. The coupon may be in a leaflet/brochure, form part of the packaging on a consumer product, or be contained in a magazine, catalogue or newspaper. Redemption involves two aspects: the value of the coupon when redeemed and the handling fee paid to the retailer. Whereas printing and distribution can be regarded as fixed costs since they are incurred whatever the response, the cost elements concerned with redemption are variable according to the number of coupons actually redeemed.

The question of the degree of impact should be carefully controlled since there is a limitation to the response from a single household. Furthermore, the agent or distributor, when he is calculating the cost of the sales promotion, must recognize the fact that a certain amount of positive response will come from established regular customers, thus depriving the distributor of part of the profit which he would receive from normal turnover. The whole object of employing coupons as a sales promotion may be entirely negated by repetition, unless the later promotions follow a very long time after the first. If coupon promotions are frequent, regular buyers of the product hold back their purchases until the next issue of coupons and then lay in stock. The manufacturer and the distributor thus get an entirely false impression of the impact of the scheme and the real pattern of distribution flow is badly distorted.

4.15.2 Self-liquidating offers

These arise when the consumer is invited to submit proof of purchase of a specific product, such as a label, box top or wrapper, together with a sum of money, in exchange for an article which is described as a special offer. It could be a promotion which is not related with the product, e.g. cereal box tops enable the consumer to buy a child's toy from the specified source at a special discount, or free travel for one or two people by rail, or coach, could be offered on payment to the sponsor of a modest sum plus, of course, the requisite box tops or wrappers.

The manufacturer purchases these articles in bulk at a discount and passes on the benefit of this reduced price, less the expense of the promotion, to the consumer. The manufacturer benefits from the increased turnover and the consumer benefits by obtaining the special offer at reduced price. As the promotion is accomplished when the consumer responds to the offer, it is termed 'self-liquidating'. The scheme is usually supported by substantial advertising and/or extensive point-of-sale displays.

4.15.3 Bargain packages

This involves selling a product at a reduced price for a specified period with a view to encouraging new customers to sample the product and to create extensive point-of-sale displays. While engaging in such tactics the manu-facturer must ensure that despite the reduced price, distributors' margins remain broadly the same. Moreover, new customers buying the product must be encouraged by the retailer to buy the product on a regular basis thereafter.

4.15.4 Gifts

For a variety of reasons, directly or indirectly associated with export promotion, the cost of gifts has to be prebudgeted 'below the line'. Basically such promotion falls into one of the following three categories:

1 Establishing good relationships with foreign agents and expatriate staff, where there is a regular pattern of distribution gifts in kind. This occurs when the distribution coincides with dates and events in the UK e.g. Christmas, when most exporting manufacturers send out a token of goodwill such as a diary; or when some outstanding event in the firm's history is being celebrated, such as a centenary year. Firms which take pride in doing things properly also send presents to agents at traditional times for making gifts in the foreign country such as the Muslim New Year; they should do this every year.

2 As part of the good personal relationships between the firm's export staff and agents abroad, gifts are sent – not in a regular pattern, but when something special warrants it, i.e. some special event in the agent's life or in the development of the agency. For example, if the agency is a family partnership and one of the younger partners gets married a gift is paid for by the firm, though as a present from the export manager: if a senior partner dies, arrangements should be made for flowers to be sent.

Under the same auspices are special presents given to trainees who complete a successful course; a kit of tools to a serviceman or a briefcase to a salesman, bearing the name of the firm, and possibly including an inscription to remind the man of his association with the firm.

3 A wide variety of gifts may be sent out to agents in foreign markets for them to use for promotion purposes; in order to prevent misuse, the agent is asked to pay half the cost, or to buy them at a subsidized price, though this can be very low owing to bulk-purchasing by the principal. The items are more usually of the 'advertising novelty' type. At a suitable juncture the agent should give them to the wholesalers and/or retailers who sell the products, or to useful contacts, e.g. civil servants, employees of Chambers of Commerce or bank officials, where goodwill is important.

The principal's name or brand image is usually featured with some prominence on these items. Included are calendars, pocket diaries, manicure sets, ball pens, ashtrays, etc. In less sophisticated markets, supplies of these novelties are given by the agent to retailers or are sold to them at the subsidized price so that they can use them at point of sale. The markets in question are those where retail price maintenance is not practised (it may be illegal) and the recommended price is not generally applicable. In such markets coupon offers are seldom used. If the retailer puts a price ticket on the product he would never sell it, since all the sales are subject to bargaining. The giving of a present costing 10 cents often clinches the sale which would otherwise only be achieved by a further reduction of 25 cents after more haggling. Advertising novelties come within this class (especially the cheaper items) and are given away to make the brand more widely known or as a form of 'reminder advertising'.

4.15.5   The sampling technique

This is a method whereby a small quantity of the product is given to the consumer with a view to obtaining his approval and securing his regular patronage. The cost of effecting a sample promotion involves the following elements:

1 The cost of production of the sample, including the cost of obtaining smaller containers to carry the sample.
2 The cost of distributing the sample.
3 The amount of sales revenue lost by sampling to regular customers.

4.15.6   Display

This concerns the strategic placing of the product at the point of sale and forms a vital part of merchandising, which also involves planning and a positive selling attitude towards the product. The function of merchandising is to draw the customer towards the product and, having attracted his attention, to punch home the initial advantage by means of a strong sensory appeal. Basically, merchandising is the function of the distributor rather than the manufacturer but, because the manufacturer is competing strongly for a share of a highly organized market, he is usually compelled to participate in this vital aspect of sales promotion.

The exporter should consider alternative aspects of sales promotion:

1 The offensive or attacking strategy where the manufacturer seeks to increase sales volume by means of the promotion.
2 The defensive tactics where the manufacturer participates in sales promotional activity to avoid losing ground by virtue of the fact that his competitors have launched promotions.

The extent to which the foregoing sales techniques are applied varies by country but the more sophisticated the market, the more likely it is that they will be used.

4.16   BRAND NAME

During the past twenty years, more attention has been directed towards the development of the brand name concept. It is a means of distinguishing a particular company's product/service in the market place and thereby differentiating it from its competitors. Invariably it is protected by trade marks, but equally invariably it is an intangible asset. It does not feature on the balance sheet. Overall it results in: a brand image – the general marketplace perceived assessment of a particular product/service; brand loyalty – the process of the marketplace supporting indefinitely a company product/service; and brand marketing – the process of promoting a company in the market place using the brand name. Examples of brand names include Kit Kat, Guinness, Coca-Cola, Double Diamond and St Michael.

The development of the brand name requires careful objective market research and evaluation. Moreover, it should involve senior management in its development and ideally must satisfy the following objectives:

1 It is able to sell at a premium price in the competitive market place. If the product/service fails to do so, the brand is a failure.
2 It is supported by an effective, strong marketing strategy. However, advertising cannot sustain inferior brands.
3 It is supported by good quality production and distribution facilities. This involves particularly quality control to ensure the product reaches the buyer in a good condition.
4 The product/service must have quality and points of distinction which separate it from the competitor and thereby makes the product/service outstanding. This needs to be emphasized in the marketing strategy.
5 It must be constantly repositioned in the market place to take account of changing market demands. This may arise through technology, increased competition or demographical changes. Overall, the strategy adopted in one overseas market is likely to be different to that in another.
6 It must be able to satisfy various financial ratios. For example, a return on capital of 20% should be sought.
7 The brand name should be clearly understood in the market place and not prove offensive. Exporters entering new markets should clearly check out this point.
8 It should accord with the market image of the company. This is an important consideration.

Effective brand management involves global marketing targetted to a receptive audience. This is likely to involve – due to the demographical and socio-economic considerations, and culture aspects – a varying marketing strategy in each overseas territory. For example, marketing a washing machine through a brand name is likely to interest the socio-economic categories of ABCD in West Germany, whereas in Thailand with a much lower GDP and living standards, it would only interest the AB socio-economic category. This requires adequate market research to be undertaken in the overseas territory to determine the market profile. It may result in the change of the brand name to reflect culture, language and religious needs.

Brand marketing is a very specialized area of marketing. Overall, developing a brand product or service is providing a value-added benefit to that product or service and, in so doing, reflecting it in the price. Hence it is a premium price above the level of its competitors and not subject to any discounted sales technique.

Developing a brand product requires continuous and heavy advertising to build up and sustain the brand image. It involves a quality product or service and, through continuous effective advertising, builds up a quality perception of the product by the consumer. It also develops brand loyalty through perceived quality in the brand image by the consumer. This is achieved in the product mix, embracing its specification and packaging. Moreover, branded products involve the logo to symbolize the brand. It may be a product or range of products.

Brand marketing requires skilful handling in the overseas markets, and every market requires to be carefully researched and evaluated to determine the most effective strategy. Particular attention must be given to culture and the ability of the consumer and the end-user's profile. Overseas markets differ widely in their acceptance of branded products and market research should reveal the appropriate target market strategy.

To conclude, brand management is a specialized area of export marketing. To introduce an unknown brand name in a market involves a heavy advertising commitment. It must be thoroughly researched and test marketed.

4.17   INNOVATIVE MARKETING

During the past decade the successful marketeer has been innovative. This may be on pricing, product development/specification or marketing. Overall, it places the marketeer in an advantageous position in the market place and lends itself to premium pricing.

Innovative marketing is the process of introducing something new/ unique to the market place and given below are examples in the area of pricing, product development/specification, and marketing technique.

4.17.1   Innovative pricing

This is used when a new pricing composition arises in the market place. Recent examples include the provision of interest-free credit to the buyer of a household unit such as a refrigerator, washing machine or lounge suite, subject to a down payment and monthly payments over a specified period. It may involve a purchase price of £1000 with a down payment of £100 and nine monthly payments of £100 with no interest charge thereon. Another example is to offer a low price package out of season, such as selling next year's calendars in June some six months prior to their commencement date.

4.17.2   Innovative product development/specification

This is the most common situation, and requires very careful handling to ensure the seller does not lose control thereby maintaining a prime position in the market place. An example is an electric car with a rechargeable battery, range of 2000 kilometres and speed of 50 kph. Another example is decaffeinated tea. The seller can patent the product, but this has to be on an individual market basis which takes time. Again, the product commands premium pricing, and overseas markets must be researched to establish market demand and profile. The adequacy of distribution also needs to be established along with market entry options, and the seller/manufacturer production resources. Planning is a vital ingredient in the marketing strategy. It may be unwise to enter into a licensing agreement for an overseas production base with royalty payment, as the risk of losing control and preserving quality control and confidentiality of the techniques are very real. However, situations do emerge where overseas licensing agreements are successful, but they are the exception.

4.17.3   Innovative marketing

This arises through a new advertising technique. It may be the development of a retail technique when three products are offered for the price of two in a low demand period in order to clear excessive stocks and maintain cash flow. Examples include the car distributor offering insurance cover for one year in the price; the tailor offering 20% discount on the next garment purchased subject to a minimum price; the car dealer offering 10% discount to all couples married in the past two years on the purchase of a car. Again, the market must be researched to determine market acceptance and likely market volume to establish whether the project is worthwhile.

Innovative marketing is an area which can aid the development of a business. It is desirable to maintain a high profile in the market place and this way the seller retains complete control. It requires good market research and careful planning from the production stage to the consumer. Advertising agencies can help in the successful development of sales in the market place. Overall results should be monitored regularly and the marketing plan reviewed in the light of sales performance.

4.18   NICHE MARKETING

The successful entrepreneur continuously studies the markets in which the company operates and those in which it has a potential of market entry of viable development. In so doing, the entrepreneur studies especially the strengths and weaknesses of the competition, consumer behaviour, market trends and gap analysis.

Gap analysis is the process of finding/identifying service gaps in the market and, in so doing, developing new products/ideas, or for generating new product ideas in areas of unfulfilled needs. This involves continuous market research and test marketing followed by product/service development. The need to test-market the product/service is paramount to ensure its consumer acceptance/evaluation and thereby provide the entrepreneur with the opportunity to modify the product/service. Such modification can vary by culture and overseas territory. It can also vary by socio-economic category and demographic factors.

Niche marketing is the outcome of gap analysis and involves the promotion of new products such as an electric car or the developing of a new product within an existing range already operative in the market. An example of the latter is found in the car industry where a car manufacturer offers the consumer saloon/hatchback models in the 1100–2300 cc range, but no sports versions. The demographic analysis reveals that 30% of all car buyers are under 30 years of age and would be receptive to a sports model version.

Niche marketing involves innovation and given below are the features which flow from niche marketing:

1 It gives the company a high market profile.
2 It permits premium pricing to be adopted which can be maintained until fiercer competition arises.
3 Emerging from item (2) it permits a high 'mark up' to be recorded on the product/service, thereby generating above the norm levels of profitability.
4 It is a high risk area which can be lessened through effective market research and test marketing.
5 Niche marketing may not be acceptable in every overseas market and it needs to be approached with caution.
6 Problems can arise in meeting excessive demand in the early stages of the product's life prior to the competitors becoming established, and price wars developing, thereby lowering profit margins.
7 It generates a company market exposure as the consumer focuses attention on the new product/service. This also exposes the company's other products/services, thereby increasing their sales through skilful marketing.

During the next decade niche marketing will become more significant in an increasingly competitive environment. It tends to flourish most in homogeneous markets and the single market entity in EC, operative in 1992, with one patent and product approval/certification system will provide a unique opportunity for the enterprising entrepreneur.

5 Export finance

The ability to sell goods abroad no longer depends solely on quality, delivery and price; a new factor of growing importance is the ability and willingness to grant credit. The granting of credit terms, which are lengthening as the dominance of buyers increases, means that the exporter must wait longer for payment. This automatically reduces cash flow and sooner or later forces the exporter to seek assistance from his bank. Hence, the financial aspects of selling goods abroad are likely to assume increasing importance.

The criteria of the method of payment chosen by an exporter and specified in the contract of sale and reflected in the export/commercial invoice will have regard to the following:

1 available financial options;
2 political situation in buyer's country;
3 nature of relationship between buyer and seller;
4 currency situation;
5 terms of contract of sale;
6 exchange control regulations – if any.

Basically no two businesses have the same pressure – or lack of it – on their cash flow. Different commodities, products, services and projects can all require their own particular financing facilities. An appraisal of the range of short- and medium-term financial resources are found in Tables 5.1 and 5.2.

We will now examine briefly the various options available to the exporter/seller.

5.1 PAYMENTS ON 'OPEN ACCOUNT'

With the open account method of payment the main advantage lies with the importer, whereas the exporter has far less security. To adopt it, the seller must be satisfied that the buyer is entirely creditworthy.

However, much of the UK's trade with Western Europe and the USA is conducted on open account terms, and it is difficult for an exporter to resist the pressure from the buyer to trade on these terms, other than for the first one or two orders.

Open account trading is an arrangement whereby the seller sends the goods and shipping documents direct to the buyer, thus enabling him to take delivery and dispose of the goods – payment being made some time later.

If the goods are to be sold on open account terms, it is sensible to have a clear sales contract showing exactly when payment is to be made. It might, for instance, indicate that this should be effected on receipt of the goods, or of the documents, or perhaps thirty days after receipt of the documents, by the buyer.

Regular monitoring should then highlight occasions when the buyer is not adhering to the agreed settlement terms.

It naturally follows that the seller must have absolute trust in the integrity of the buyer, which is usually based on an established relationship or satisfactory status reports obtained at regular intervals. In addition, there must be confidence that regulations and availability of foreign exchange in the buyer's country will not prohibit or delay the transfer of payment.

It is especially popular between established exporters/importers who have a good and continuous trading relationship.

When using open account trading there are several ways by which the buyer can make payment, and stipulating the most favourable method can make a significant difference to cash flow and business performance.

5.1.1 Buyer's cheque

The buyer's own cheque is the most advantageous way for an importer to settle since he is taking up to a month's extra credit in the time taken in the post for the cheque to reach the seller, to be paid into the seller's bank, and be sent through the international banking system, before ultimately being debited to the importer's account in his own country. Further delays will arise if exchange control authority has first to be obtained in the importer's country.

The seller can arrange with his bank to collect the cheque, in which case he does not receive credit to his account until his bankers have received advice of final payment of the cheque in the buyer's country. Alternatively, he may arrange for the cheque to be 'negotiated/purchased with recourse'. The bank will then make the funds available before the cheque has been paid, although retaining the right to charge back the customer's account should the cheque be unpaid.

Since the seller's bank is effectively making funds available before it has received the credit, an interest charge will be made for the estimated period the bank is out of funds. In the case of foreign currency cheques, this is normally done by a small adjustment to the rate of exchange.

Table 5.1 Short-term international trade finance

Facility	Normal credit period	Usual minimum amount	Basis of interest rate	Other charges	General Comments
Overdraft (on sterling account)	Up to 12 mths, renewable	–	Base rate plus agreed margin	As negotiated	Flexible, revolving facility
Overdraft (on currency account)	Up to 12 mths, renewable	–	Lloyds Bank Offer Rate for relevant currency plus agreed margin	As negotiated	An alternative to sterling overdraft when currency receivables are available to repay
Foreign currency loan	30 days minimum	Negotiable – dependent upon currency	Lloyds Bank Offer Rate for relevant currency plus agreed margin	As negotiated	Same as currency overdraft but for longer-term projects
Finance for exports scheme	Up to 180 days	Normally eligible export turnover of £1m plus. Minimum invoice value of £3000. No maximum	Base rate plus agreed margin	Invoice charge, arrangement fee, and collection charge	Backed by ECGD guarantees. Non-recourse finance up to 90% of invoice value
Smaller exports scheme	Up to 180 days	Normally eligible export turnover of less than £1m	Base rate plus agreed margin	Service charge ranging from 0.5–2.5% of factored turnover	Various schemes are available to suit all companies. Finance can be up to 85% of invoice value dependent upon scheme. Available for sterling and currency items

				Collection charges	
Negotiation/advance against collections	Up to 180 days	—	Base rate plus agreed margin	—	With recourse finance may be up to 100% of value of bill of exchange or documents
Discounting bills of exchange under letters of credit	Up to 180 days	—	Sterling bills – market rate plus margin. Currency bills – Lloyds Bank Offer Rate plus margin	Acceptance commission	No recourse to customer as bills of exchange drawn on Lloyds Bank
Discounting bills of exchange (where not drawn under letter of credit)	Up to 180 days	—	Sterling bills – market rate plus margin. Currency bills – Lloyds Bank Offer Rate plus margin	—	With recourse, at discretion of bank
Acceptance lines of credit	Up to 90 days	Normally £100 000 Maximum £1m per bill	Eligible bank bill discount rate or market rate	Acceptance commission	Revolving facility within agreed limit linked to discount rate as an alternative to base rate
Produce loan	Short term, period negotiated individually	—	Base rate plus agreed margin	As negotiated	Amount financed can be up to 80% of value of goods
Forfeiting	Up to 2 years	£50 000	Market rate linked	Commitment commission	Non-recourse
Buyer finance	Up to 2 years	£250 000	LIBOR plus agreed margin	Arrangement fee	Non-recourse

Reproduced by kind permission of Lloyds Bank PLC.

Table 5.2 Medium-term international trade finance

Facility	Normal credit period	Usual minimum amount	Basis of interest rate	Other charges	General comments
Premier revolving loan	Up to 5 years	£100 000	Mix of: Sterling base rate plus agreed margin; Sterling LIBOR plus agreed margin; Eurocurrency LIBOR plus agreed margin; Eligible bank bill discount rate	Arrangement fee, and other fees as negotiated	Flexible revolving facility
Premier deferred loan	Up to 3 years	£100 000 maximum £5m	Base rate plus agreed margin, or fixed interest rate	Arrangement fee, and other fees as negotiated	Repayment of interest and capital can be deferred for up to 3 years
Premier term loan	Up to 15 years	£100 000	Choice of: Sterling base rate plus agreed margin; Sterling LIBOR plus agreed margin;	Arrangement fee, and other fees as negotiated	Medium- to long-term finance. It is possible to postpone capital repayments

	Term	Amount	Interest rate	Costs	Features
			Eurocurrency LIBOR plus agreed margin; Eligible bank bill discount rate		
ECGD supplier credit	2–5 years	£10 000	Preferential fixed rates in line with international agreements for officially supported medium-term export credits	ECGD premium. Arrangement fee, and bank charges as negotiated	Finance for UK capital goods up to 85% of contract value. Non-recourse
ECGD buyer credit	2–8½ years	£2m	Preferential fixed rates in line with international agreements for officially supported medium-term export credits	ECGD premium. Arrangement fee, and bank charges as negotiated – usually payable by buyer	Project related finance up to 85% of contract value. Non-recourse
Buyer finance	2–5 years	£50 000	Preferential fixed rates in line with international agreement for officially supported medium-term export credits	ECGD premium. Arrangement fee	Finance for UK capital goods up to 85% of contract value. Not project related. Non-recourse
Forfeiting	2–5 years	£50 000	Market rate linked	Commitment commission	Non-recourse

Reproduced by kind permission of Lloyds Bank PLC.

5.1.2   Banker's draft

Another method is the banker's draft, where an importer can purchase from his bank a draft in favour of the exporter, drawn on a bank in the exporter's country, either in sterling or foreign currency.

Unlike the situation where he issues his own cheque, the importer pays his bank for the draft at the time of issue, but, from the exporter's point of view, there is still the delay in the post before such a draft reaches him. However, once received, the draft can be cleared quickly if it is payable in the exporter's own country.

However, a bank draft is not a guaranteed payment. It is a cheque drawn by one bank on another, with all the characteristics of a normal cheque. With the prevalence of forgeries, an exporter is still relying on the integrity of the importer from whom he receives the draft. As with a cheque, the standing of the drawer (the bank) is also a consideration.

Hence the seller must consider these points, and relate them to the context of the trading situation and countries concerned.

The International Money Transfer and Express International Money Transfer are the quickest means of making payment, and result in the exporter receiving cleared funds direct into his bank account. The importer instructs his bank to make payment through the banking system and usually the exporter will indicate on his invoice his account number and the branch of the bank where his account is held. The importer's account is debited by his bankers. Many of these payments are made via SWIFT. This involves the buyer's bank instructing a bank in the seller's country to make the payment. This instruction can be sent by mail, telex or through the Society for Worldwide Interbank Financial Telecommunications. SWIFT is an automated interbank system for transfers and other communications. It offers a secure, standardized and rapid method for members (the banks) to make financial transactions between themselves.

In the case of larger amounts, and where cashflow and interest are factors to be considered, payment may be made by Express International Money Transfer. The buyer's bank then gives instructions to a bank in the exporter's country, either by coded cable/telex, or by a priority SWIFT message.

In both cases, bank charges can be met either by buyer or seller – depending on the agreement between them – and the additional cost of a cable may well be outweighed by the savings in interest for an exporter.

Finally, the fastest method of making payment, but usually the most expensive, is the Telegraphic Transfer. In such situations the buyer's Bank cables, telephones or telexes the exporter's Bank instructing them to pay the seller the agreed amount.

5.2   BILLS OF EXCHANGE

If 'open account' terms have not been agreed, the exporter has to arrange for collection of the amount due. One way in which this can be done is by drawing a bill of exchange, the traditional instrument for claiming that which is due from a debtor. Bills of exchange can be used in international trade involving practically all countries of the world. Indeed, in some countries a trader would be unwise to forgo the protection a bill can provide.

The use of bills of exchange presents several advantages:

1 The bill of exchange is an instrument long recognized by trade custom and by the law, so that it is governed by an established code of practice.
2 A bill is a specific demand on the debtor, which the latter refuses at his peril.
3 The bill is a useful instrument of finance.
4 The bill provides a useful mechanism for granting a pre-arranged period of credit to an overseas buyer. Thus if an exporter has to offer his client a period of credit of 90 days, the bill can be drawn at 90 days after sight.
5 The bill permits the exporter to maintain a degree of control over the shipping documents by making their release subject to payment or acceptance of the bill. Nevertheless, it should be noted that the drawing of a bill of exchange does not guarantee payment; bills too can be dishonoured.

In normal circumstances the exporter draws a bill of exchange, attaches the shipping documents to it and lodges the whole with his bank, giving very precise and complete instructions as to the action to be taken in certain circumstances; whether to forward the bill by air mail and ask for the proceeds to be remitted by cable or air mail; whether the documents are to be released against payment or acceptance of the bill; whether the bill is to be 'protested' if dishonoured; whether the goods should be stored and insured if not taken up by the buyer; whether rebate may be given for early payment; and the party to whom the collecting bank may refer in case of dispute.

The exporter's bank will forward the bill and documents to its correspondent bank in the buyer's country, passing on exactly the instructions received from the exporter. Acting as collecting bank, the correspondent will present the bill to the buyer and release the documents in accordance with the instructions received. If the arrangement called for payment to be made immediately, then the bill of exchange will be drawn at 'sight' and the instructions will be to release the documents against payment (D/P). If a period of credit has been agreed, then the bill will be drawn at, say '90 days sight' and the instructions will be for the documents to be released against acceptance of the bill by the buyer (D/A). In this case, the buyer signs his acceptance across the face of the bill, which now becomes due for payment in 90 days, and he receives the documents of title to the goods. The collecting bank will advise the remitting bank of the date of acceptance and hold the bill until maturity, when it will be presented to the buyer for payment. In the event of dishonour, the collecting bank will arrange 'protest' by a notary if it has been instructed to do so. This procedure provides legal proof that the bill was presented to the drawee and was dishonoured, and enables action to be taken in the courts without further preliminaries.

The procedures and reponsibilities of the banks and other parties are laid down in the Uniform Customs and Practice for Documentary Letters of Credit (1983) Paper issued by the International Chamber of Commerce (No. 400), and accepted by major banks throughout the world.

The method of collecting payment described above is based on the documentary bill, but, in certain circumstances, use may be made of a 'clean' bill, that is, a bill to which no documents are attached. Such bills may be drawn for the collection of monies due for services or for any debt which does not relate to goods. A clean bill may also be used to obtain payment for goods sent on 'open account', especially where payment is overdue.

5.3 DOCUMENTARY LETTERS OF CREDIT AND ALLIED DOCUMENTS

A documentary letter of credit has been defined as an instrument by which a bank undertakes to pay the seller for his goods providing he complies with the conditions laid down in the credit. Apart from requiring 'cash with order', the most satisfactory method of obtaining payment is by means of a documentary letter of credit. It provides security of payment to the exporter and enables the buyer to ensure that he receives the goods as ordered and delivered in the way he requires. It is an arrangement whereby the buyer requests his bank to establish a credit in favour of the seller. The buyer's bank (the issuing bank) undertakes, or authorizes its correspondent bank in the exporter's country, to pay the exporter a sum of money (normally the invoice price of the goods) against presentation of specified shipping documents. It is a mandatory contract and is completely independent of the sales contract. It is concerned only with documents and not the goods to which the documents refer. Liability for payment now rests with the issuing bank and not the buyer. Such credits are usually 'irrevocable', which means that they cannot be cancelled or amended without the agreement of the beneficiary (the exporter) and all other parties. The exporter can thus rely on payment being made as soon as he has shipped the goods and produced the necessary documents. The security provided by an irrevocable credit may be further enhanced if the bank in the exporter's country (the advising bank) is requested by the issue bank to add its 'confirmation'. The exporter then has a 'confirmed irrevocable credit' and he need look no further than his own local bank for payment. If a credit is not 'confirmed', liability for payment rests with the issuing bank abroad, although the advising bank would usually be prepared to negotiate with recourse.

A documentary credit contains a detailed description of the goods: price per unit and packing; name and address of the beneficiary; the voyage, that is, port of shipment and port of destination; whether the price is FOB, CFR or CIF (free on board, cost and freight or cost insurance freight); and whether part shipments and transhipment are allowed. In some cases, the ship will be named. Details of insurance (if CIF), and the risks to be covered, will also be shown. The credit will specify a latest date for shipment and an expiry date, which is the latest date for the presentation of documents. It will also stipulate a time limit for presentation measured from the issue date of the bills of lading; in the absence of such a stipulation, banks refuse to accept documents presented later than 21 days after issuance of the bills.

The documents usually required are the following:

1 Commercial invoice – the amount must not exceed the credit amount. If terms such as 'about' or 'circa' are used in connection with the amount of credit or the quantity or the unit price stated in the credit, these are to be construed as allowing a difference not to exceed 10% more or 10% less than the amount or unit price to which they refer. The description of the goods on the invoice or packaging must be precise, and must agree with the credit. An essential part of the description are the marks or numbers on the packaging; these must appear on the invoice, which must be in the name of the buyer.
2 Certificate of insurance or insurance policy.
3 Pre-shipment Certificate – if required.
4 Quality certificate – if required.
5 Weight certificate – if required.
6 Air Waybill.
7 Certificate of origin.
8 Draft bill of exchange – a written order for payment.
9 Transport documents – clean shipped on board bill of lading, embracing ocean bill of lading or a bill of lading covering carriage by sea, combined transport bill of lading; or a post receipt; or certificate of posting.

It is important that the exporter is fully conversant with articles Nos 22–42 of documents required under documentary credits contained in the *Uniform Customs and Practice for Documentary Credits*. The exporter is advised to consult his bank for guidance.

Besides the basic irrevocable credit there are revocable credits which, as the name implies, can be cancelled or amended at any time without notice to the beneficiary. They do not constitute a legally binding undertaking by the banks concerned. Once transmitted and made available at the advising bank, however, their cancellation or modification are only effective when that bank has received notice thereof and any payment made before receipt of such notice is reimbursable by the issuing bank. The value of these credits as security for payment is plainly doubtful. They are used mainly between parent and subsidiary companies, where a continuing series of shipments is concerned, or as an indication of good intent.

Where a buyer wishes to provide his supplier with the security of payment afforded by a documentary credit, but at the same time requires a period of credit, he may instruct his bank to issue a credit calling for a bill of exchange drawn at so many days after sight instead of the usual sight draft; this would, of course, be an irrevocable credit. In this case the beneficiary would not receive immediate payment upon presentation of the documents as under a sight credit, but his term bill would be accepted by the bank. It could then be discounted in the money market at the finest rates. Thus the beneficiary would still receive payment, but the buyer would not be called upon to pay until the bill matured.

Given below is the documentary credit cycle.

1 Buyer and seller enter into a contract of sale calling for settlement by documentary credit.

2 The buyer (applicant) requests his bank (issuing bank) to issue a documentary credit in favour of the seller (beneficiary). The documentary credit outlines the terms and conditions under which payment or negotiation or acceptance may be made.

3 The documentary credit is sent to a bank in the beneficiary's country (advising bank) for onward transmission to the beneficiary.

4 The seller should check the documentary credit to ensure that he can comply with all the terms and conditions.

5&6 The seller ships the goods and presents his documents to the negotiating bank for settlement.

7 The negotiating bank examines the documents against the credit and, if in order, settles with the seller.

8&9 The negotiating bank forwards the documents to the issuing bank, claiming reimbursement as agreed between the two banks.

10&11 The issuing bank examines the documents and forwards them to its customer, the buyer, who pays for them in due course.

Given below is a check list to ensure the letter of credit agrees with the terms of sale:

1 Does it state that it is subject to UCP?

2 Is it irrevocable, preferably with the added confirmation of the advising bank?

3 Are the terms of settlement clearly expressed and satisfactory?

4 Where is it available? If you cannot get settlement in your own country, payment for your goods will be delayed and your security of payment reduced.

5 Does it describe correctly the good, their weight, quantity, etc.?

6 Are there any spelling errors? If there are, they should be taken up immediately with the advising bank. Any needed amendments of the credit should then be communicated to your buyers.

7 Are the terms for despatch of the goods, e.g. FOB, CIF, etc., as agreed in your sales contract?

8 Are all the transport details correctly stated such as place and time of despatch, the destination, the method of carriage?

9 Are part shipments and transhipments allowed?

10 Does it call for the correct transport documents for the method of carriage to be employed?

11 Does it state what insurance risks, if any, are to be covered and whether a policy or a certificate is required?

12 Does it require any special declarations, or endorsement or certification of documents, including references to export or import licences?

13 Can you comply with the credit terms, particularly as regards despatch and presentation time limits and documents stipulated, bearing in mind possible difficulties and delays in obtaining outside certifications?

The subject of export documentation is dealt with in Chapter 12 of *Elements of Export Practice* (see Appendix A).

5.3.1 Transferable credits

These arise where the exporter is obtaining the goods from a third party, say the actual manufacturer, and, as the middleman, does not have the resources to buy outright and await payment from his overseas customer. The credit is established in favour of the middleman (the prime beneficiary) and authorizes the advising bank to accept instructions from the prime beneficiary to make the credit available, in whole, or in part, to one or more third parties (the second beneficiaries). The second beneficiary is then notified of the credit on the original terms and conditions, except that the amount and unit price are reduced and the shipment and expiry dates shortened. The original credit relates to the price the buyer is paying to the prime beneficiary, but the latter will be obtaining the goods at a lower price, hence the reduction in amount. When the second beneficiary presents the shipping documents, he obtains payment for his invoice price, and the prime beneficiary is called upon to substitute his own invoice and receive the difference (his profit). The negotiating bank then has documents in accordance with the original credit.

Where more than one second beneficiary is involved, the credit must permit part shipments. If the prime beneficiary does not wish his buyer and supplier to be aware of each other, he may request that his name be substituted for that of the opener on the transfer credit, and that shipping documents be in the name of a third party blank endorsed.

However, a transferable credit can only be transferred once – that is, it cannot be transferred by the second beneficiary to a third.

It can only be transferred in accordance with the terms and conditions of the original credit, with the following exceptions:

1 The beneficiary may substitute his name and address for that of the applicant for the credit.

2 The amount of the credit and any unit prices may be reduced, thus enabling the first beneficiary to allow for his profit.

3 The expiry date of the credit, the last date for presentation of documents after issuance of the transport document, and the latest date for shipment may all be brought forward.

4 The insurance cover may be increased to provide the amount of cover required in the original credit.

The middleman is able to take his profit out of the credit as first beneficiary by substituting his own invoices for the invoices of the second beneficiary (supplier) when they are actually presented for payment under the transferred portion of the credit. In this case, the paying bank acts for both beneficiaries. It must check that the first beneficiary's invoices, together with all the other documents presented by the second beneficiary, comply with each other and with the terms and conditions of the original credit. If so, payment is made to the second beneficiary for the value of his invoices, and the first beneficiary is paid the difference in value between his invoices and those of the second beneficiary.

5.3.2 Back to back credits

Back to back credits arise in circumstances similar to those of the transferable credit and particularly where both the supplier and the buyer are overseas. In this case, the middleman receives a credit in his favour from the buyer and asks his bank to establish a credit in favour of his supplier against the security of the credit in his own favour. Hence there are two separate credits instead of one as in the case of a transferable credit, and this can create problems in the matching of documents and credit terms.

5.3.3 Revolving credits

Revolving credits are used where a series of shipments of roughly the same value are made at intervals and the parties wish the programme to proceed without interruption. A credit is established for a certain sum and quantity of goods with a provision that, when a shipment has been made and documents presented and paid, the credit is automatically renewed in its original form so that another shipment can be made. They help speed and simplify transactions because they do not have to be renegotiated every time documents are presented for payment. Such credits can be revocable or irrevocable, and are usually subject to a time limitation. They can also be cumulative or non-cumulative.

With a cumulative revolving credit, any amount unused from one month can be carried forward to the next. Thus, if the credit limit is for £100 000 per month over a 6 month period, the total value of the credit would actually be £600 000. With a non-cumulative revolving credit, any unused amount is not carried forward and so only the monthly limit, say £100 000, is available to the borrower.

5.3.4   Acceptance credit

Acceptance credit involves the process of specific banks providing acceptance credit involving the adoption of a bill of exchange drawn on any of its members. The 'Bank Bill', as it is called, permits funds to be drawn for a set period and amount, and is particularly useful to importers of raw materials or components who have to meet their costs before the finished goods are sold. Usually a minimum amount is imposed when financing the scheme.

It operates on the basis that the importing company draws a bill of exchange up to an agreed value for payment at a specified date in the future, and the bank arranges for the bill of exchange to 'be discounted' in the money market to one of the discount houses that specializes in this business. The sale proceeds are credited to the importer, making funds immediately available to him. When the bill of exchange matures, the bank pays it and debits the importing company's account for the amount.

5.3.5   Deferred payment credits

These are becoming increasingly popular where a period of credit has been agreed between buyer and seller, but the issuing bank and buyer do not wish the credit period to be represented by a bill of exchange. This is usually where, under local law, bills of exchange attract stamp duty.

Consequently, when documents are presented 'in order' by the seller the bank does not accept a bill of exchange but instead gives a letter of undertaking to the seller advising him when he will receive his money. The main drawback with this is that should the exporter wish to receive his money straight away, he does not have a bill of exchange to have discounted. Such credits are very common in Spain and Italy.

5.3.6   Standby letters of credit

This type of credit differs from other types in that the buyer and seller hope it will never be drawn upon. They are often used as security for open account trading where the seller requires some kind of 'back up' in the event of the buyer not paying for the goods. They normally require the issuing bank to make payment to the seller upon presentation of documents evidencing non-payment by the importer.

They are also commonly used in some countries as a substitute for a bank guarantee which, due to the regulations in that country, are not generally acceptable. A prime example of this is the USA.

In such instances, standby letters of credit have the advantage of being subject to the Uniform Customs and Practice for Documentary Credits Brochure 400, whereas at the moment there are no internationally agreed regulations for bank guarantees.

5.3.7   Counter trade

Counter trade – loosely known as barter – is a form of foreign trade in which the sale of goods or services to a country is limited contractually to an obligation to buy goods or services from that country. It is practised in over 100 countries and particularly common in less developed countries (LDCs) and Eastern Bloc countries. Counter trade negotiations closely involve international banks.

Pressure for this type of trade arises through lack of convertible currency, political pressures and the desire to use the marketing skills of the West to sell their goods. Recently, even certain developed countries have been seeking counter trade deals.

The main forms that this trade takes are as follows:

(a) *Barter*   This is the direct exchange of goods for goods under a single commercial contract without the involvement of money, which has been conducted from time immemorial. Its practice in modern times is fairly rare. LDCs sometimes barter their primary products such as oil and timber for consumer products or capital equipment.

(b) *Counterpurchase*   This is more common in international trade between western developed countries on the one hand, and the LDCs and the centralized East European economies on the other. It differs from barter in that the payment for imports into an LDC is met from the proceeds of an export contract. Two separate contracts exist under normal commercial terms, one for the goods exported to the LDC, and one for the counter-purchase goods. Both contracts are normally concluded between unrelated parties with the convertible currency realized under the counter-commodity contract being used to settle the original export.

As a variation of this concept, the goods exported can be settled in a minor currency, with the exporter agreeing to buy the goods from the LDC in return for a major trading currency, up to a given percentage of the main contract. The second contract may be with an entirely different company or foreign trade organization within the LDC or East European country.

(c) *Compensation or buy-back trade*   This is tied to the sale of capital equipment and plant, and involves the buy-back of the product produced by the original equipment. This type of arrangement usually involves large projects for, say, chemical or fertilizer plants.

(d) *Switch deals*   These result from imbalances on clearing accounts set up between central or government-owned foreign trade banks under bilateral trade agreements. They are arrangements whereby intermediaries are able to utilize clearing account credits to finance exports from third countries, thus restoring equilibrium to the clearing account.

5.3.8 Factoring

The practice of using factoring companies by exporters is very much on the increase. Their prime function is to administer the sales ledgers and collect payments once the goods have been shipped. Such factoring companies provide a complete range of services which cover those aspects of exporting, so leaving the manufacturer free to concentrate on export production and sales. For a small service charge of between 0.75% and 2% of turnover, they will provide multi-currency and multi-language sales accounting, backed by credit management, which is exercised in the customer's country by the factor's own employees or agents. Also included in this service charge is 100% protection against losses due to the insolvency of the customer and, in some cases, protection against political risk and exchange rate fluctuations. Factoring cannot effectively meet the particular needs of every industry and the most suitable companies are likely to have an expanding turnover in excess of £100 000 and to be selling consumer goods, light industrial products or services on short-term credit.

The advantages of using a factoring service are: the saving of time in running a sales ledger, the savings on cost of postage, telephones and telex and overseas bank charges; involvement with only one debtor – the factoring company; the availability of credit facilities for the buyer on 100% of the value of approved sales; the removal of responsibility for collecting overdue accounts or making provision for bad debts by the seller; the ability to predict the seller's cash flow with confidence; the facility of the seller to draw cash in advance of payments being received from the buyer; and, finally, the ability to obtain cash discounts from suppliers using money generated from the advance payment facility.

It is usual for a company to have a minimum annual sales turnover of £100 000 before a factoring service becomes an economical proposition for either party. The range of industries where factoring services have been used successfully includes textiles, clothing, food distribution, consumer durables, engineering and electronic equipment.

Export factoring services are generally used by companies selling to Europe, USA and Canada. However, it may be possible for a company exporting to other countries to obtain a factoring service provided that the countries concerned are thought suitable.

5.3.9   Forfeiting

Forfeiting is a method of international trade finance involving the discounting of bank-guaranteed overseas trade bills or notes. It has no recourse to the exporter as he surrenders or relinquishes his right in return for cash payment from the forfeiter. In such circumstances the exporter agrees to surrender his rights to claims for payment on goods or services which have been delivered to the buyer. Any type of trade debt can be forfeited (i.e. surrendered for cash) but the most common is trade payee – bill of exchange accepted by the buyer or promissory notes from the buyer. A forfeiter can provide finance for any type and duration of trade transaction but usually credit is provided for the export of capital goods which require finance for periods of between three and seven years.

(a) *Computerized international banking: MidTrade*   A survey carried out two years ago among importers and exporters in the UK showed that the services being provided by the major banks were lacking in important areas.

In particular, these customers complained about import letters of credit and export collections. Concern was voiced about levels of accuracy in the banking system and consequent delays in both documents and flow of funds. Importers had difficulty in monitoring their Letters of Credit (L/C) once they had left the UK and exporters had trouble getting information regarding the status of outstanding bills. The problems were compounded by the vast administrative job involved in processing tens of thousands of Letters of Credit (L/Cs) and collections were paper-intensive, resource-consuming and error-prone.

The Midland Bank recognized that the internal and external problems were interrelated and that the development of an integrated computerized processing system would benefit both the bank and its customers. The result is MidTrade; an automated processing and information system that allows for the transfer of previously paper-based records on to computer. MidTrade was launched in February 1989 after a major collaborative effort between the operations, systems and marketing departments of the bank. A major financial investment was involved but customers are not charged extra to pay for the improvements in service and benefits that the system brings.

A mainframe computer is accessed directly by terminals at Midland Bank premises in nearly 40 strategic locations. Details of L/Cs and collections are input by operators and can be updated or accessed at the touch of a button. From one single entry that is checked; data is replicated by the system to produce all necessary advice letters, payment messages and accounting details. The integrated nature of the system with the bank's communications and accounting systems negates the need for re-keying and hence reduces errors to the absolute minimum.

These features have provided solutions to the problems previously experienced including greater accuracy, Midland's staff able to respond quicker to customer enquiries – up-to-the-minute details can be called up on screen while the customer is on the phone, and finally, there is a faster flow of advices of L/Cs to beneficiaries overseas, which enables them to begin manufacture or ship the goods earlier than might otherwise have been the case.

There are other benefits specific to export collections. MidTrade automatically generates tracers – enquiries of overseas banks – which can often lead to cash proceeds arriving up to 14 days sooner than they would otherwise have done, and consequently saving money for Midland's exporting customers. For example, with interest costs at 15%, if £25 000 arrives one day earlier, it saves the customer more than £10.

To make the export collection process even quicker, customers can send their documents and instructions directly to the overseas bank, and send a copy of the instructions to Midland for entry into MidTrade. The system also accepts SPEX generated documentation.

Comprehensive monthly export collection status reports are made available to Midland's major customers. These reports highlight details of unaccepted and overdue items, country and customer payment performances together with summaries of country and currency exposure.

Benefits specific to import letters of credit include sight and term status reports that enable customers to follow the full life-cycle of a transaction in addition to providing currency exposure and facility usage detail. Customers benefit from the improvements in the critical areas of accuracy, speed, timeliness and the ready availability of information.

The benefits are not confined to customers, of course. The original problems were Midland's as well, and the bank too benefits from the solution. The availability of MidTrade enables the bank to manage its own work more efficiently, to save staff time for more customer attention and to develop its share of competitive import and export markets.

The MidTrade facility is a market leader. In addition to it being fully integrated and so obviating the need to re-key transactions; access to the system by its operators extends to nearly 40 international banking centres throughout the UK and customers will be able to direct all their transactions via their local centre. The provision of local access in this way answers hitherto unfulfilled customer demand. Other advantages include import

L/C customers will be able to access MidTrade direct from terminals in their own premises with the loading of information being made off-line. There will be no need to post or deliver instructions to the bank. Once the details are entered by the customer, they will be retained and reproduced as necessary by the system. There will be no need for Midland operators to print out hard copy and then re-key before transmission overseas, as is the case with many other systems. Midland's other MidTrade-related plans for the future include developments in electronic data interchange and electronic mail.

There is no doubt the system will grow in popularity as the exporter realizes the benefits that MidTrade offers on the market.

5.4 FINANCE GUARANTEED BY THE EXPORT CREDIT GUARANTEE DEPARTMENT

As the various sources of export finance mentioned above have proved insufficient and costly and have not always been readily available, special arrangements for short-, medium- and long-term finance have been concluded between the banks and the Export Credit Guarantee Department (ECGD).

ECGD is in the insurance business, covering the exporter against losses on export contracts. It is just as easy for buyers in the European Community, America, or Australasia to fail, as it is for those in some further-flung market that the exporter instinctively feels is risky. ECGD protection gives the exporter the confidence to expand overseas business. Exporters insured against risks of non-payment can work to a much bolder export policy; taking on new buyers and breaking into new markets, without the fear of crippling losses. ECGD insurance can also support export finance, improving the exporter's liquidity by giving access to export funds from banks and other institutions, often at favourable rates of interest.

ECGD has the experience of almost 70 years' service to the export industry, and has an extensive database of overseas traders and credit risks. It has numerous contacts overseas and insures a wide diversity of risks.

Some 80% of the exports covered by ECGD are standard, or near-standard goods made in the UK and sold on credit terms of up to 180 days. These, together with goods regarded as capital expenditure items which are sold on longer terms of credit, or which take more than 12 months to manufacture, are handled by ECGD Insurance Services through a network of Regional Offices and the Head Office in Cardiff. In the past three years, over £2 billion has been paid out in claims to exporters who have not been paid by overseas buyers. Had these UK companies not taken out ECGD credit insurance, they might have gone into liquidation, or become more vulnerable to a takeover bid. The reasons the exporters did not receive payment are many and various. There could be any of the following: default or insolvency of the buyer; exchange problems – a currency crisis in the buyer's country, for example; difficulties in remitting moneys, due to a change of government; or a change of local currency regulations.

ECGD insurance gives the exporter peace of mind by covering both 'buyer risks' and 'country risks' in the same policy. ECGD can meet the needs of any exporter – from the smaller companies, usually new to exporting, who need full and overall protection, to the more sophisticated, usually larger company looking for a specific form of insurance tailor-made to cover particular aspects of its operations.

If the exporter's business is mainly regular shipments of 'off the shelf' consumer products or fairly standard specification engineering goods, or if they are made in the UK and sold on credit terms of up to six months, then the most appropriate policy for the exporter would be an ECGD Short Term Guarantee. With this policy, the exporter can insure either the whole of the export turnover or an agreed proportion of it. The exporter is insured against loss from a wide range of causes. They come under two broad headings – Buyer Risks and Country Risks. A Short Term Guarantee usually insures the exporter against both in the same policy. Buyer risks include: the insolvency of the buyer; the buyer's failure to pay within six months after the due date for goods accepted; and the buyer's failure or refusal to accept goods despatched which comply with the contract. Country risks include: difficulties and delays in transferring money from the buyer's country, for example due to a general moratorium on external debt by the government of the buyer's country, or a third country through which payment must be made; any other action of the government of the foreign country which wholly, or partly, prevents performance of the contract; political events or economic, legislative or administrative measures occurring outside the UK which prevent or delay transfer of payments; war, civil war and the like, outside the UK, preventing performance of the contract, where the cause of loss is not normally commercially insurable; and cancellation or non-renewal of an export licence or the imposition of new restrictions on export, after date of contract. Also, when ECGD has confirmed that the buyer is a public buyer, the failure or refusal to fulfil any of the terms of the contract. The exporter is normally covered for 90% of loss in cases of buyer default or insolvency and 95% for the country risk.

ECGD Insurance Services can protect many other businesses, goods and services. For example, services provided for an overseas customer, such as professional assistance, refits, conversions and repairs; royalties on licensing or franchising agreements; cover for sales through overseas subsidiaries; constructional works contracts; and goods sold after export from stock held overseas or after exhibition. There is a Multi-Sourcing Endorsement for the Short Term Guarantee which gives cover for UK manufacturers and merchants dealing in foreign goods and UK merchants trading goods or commodities between other countries.

Goods that are sold on terms longer than 6 months, or which take more than 12 months to manufacture can have similar protection with an Extended Terms Guarantee. Cover is available for exports invoiced in a wide variety of currencies, too. If the exporter is using the forward exchange market, ECGD can agree that claims may take account – within limits – of any additional losses in meeting the forward exchange commitment.

The system operates on the basis that an exporter takes out a policy, increasing cover on the existing buyers if they increase their orders, or arranging cover for any new buyers ordering from the exporter. Most applications are cleared within 24 hours.

Premiums depend on what cover is being provided for which countries. ECGD have a flexible premium rate system and lower rates may be given to those exporters who bring a wide spread of risk.

Cover usually starts on the shipment date. However, for exporters producing specialized goods for a particular buyer, or goods which would not have a ready market elsewhere if things went wrong, pre-credit risk cover – from the date of contract – can also be provided for a small increase in premium. Claims are paid in accordance with the guarantee provisions. The time at which claims are paid varies according to the cause of the loss, but provided a fully-documented claim is submitted promptly and is accepted, payment is normally made: immediately on proof of your buyer's insolvency, six months after due date of payment for a protracted default on goods accepted; one month after resale if the original buyer has failed to take up the order; or four months after due date for most other causes of loss.

ECGD insure hundreds of exporters in the invisible sector, and the quality of cover is just as good as that available to cover sale of goods.

ECGD also provides cover to the exporter engaged in a whole range of services classified as invisible exports including contracts to: accommodate; advise; arrange; broke; consult; convert; create; design; draft; draw; franchise; insure; lease; license; map; overhaul; perform; process; refit; repair; survey; teach; train; transport; treat; or write for overseas principals.

ECGD make every effort to tailor individual policies to individual needs. The exporter can insure all, or an agreed proportion of, the insurable business. The greater the spread of risk the exporter offers to ECGD, the lower the premiums are, as a rule. Normally, the services the exporter requires are unlikely to involve credit of more than 180 days from invoice date, but ECGD cover is very flexible on pre-invoice periods if the exporter wants cover to start earlier.

Cover starts either from the date of the contract, or from the date of submission of the invoice for the services performed. The exporter can insure against loss from a wide range of causes. These come under two broad headings – Buyer Risks and Country Risks. The Services Guarantee insures the exporter against both in the same policy, as earlier described.

It may well be that the services the exporter provides are large one-off contracts or have a very long horizon of risk e.g. several years between contract and final payment, or are unlikely to be repeated. This is often the case in major consultancy work. ECGD's Project Group can supply a policy, underwritten individually, giving specific insurance for a particular contract. This type of insurance is usually arranged at the same time as the contract is being negotiated.

The people to approach for export finance are banks, export finance companies and other trade finance institutions. ECGD cover often helps the exporter get finance because it represents very attractive security. There is a great deal of flexibility here. The security can range from simple assignment of the policy monies to joint policy holding with the exporter's finance provider, who may even agree to manage the exporter's policy as an additional service. The policy can be easily adapted for finance in respect of selected contracts as they arise, or pre-defined contracts depending on arrangements with the exporter's chosen source.

When goods and services are sold on credit terms of two years or more, ECGD can provide a guarantee direct to the financing bank. This is complementary to the basic insurance guarantee. With the guarantee in place, the bank will advance finance at a special fixed rate of interest.

To conclude our treatment of export finance the reader is advised to study the financial press every day to keep up-to-date on new developments and facilities available from the financial market, government agencies and other sources.

6 *Costing and pricing*

The need to have reliable costing data is important to ensure an adequate return on investment so that the overall operation remains viable. Moreover, such costing techniques require constant reappraisal to take account of any changed circumstances. For example, the price of materials may rise sharply following a drop in the value of sterling; improved production techniques may have been introduced thereby lowering unit cost; or distribution cost may have risen due to the revised production arrangements involving more inter-factory transfer to complete the product assembly.

Pricing requires much skill and a good knowledge of the market, together with reliable market analysis data. The export marketing manager must be fully aware of both the strengths and weaknesses of the product within the overseas market place, and also the likely customer profile. Such data analysis must be reconciled with many other factors, particularly competition and long-term market prospects. Price determination is a complex evaluation and each situation must be treated on its merits. Moreover, when the time comes for the annual price review it is important that a straight percentage increase is not applied across the board on every overseas market. Rather, selective price increases should be sought to reflect market sensitivity, general competitiveness and customer resistance to such an increase.

Statistical data are important as a means of providing information on which management can make judgements and decisions on pricing, product development, market share improvement, budgets, etc. Many official statistics are available from a wide variety of sources, and such data can be employed usefully in many circumstances, such as in devising market reports in continuous evaluation of the market results, market analysis and consumer profiling.

In our study of export costing and pricing it is appropriate to consider the various options which exist regarding entry into an overseas market:

1 Selling to overseas governments through their buying offices.
2 Submitting tenders to foreign governments and private consortia.
3 Selling to foreign subsidiaries.

4 Selling to home-based organizations for their overseas subsidiaries.

5 Accepting orders from independent export/import agents.

6 Participating in trade fairs and exhibitions. This is an important medium through which to support direct marketing, via the Department of Trade and Industry, local Chambers of Commerce and trade associations.

7 Engaging an export agent, which is ideal for small companies and for the more remote markets.

8 Utilizing the expertise of another UK company which is well established in the overseas market place, and retailing the product through them, thereby improving their promotion prospects and strengthening their market share.

9 Setting up a joint selling company in the overseas market which will have the benefit of utilizing the local company expertise and thereby strengthen the prospects of developing the market.

10 Selling through intermediaries such as agents on an *ad hoc* basis.

11 Joining a consortium with other related manufacturers. This may be a consortium of UK companies or, more likely, have a multinational company structure. It is common in the turnkey arrangement and especially in the development, construction and commissioning of engineering projects as found, for example, in a hospital project in the Middle East. (A turnkey is an export sales corporate contract whereby the seller (exporter) undertakes to supply the goods and commissions them on the site as specified by the buyer.)

12 Conducting sales on a barter basis: products in exchange for raw materials or other manufactured products. This could involve a bilateral trade agreement. It is more common with Eastern Bloc, Middle Eastern and Third World countries. Negotiations are difficult and guidance should be sought from the Department of Trade and Industry.

13 Engaging in the direct selling technique by setting up a regional or national sales branch office or subsidiary. This arrangement can emerge following a successful launch and development of the product when it is felt that a local branch office with personal service could further develop the market.

14 With a joint selling company consider joining a local, third company.

15 Set up sales forces with home-based salesmen or expatriate salesmen, national salesmen, or a combination of these. Such a venture will require particular attention to recruitment and training.

16 For new products, new outlets and new areas, 'commando' or 'missionary' salesmen could be used. This could be an additional requirement to item (15).

17 Use dealers and distributors of other manufacturers to sell non-competing products from their warehouses and for display in their showrooms.

18 Direct marketing through mail shots/catalogues, etc.

A combination of selling techniques may be employed to suit the individual market and product type and range. The techniques must be cost-effective and the foregoing options must be considered in the product costing analysis. Policy should be altered when appropriate to keep up with changing trends.

6.2   EXPORT PRODUCT COSTING

Before we examine the factors influencing choice of export product price, it is important to consider the question of the export product cost structure, involving the direct cost and the indirect cost.

Direct costs embrace all those elements in the product manufacture including labour, raw materials, component parts, salaries, heating, lighting, general maintenance of the factory building and plant (including an element for depreciation/amortization) and any other ancillary cost which could be directly allocated to the product. This could include warehousing/storage, distribution involving inter-factory transfer handling and assembly.

The indirect costs embrace all those elements which can be identified with the production of the items. Again, it can be broken down into three main elements of indirect labour, materials and other indirect expenses. Indirect labour cost would include design cost, production specification, and general administration. Cost of materials would include allocation of stationery and stores expenses. Other allocated indirect expenses are computer allocation running cost, transport, insurance, capital changes and security.

The outcome of this cost analysis, which will vary by product and by individual company, will give the total product cost without any element for promotion, distribution, profit, etc.

6.3   PRODUCT PRICE DETERMINATION

The subject of product pricing is a complex one, and situations are likely to vary extensively by company, commodity market and the factors on which the price is ultimately based. Experience, business acumen, professionalism at all levels and market pricing techniques will all play their part. Above all the price charged by the exporter must produce a profit after the specified launch time.

Basically there are three main approaches to fixing the final product price:

1 There is the purely academic approach of the economist. This involves a basic understanding of the more sophisticated pricing policies of integrated marketing.
2 The second option involves the concept of competition bidding. This policy is adopted more by the larger companies which are involved in a tender for a large contract. The make up of the tender involves many elements and various companies, often multi-national in structure. Moreover, many subcontractors are involved.

3 The third option is primarily the business acumen approach. It involves the consideration of many factors to produce the most acceptable product price in the market place.

It is relevant to mention here that the cargo delivery terms such as FOB, ex works and CIF will determine the total cost to buyer; Chapter 8, dealing with Incoterms 1990, should be read in association with this chapter. All the constituents of the varying cargo delivery terms must be fully understood.

Given below are the factors which influence the determination of the export product sales price:

1 Direct cost of commodity production.
2 Indirect cost of commodity production. It must be stressed, as outlined earlier, that the various items which are included in this item and the previous one will vary by individual company and commodity. Experience will dictate the best criteria on which to formulate such cost.
3 Promotion cost. This will reflect cost found in the advertising budget and a portion of the sales office expenditure.
4 Packaging charges. Usually the seller (exporter) has to reflect the packaging cost of an international consignment in any quotation.
5 Cargo insurance is a cost borne by the buyer under the C & F, FOB and ex works terms. Usually the buyer makes his own insurance arrangements, but the buyer can request the seller to do so, in which case the buyer would reimburse the seller.
6 Physical distribution charges represent a significant expenditure and again the cargo delivery term would determine the extent of the commitment of the seller and buyer. For example, under FOB Southampton, the seller meets all transportation cost until the goods are placed on board the vessel – at which point the residue of transit cost is borne by the buyer. This includes sea freight, cargo handling, customs clearance, any consular invoice, despatch from the port to the buyer's premises, cargo insurance, etc.

Distribution options are tending to be made more by the buyer (this is reflected in the increasing number of cargo preference laws as detailed in Chapter 14 of *Economics of Shipping Practice and Management* – see Appendix A). Nevertheless, the seller still has the opportunity to decide the most favourable transport mode in a high percentage of export sales contracts, and this allows him to choose the most favourable one in the circumstances. It involves the evaluation of many options and is fully considered in Chapter 11 of *Elements of Export Practice*.
7 Method of payment of the goods. Again the cargo delivery terms will determine the stage at which the buyer must effect payment of the goods to the seller. In broad terms, subject to all the arrangements proving satisfactory, this will arise when the goods have been passed over to the buyer, at which point he accepts all responsibility, liability and cost of the

onward transit to the destination. Under FOB the process of securing payment commences when the goods have been placed on board the specified vessel in accord with the cargo delivery terms and when all arrangements are in order.

Export finance is dealt with in Chapter 5, whilst exchange rates are dealt with elsewhere in this chapter (section 6.4). Particular attention needs to be given to this element of the cost evaluation; if in doubt, contact your local bank.

8 Contingency charges. These will embrace any standing cost of general administration charges, any special cost particularly relevant to the product, such as product design modification to meet a new market need.

9 Profit element. This is also based on a percentage cost of the combined direct and indirect cost of the product. Again the technique will vary and may be assessed on the overall cost of the commodity including the despatch cost.

It will be appreciated that the foregoing cost constituents will produce an ideal figure for a favourable market, which will embrace an acceptable level of profit. However, international marketing involves a number of other factors which will influence the ultimate price in the market place.

1 Selling techniques. All methods of selling a product involve a possible variation in the distribution arrangements which can affect the distribution cost. Likewise the actual selling technique can vary; for example a commission element might have to be included in the cost analysis.

2 The degree of competition. Market analysis and market research will reveal the influence of pricing in the market place. It is quite possible that the price may have to be trimmed to enable the commodity to be competitive. This will lower the profit margin and could result in a review of the distribution, promotion and production arrangements. For example, more aggressive marketing could result in improved sales, thereby generating a need for a faster rate of production and subsequently more economical production and distribution costs. Thus, an acceptable profit level at a competitive price could be achieved.

3 Existing market. The market research will detail the profile of the existing market. This will pinpoint the strengths and weaknesses of the product in the market place and whether, for example, more money should be spent to improve its packaging image in the retail outlets.

4 The potential market. If the market potential is large, it will justify above-average promotion cost to stimulate a quickening market share growth.

Our examination of product price determination would not be complete without mention of the economic forces of supply and demand. In broad terms such factors will continue to play a role in price determination and this applies particularly to the market profile. Industrial countries tend to

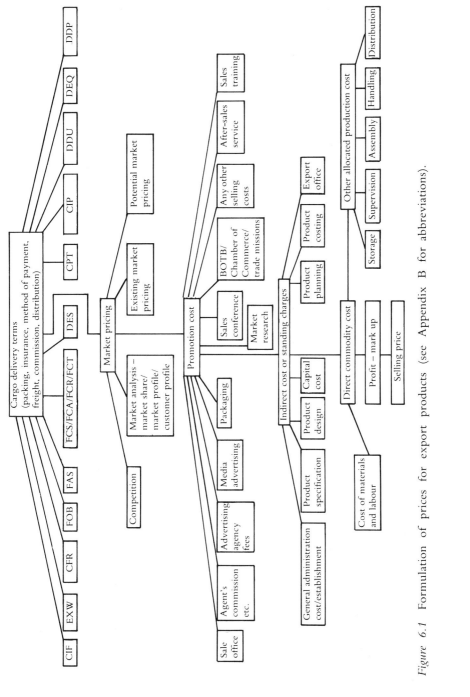

Figure 6.1 Formulation of prices for export products (see Appendix B for abbreviations).

be more organized commercially, with better communications and a much higher income per capita. A further point to bear in mind is the sales cost element of the product price. After-sales service can prove expensive in a competitive market, but is essential if standards are to remain high. Likewise, many overseas markets require a different specification to the UK home market product. This requires careful costing and the maximum production run possible to lower unit cost. Figure 6.1 features the constituents of product price determination in an overseas market.

6.4 INTERNATIONAL EXCHANGE RATES

The costing of the export product involves international exchange rates and it is important to have an understanding of the impact of their fluctuations and the various options open to counteract them, taking into account the way the market operates.

Foreign exchange rates concern the means whereby foreign debts may be settled, means of payment and the services of banks and brokers. Settlement of debts between people in the same country is quite simply effected by the payment of money, which one possesses and the other is prepared to accept. He will accept it because it is the national currency and legal tender supported by law. Where the payer and receiver live in different countries and use different money, the problem is to enable both parties to deal in their own currency. This is resolved by the foreign exchange system whereby the money of one country can be exchanged for the money of another.

6.4.1 Rate of exchange

The price of one currency in terms of another is called the rate of exchange. It is the number of units of one currency that will be exchanged for a given number of units of another currency. The rates quoted for buying and selling currency on the foreign exchange market are called market rates, and these are quoted by one bank to another, usually through the intermediary of a foreign exchange broker. The market has no centre in the same way as the Stock Exchange or the Baltic Exchange have, but consists merely of a network of telephonic communication between the dealers (the banks) and the brokers. Deals in the market are conducted by word of mouth and overseas deals are conducted by authenticated cable. The list of rates in the financial press each morning shows the spread of rates over the previous day and the closing selling and buying rates. The rates are quoted in pairs: the higher indicates the market's buying rate and the lower the market's selling rate, and business is done between the dealers at approximately those values. A banker who is asked to buy or sell foreign currency relies upon the market for his cover and the price at which he can obtain this cover are market prices. Hence, in quoting to his customer, he bases his prices on those ruling in the market, while allowing himself a margin for profit. Bank dealers must ensure that their purchases of any currency are approximately equal to their sales of that currency.

The market rates quoted in the press are the 'spot' rates, i.e. those quoted for transactions which are for immediate completion, or at latest within two working days from the date of the deal. Currency is a commodity and like any other commodity its price will be governed by the interaction of supply and demand and therefore by the short-term and long-term factors which influence buyers and sellers. The short-term factors fall into two classes.

(a) *Commercial operations*   The exchange of commodities which is called 'trade' gives rise to an exchange of currencies in that the seller requires payment in his own currency and so the buyer needs to purchase some of the seller's currency with his own. Trade, however, is not simply between two nations: each nation trades with many others and debts due by one nation to another may be offset by debts due to the first nation by a third. The payments to be made across the exchanges for purchases (imports) and to be received for sales (exports) determine the demand for, and supply of, a currency. The difference between sales and purchases of commodities is the 'balance of trade'.

Account must also be taken of what is known as 'invisible' trade, i.e. payments received or made for services and other intangible items. Examples of invisibles are: freights for transport by sea or air, insurance premiums, commissions and brokerage, banking earnings, tourist spending, profits from branches or subsidiaries of home firms and government disbursements, loans and interest payments. Where the balance of trading in visible and invisible items shows an excess of purchases over sales, there is an excess of supply of its currency over the demand and in consequence its price will fall, i.e. the rate of exchange will depreciate.

(b) *Financial operations*   These come under a variety of headings:

1 Stock exchange operations – purchase and sale of securities on foreign exchanges (bourses) by private or corporate investors in order to earn interest or hold for capital appreciation. These are portfolio investments as opposed to 'industrial' investments which represent capital placed by manufacturers in subsidiary or associated enterprises abroad.
2 Banking operations – transfer of funds by bankers for investment or deposit in foreign centres.
3 Speculation – operators taking a view on the way in which the rate of exchange of a particular currency will move, a view usually based on some political event or natural event which might affect the future value of the

currency. According to the view taken they will buy or sell a currency anticipating a rise or fall in value. A similar effect, arising from anticipation of future movements in exchange rates, is known as 'leads and lags', where a debtor will pay a debt due in foreign currency before it is due if he expects that currency to appreciate in value (lead), or delay payment if he expects the currency to depreciate (lag).

4 Interest payments – interest on loans and dividends on investments.

5 Loan payments – arising from the issue of loans by one country to another. The raising of a loan in one country on behalf of another means there will be a payment across the exchanges from the lending country to the borrowing country which will cause the rate of exchange of the lending country to move unfavourably and that of the borrowing country to move favourably. This effect would be offset if the proceeds of the loan were used to purchase goods or services from the lending country. When the loan is repaid, the reverse effect will take place. Because the proceeds of the loan are often spent in the lending country and therefore increase its export trade, it is said that 'every loan creates an export'. This is not necessarily so unless it is a 'tied' loan, i.e. one which is granted on condition that the proceeds are used to purchase goods in the lending country.

6 Inter-governmental transfers – governments borrow from, and lend to, each other in the same way as private individuals and trading companies, and the payments which arise from such loans have the same effect as detailed above.

7 Exchange control – operations in the foreign exchange market by governments in order to control exchange rate movements by varying the relation between supply and demand. These operations are usually directed to keep fluctuations to a minimum. Sometimes, of course, a government may deliberately seek to raise or lower the exchange rate of its currency.

8 The long-term factors. Over a long period the factors which influence exchange movements are those which produce changes in the internal value of a currency, i.e. its domestic purchasing power. Exchange rates tend to reflect the purchasing power parity between two currencies and so it follows that if the volume of a currency is increased (inflation) or decreased (deflation), or if the credit conditions are changed so as to cause prices to rise or fall in the country concerned whilst prices in other countries remain stable, there is a tendency for the exchange value of that currency to move to a new level.

6.4.2   Forward exchange

In the present climate of 'floating' rates of exchange and the increasing amount of business done on credit terms, it is quite likely that a trader may find that he is due to pay his supplier in the latter's currency at a future date or to receive foreign currency at a future date from his buyer. He is, therefore, unaware of the amount in sterling he may have to pay or receive – he is in an open position subject to any changes in the exchange rates which may take place between now and the date on which payment is to be made or received. To protect himself against this exchange risk, the customer may take advantage of the 'forward exchange' market. No trader should leave an exchange risk uncovered. The cover is obtained by entering into a forward exchange contract with the bank. This contract is an operation in exchange whereby a rate is fixed at once for a purchase or sale of one currency for another which is to be completed at some fixed, agreed future date. It is immediately firm and binding between customer and banker and performance must take place, with any unused portion cancelled by 'closing out'. Once a customer has entered into a forward contract he knows immediately how much he will have to pay or receive in due course.

Forward contracts may be 'fixed' or 'option'. A fixed forward is a contract where a specific date is agreed for performance to take place. A forward option is where the customer is unable to be certain on which date in the future the transaction will take place; instead a specific period of time is agreed during which performance is to take place. The actual date within the option period is chosen by the customer. The reader should especially note that the 'option' is not whether the customer deals or not (he is committed) but when he takes or delivers the currency concerned.

6.4.3 Forward rates

The rates for forward exchange deals are quoted at so much premium of discount on the spot rate, i.e. so much below or above spot. Sometimes they are quoted as 'par' with spot. The forward rate adjustments are quoted in the press below the market spot rates mentioned above. If a forward rate is quoted at a discount, then the currency is cheaper to buy forward than spot. Conversely, if it is at a premium, the currency is dearer forward. To calculate the rate to apply to a forward deal where the forward adjustment is a discount, the discount will be added to the spot rate; where it is at a premium the premium will be deducted from the spot. If a customer is unable to complete a forward contract when the agreed date is reached, the transaction may have to be closed out as follows: a customer who has contracted to buy foreign currency but finds that he does not require it will still have to take delivery of the currency at the agreed forward rate and then sell it back to the bank at the ruling spot rate. A customer who has contracted to sell foreign currency, but does not receive it and therefore cannot deliver, will have to buy the currency at the ruling spot rate in order to deliver it to the bank at the agreed forward rate. In practice, the bank would merely debit or credit the customer with the difference. Where circumstances cause a delay in fulfilment of a contract, it may often be extended by arrangement with the bank at an adjusted rate.

Forward rates will fluctuate as the spot rate fluctuates (the forward rate is an adjustment of the spot rate). The forward margin adjustments (discount or premium) are not the result of the market's forecast or expectation of what rates are likely to be in the future, but are a reflection of the difference in interest rates ruling in the two centres. Forward rates tend to be at a premium when interest rates are lower in the foreign centre than in the home centre, and conversely, they tend to be at a discount when interest is lower in the home centre than in the foreign centre. The forward margins are usually quoted in the press for one, three and six months forward, but by arrangement with the bank it is possible to cover for longer periods, depending on the currency concerned.

With reference to the 'closing out' procedure, where the need to close out is due to the failure by the foreign buyer to pay and the transaction is covered, for example, with a credit insurance company in the UK, the latter will also cover any loss due to the difference in rates in closing out, as well as the loss by non-payment.

It is appropriate to consider some of the principles which exporters are recommended to follow when they expect to receive foreign currency over a period of time, relative to their international financial settlement arrangements. This will enable the exporter to take objective foreign exchange decisions. The following criteria arise when the currency to be received is strengthening in its value.

1 It is better to have retained proceeds in foreign currency on interest-bearing accounts to maximize the conversion into sterling at a more propitious exchange rate.
2 The flexibility of being able to review the rates at regular intervals, and decide whether to roll over the currency deposit for another period or to sell it for sterling, produces favourable results.
3 Borrowing currency which subsequently hardens tends to produce less favourable results. Within this context, it should be noted that interest on borrowing has to be paid in the same currency, which meantime has revalued (become more expensive). High interest rates of borrowing, coupled with revaluation of interest payment, tend to reduce the funding benefit from such an exercise.
4 Forward cover taken out when the exchange rates are higher than the previous six months tends to produce a loss of benefit in cash flow terms to the exporter. Moreover, when the forward rate is quoted at a discount against sterling at the time, it gives the exporter a less favourable exchange rate than the spot rate ruling. However, in the event of the forward rate being quoted at a premium against sterling, the exporter may have received the benefit in the form of a better rate than the current spot rate.

When the currency to be received weakens, the following criteria apply.

1 It is better to retain proceeds of a weakening asset in a currency deposit

account since the interest earned – even if higher than comparable sterling interest rates – is usually not sufficient to compensate for the movement in the exchange rate.

2 Spot sales of a weakening currency reverse any profitable trend.

One must appreciate that the foregoing criteria can vary with circumstances and must be regarded only as broad guidelines. From these guidelines, it will be seen that through the foreign exchange market the ordinary trader can protect himself against any fluctuations in the exchange rates. There are, however, some activities where the movement in exchange rates, both spot and forward, give rise to problems, i.e. where a variety of costs (payments) arise, some in one's own currency and some in other currencies, and revenue is derived from a variety of sources, in several currencies. A particular example of this problem is found in connection with freight charges.

It has been convenient for a conference's rates of freight to be expressed in a single currency called the 'tariff currency' (usually US dollars). Nevertheless freight can be paid in some other currency; understandings have to be reached on the basis of conversion of freight from the amount in the tariff currency to the amount in the currency in which the freight is actually paid. Where adjustments in relevant currency values have resulted in a reduction in value of rates of freight and/or increases in shipowner's operating costs, it has been the practice of conferences to increase tariff rates of freight or to introduce or increase a currency adjustment factor (CAF).

There has been a tendency to regard the CAF as a means of keeping ratios of past rates of exchange fixed once and for all. As a result of the different rates of inflation in the various countries, the terms of trade have changed, but this fact has not been taken into account when calculating the sea freight. The present ratio of currencies, however, has changed considerably. When the value of sterling was falling the system favoured the UK exporter in terms of freight rates; however, when sterling began to appreciate, shipowners in other countries introduced a currency adjustment. The situation had become more complicated when rates of exchange were allowed to float and the dollar was effectively devalued. The system which had stood the test of all the upheavals in exchange rates began to show signs of strain. The heart of the problem is that if there were a parity of CAFs it would be to the disadvantage of UK shippers, but continental shippers argue that if basic rate parity is maintained, then CAF parity should also be the rule. If the present CAF disparity is permitted then basic rate disparity should also be introduced.

The different conferences serving different areas of the world have reacted to changing circumstances in different ways, and a final solution to the problem has still not been found.

A list of the world currencies is given in Appendix F.

6.5 STATISTICS

Our study of export marketing would not be complete without consideration of statistics, which tend to play an increasingly important role in developing the overseas markets. The evaluation of statistics falls into two broad divisions: (1) the actual statistics produced by the various governments, trade organizations, etc., worldwide, and (2) the range of statistical techniques which exist and can be usefully applied to develop international trade (see *Elements of Export Practice*, Chapter 15).

6.5.1 Requirements for statistics in market analysis

The export marketing manager can obtain much useful statistical data by studying the various statistics produced by governments, trade associations, the Department of Trade and Industry, COI, Chambers of Commerce, banks – not only the UK-based international banks but also the national banks overseas which have a London office, and various economic reviews and bulletins produced by OPEC, UNCTAD, EC, OECD, IMF, ICC, etc. The role of these organizations, and their involvement in trade, is significant in overseas market development (see *The Economics of Shipping Practice and Management*). Numerous economic agencies exist throughout the world which produce economic reviews and bulletins, often on a quarterly basis. Undoubtedly one of the most important is the Economic Intelligence Unit (EIU) which produces 81 different reviews, issued quarterly and covering 160 countries. These contain much economic and statistical data. In addition the EIU produces special reports giving an authoritative analysis of major issues and problems that directly concern the internationally orientated manager and administrator. Each EIU special report is devoted to a single major topic. Details of their publications are available from The Economic Intelligence Unit Ltd, Spencer House, 27 St James Place, London SW1A 1NT. Such reports can prove invaluable in determining market trends and in undertaking statistical analysis within a specified market or commodity.

The following statistical data should be sought in a market analysis, but the importance of each set of information will vary according to individual circumstances.

(a) *Economic structure* This will give statistical data about the gross domestic product (GDP) and its constituents. This will include, expressed as a percentage of the GDP, the following components: manufacturing; commerce and finance; construction. Details should be obtained of the population and gross domestic product per head of population. Information should be sought about the public direct foreign debt.

(b) *Imports and exports* Details of the commodity and the importing

(b) *Imports and exports*   Details of the commodity and the importing nations should be sought. Ideally figures spanning three years should be sought to enable a trend to be devised.

(c) *Economic outlook*   This is an important area as it will feature trends and business opportunities for the enthusiastic exporter. It will deal with the political scene both nationally and internationally; any currency rate exchange trend in respect of devaluation or revaluation of the currency and its impact on trade; the GDP trend; production and investment; personal consumption; and any economic growth or decline. Mention will be made of any relaxation or embargo on trade, together with any home trade protection policies. For example, if one wishes to look at a report covering trends in industrial production, it would deal with the main industries of the economy, which are likely to be metals (not steel or ferrous); chemicals and rubber; metal manufactures and engineering; textiles; food and drink, etc.

(d) *Economic trends in statistical terms*   The following statistical data, featuring the economic trends, are usually available from official government sources. A detailed analysis can usually be obtained in certain areas, particularly in commodity analysis.

1 Industrial production. This is a global figure which usually covers all industries, but can be specific to individual industries of marked significance to the economy. It is a major barometer of the general economic prosperity of the country. It is usually produced monthly on an index basis. If the exporter was, for example, interested in the car industry, the monthly index would reveal production output trends, output by individual manufacturers and, possibly, output of individual model ranges. The manufacturer would segregate home and imported products. Great care must be exercised in the use of such statistics because many car manufacturers are multi-national and hence not all of their models are home-produced, in part or in whole.

2 New orders received. In broad terms this is major contracts awarded. Again, it is index-compiled and best shown on a histogram, plotting each month's results against the index.

3 Employment. Each month this information would give the numbers employed and unemployed, and the number of job vacancies. The data might be broken down by region/area/town or by sex. Further monthly analysis would give the workforce found in each of the major industries.

4 Wages and prices. This is usually hourly earnings and the cost of living. Again, it is usually index-compiled, and the hourly earnings can be split according to sex or industry.

5 Foreign trade. These data segregate exports and imports and visible and invisible trades. They indicate whether a trade surplus or deficit was incurred on a monthly basis.

6 Reserves. The national reserves figure would be produced each quarter, and it would feature the gold element in the total reserve figure.

7 Exchange rate. Most countries give details of their exchange rate, particularly in relation to other major world currencies (again on a monthly basis).

8 Trend of gross national product. These data (usually produced by the national bank) give an analysis on an annual basis at current prices, constant prices in 1988, and a measure of the real change between the two sets of data. Similar data are produced per capita during this period. Overall, it enables trends to be produced.

9 Origin of national income at factor cost. This is an annual analysis of the national income by industry. It includes agriculture, mining, construction, public utilities, transport and communications, government services and net income from abroad.

10 Composition of national expenditure. This reveals the extent to which the government features in a nation's expenditure. It includes private sector consumption, government current spending, change in stocks, etc. It is usually produced annually.

11 Distribution of national income at current prices. This would give details, annually, of gross income by employed persons, and other incomes.

(e) *Statistics for specific areas of commerce*   Statistics are usually available for the main industries in various countries, and they amplify the index of production data mentioned earlier. Examples of such information, usually produced by the government statistical unit, are given below. The data are also usually available from the Department of Trade and Industry and COI.

1 Agriculture and fishing. Annual details of the tonnage yield and yield per hectare of the main crops: wheat, rye, sugar beet, potatoes, etc.

2 Dairy production. Production details, annually, of milk, butter, cheese, condensed milk, dried milk, etc.

3 Mining, fuel and power. Minerals and energy sources, including coal, crude oil, natural gas, manufactured gas, electricity, nuclear energy, etc.

4 Manufacturing industry and construction. This would amplify particularly the index of production by annual output (tonnes) by individual industry. It could include house building (segregating those buildings just started from completed dwellings). An interesting statistical analysis is the employment in each industry and the corresponding production value, segregating the value of exports.

5 Transport and communications. Details of the country's transport resources by ship, rail, road and air. Communication details would include the number of telephone subscribers and television receivers. The latter would be useful in evaluation of the advertising media.

6 Advertising media. Circulation figures of each national newspaper, major

regional newspapers, and magazines and technical journals and the readers'
socio–economic category and demographic data. Similar data are usually
available for TV and radio. Also, viewing and listening figures for
television and radio, respectively.

7 Government finance. This usually involves three main statements. The
first includes the central government revenue and expenditure. It will reveal
not only the overall expenditure and revenue levels, but also whether they
were in deficit or surplus in any year.

The second concerns the main sources of tax revenue such as income tax,
wages tax, corporation tax, turnover tax, import and excise duties, etc. Of
course, the forms of taxation vary by country. Thirdly, central government
expenditure. This includes defence, transport, education, science, social
services, housing, national debt, industry and public works.

8 Financial statistics. These include total money supply, currency in circulation, deposits, advances by the commercial banks to the private sector,
official discount rate, three months treasury bill rate, yield of undated
government bonds and share prices indices. Such statistical data are usually
issued monthly. Annual figures over a five-year period, producing a useful
trend, may also be available.

Additionally, wages and prices indices are available in different forms of
analysis. It is usual to have the hourly wage rate index and annual salary
scale for all workers published monthly and annually to produce meaningful
trends. Separate data of similar composition are produced for manual
workers. Consumer price indices are devised in most countries to cover
individual selected items such as food, and often there is an all-embracing
index, usually referred to as the cost of living index. Indices are also
provided for investment goods.

9 Foreign trade and payments. Such statistics are of great interest to the
exporter. Figures are usually produced monthly and annually on the value
of exports and imports, together with an index on the volume of exports.
Data are also available on the main trading partners of a country, in terms
of both value and of per cent of total trading. A similar list of main exports
and imports is given. Details are also given, monthly and annually, of the
balance of payments. This includes trade balance, invisibles balance, balance
on current account, capital balance (excluding banks) and change in official
reserves. Data on exchange reserves include gold foreign exchange (net),
special drawing rights (SDR) from IMF, IMF reserve position (net) and
commercial banks (net).

The foregoing commentary on available published, official statistics must
not be regarded as exhaustive. If an exporter is anxious to obtain statistical
data relevant to his existing or potential market, it is always wise to contact
his international bank, the Chamber of Commerce or the Department of
Trade and Industry.

It is appropriate to list a number of areas where statistical data can prove useful in determining market development. Such data could be related to some of the statistical data described earlier.

6.5.2   Actual market research analysis

(a) *Who uses the product?*   This would involve analysis of the market response to the product (see Table 6.1).

Table 6.1   Market product response

Area	Number of interviews	Positive	Negative	Percentage positive
A	250	125	125	50.0
B	250	130	120	52.0
C	500	410	90	82.0
Total	1000	665	335	66.5

A significant feature is the varying positive product use response rate, which favours area C (82%).

(b) *Use of brand loyalty*   This involves the market response to a particular brand for a product (see Table 6.2).

Table 6.2   Brand loyalty analysis

Area	Number of purchases	One brand	Two brands	Three brands or more
A	400	150	200	50
B	600	250	260	90
C	500	300	150	50
Total	1500	700	610	190

It is apparent that a high percentage of customers bought two brands. This may have been due to a limited range of items in any one product brand, price differential, quality differential, or simply that one brand for a particular product was a well established market leader. Further research would be necessary to determine the reason for brand choice.

(c) *Amount of product purchased*   This is useful to determine trends and facilitate stock control (see Table 6.3).

Table 6.3   Product sizes – consumer analysis

Area	Number of purchasers	Small size	Medium size	Large size
A	400	175	125	100
B	350	150	125	75
C	500	200	200	100
Total	1250	525	450	275

Further market research would suggest reasons for the differing results in each of the three areas. It could be related to consumer purchasing power, high degree of unemployment in one particular area, or method of retailing.

(d) *Factors of appeal*   This type of statistical enquiry can be allied to many reasons, and Table 6.4 is an example of a consumer product choice analysis, embracing price, packaging, economy in use and so on, of a washing-up liquid.

Table 6.4   Choice of product purchase – first preference

Area	Number of purchasers	Price	Packaging	Economy in use	Hand protection	Colour of liquid
A	200	50	45	75	15	15
B	300	75	25	100	75	25
C	400	100	50	150	60	40
Total	900	225	120	325	150	80

Clearly price and economy of use are the dominant factors in product choice.

(e) *Frequency of purchase*   The analysis shown in Table 6.5 reflects consumer purchasing power and, if frozen foods are involved, the number of households which have a deep freezer.

Table 6.5 Market analysis of product frequency purchase

Area	Size of purchase	Number of purchasers	Rate of purchase		
			Weekly	Fortnightly	Monthly or longer
A	Small	200	100	75	25
	Medium	50	30	10	10
	Large	70	40	15	15
B	Small	170	70	70	30
	Medium	120	10	100	10
	Large	70	15	40	15
C	Small	70	10	40	20
	Medium	50	10	25	15
	Large	100	20	60	20
Total		900	305	435	160

7 Budgetary and marketing control

Budgetary control, together with the associated marketing and sales plan, are essential in modern business management techniques. Basically, this is management by objectives (MBO) and enables the management at all levels to monitor current results against agreed budget levels, and to take remedial measures when necessary. It is not only a financial discipline, but also sets agreed, reliable targets from the marketing standpoint. In so doing, it is an essential aid to profitability and to the development of a situation whereby the export company, large or small, can go forward with business confidence to improve their profits further. It also identifies the strengths and weaknesses of the existing strategies.

7.1 BUDGETARY CONTROL

Budgetary control generates maximum profitability to the export company and, in so doing, attracts investment which is so vital to the long-term future of the company. Advantages of budgetary control are given below:

1 It enables a strict control to be exercised on expenditure.
2 It permits the export company to devise a cash flow forecast and thereby enables the best use to be made of monthly cash surpluses and the best plan to be drawn up to meet deficit situations. For example, substantial cash surpluses make it possible to seek short-term investments.
3 It encourages optimum use of company resources and promotes good housekeeping.
4 It ensures that all personnel, through their managers, work towards the objectives of the company.
5 It enables management to work towards objectives and in so doing it focuses resources towards this aim.
6 It allows the company to achieve the most favourable financial results and adopts a 'value for money' policy on expenditure, thereby avoiding abortive spending.
7 All management personnel within the company are aware of the objectives

Table 7.1 Manufacturing company budgeted trading results for January 1990: Export Division

Expenditure	Explanations							Income	Actual-Budget-Variation from budget	Explanations			
	Actual	Budget	Variation from Budget	Market fluctuations	Staff costs	Currency variation	Other			Market fluctuations	Currency variation	Late delivery	Other
Export Office								*Country A*					
Staff Expenses								Commodity A					
Overseas Travel								Income					
Hire of Equipment								Volume					
Office Rental								*Product					
								cost					
								Net income					
Advertising								*Country B*					
TV								Commodity B					
Brochures													
Exhibitions													
Trade Missions								Income					
Commercial Radio								Volume					
Newspapers								*Product					
Journals								cost					
Sponsorships								Net income					
Market Research								*Commodity C*					
Agencies								Income					
Desk Research								Volume					
Field Research –								*Product					
Specific Assign-								cost					
ments								Net income					
								Total income					

Net trading
surplus/loss

Product Development

Staff Expenses
Product research –
consumer/industrial
Research and
development –
specific products

Overseas Territories

Country A

Staff Expenses
Office Rental
Advertising
Agent's Commission
Miscellaneous

Country B

Staff Expenses
Office Rental
Advertising
Miscellaneous

Miscellaneous

Legal Advice
Insurance
Compensation
Other

Total Expenditure

NB ★ The breakdown of the individual product cost would be compiled by the Production Director and identified in the budget. Each overseas territory would have a separate budget which would be consolidated into the Export Director's budget.

which will result in increased profitability and commitment. This encourages *esprit de corps* and develops management potential on a profit-centre basis.

8 By using strict financial controls, it enables up to 3% to be saved in total expenditure through better management techniques and control. It reduces working capital limits and encourages positive cash flow. It also facilitates effective management control of the settlement of international currency exchange accounts.

9 It enables personnel in the company to be measured in terms of their work performance by gauging the results against the budget. Such results must be judged objectively against the background of the results achieved.

10 By monitoring performance, i.e. expenses against budget, on a regular basis, the need for remedial measures can be spotted and they can be carried out quickly. Overall, it helps the level of profitability to be sustained.

11 It encourages cost-consciousness throughout the export company, particularly amongst management personnel who are committed to budget realization (see Table 7.1).

The export marketing manager, when formulating his sales budget and marketing and sales plan, would liaise very closely with sales personnel and/or agents directly responsible for securing the business. Attention must also be given to the economic and political background likely to obtain throughout the time which has been budgeted for, and any subsequent developments which might cause the company to increase or lessen their marketing effort in such areas. This could include: any trade protectionism policies likely to be introduced; new technical or safety code regulations discriminating against imported products; new exchange control regulations; predicted growth in gross national product (GNP); variation in exchange rates; relaxation of trade/custom barriers; inflation and unemployment; variation in the government's five-year economic plan; level of money supply for consumer goods; and, finally, any general economic trends. Reports of marketing/trade opportunities are produced regularly by international banks; exporters are well advised to consult them when necessary.

The budget is compiled for one year and the income and expenditure spread throughout the period either on a four-weekly or monthly basis. This enables the results to be monitored each month.

The sales and expenditure budget represents the income produced from overseas sales and the expenditure emerging from the export office, which falls under the control or influence of the export director/export marketing manager.

The income will emerge from overseas sales, and this can be recorded on the basis of country, region or commodity. It will represent the price recorded in the export sales contract. The sales budget is likely to be broken down ultimately to individual sales personnel, agents, distributors, etc., thereby reflecting the sales technique used. The expenditure budget is likely to be more comprehensive and could include the following elements.

1 Cost of running the export marketing, export sales and shipping offices. Each may be costed separately. For example, the justification for a large shipping office may rest on the fact that all the distribution arrangements are made directly with the shipowner or airline so that all the documentation and transportation arrangements are handled 'in house'. This would avoid the use of a freight forwarder who would raise a commission on his services. Similarly, a team engaged on advertising and/or market research could be justified on the basis that it avoids resorting to the advertising or market research agency. In some companies, use is made of such services in other departments and the cost 'off-charged' to the export office. The justification for a team of personnel engaged in market research or advertising depends on the volume of work and the nature of the short-term and long-term overseas business.

2 The budget will reflect the production/manufacturing cost of the commodity sold overseas. Additional expense could include packaging and any transportation insurance cost borne by the seller under the terms of the contract of sale (Incoterms 1990).

3 Promotion cost can form a significant part of the overall budget, but much depends on the selling technique used. (Some of the numerous selling techniques and promotion aids are shown in Figure 7.2.) It is a question of which is nearest to the ideal, having regard to market conditions, especially the competition. It is important that such a budget be carefully controlled to ensure it is not overspent and maximum benefit is derived from the money spent on the selling aids adopted. The actual results, both in terms of expenditure and income should be monitored against the budget on, for example, a monthly basis. The budget predictions should be reviewed about every four months and any adjustments made. For example, if a political situation emerging in one of the overseas markets is resulting in lower sales, an adjustment should be made on income predictions and the advertising programme in the area should be curtailed.

Each annual budget should be presented to the company directorate by the export director for approval with a supporting commentary on its salient features and assumptions. This is usually undertaken some three months before the commencement of the budget period i.e. September/October for the budget year starting on 1st January. Details of the data to be incorporated in the budget commentary are given below:

1 Overview of the market profile and opportunities/threats in the various overseas territories. This will include competition, consumer buying behaviour, legal/political situation, and so on.

2 Outcome of market research and market trends. This will include product specification, adequacy of promotion, non-price areas such as warranty, spares availability, price sensitivity, and so on.

3 Basis of assumptions made in the budget plan such as the level of exchange rates, economic growth, level of inflation, GNP, GDP, and market competition. Exchange rate forecasts are usually available from international banks, together with other financial and economic data.

4 Overview of previous years' results and salient features emerging therefrom. Many data are available through the sales analysis.

5 New developments such as relaxation of import controls, execution of economic five-year plan, new product launch, extension of product range or modification of existing products.

6 Basis of the pricing strategy to be adopted in the individual markets, having regard to competition, manufacturing cost and contribution to overheads, exchange rate levels, and mark up (profit).

7 Basis of the market sales volume. An increase of 10% over the previous year for a commodity is budgeted based on improved promotion techniques and more retail outlets, coupled with market research findings.

8 Market entry options such as distributors, agents, overseas subsidiaries, and their variation compared with previous years, together with the reason for such changes.

9 Impact on company resources to handle any budget growth/decline compared with previous years. This may involve: increased investment in plant, more research and development of new product technology, recruitment of more technicians on the factory floor to cope with increased production, and sales executives to process market penetration; method of investment and cost and finally an action plan.

10 Advertising budget, its salient features and comparison with previous years, especially in regard to its effectiveness.

11 Export office budget in terms of personnel, overseas travel account and adequacy of resources to cope with market opportunities. This will include the shipping office and its cost-effectiveness compared with the use of a freight forwarder. Ideally the office should be fully computerized.

12 The budget should 'key in' with the company's five-year business plan, and any variation must be fully explained.

13 Comment should be made on the future, especially risk and opportunity areas such as currency devaluation, major orders being secured, and so on. Risk analysis is an important feature in the budget commentary especially in the areas of exchange rates, credit control, sales forecast, import controls and political situations. Its emphasis will vary by product/market.

14 The level of profitability will be critically examined by the company directorate, and continuing growth will be expected.

An example of the constituents of a budget plan are found in Figure 7.1. It involves two countries and three commodities. The early part of the plan features the income, expenditure price and volume aspect, whilst the latter part deals with the political/economic considerations involved and various analyses.

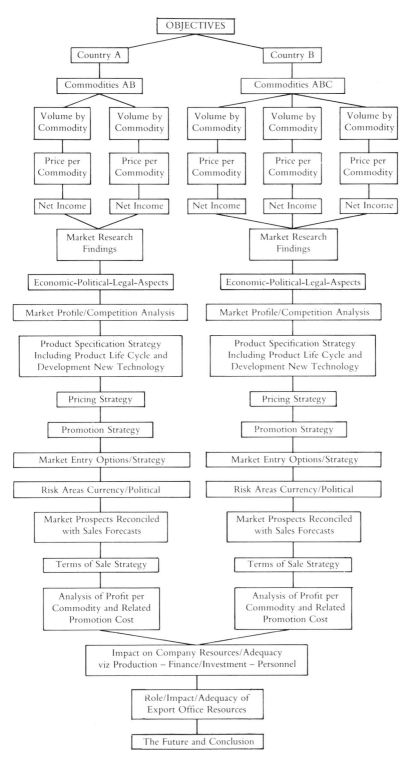

Figure 7.1 Export directors budget plan constituents commentary.

7.2 EXPORT MANAGEMENT

It is important that the export management structure and its constituents fulfil the needs of the overall company policy and objectives, as contained in the business plan. Overall, it involves the efficient use of resources.

The following points are, however, especially relevant.

7.2.1 Planning

This involves the identification of problems, opportunities, and formulation and realization of objectives within a timescale and financial structure. It embraces those departments involved in the export sector including finance, production, personnel, research and development, engineering, etc., plus, of course, the export director's team. Special attention should be given to the attainment of objectives and performance monitoring.

7.2.2 Organizing resources

This embraces the identification and selection of possible solutions. It could arise in the production cycle, where the schedule has to be modified to meet an urgent export order or the introduction of another shift in the factory changing from a one- to a two-shift system with ramifications on labour resources, availability of raw materials and components, transport, warehouse provision, and so on.

7.2.3 Co-ordinating activities

This embraces effecting the decision and co-ordinating the activities of all those involved on a cost-effective basis within the objective and strategy laid down. An example is the execution of a major export contract and the formulation of an overall plan usually undertaken on a critical path analysis technique basis.

7.2.4 Directing towards objectives

This can arise in the research and development department whereby the export director, through the management team and overseas market research findings, provides the requisite input and guidance/direction.

7.2.5 Controlling activities

This is to ensure that the plans devised are monitored/measured in regard to their performance/effectiveness, and the objectives are being realized; otherwise, remedial measures are taken. An example is the execution of the marketing and sales plan.

Full use should be made of computer technology in all areas of export management. This includes developing adequate management information – feedback systems on a continuous basis.

Management policy ultimately is profit motivation and this must feature uppermost in management strategy and execution. An adequate return on capital must be realized. Markets or circumstances which have a high risk potential attract a high return, whilst those of a low risk potential generate a low return.

To conclude, export management involves much diversity. Each decision taken involves a monetary value arising therefrom, and permits comparisons to be drawn in the decision-making process between individual markets and circumstances. Moreover, full use should be made of the planning process and computer technology.

7.3 MARKETING AND SALES PLAN

The marketing and sales plan should be devised annually by the export marketing manager and is usually prepared in September/October for the following year. It basically sets out the marketing objectives of the export marketing department; it is formulated in consultation with the export sales manager and shipping manager and approved by the export director. The plan should 'key in' with the budget both in terms of expenditure (including advertising and staff expenses) and income from sales overseas.

The plan outline is found in Figure 7.2 and it must be stressed that each exporting company will give varying emphasis to parts of it, according to circumstances. Above all, it must set realistic goals. Like the budget, the objectives of the plan must be reviewed about every four months.

The marketing and sales plan should be regarded as the expression by the management of the techniques to be used to secure the business predicted in the plan and the sales budget. All personnel involved in its execution should ideally have a copy, especially those in direct selling. Furthermore, such personnel should be given the opportunity to contribute to its formulation and be present when the export marketing manager reviews it from time to time. The export director or export marketing manager should give a presentation of the plan to relevant company personnel, including those in the production department, so that they are well aware of their obligations to supply the specified products to the overseas markets at the right times.

A commentary on the constituents of the plan, as found in Figure 7.2 now follows:

1 The marketing objectives must be clearly outlined. This can be undertaken on the basis of country, region or commodity, or a mixture of these, to suit the selling techniques of the company.

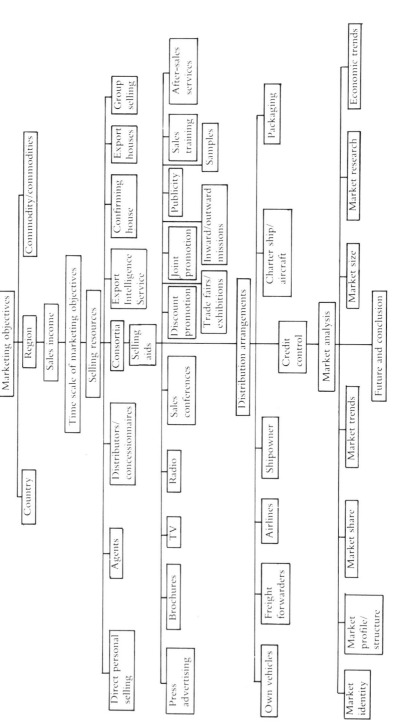

Figure 7.2 Marketing and sales plan.

2 The budgeted sales income may again be categorized by country, region or commodity. This will 'key in' with the sales budget and individual sales personnel should be identified with their contributions to the sales budget. Alternatively, an agent or an export house might be responsible for certain aspects of sale.

3 The timescale of the marketing objective is especially important for the promotion and production departments. The sales promotion plan will require a lead-time of six months, and the production department need a longer lead-time to ensure adequate stocks are available to the correct technical or safety specification.

4 The available selling resources form an important part of the plan. They may involve one or more of the following: direct personal selling using staff employed by the company, based either in the seller's or buyer's country; engagement of agents (a common arrangement); appointment of a distributor or concessionnaires; becoming a member of a consortium of companies formed to tender and execute a project and promote similar products overseas; scrutiny of the Export Intelligence Service which invites subscribers to tender for contracts, agents seeking UK principals, early notification of projects overseas and many other items offering new trade opportunities; confirming houses; export houses; and finally, group selling. To ensure that sales personnel are aware of their objectives, broad indication of the income and volume of each selling resource should be quoted, if practicable.

5 Extensive selling aids to promote the product are available today. The scale of the use of such techniques will depend on the cost and predicted market response, the facilities available in the buyer's country and the market potential, together with the exporter's sales budget. Items available include: press advertising; brochures; television commercials; radio commercials; cinema presentations; sales conferences to launch or develop the product; discount promotions offering a special low price during a specified promotion period; participation in trade fairs/exhibitions; joint promotion with an agent; inward or outward missions involving the Department of Trade and Industry, trade associations or Chambers of Commerce; general publicity involving press releases etc.; provision of samples; sales training; and, finally, after-sales service, which is very important with technical products. Each item to be featured should be costed and the expenditure should not be exceeded.

6 The distribution arrangements for the goods will reflect the terms of the export sales contract. A freight forwarder might be requested to undertake all the distribution and associated arrangements of the seller's own transport, including customs clearance, documentation needs and financial settlement. All the distribution arrangements could be entrusted either with an airline or shipowner in liaison with the export shipping office; a ship or aircraft could be chartered for a special assignment. Packing arrangements must be considered. One cannot predict completely the cargo delivery arrangements, and the shipping office workload will vary accordingly. The more expert the shipping office becomes in processing the export consignment, the less work they will entrust to the freight forwarder, which will reduce commission payments and exercise more direct control over distribution.

7 The credit control arrangement ensures that payment is executed in accord with the terms of the export sales contract; this is a responsibility of the shipping office.

8 The market analysis gives a broad assessment of existing markets and their opportunities, together with forthcoming developments which could improve the company's market share.

9 In conclusion, the plan should point the way to opportunities for future business development. It should also encourage maximum support and co-operation from all concerned with the plan.

7.4 MARKET FORECASTING

A market forecast plays an important role in formulating future strategy with regard to both the product and the market. The following points are relevant:

1 Senior management and sales personnel need to know the likely profit and development of the market in the future, in order to plan their export strategy and on which areas to concentrate their marketing resources.

2 The advertising agency relies heavily on statistical data, especially those relative to market trends and shares. Forecasting features prominently, and it is likely market research/advertising agencies will be in the most favourable situation to produce many of the data for such forecasts through their probable long association with the market and a range of commodities.

3 The agent will have many useful data on the market situation and again could contribute these to a realistic forecast. The agent must be kept informed of company policy, especially in the area which he serves. Close liaison between agent and exporter will facilitate the realization of market objectives as expressed in the budget. Regular overseas visits are desirable.

Market forecasting of an international market is a difficult task. It involves obtaining as many statistical data as possible from a broad spectrum of sources including: trade associations; COI; trade journals; market reports produced by various international banks; Department of Trade and Industry sources; Chambers of Commerce; official statistics produced in the overseas market; and data obtained from agents or advertising agencies.

The forecaster must be well acquainted with the economic, political, cultural and business background of the overseas market. Moreover, the forecast must reflect any likely change in exchange rate, import controls, more intense competition, more onerous technical specification; cargo delivery terms which vary by export sales contract; change in overall distribution arrangements; any free trade or bilateral trade agreement; risk analysis evaluation and revised arrangements with the agency. Full use must be made of the various statistical techniques available to produce trends, and any change in a government's policy should be noted.

It will be realized that market forecasting is a task which involves market analysis, market research and statistical processing, in addition to sound judgement and a good comprehension of the market. It can only be achieved by building up a lot of reliable data, and this means making the maximum use of information available within the manufacturing company, particularly that obtained through sales outlets.

Given below are the various stages in compiling the sales forecast and relating it to the manufacturer's evaluation of the overseas market development policy.

1 Company objectives. These would be found in the company's business plan covering a period of up to five years.
2 Collection and assembly of data and market information.
3 Analysis and evaluation of data.
4 Determination of possible market share of the product(s).
5 Formulation of the sales forecast, using data from item (4).
6 Relating the data to cost, investment and predicted profits.
7 Taking account of possible changing market conditions through change in government, tighter import controls, more competition, etc. It is possible
that over a five-year period, two sales forecasts would be produced, one of which would be particularly pessimistic and take account of possibly more intense competition and tighter import controls plus a devaluation of the consumer currency.
8 Reviewing the forecast periodically and making necessary adjustments to maintain a realistic, up-dated sales target. Such a review is annual, or when a particular circumstance arises which warrants a review of the market prospects, such as tighter import controls or heavier personal taxation which reduces consumer demand and personal money supply.
9 Producing a commentary on the circumstances and reasoning behind any significant change in the sales forecasts. This is produced at yearly intervals throughout the sales forecast period.
10 Taking account of the various stages of the life cycle of the product and any intensification of competition, particularly through a more technically-advanced product being introduced to the market by a competitor.
11 Risk analysis evaluations which would include political situations, import controls, exchange rates, credit control, and includes items (7), (8), (9) and (10).

8   *Incoterms 1990*

Our study of export marketing would not be complete without a brief examination of the role of the International Chamber of Commerce (ICC) and the way in which it facilitates development of international trade. One must realize that an international trade deal can involve up to four contracts and the businessperson must have a broad understanding of each of them. The four contracts are: the contract of carriage, the export sales contract (usually involving Incoterms), the insurance contract and the contract of finance. In particular, the overseas salesman must understand the various cargo delivery terms (devised by ICC) which exist, and their international interpretation. Similarly, the rules are designed to simplify and facilitate commercial documentary credits operations. Such data must be fully understood when negotiating the export sales contract; they have been devised in a way that tries to ensure, through international acceptance, that there is no doubt about their interpretation by either party to the contract.

8.1   INTERNATIONAL CHAMBER OF COMMERCE (ICC)

The fundamental role of the ICC is to promote the world economy, with particular emphasis on the expansion of international trade and investment. National economic growth is encouraged to generate expansion of world trade. The objective of the ICC is the integration of the business community's approach to world economic progress and problems.

  The ICC is represented in 96 countries and works through all its National Committees and Councils. Its headquarters is in Paris. Details of the various ICC studies and activities include: multi-national enterprises; ethical practices relative to business transactions; International Bureau of Chamber of Commerce; ICC–UN, GATT (United Nations General Agreement on Tariffs and Trade), economic consultative committee; international monetary relations; expansion of international trade; international investment and economic development; commission on insurance problems; commission on law and practices affecting competition; international arbitration; marketing (advertising and distribution); international commercial practice; and banking techniques and practices.

The range of these activities demonstrates the breadth of influence of the ICC today in promoting world trade using a soundly based ethical, economical and financial code of practice.

The role of the ICC is becoming more prominent. There will be increasing integration of the world economy; the continuing preparation of codes of ethics or good conduct for international business practices; the facilitation of international trade and investment through the harmonization and standardization of trade practices; and the provision of a central forum for discussing policy problems being faced by businesspeople in communities throughout the world and where agreed viewpoints and solutions can be approved.

The overseas salesperson should keep up-to-date with the ICC international business codes and terms of sale, and their interpretation.

The role of Incoterms is to give the businessperson a set of international rules for the interpretation of the more commonly used terms such as FOB, CIF, ex works, etc. in foreign trade contracts. Such a range of terms enables businesspeople to decide which is most suitable for their needs, knowing that the interpretation of such terms will not vary by individual country. The most recent terms formulated by the ICC are called 'Incoterms 1990'.

A fundamental aspect featured in Incoterms 1990 is the reference to the provisions of ICC UNCID and EDIFACT. It states that if so agreed between the buyer and seller, where the seller is required to carry out an activity for which documentary evidence is required, such as an invoice, insurance certificate, transport document, document required for administrative purposes or any other document stipulated in the contract, the required document may be substituted by electronic data interchange (EDI) by or on behalf of the seller in a form agreed between the buyer and the seller, taking note of the provisions of the ICC UNCID (UNECE WP R483) and EDIFACT (ISO Standard 9735).

There are three main areas of uncertainty in international trade contracts and their interpretation. These are: the uncertainty as to which country's law will be applicable to their contracts; the difficulty emerging from inadequate and unreliable information; and the serious problem of the diversity of interpretation of the various trade terms. The last point can involve costly litigation and loss of much goodwill when a dispute over the interpretation of such terms arises.

Incoterms, which are constantly updated by the ICC, tend to overcome such problems but it must be recognized that it is not always possible to give a precise interpretation. In such situations, one must rely on the custom of the trade or port. Businesspeople are advised to use terms which are subject to varying interpretations as little as possible and to rely on the well established, internationally accepted terms. To avoid any misunderstandings or disputes, the parties to the contract are well advised to keep trading customs of individual countries in mind when negotiating their export sales contract. However, parties to the contract may use Incoterms as the general basis of their contract, but may specify variations of them or additions to them relevant to the particular trade or circumstances. An example is the term CIF (cost insurance freight) plus war risk insurance. The exporter would base his quotation accordingly. Special provisions in the individual contract between the parties will override anything in the Incoterm provisions.

An especial point to bear in mind is the need for caution in the variation, for example, of C & F (cost and freight), CIF (cost insurance freight) or Customs Duty Paid. The addition of a word or letter could change the contract and its interpretation. It is essential that any such variation be explicitly stated in the contract to ensure each party to the contract is aware of its obligations and acts accordingly.

The buyer and seller parties to the contract must especially bear in mind that Incoterms only define their relationship in contract terms, and has no bearing directly or indirectly on the carrier's obligations to them as found in the contract of carriage. However, the law of carriage will determine how the seller should fulfil his obligation to deliver the goods to the carrier on board the vessel as found in FOB, C & F and CIF. A further point for the seller to bear in mind is that there is no obligation for him to procure an insurance policy for the buyer's benefit. In practice, however, many contracts request the buyer or seller to so arrange insurance, from the point of departure in the country of despatch to the point of final destination chosen by the buyer.

The use of bills of lading is now becoming less common in the liner trade and is being replaced by non-negotiable documents such as sea waybills, liner waybills, freight receipts and combined or multi-modal transport documents. Ultimately the transmission of such information will be by automatic data processing techniques. Further details are found in *Elements of Export Practice*, Chapter 12. SITPRO are very much involved in such developments.

8.2 FACTORS DETERMINING CHOICE OF INCOTERMS

Personnel involved in negotiating the sales contract have a wide choice in selecting the cargo delivery terms most acceptable to the sale. The prime consideration is to ensure that each party to the contract is clearly aware of their obligation to ensure the consignment is despatched without impeding the transit arrangements.

The following factors are relevant in the evaluation of the choice of the cargo delivery term:

1 Basically the buyer is the stronger party in such negotiations, especially as he has to fund the carriage charges directly through his payment to the carrier under FOB or indirectly through CIF to the seller.

2 The buyer has the opportunity of controlling the transit arrangements when he concludes the arrangements and funds them direct with the carrier. He may, through other contracts, be able to get a discount through the volume of business generated to the trade or route.

3 An increasing number of Third World countries, COMECON and Eastern Bloc countries now follow a policy of directing all cargoes onto their national shipping line or airline. This saves hard currency and develops their shipping and airline companies.

4 The seller, under CIF terms, can maximize the national income from such a sale and thereby despatch the consignment on the seller's national shipping line or airline, and likewise obtain insurance cover through brokers.

5 In recent years an increasing volume of business has been air-freighted and much of the traffic is passing under air-freight consolidation terms involving freight agency sponsorship (see *Elements of Export Practice* p. 71–3). Such developments must be reconciled with the most suitable cargo delivery terms.

6 Both seller and buyer should consider carefully the overall benefits and obligations resulting from any cargo delivery terms.

Incoterms 1990 can be classified into recommended usages by mode of transport: all modes (i.e. combined transport) EXW, FCA, CPT, CIP, DAF, DDP, DEL; and conventional port port/sea transport only FAS, FOB, CFR, CIF, DES, DEQ.

Incoterms 1990 reflect the changes and development of international distribution during the past decade, especially the development of combined transportation and associated documentation together with electronic data interchange. The exporter, in analysing each term, should identify the following aspects:

Seller
1 Supplying good(s) in conformity with the contract.
2 Licences and authorizations.
3 Place of delivery (not delivery of the goods).
4 Carriage of goods contract and insurance.
5 Documentation and notice to the buyer.
6 Transfer of risks.
7 Transfer/division of costs.
8 Checking, packages, marking.
9 Other obligations.

Buyer
1 Licences and authorizations.
2 Notices, receipt of documents.
3 Taking delivery.
4 Transfer of risks.

5 Transfer/division of costs.
6 Other obligations.

Overall, the most decisive factors to employ in determining the most acceptable Incoterm are experience of the trading market and the development of a good business relationship between seller and buyer.

8.3 INCOTERMS 1990

8.3.1 Ex works (EXW)

This term means maximum involvement by the buyer in arrangements for the conveyance of the consignment to the specified destination. The exporter merely makes the goods available by an agreed date at his factory or warehouse. The seller minimizes his obligations, whilst the buyer obtains the goods at the lowest possible price by arranging to use his national shipping line or airline and by securing insurance cover in his own country. This eliminates the need to fund such provisions using hard currency, and thereby improves the importer's trade balance. This practice is much on the increase nowadays, particularly by Third World countries and COMECON and Eastern Bloc nations. The seller's obligations cease when the buyer accepts the goods at the factory or warehouse. The term provides two options: Ex works cleared for export, and Ex works uncleared for export. The following is based on uncleared for export.

The principal obligations of the seller include: to supply the goods in accord with the contract of sale; to make available the goods to the buyer at the customary delivery point, i.e. works or factory, or as specified in the contract of sale, to enable the goods to be loaded on the transport unit arranged by the buyer; to provide at his expense the necessary packaging suitable for the transport of the goods of the contract description; to give the buyer prompt notice when the goods will be available for collection; to pay the cost of any cargo scrutiny, e.g. checking quality, counting or weighing prior to placing the goods at the disposal of the buyer; to bear all risk and expense of the goods until they have been placed at the disposal of the buyer as specified in the contract of sale; to render the buyer on request every assistance to provide, in the country of delivery or cargo origin, all the relevant documentation required in the process of exportation. Further, although the seller is not responsible for loading the goods in the vehicle provided by the buyer, it is normal practice for the seller to assist the buyer in loading, at the risk and expense of the buyer. Equally, the seller may be asked to provide the export declaration, which would also be at the buyer's risk and expense. Furthermore, in some circumstances, the buyer located outside the exporting country may not apply for an export licence, thus the seller may also be asked to obtain the export licence, at the buyer's risk and expense.

Obviously, the responsibilities of the buyer are more extensive. These include: to take delivery of the cargo and to pay for the goods in accord with the contract of sale terms; to bear all the cost and risk of the goods from the time they have been placed at his disposal by the seller in accord with sales contract terms; to fund any custom's duties and taxes arising through exportation; to bear additional costs incurred and related risks inherent through the failure of the buyer to give instructions about the place of delivery within the prescribed period; to fund all costs in obtaining the documents required for the purpose of importation and exportation and for passing through the countries of transit. In regard to Ex works cleared for export, the seller is responsible for providing all the requisite documentation and processing the cargo through customs clearance at his expense. When the goods have been cleared through customs, they are handed over to the buyer.

A fundamental point to bear in mind applicable to all Incoterms 1990 is the responsibility of the seller in regard to packaging. It obliges the seller to provide, at his expense, journey-proof packaging suitable for the transport of goods of the contract description – unless it is the custom of the particular trade to despatch goods of the contract description unpacked. All such packaging is to be marked appropriately.

8.3.2   FOB (free on board) – including name of port shipment

Under such terms the goods are placed in the ship by the seller at the specified port of shipment detailed in the sales contract. The risk of loss of, or damage to, the goods is transferred from the seller to the buyer when these goods pass over the ship's rail. Under such terms the seller bears all the cost and the risk of conveyance up to the ship's rail and the buyer accepts the residue of the transit cost, including sea freight and insurance. This term is used frequently in international trade and is to the advantage of the buyer inasmuch as the cargo can be conveyed on his national shipping line, thereby ensuring it is funded by the national currency. Insurance provision can likewise be arranged in his own country with similar benefit.

The principal seller's obligations found in an FOB sales contract include: to supply the goods in accord with the contract of sale; to deliver the cargo on the named vessel at the specified port of shipment within the agreed period/on the agreed date and, in so doing, promptly inform the buyer; to provide, at his expense, any export licence or other governmental authorization necessary for the export of goods; to bear all costs and risks of the goods until such time as the cargo has effectively passed over the ship's rail at the named port; to provide at his expense the customary packing of the goods unless it is the custom of the trade to ship the cargo unpacked; to pay the cost of any cargo scrutiny prior to the delivery of the cargo; to supply at seller's expense the requisite transport documentation as proof of delivery of the goods on board the named vessel; to provide the buyer, on request and at his expense, with the certificate of origin; and to supply the buyer, on request and expense every assistance to obtain transport documentation and other documentation issued in the country of shipment or origin necessary for the importation process both in transit countries and the destination country. A point to emphasize is the need to have a clean 'on board' transport document, which may be a negotiable bill of lading, a non-negotiable sea waybill or electronic data interchange message equivalent thereto, to cover the contract of goods and to be dated within the period agreed for shipment. When such a transport document is issued in several originals, a full set of originals must be tendered to the buyer. If the transport document contains a reference to the charter party, the seller must also provide a copy of the charter party document.

The buyer's responsibilities are extensive. These include: to arrange, at his own expense and risk pre-shipment arrangements with a shipowner/agent and, in so doing, give full details to the seller; to bear all cost and risk of the cargo from the time they have passed over the ship's rail at port of shipment and to pay the price as specified in the sales contract; to bear all the cost and risk emerging from the failure of the shipowner to fulfil the contracted pre-shipment arrangements (such as the cargo being shut out) – this is subject to the seller making the cargo available at the loading berth in accord with the sales contract; in the event of the buyer failing to give pre-shipment details to the seller within the prescribed period, all additional cost and risk to be borne by the buyer; and to pay all cost to the seller to obtain bills of lading, certificate of origin, consular documents and any other documentation required to process the cargo through importation both in transit countries and in the country of destination.

8.3.3   CFR (cost and freight) – detailing the port of shipment

Under this term the seller must pay the costs and freight necessary to bring the goods to the named destination, but the risk of loss of or damage to the goods, as well as of any additional expenses, is transferred from the seller to the buyer when the goods pass over the ship's rail in the specified port of shipment. This is identical to CIF except that the seller is responsible for funding and arranging the minimum cargo insurance.

The seller's obligation in CFR include: to supply the goods in accord with the contract of sale terms; to arrange and pay for the conveyance of the goods to the specified port of destination by the customary route and fund any unloading charges at the destination port; to provide and pay for any export licence or other governmental authorization necessary to export the cargo; to arrange and pay for, on specified date or period, the cargo loading at the agreed port – if no such loading date/period is quoted, such a task to be undertaken within a reasonable period; to bear all the cargo risk until such time as it passes over the ship's rail at the port of shipment; to supply promptly and pay for the clean on board transport document to the agreed destination port, together with any invoice of the goods shipped; to provide and pay for the customary packing of the goods unless it is the custom of the trade to ship the cargo unpacked; to fund any cargo scrutiny prior to loading the cargo; to pay any cost of dues and taxes incurred relative to the process of exportation in respect of the cargo prior to shipment; to provide the buyer, on request and at the buyer's expense, a certificate of origin and consular invoice; to render the buyer, on request and at the buyer's expense/risk, every assistance to obtain any documents required in the country of shipment, or transit countries, necessary for the conveyance of the cargo to its destination.

A point to note, especially with the CFR term, is the clean on board transport document may be a negotiable bill of lading, a non-negotiable sea waybill, or electronic data interchange message equivalent thereto, to cover the contract goods and be dated within the period agreed for shipment. When such a transport document is issued in several originals, a full set of originals must be tendered to the buyer. If the transport document contains a reference to the charter party, the seller must also provide a copy of the charter party document.

The factors relevant to the buyer include: acceptance of the documents as tendered by the seller – subject to their conformity with the terms of the contract – and payment of the goods etc., as specified in the contract of sale; to receive the goods at the port of destination and, with the exception of the sea freight, all the cost and charges incurred during the voyage(s); to fund all unloading expenses at destination port including lighterage, wharfage etc. unless such costs have been included in the freight or collected by the shipowner at the time freight was paid; to undertake all the risk when the cargo has passed over the ship's rail at destination port; in the event of the buyer failing to give instructions – by the specified date or within an agreed period – relative to destination port, all additional cost and risk will be borne by the buyer subject to the goods being duly appropriated to the contract; to pay all the cost to obtain the certificate of origin and consular documents; to meet all charges to provide any other documentation specified relative to processing the consignment in the country of shipment or transit countries; to pay all customs duties and other taxes raised at the time of importation; and obtain and pay for any import licence or related documentation required at the time of importation.

If the goods are sold 'CFR landed', the seller bears the cost of unloading, including lighterage and wharfage charges. In the CFR contract sale the buyer can arrange the cargo insurance in his own country, thereby saving foreign currency. Many importers are tending to favour this arrangement.

8.3.4   CIF (cost, insurance freight) – with the named port of destination

This is a commonly used cargo delivery term arrangement and is not identical to CFR: there is the addition that the seller is obliged to procure minimum marine insurance against the risk of loss of or damage to the goods in transit. Basically, the seller contracts with the insurer and pays the insurance premium.

The salient features of the contract as far as the seller is concerned include: to supply the goods in accord with contract of sale terms; to arrange and pay for the carriage of the goods to the specified destination port by the customary route and to fund any loading charges at the destination port; to provide and pay for any export licence or other governmental authorization necessary to export the cargo; to arrange and pay for, on specified date or within an agreed period, the cargo loading at the agreed port – if no such loading date/period is quoted, such a task to be undertaken within a reasonable period; to inform the buyer promptly when loading is completed; to arrange and pay for insurance of the cargo in a transferable form against the risk of loss or damage during the transit – such terms shall be FPA (free of particular average) and embrace the CIF price plus 10% and the insurance will be in the currency of the contract; to bear all the risk of goods until they have effectively passed over the ship's rail at the port of shipment; to supply to the buyer promptly, at the seller's expense, a clean on board transport document to the agreed port of destination and insurance policy or certificate of insurance; to provide and pay for the customary packing of the goods unless it is the custom of the trade to ship the goods unpacked; to pay the cost of any cargo scrutiny prior to loading the cargo; to bear any cost of dues and taxes incurred relative to the process of exportation in respect of the cargo prior to shipment; to provide the buyer, on request and at the buyer's expense, a certificate of origin and consular invoice; to render the buyer, on request and at the buyer's expense/risk, every assistance to obtain any documents required in the country of shipment or transit countries necessary for the conveyance of the cargo throughout the transit.

A fundamental point to bear in mind is that the seller must, at his expense, supply the buyer without delay a clean on board transport document for the agreed port of destination, as well as the invoice of the goods shipped, and transfer the right to dispose of the goods to the buyer. The transport document may be a negotiable bill of lading, a non-negotiable sea waybill, or electronic data interchange message equivalent thereto, and must cover the contract goods and be dated within the period agreed for shipment. When such a transport document is issued in several originals, a full set of the originals must be tendered to a buyer. If the transport document contains a reference to the charter party, the seller must also provide a copy of the charter party document.

The responsibilities of the buyer include: acceptance of the documents as tendered by the seller (subject to their conformity with the terms of the contract) and payment of the goods, as specified in the contract of sale; to receive the goods at the agreed destination port and to bear, with the exception of the freight and minimum cargo insurance, all costs and charges incurred during the voyage(s); to fund all unloading expenses at the port of destination, including lighterage, and wharfage, unless such costs have been included in the freight or collected by the shipowner at the time freight was paid; to undertake all the risk when the cargo has passed over the ship's rail at the destination port; in the event of the buyer failing to give instructions, by the specified date or within an agreed period, relative to the port of destination, all additional cost and risk will be borne by the buyer subject to the goods being duly appropriated to the contract; to pay all the costs in obtaining a certificate of origin and consular documents; to meet all charges to provide any other documentation specified relative to processing the consignment in the country of shipment or transit countries; to pay all customs duties and other taxes raised at the time of importation; and obtain at his expense any import licence or related documentation required at time of importation.

A point to bear in mind from the buyer's standpoint is that if the goods are sold 'CIF landed', the unloading cost, including lighterage and wharfage charges, are borne by the seller.

The CIF terms enable the seller to obtain the maximum income from the sales contract with the insurance and freight charges contributing to the invisible exports if the goods are carried on the national shipping line and the insurance is effected in the country of origin.

8.3.5   Delivered ex ship (DES) – detailing the name of port destination

This sales contract term is not used extensively. It obligates the seller to make the goods available to the buyer on board the vessel at the destination port as specified in the sales contract. The seller has to bear the full cost and risk involved to bring the goods to the destination port.

The seller's main obligations include: to supply the goods in accord with contract of sale terms; to make the goods available to the buyer on board the vessel at the agreed destination port to enable the cargo to be conveniently discharged; to bear all the risk and expense of the cargo conveyance to the destination port until promptly collected by the buyer; to provide and pay for the customary packing of the goods unless it is the custom of the trade to ship the goods unpacked; to pay the cost of any cargo scrutiny prior to collection of the cargo by the buyer; to promptly inform the buyer of the expected date of arrival of the vessel and to provide the buyer with a bill of lading and any other documents necessary to enable the buyer to take delivery of the consignment; to provide the buyer on request and at the buyer's expense the certificate of origin and consular invoice; and to render the buyer on request and at the buyer's expense every assistance to provide the requisite documentation issued in the country of shipment and/or origin required for importation in the destination country or transit countries.

The buyer's obligations are less onerous and include: to take delivery of the cargo and pay the requisite cost as specified in the sales contract; to bear all the risk and expense from the time the cargo has been placed at the disposal of the buyer on board the vessel awaiting discharge at the destination port; to bear all the cost associated with the provision of documentation obtained by the seller necessary for the importation of the goods both in destination and transit countries; to obtain at the buyer's expense all licences or similar documents necessary for the importing process; and to bear all customs charges and other duties/taxes incurred at the time of importation.

8.3.6   Delivered ex quay (DEQ) – detailing the name of port of destination

Under this term, the seller arranges for the goods to be made available to the buyer on the quay or wharf at the destination port detailed in the sales contract. The seller has to bear the full cost and risk of bringing the goods to the quay.

Basically there are two delivered ex quay contracts in use, namely delivered ex quay duty paid, and delivered ex quay duties on buyer's account, in which the liability to clear the goods for import is met by the buyer rather than the seller. It is important that the full description of each term is given to avoid ambiguity and subsequent dispute: for example, it should be clear whether the terms are 'delivered ex quay duty paid' or 'delivered ex quay duties on buyer's account'. Sometimes the buyer also undertakes responsibility for import clearance, in which case this should be specified in the contract of sale. If the seller wishes, this should be specified by adding the words 'exclusive of VAT and/or taxes'.

The seller's obligations include: to supply the goods in accord with the contract of sale terms; to make the goods available to the buyer at the specified quay or wharf within the period given in the sales contract and to bear all the associated risk and cost; to provide and pay for any import licence and bear all charges through importation of the goods and delivery to the buyer; to provide and pay for the journey-proof packaging of the goods unless it is the custom of the trade to ship the cargo unpacked; to pay the cost of any scrutiny immediately prior to the goods being placed at the disposal of the buyer; and at the seller's expense to provide the delivery order or other relevant documents necessary for the buyer to take delivery of the goods.

The buyer's task is twofold: to take delivery of the goods as specified in the contract; and to bear all the expense and risk of the goods from the time the cargo has been effectively placed at the disposal of the buyer. Both DES and DEQ are ideal for commodities or trades involving grain, proteins, seeds, timber and so on.

8.3.7   Delivered at frontier – specifying the name of frontier delivery point

Under the 'delivered at frontier' term, the seller's obligations are concluded when the goods have arrived at the named frontier point or customs examination border. It is usual, to avoid ambiguity, to quote the two countries separated by the frontier. This term is used primarily for rail- or road-borne traffic, but can be used for other transport modes in varying circumstances. Its use could become more common through the development of the combined transport operation for international consignments.

The seller's main obligations include: to supply the goods in accord with contract of sale terms at the seller's risk and expense; to place the goods at the disposal of the buyer at the specified frontier point within the stipulated period and, in so doing, provide him with the necessary customary documentation including consignment note, export licence, delivery order, warehouse warrant, etc., to enable the buyer to take delivery of the cargo; to fund any customs charges and other expenses incurred up to the time when the goods have been placed at the buyer's disposal, and bear all the risk throughout this period; to obtain and pay for all documentation necessary for the exportation of the cargo, including transit countries' needs and placing them at the disposal of the buyer as appropriate; to fund all transport cost (including incidental charges raised during the transit) up to the nominated frontier point; if no particular frontier point is quoted, the seller may choose the one which is most convenient to him provided he notifies the buyer promptly and it offers adequate customs and other facilities to enable the contract to be executed satisfactorily by both parties; to supply the buyer on request the through consignment note embracing the origination and destination place in the importing country – such a request to be executed by the seller on the condition he incurs the risk, or expense other than is customary to incur; in the event of the goods being unloaded on arrival at the frontier point, such cost to be borne by the seller, including lighterage and handling charges (this would also apply if the seller used his own transport); to notify promptly the buyer the goods have been despatched; to provide and pay for the customary packing of the goods unless it is the custom of the trade to ship the cargo unpacked; to fund any cargo scrutiny necessary to transport the goods to the specified frontier point; to bear any additional cost incurred to place the goods at the buyer's disposal; and render to the buyer, on request and at the buyer's expense, all reasonable assistance to obtain documents inherent in the importing process in the destination country.

The buyer's obligations include: to accept delivery of the goods at the specified frontier point and accept all transportation/handling costs therefrom; to meet the risk and custom duties and other costs incurred from the time the goods have been placed at the buyer's disposal relative to the process of importation of the cargo; to fund incidental expenses incurred to unload the cargo at the specified frontier point; in the event of the buyer not taking delivery of the cargo, duly put at his disposal in accord with the sales contract, the buyer will pay all additional cost and bear all the risk resulting therefrom; to obtain, at his expense, any import licence and other documentation required to process the cargo through importation; to fund any additional expense incurred by the seller to obtain the consignment note for the buyer, which could include documentation; and to supply the seller on request with details of the ultimate destination of the goods; to fund any expense incurred by the seller to provide the buyer with any export third party certificate of conformity of the goods stipulated in the contract of sale.

In addition to the foregoing cargo delivery terms which can be regarded as the most popular there do exist a number of others which are found in Incoterms 1990. A brief commentary on them follows.

8.3.8   Delivery duty paid or unpaid – quoting destination name and country of importation

Under this term is provided the option for the buyer/seller to specify duty paid or unpaid at the named place of destination in the country of importation. The seller is also given the maximum obligation regarding cargo despatch arrangements. Under such terms, the seller is responsible for the conveyance of goods, at his own risk and expense, to the destination in the buyer's country named in the contract of sale. This includes the task of processing the cargo through both exportation and importation, embracing the payment of duties and taxes, if agreed with the buyer, including customs clearance and loading/unloading, together with the related documentation, which the buyer usually obtains, as necessary, on request but at the buyer's expense. The seller may use his own transport throughout the conveyance.

The buyer's role is to accept the goods at the named place of destination, and he is responsible for all subsequent movement costs of the goods, including handling and, if agreed, duties taxes and, where necessary, any import licence. Any form of transport may be used. If the parties wish the seller to clear the goods for import, with some of the cost payable upon import of the goods, such as VAT, excluded, this must be made clear with the addition of the words 'exclusive of VAT and/or taxes'.

If it is necessary or customary for the goods to be unloaded, discharged or landed upon their arrival at the named place of destination for the purpose of putting them, duty paid, at the disposal of the buyer at that place, the buyer bears and pays the expenses of such operations, including any lighterage, wharfage, warehousing and/or handling charges. This would be subject to the agreement of the buyer and seller. This term is ideal for any transport mode.

8.3.9   Free carrier – quoting named point of transfer of goods

This term is primarily for the combined transport operation such as a container, or roll on/roll off operation involving a road trailer and sea ferry operation, and for air including air/sea, sea/air, road/air, etc. The term is based on the FOB principle except that the seller fulfils his obligations when he delivers the goods into the custody of the carrier at the named place found in the sales contract or subsequently agreed by the parties. This is likely to be used by a freight forwarder engaged in the international road haulage business. The risk of loss of or damage to the goods is transferred from the seller to the buyer at the time the nominated carrier accepts them at the prescribed place and not at the ship's rail as with FOB. When the seller has to render to the buyer or other person prescribed the bill of lading, waybill, or carrier's receipt, as evidence of the delivery acceptance of the goods, the seller's contractual obligations are fulfilled.

This term may be used by various modes of transport such as FCS-sea, FCA-air, FCR-rail, and FCT-road. The seller fulfils his obligations when he delivers the goods into the custody of the carrier at the named point: 'the carrier' means any person by whom, or in whose name, a contract of carriage by road, air, rail, sea or combination of transport modes has been made. The seller, at his risk, must supply and deliver the goods into the charge of the carrier named by the buyers on the agreed date. The seller must provide any requisite export licence and customary packaging, and supply the buyer with the customary transport documents as proof of delivery of the goods to the carrier. The buyer must bear all the cost and risk of the goods from the time they have been delivered to the carrier.

8.3.10   Freight carriage – paid to a named destination (FPT)

Under such a term the seller pays the freight for the carriage of the goods to the named destination. The buyer's risk commences when the goods have been delivered into the custody of the first carrier who is the carrier responsible for the first section of the transport carried out under the transport document issued according to the contract even in a domestic/ local transport journey. Moreover, at this point the buyer accepts full liability for any additional cost incurred in the conveyance of the goods. On request the seller may have to provide a bill of lading, waybill or carriers receipt to the buyer or other person prescribed at which stage the seller's obligations are fulfilled. In common with the previous delivery term, it is ideal for the multi-modal transport operation which includes roll on/roll off and container movements.

8.3.11   Freight carriage and insurance paid to the named point of destination

This term is identical to the previous item except that the seller also funds the cargo insurance. Again it is ideal for the combined transport operation and the seller's liability ceases when the cargo has been accepted by the first carrier at the named place and any requested bill of lading, waybill, or carrier receipt has been handed over.

The importance of all who are involved in negotiating sales contracts and executing them, understanding the foregoing cargo delivery terms cannot be overstressed.

In concluding this chapter, I would particularly like to thank the International Chamber of Commerce and recommend readers involved in the export/shipping business to study the ICC publication No. 350, entitled *Incoterms 1990*, which gives the information in much greater detail. Additionally, those export personnel engaged in the commercial documentary credit operations are recommended to study ICC publications No. 400 *Uniform Customs and Practice for Documentary Credits* and No. 415 *Guide to Documentary Credit Operations*.

9 Export selling

9.1 FACTORS TO CONSIDER IN THE EVALUATION OF THE MOST ACCEPTABLE METHOD OF SELLING PRODUCTS OVERSEAS

The exporter may be fresh to overseas business, endeavouring to determine the most suitable method to sell the product. Alternatively, a manufacturer may be seeking to extend his overseas selling to markets in neighbouring countries, or could be carefully reviewing his present selling techniques in a particular overseas market with a view to devising a more effective, cost-cutting, dynamic and direct sell. Various organizations exist which can offer help in such circumstances, and these include Chambers of Commerce, international banks, trade associations, export club members, and the BOTB. An increasing number of exporters now circulate a news bulletin to their overseas agents and distributors detailing the latest developments in their company and any future plans which may interest the overseas buyer.

Various factors must be considered in deciding the most suitable method of selling overseas:

1 The type of product(s) involved, and the product quantity and the potential annual income from sales. This would be evaluated during the first three to five years of the operation, and would be detailed in a five-year business plan.

2 The market profile. This is an important area and the fullest information should be sought. It is allied to a number of other points contained in this list.

3 The degree of competition in the market place, and especially how the product compares with other products in the field and their marketing techniques.

4 Any statutory regulations, which might mean that the product has to be distributed and/or sold in a particular way through accredited government agencies.

5 The long-term future of the market. If the market prospects are exceptionally good with the potential for high sales and high profit levels, it may prove worthwhile to invest more heavily in the venture and engage in an

active selling technique at the outset rather than allow the agent to retail the product in a more passive way.

6 The general political and economic situation in the country. An unstable government tends to present risk to the exporter through sudden import restrictions and other measures designed to preserve the home economy. In such circumstances, the exporter may be wise to limit the level of investment in such a venture.

7 Any marketing/selling arrangement with another company or group of companies.

8 The overall physical distribution cost. This may be the cost of a fully loaded container, serving a distributor depot overseas, or the more expensive unit cost of using a break bulk/groupage container service where the products are delivered direct to the retailer. The economics of distribution need careful evaluation, as fully explained in section 12.3 relative to transport distribution analysis.

9 An increasing number of multinational companies now exist who manufacture/assemble their products in the overseas market and engage in direct marketing/retailing (see sections 4.4–4.7). This tends to aid competitiveness of the product and provides employment opportunities for the nationals which overseas governments naturally welcome. Additionally, some countries provide financial assistance in the construction of such manufacturing/ assembly plants and welcome the professional, technical expertise which can be passed on to their nationals.

10 Market research will indicate the most suitable selling technique with regard to the competition, price level, customer profile, level of profitability, and the strengths and weaknesses of the product in the market place.

11 A market analysis reveals market trends and areas where growth is likely to be at its highest. The latter may be identified with a customer profile which is receptive to a particular selling technique, such as a mail shot.

12 The overall economics of the task should be examined relative to the selling technique allied to the distribution/marketing arrangements which include servicing the market. Each option requires careful consideration, with some options producing quicker throughput of product, quicker turnover; less goods and capital tied up in transit and/or in the warehouse awaiting distribution; less risk of stock deterioration through quicker turnover of goods; lower insurance premium; and quicker payment for the merchandise.

13 Any trading/distribution/marketing/selling regulations which may apply to retailing products in another country. Some countries may operate through a licensing system, whilst others have stringent local trading regulations which may be more severe on imported products. The Department of Trade and Industry, through the overseas diplomatic post, can offer good advice.

14 The resources of the company for an overseas sales force. If the exporter is keen to have his own sales force, the cost must be carefully evaluated, including any training, recruitment of personnel or utilizing personnel already in the company. Undoubtedly, the directly controlled sales force can prove the most forceful and effective, but its cost can prove to be high in comparison to a good agent on commission.

It should be appreciated that the individual exporter's evaluation of the most acceptable selling technique will vary extensively, and not all the foregoing items will always be relevant. Items (1), (2), (3) and (12) are usually the most decisive ones. Undoubtedly, at some stage, a cost analysis should be undertaken of the product to determine the unit cost incurred in reaching the consumer, including packaging, distribution, marketing and selling. The cost analysis should be closely allied to the volume of sales. For example, one may find that it is more expensive to retail a product than a competitor does, but if the profit margin is reasonable, and it is generating annually more sales growth and market share improvement, such an arrangement should remain unchanged. Overall, in any evaluation the market report (see section 4.3.1) should prove a very useful aid to determine market prospects, market profile, market size and the overall situation both in the short and long term. Additionally risk analysis, profitability and market entry option (see section 6.1) must be closely evaluated.

To conclude our examination of overseas selling techniques one must not forget that the following factors must be borne in mind when the sale has been secured:

1 The technical and design specification must be in accord with the buyer's needs, and the quotation and the method of payment must be acceptable, including the currency.
2 It is essential that the delivery date be met. Industrial disputes, delayed transits and non-availability of raw materials create a bad impression for the buyer (importer) who has a deadline to meet in getting the product in the market place. It is the ultimate responsibility of the export office to ensure that no such problems arise, and, if any signs emerge suggesting that a delay might occur, early remedial measures must be taken. Many exporters faced with such situations use air freight to distribute the goods to meet the delivery date rather than rely on the slower and less expensive sea transport.
3 Adequate attention must be given to after-sales service. Any technical manuals should be provided, and spares should be easily available (see sections 4.6 and 4.7). This important area requires close attention.

It will be appreciated that selling direct to the local buying office, the export house/merchant, confirming house, etc. situated in the exporter's country is basically a local sale. All the export documentation and transportation arrangements are undertaken by the buyer. The level of profit per item sold is lower, and the seller is not aware of the end user to undertake any market research or product development. Payment for the goods is usually prompt, with no credit risk.

In regard to selling to the agent, distributor, overseas sales office or subsidiary, the exporter is subject to the prolonged payment arrangements and credit risk. Moreover, he/she is required to have an export/shipping office to handle the physical distribution and channels of distribution arrangements. The exporter knows the end user and therefore can undertake market research and product development. Also, the level of profit per unit sold tends to be higher and customer loyalty, but the exporter incurs high cost to enter and serve the market.

The exporter has the other option of developing local manufacture in the buyer's country through licensing, joint venture, contract manufacture, full manufacture, etc. These all involve close supervision and usually eliminate the need to have a shipping office to undertake the transportation arrangements. Financial commitment is also much stronger. A similar situation arises under mergers and acquisitions (see also section 4.14).

The need to execute the order efficiently, in accord with the export sales contract, cannot be overstressed (see section 8.2).

9.2 SALES NEGOTIATION

The process of concluding a sale in an overseas territory involves many skills and each situation varies by product/service, culture, competition, language, after-sales service, import regulations, market profile/attitudes, protocol, and so on. Personal relationships, the exporter's company profile/ reputation, and complete professionalism are all paramount considerations. Each situation requires a different strategy and market research will facilitate the successful sale negotiation.

Overall, there are seven basic steps in the sales process as detailed below:

1 Making contact with the potential buyer. This arises through direct or indirect market entry. It includes: outward/inward trade missions; trade exhibitions; overseas visit; mail shot; advertisements in trade magazines; enquiry by telex/letter, telephone; and so on.
2 Arousing interest. This requires the seller to devise a strategy which will interest the importer. Accordingly, the seller must quickly identify the importer's needs and mould the negotiations around them. These may be on price, specification, design, product performance, productivity, delivery time-scale, innovation or finance. A sales person able to solve a buyer's problem by providing equipment at a competitive price and aiding the importer to develop his business profitability is likely to obtain customer loyalty and repeat business.
3 Creating preference. The seller must, through analytical evaluation, be able to establish the strengths and weaknesses of the product/service

compared with the competition and, in so doing, be able to conduct the sales negotiation in the most favourable light. This especially involves developing the main advantages of the product/service with particular emphasis on the points which interest the buyer as established from item (2). Product samples, demonstrations, and videos all help to present a favourable image. The sales person must decide whether to adopt a soft sell or hard sell attitude. Much depends on the situation and the product position in the market place, and especially the level of competition. Overall, this stage can take some time, especially if the client requires product samples for quality testing and consumer research. The scale of the presentation will depend on the size of the potential order and level of competition.

4 Making a specific proposal. This is the culmination of the earlier negotiations, and involves the complete package including product specification, price, terms of sale, finance, delivery date and product approval certificate of importing country and so on. It is most desirable the seller leaves room for further manoeuvre in the proposal to take account of any unforeseen situations such as price reduction, earlier delivery date, colour change, better packaging and so on. It is usual to give a time limit on the quotation, which can vary from 30 to 90 days.

5 Closing the sale. This requires the buyer to accept the seller's original or modified offer. It is usual for the seller to check carefully the buyer's acceptance to ensure it contains no counter offers and it accords with the seller's terms of sale. It is possible the sales contract may include an option on a further order in the light of market considerations and product performance/acceptance.

6 Retaining the business. This is a critical area for the sales person. Personal visits are desirable on a regular basis in most situations, but much depends on the product and the nature of the sale. This can be supplemented by the despatch of sales bulletins and company profile development. Such data will keep the buyer in touch with the seller's business and product developments/ activities. Any sales conference or trade exhibition notification should contain an invitation to the buyer. Overall, the buyer must be given the impression that he is an important customer receiving special treatment to ensure the buyer's business can prosper through supporting seller's product/ service. It should be a partnership of trust and mutual development: complete professionalism must be displayed by the sales person to create a good image.

7 Endeavour to have a draft discussion plan with options risk areas and their options and strategy formulation.

The time-scale of the sale negotiation will vary considerably, and can extend from several days to, in extreme situations, two/three years. Usually the capital goods market takes much longer and involves more detailed negotiations extending to both sales and technical personnel. In a free market economy (free of government controls) the time-scale is quicker and there is less extensive bureaucracy. This applies to most westernized economies. In regard to centrally-controlled economies such as China, USSR, Eastern Bloc countries, bureaucracy reaches its peak and is usually subject to bi-lateral trade agreements. In many of the African states, in South America and on the Indian sub-continent, exchange control regulations are severe and an increasing number of deals are conducted under counter-trade terms. Much can be learnt with regard to culture profile and selling techniques by contacting another company active in the overseas territory to obtain an overview of the situation. This exchange of data can often arise through joining an export club, Chamber of Commerce or trade association.

It will be appreciated that selling is a diverse activity, but given below is a check list of points to consider in sales negotiations – each situation it is stressed will vary by individual circumstances.

9.2.1   Before negotiations

(a) *Sales material*   The seller must provide as much material as possible before negotiations begin, including company reports and articles published outside the company. If resources are available, prepare films and slides dubbed in the buyer's language. Overall, such data will provide a company profile with emphasis placed on the company's position in the market place. This may be with a market-leader with many innovative qualities, or as a large multi-national, well-established and respected worldwide with enormous resources in technology, high calibre personnel, production, research and development, marketing and so on. In the small company a slide presentation is useful, especially when adequately supported by brochures and articles. It could take the form of a joint presentation with another company such as the bedroom furniture manufacturer working alongside the furnishings/curtain producer. Stress should be placed on the major features of the product which are likely to interest the buyer following the market research findings.

(b) *Market research*   The enquiry/presentation should be aided by market research findings conducted by the exporter involving desk and, where appropriate, field research. This should identify culture analysis, market profile, competition, import regulations, distribution, political situation, short- and long-term market prospects, finance, risk analysis and so on. Trade associations, Chambers of Commerce, and BOTB can help in this area. Adequate market research cannot be overstressed: this will ensure the correct viable export marketing strategy is devised, having regard to company resources and the overseas market potential.

(c) *Interpreters*   To the sales team not competent in the language of the buyer, it is most desirable that the services of an interpreter be secured. Often the interpreter will also assess the success or otherwise of the negotiations, and give advice on protocol and culture of the country.

(d) *Adequate briefing*   All members of the export negotiating team, which may range from the individual sales person to a group of personnel covering sales, technical engineer, etc. should be provided with a brief prepared in house. All such personnel should have a business card for presentation, ideally double sided – one in English and one in the language of the buyer, i.e. Arabic, German, Italian, etc. Prior to the overseas visit, perhaps up to six weeks in advance, in house meetings should be conducted to formulate strategy and adequacy of company resources to handle the order. This will embrace production, pricing, design, research and development, overview of the overseas market including existing clients, and 'swop' (strengths–weaknesses–opportunities–strengths) analysis of the product/service reconciled with market situation. Particular emphasis should be given to product-specification aspects which interest the buyer, and pricing/production/delivery time-scale options based on size of order and period of shipment profitability and risk analysis. All such meetings should be led by the export sales director/manager in charge of the delegation.

9.2.2   During negotiations

The following should be borne in mind as a guide to the conduct appropriate during negotiations.

1 Greet your client with the appropriate culture of the overseas territory which, in Thailand for example, means putting one's hands together and bowing the head. Also use the appropriate greeting in the buyer's language. This quickly establishes a favourable relationship and confirms to the buyer that his visitor has taken the trouble to learn something of the culture of the country. Such information can be obtained through a cultural briefing prior to the departure of the export sales person. A small gift representing the culture of the seller's country is usually appropriate. It is usual to exchange gifts as a mark of personal friendship and understanding. On arrival at your host's office, accept their hospitality in regard to the national custom, such as in the form of refreshment.

2 Establish a personal relationship with members of the buyer's team. Enquire about their hobbies, interests and family backgrounds and do not be offended if you are asked about religion and other matters which might be considered inappropriate elsewhere. Exchange views in a cordial and diplomatic manner and endeavour to understand the basis of the buyer's views having regard to the cultural environment and political situation.

3 Ideally open the meeting by discussing common ground and establishing what you hope the talks will accomplish. Put your position (seller) in writing when appropriate as a sign of the importance you attach to the negotiations. Save points of contention until firm groundwork has been laid.

4 When negotiating in English in an overseas territory where English is not the national language (such as in Arab States, Japan, China, etc.), do not assume that the person with the best command of English is the most important member of the team. Negotiators (sellers) who address comments to this person risk insulting more senior members who do not speak English. In social and business situations, address the entire team.

5 Maintain a formal posture throughout the negotiations. Casual dress is unacceptable in negotiations. The sales person must be well-groomed and neatly presented, with the men wearing suits appropriate to the climatic conditions. Short-sleeve presentation is not usually acceptable. Do not use first names at the first meeting, and only subsequently when the level of friendship warrants it and it is an acceptable practice as a custom of the country to do so.

6 Be prepared for periods of silence at the meeting, and do not rush to fill the gap. Silence can be a sign that the importer's team is considering an important point; it may also be a sign of respect.

7 If the seller's question is met with silence or an evasive response, do not pursue the point immediately. Reflect on why the question got that response, reformulate it to avoid the sticking point, and ask it later – maybe at the next meeting.

8 Start each session with a review of the main points agreed to in the previous session. Debrief each member of the sales team after every session.

9 The sales person must avoid excessive praise of the product or service: avoid also references to a generous offer. This attitude could be adopted in subsequent meetings, but its timing requires evaluation and will vary by culture and overseas territory. For example, the Japanese are likely to consider hard sell tactics or aggressive confrontational behaviour as bullish.

10 Communicate clearly and avoid using idioms. Large numbers can easily be mistranslated: keep them to a minimum and write them down.

11 If the negotiations stall, try to find a third party who has had success with the buyer's team and, in so doing, endeavour to establish what can be done to break the deadlock.

12 Do not mix business with pleasure. When the negotiating teams dine together or go for a night out on the town, do not discuss business items.

The foregoing list should not be regarded as exhaustive, and the following considerations are especially important.

1 Adequate planning is essential in regard to the overseas visit, discussion and strategy.

2 Be professional at all times. Ensure all members of the sales team are competent and have authority to make decisions at the meeting(s).

3 Sound preparation, including market research, for the visit in all its areas is paramount. This involves a Company Portfolio perception analysis of the buyer. An itinerary should be prepared (see section 11.2) on the overseas business visit.

4 Develop the quality of perseverance and stress continuously the salient features of the product/service which the sales literature is promoting and which has been identified as interesting to the buyer. An adequately researched customer profile will produce useful data and guidelines.

5 An acceptable personality of the team is desirable with the quality of diplomacy and the ability to get on with the importer.

6 Deal with all unanswered questions promptly and professionally, ideally within 48/72 hours. All requests for additional samples or modified samples should be treated with priority and arrangements put in hand shortly after the meeting by telex with the UK company office.

7 Exercise patience over the buyer's decision-making process, but maintain personal contact by telephone and/or visit. Regular visits of three-monthly intervals – depending on the market – encourage good relationships and enthusiasm.

8 Display commitment to the buyer. Regular contact as in item (7) and the despatch of sales bulletins all help to facilitate business development.

Factors to be considered in developing an effective overseas selling technique include adequate planning and preparation. This includes market research of the level of competition and the buyers/consumer profile and behaviour. The need to have the personality and character to get on well with the buyer is essential as it is to develop a strong professional relationship with a view to aiding the buyer's business development in a competitive environment. This does include the exporter's persistence to obtain the sale which may be prolonged and tedious. At all times the sales person must be completely professional and always dressed smartly and appropriately for the occasion, whether it be at the negotiating table or on a leisure trip. The theme throughout must be to retain and develop the client's interest in the exporter's product/service and in so doing present it in a balanced manner but a favourable light. Research will determine the features which most interest the buyer and this should feature adequately in the presentation. Overall, this technique will help the buyer evaluate the product/service more favourably and thereby facilitate securing the sale.

To conclude, successful negotiation is usually realized through the most thorough preparation and market research to determine what the customer requires and on what terms. The nature of the market and the product/service will be dominant factors, coupled with the level of competition. Pricing and delivery are important together with a commitment to the market displayed through regular visits and communication.

9.3   AGENTS AND DISTRIBUTORS

The narrow definition of 'agent' in export practice is that he is a party who acts for the exporter, the latter being the principal. He does not make a profit, but is paid a commission on all orders secured, for which his principal obtains eventual payment. Usually, such an agent works for a number of principals which offer a cohesive group of products, but not so as to be in direct competition with each other.

9.3.1   Agency systems

There are variations in the type of agency which works on a 'commission only' basis according to what the parties consider suitable to the product and the market, of which the following are examples:

(a) *Fee or retainer*   When it is clear from the outset that it will take some time before the product gets established in the market, and thus before the agent can earn a worthwhile commission, it is up to the principal to offer some alternative financial inducement to motivate the agent until straight commission becomes a viable proposition. Where the agent is selling a range of products for one principal on a commission basis, the agent may be offered a fee to launch a new product which, although within the general range, is an untried newcomer to the market – or some entirely fresh range of products.

(b) *Expenses incurred by the agent*   These may be paid by the prncipal or shared between the parties on an agreed basis. This introduces variation from the 'commission only' type of agency. Such expenses may be a 'once only' arrangement such as setting up show-room facilities. Alternatively, they may be continuing, involving, for example, the agent being charged with reading local technical journals and buying them for the principal when appropriate information appears. Some special variation of the 'commission only' arrangement can be introduced to cover the agent's outlays or to share them in special circumstances, such as an exhibition or some exceptional venture in local publicity.

(c) *Stockist agencies*   In this case the agent fixes the selling price but undertakes to buy for his own account – the difference between buying and selling price covers cost and profit. This could improve sales turnover significantly where the goods are such that the demand is always for prompt delivery; for example, components for automobile repair services in a foreign country.

(d) *Service after sale*   With technical products it is often necessary to provide a manufacturer's guarantee. This is undertaken by the agent who sells on commission and may include a repair service outside the manufacturer's guarantee arrangements. This involves stocks or parts being carried in the market by the agent and, usually, workshop facilities. The details of the arrangement between the parties varies widely according to individual circumstances. The principal may supply free spares, or send them on a consignment basis. Alternatively, the agent may be required to equip a workshop and carry spares at his expense.

(e) *Consignment stocks*   The market where sales are made must have goods available for immediate delivery as soon as the commission agent concludes the sale. Such stocks can be entrusted to the agent providing he owns or rents suitable warehousing space. Such an agent must be of outstanding integrity and sound financial standing. Moreover, one must ensure that the law of the country involved recognizes the continuing legal ownership by the principal of goods physically held by the agent. The alternative is for the stock to be held by an independent warehouseman in the name of the principal, who then sends delivery orders to the buyers to enable them to call on the warehouse for release of the goods ordered through the commission selling agent.

(f) *Salaried agent*   The agent is resident in the country of operation and is paid a salary, with or without expenses and fringe benefits, by his principal. This may prove suitable where the products are capital goods or when the principal is a firm of consultants (or a consortium). Such an agent could keep the principal in touch with conditions in his territory and advise on local opportunities and official tenders over a period of years. For example, he could tender on behalf of his principal for medical equipment or navigational facilities in harbours.

(g) *Distribution agent*   Some markets are dominated by one large firm which dwarfs its competitors; but the market potential cannot be fully exploited unless the smaller concerns are enticed into the sale of the products. The large firm, acting as a distributor, can also secure orders for shipment direct to the small ones. Such transactions are remunerated on a commission basis. However, it may prove in practice that the small firms are squeezed out of effective marketing because of the increase in the price they charge to cover the agent's commission. At best they are somewhat restricted in their activities.

Finally, particular attention must be given to the drafting of the terms of an agency contract and the services of a lawyer should be sought.

(h) *Export management agency*   The function of the export management agent is to act as the manufacturer's export department, either for all markets abroad or for a selected number, clearly agreed in advance. He is briefed about the products, both technically and with regard to future production flows and possible changes in quality and quantity. Price is agreed and a rate of commission fixed, with or without some contribution to the agent's expenses (generally, or for specific purposes such as travel) or a fee plus commission is payable on results. It is usual for the export management to be authorized to appoint agents in foreign territories within the agreed sphere of operation. On the other hand, the management does not usually incur any financial risk – the manager would not be expected to put through orders from parties of doubtful standing, and would advise the manufacturers about financing the business. This avoidance of financial implication is not, however, invariable; thus the merchants who operate manufacturer's agency departments often take over the goods ex-works or FOB.

Some care must be taken to differentiate between this form of agency and the group sales concept detailed in section 9.9. In the latter case, the manufacturers form the sales grouping and decide what to sell overseas whilst in an export management agency situation, the agency takes over the exporters function and decides what shall comprise his group of products to be marketed overseas.

(i) *Del credere agent*   An agent selling on a commission basis (whatever the other terms of reference) who undertakes that orders passed to the principal will be paid for in due course by the buyers, is called a del credere agent, i.e. a credit risk is undertaken. Great care is necessary in defining the responsibilities and rights of this special type of agent, and when and how he is paid his del credere commission. Thus, the principal must be certain to instruct the collecting bank when a document is lodged with a del credere agent named as 'case of need'. In such a situation, if the buyer refuses the bill, does the agent have authority to take possession of the documents and/ or the goods?

It must be stressed that a wide variety of types of agents exist and the foregoing are the primary ones. Moreover, one must bear in mind that there are certain similarities in the role of the agents, confirming houses and export houses. The latter two are described later in this chapter.

It is appropriate, however, when examining the role of the agent, to consider the distributor. For example, the manufacturer markets some of his products in some territories through commission selling agents, but in other areas through importers/stockists/distributors, who buy the goods for their own account and earn a profit (not a commission) as a basis of their remuneration. The role of the distributor in the overseas market has become increasingly significant and the salient points of difference between the distributor and selling agent are set out in Table 9.1.

Table 9.1   Salient points of Rationale between agent and distributor

Agent	Distributor
Not financially involved	Buys for own account
Leaves importation to the buyers whose orders he passes to the principal	Imports the products
Is paid a commission at an agreed percentage on orders secured	Marks up the supply price to cover profit
Any service necessary is tendered by the buyer	Where necessary undertakes responsibility for the service
Carries no stock except for showroom purposes	Normally carries a stock
Unlikely to be involved in publicity except where required to give advice or report on impact	Likely to be involved in local publicity
May be authorized to engage sub-agents	Appoints sub-distributors
No control of resale prices	Controls selling prices in countries where retail price maintenance is possible
Leaves distribution to the buyers	Undertakes distribution in the market

It is appropriate to detail the clauses usually found in an agency agreement. The clauses may be varied to meet individual circumstances, and others may be added as required:

1 Details of parties to the contract: names, registered addresses and short title of each party.
2 Purpose of the contract. For example, it must state in specific terms that A appoints B as an agent and that B agrees to act in that capacity in accord with the terms of agreement.
3 Details of the products involved. For example, A will supply and B will sell the merchandise prescribed (give brand names).
4 Territory. The agreement must outline the geographical area over which the agent is given exclusive sales rights.
5 Precise duties of the principal.
6 Precise duties of the agent. This will incorporate any situation where other suppliers are dealt with, particularly if they are competitors.
7 Exceptions, reservations or restrictions imposed on one or both parties.
8 Method of quoting prices, e.g. whether FOB or otherwise.
9 Agent's purchase and resale. This clause will reflect the type of agency agreement involved as earlier described. For example, if the agent is buying for his 'own account' such as, when acting as a distributor, he may, subject to the manufacturer's approval: appoint sub-distributors; fix sale prices and

retail list price; and report back to the manufacturer. This clause requires careful consideration.

10 Consignments – particularly terms of delivery. This will embrace the terms under which the merchandise will be delivered, who pays for landing charges, duty, customs clearance, delivery, warehousing, stevedoring, insurance in warehouse/bond and accounting arrangements. Additionally, it should detail the goods, the arrangements for their release to the buyers and the disposal of stock on termination of the agreement.

11 Spares for general maintenance and service. This should also outline general arrangements for the disposal of the items on termination of the agency agreement.

12 Cost of cables, air mail letters and packages, telexes, and unusual expenses (not mentioned elsewhere in the agreement) and responsibility for their payment.

13 *Force majeure*. This clause excludes the principal from liability where *force majeure* prevents delivery from factory or, in respect of goods ready to leave, prevents despatch or causes diversion of the ship or aircraft carrying the cargo.

14 Permissive clause. The policy to be adopted in situations where the merchandise does not meet competitive products in styling, market suitability or price. This clause is usually found in a commission agency rather than sole distributorship and primarily arises where goods have been slow to sell and competitor's products have been superior.

15 Commission. The commission scale – whether it is a fixed or sliding rate and how it is to be credited/remitted. This requires careful deliberation, particularly at a time of floating currencies.

16 Accounting. Agent to undertake book-keeping and provide periodical statements including information on consignment of stocks, where applicable. Provision to be made for accounts to be audited/examined by the principal or his representative.

17 Overprice. This usually arises in contracts between merchant and agent concerning raw materials and semi-finished products. It embraces general conditions and whether the agent has the authority to try to overprice. Moreover, it details how the overprice is allocated between the two parties.

18 Publicity. A general agreement regarding sales literature and catalogues, local advertising and special propaganda. It should detail the apportionment of cost between the two parties to the agreement.

19 Report. The agent to submit market reports at prescribed times and likewise the principal to keep the agent informed of product development and trade generally. It will extend to production and marketing policy.

20 General conditions. Any general conditions not mentioned elsewhere in the agreement which either party wishes to introduce after mutual agreement. For example, to pledge the principal credit or not to start legal proceedings without the consent of the other party.

21 The duration of the agreement and notice of termination of agreement by either party of a prescribed period of, say, one or three months.

22 Breach of contract clause. This covers breach or default by either party or by the agent without mention of breach of principle. It also embraces a summary of determination upon liquidation, or compensation with conditions or attempts to assign benefits of contract.

23 Law and arbitration. This must indicate which country's law will apply and that disputes will be settled by arbitration in accordance with the terms prescribed in this clause. This avoids costly litigation and speeds up settlement.

24 Assignment. Neither party has the right to assign the benefits of the contract without the prior consent of the other. This may be qualified by a merger sub-clause showing what would happen if the original legal entity or party is merged into another legal entity.

The contract document finishes with space for the signature of the parties with an indication of capacity of signatories and witnesses, including formal application of the company's seal where appropriate.

In our consideration of the selection of the commission selling agency and the distributor it is appropriate to consider the points one would raise in an evaluation by questionnaire. We will deal with the commission selling agency first:

1 What is the constitution of the agency? It may be a sole trader, partnership or limited company.

2 When was the agency founded?

3 What is the capitalization of the agency, including the names and holding of the partner or directors together with their qualifications?

4 Give details of the names, ages and general background/qualifications of the sales personnel especially relevant to the manufacturer's product.

5 Give details of other agencies held. Is the manufacturer permitted to approach them?

6 Give details of the sales turnover of the other agencies held as detailed in item (5).

7 What is the average order secured in volume and value terms by commodity?

8 How many customers are regularly visited? Give details of the calls made per month per salesman and how often each customer is seen in a year.

9 What forms of promotion are advised, and what is the estimated cost?

10 What is the usual form of finance in the trade?

11 What is the agency rate of commission, and does it vary by sales volume etc?

12 Give details of any trade association or chambers of commerce of which the agency is a member.

13 Give details of the agency brokers.

14 Give any other information relevant to the commodity, such as joint publicity.

15 The agent's method of operation. For example, does he buy on his own account or keep stocks?

16 The overall size of the organization, including number of sales personnel and links with other companies.

17 Is the market coverage satisfactory, and specialist knowledge adequate?

18 Is the product range compatible with the exporter's range?

19 Is the selling organization, warehousing, administration, and communication system adequate? Is it computerized?

Details of a questionnaire to a distributor are given below:

1 What is the constitution of the distributor's business? It may be sole trader, partnership, or limited company.

2 When was the business founded?

3 Give details of capitalization of the business, including names and holdings of partners or directors and their experience and qualifications.

4 What other principals does the distributor serve, and is the manufacturer authorized to ask them to act as referees?

5 How are products of the manufacturers's type distributed in the overseas territory, and what are the arrangements for stocking, inland transport, appointing sub-distributors, show-rooms and after-sales service?

6 What are the distributor's financial conditions?

7 What are the distributor's terms for insurance of stock, goods in transit and credit risks?

8 Is it feasible to conduct any sales without using the distributor, and how would they be handled?

9 What support does the distributor require in any promotional activities, and what experience does the company have in this area?

10 Give details of the distributor's contact with wholesalers, retailers and other outlets.

11 Give membership details of trade associations, chambers of commerce etc.

12 Give details of the distributor brokers.

13 Give any other information relevant to the enquiry.

An important function of the export servicing of the agent is the method of controlling the agent: this is best undertaken through the agent contract agreement terms. Overall, the environment must be created to provide a good incentive for the agent in which to operate. This includes: good margins/commission level; marketing and promotional assistance; good communication; and quick response to enquiries and training of sales personnel. Regular visits are essential, and the opportunity should be encouraged for the agents to visit the exporter's manufacturing base and be present at the annual marketing strategy review meeting. Monthly reports on sales performance compared to budget and market developments should be provided by the agent.

Overall, both parties should fully understand their objectives, obligations and commitments. Adequate technical assistance should be provided and the exporter should have an input to all promotion material.

The Department of Trade and Industry, trade associations, and Chambers of Commerce are keen to help in obtaining a suitable agent/distributor for a manufacturer. The Department of Trade and Industry in so doing would contact the diplomatic post and obtain a shortlist for the manufacturer to consider. A personal visit to the prospective agent/distributor is most desirable and again the diplomatic post can give assistance during the visit.

The overseas status report service of the Department of Trade and Industry can also obtain information about a potential representative, and the UK exporter should check on the existence of local agency legislation. A number of countries have legislation which closely controls the arrangements for business relationships entered into by their nationals, where the nationals are to act as representatives of foreign principals. This aspect should always be investigated before concluding any agency agreement, since termination of the agreement may involve the UK exporter in considerable financial penalties and may subsequently impede further development within the market. The principal should engage a lawyer of the agent's country to help formulate the agreement.

The law relating to agency agreements is fully explained in Professor Schmitthoff's book *The Export Trade*.

When the exporter has obtained the data detailed in the preceding pages embracing the full use of desk research techniques including Trade Directories, the following procedure should be adopted:

1 A list of suitable agents/distributors situated in the overseas territory.
2 Compile in house discussions undertaken to compile a short list of potential agents/distributors featuring their profile including the name of the director or executive to be contacted.
3 Initial contact by telephone conducted in the buyer's language to determine whether agent/distributor interested; obtain more details about the company and formulate an impression of it. Details of product to be explained and brochure despatched and tentative visit date agreed.
4 Overseas visit planned and executed to determine suitability of agent/distributor and reaching a final decision. It is likely three or more agents/distributors will be seen and a day would be allocated to each to formulate impressions and negotiate draft terms before reaching a decision. The exporter would supply samples of the product to be sold and brochures – the latter translated into the buyer's language. The points raised in the questionnaire on pages 197–8 would be discussed.

5 A major factor in the final choice is the compatibility of the agent/ distributor company profile and the prospect of a good working professional relationship. Above all the need to have total commitment and being able to project the export company product adequately. Regular visits to the overseas territory by the exporter will be necessary to develop the business. Moreover, the agent/distributor can be expected to visit regularly the exporter's premises and meet key executives and the work force engaged in the manufacturing of the products exported.

6 Following evaluation of the overseas visit and maybe further checking out of the agent/distributor profile including their business performance and how they propose to handle the business, the exporter will make the final selection decision. This will involve negotiating the agreement, the salient points of which are found in pages 195–7.

9.4 CONCESSIONAIRES

These organizations operate as distributors, with a special authority granted by the manufacturer to work in a particular area of the market, usually on an exclusive basis. They tend to be expert in their field and have good contacts. The advantage to a manufacturer or exporter is that regular business is assured, but there is no direct contact with the buyer and the channels of distribution to that market will be restricted to the activities of the concessionaire. Thus a manufacturer might make what at first sight appears to be an opportunist sale to a merchant and then receive a repeat tender, coupled with a request for exclusivity for the particular territory where the merchant is active. This could, in turn, develop into a regular relationship to which the merchant became the concessionaire for that market.

9.5 CONFIRMING HOUSES

The basic function of a confirming house is to assist the overseas buyer by confirming, as principal, orders already placed, so that the exporter may receive payment from the confirming house as and when the goods are shipped. Any credit period the buyer may require is arranged and carried by the confirming house, which takes the credit risk over from the supplier. Basically, the confirming house may place the order with the supplier as agents on behalf of our principles, whereby the contract of sale is concluded direct between the supplier and the overseas buyer. Alternatively, the confirming house may buy on its own account from the supplier, making itself liable for the price and acceptance of the goods.

The order issued by the confirming house to the exporter is the 'official order'. In addition to making payment the confirming house usually arranges shipment and gives instructions to the exporter. Any communication from exporter to buyer should go through the confirming house. The confirming house is an export house and is used extensively by small and medium-sized companies involved in the export business.

9.6 CONSORTIA

These are groups of organizations which work together as a unit in order to achieve a common purpose. The consortium may operate as a group seller or a group buyer and sometimes will use a nominee in order to preserve anonymity during the negotiation of a contract. Consortia commonly tend to be engaged in bidding for large tenders, particularly where the size of the order is feasible only by employing the combined capacity of individual members.

Many consortia of this type have been set up on the initiative of the leading firms of consulting engineers, with the end products in the foreign country ranging from large dams, irrigation projects, railway modernization and extension, hospital projects, dredging undertakings and harbour installations, to such construction works in the electrical field as power generation, substations and television transmitters. Many of these projects are of the turnkey type (see section 10.4) and can best be financed in the UK with the aid of the ECGD explained in section 5.4.

Since each major undertaking of a consortium is likely to be so different in its nature from any other put out to tender by foreign governments, municipalities or other principals, it follows that many of these consortia are set up for only the one project and, when this is accomplished, they are then dissolved. Some of the parties may come together again for another undertaking, possibly then bringing in other members, but it does not often happen that the second venture is so exactly like the first one that the consortium can function again unchanged.

From the very nature of these undertakings it follows that the negotiations between the members of the consortium are protracted, difficult and complicated, before the nominee can submit the tender. This type of operation is always highly technical and, for every tender which is accepted, there is more than one where the contract is not secured. This involves having to write off the heavy expenses incurred, and the Department of Trade and Industry offer financial assistance to lessen such risk (see section 10.4).

9.7 EXPORT HOUSES

Export houses have two main functions:

1 As an export merchant buying goods outright and selling them on their own account. The merchant may buy goods from the exporter against the requirements of an overseas customer. Alternatively, the agent may buy the product and market it overseas. Finally the agent, by virtue of his international trading activities, may indulge in compensation trading, counter trade, switch deals or in any barter-type transaction.

2 As an agent, but retaining the role of the principal throughout the transaction. In such circumstances, the export house will promote the exporter's products overseas; carry the credit risk of the overseas buyer; attend to the physical and clerical work involved; stock goods at home and overseas on the exporter's behalf; follow up delivery dates or delays; deal with formalities overseas; and occasionally provide an after-sales service. Basically, the degree to which the foregoing work is undertaken by the export house will vary according to individual circumstances, and is a matter for negotiation. In the main, small or medium-sized export businesses find it more economical to engage an export house as their agent rather than to employ their own export staff or overseas representatives to undertake such work.

The payment for the foregoing services may be in the form of commission with the agent quoting the agreed export selling price to customers overseas. Alternatively, there may be some other form of remuneration to the export house negotiated by the exporter. For example, the export house may calculate the export price with the exporter on a 'cost plus profit margin' basis. The profit margin would be for the export house accountant, who is responsible not only for the product sales, but also its advertising, marketing, distribution, etc.

The export house may be a buying agent or merchant. The role of the export house varies, with the large ones undertaking virtually all the foregoing roles and the smaller ones offering a more specialized and less extensive service. Few, if any, export houses are prepared to handle all goods for all destinations. Most specialize in particular markets, types of goods, or in certain types of products for particular markets. Export houses are ideal for the small exporter, but the profit margins are low and the seller is not aware of the end user or the territories in which the product is sold. The export house may be operating through a network of agents overseas or direct with distributors. It is particularly ideal for the exporter who wishes to increase his production level and, through marginal pricing techniques, increase sales turnover. Examples include: cancellation of export orders or buyers having withdrawn import licence; recession in the home market and need to sustain production volume; spare capacity arising in season/cyclical situations; overseas market territory volume inadequate/uneconomic to develop direct market entry, but export house alternative maintains product presence; no export expertise in the manufacturing company.

In some overseas markets the only market entry is through the export house, and this applies in particular to Eastern Bloc nations. Export houses also feature in the counter trade business. The exporter interested further in export house activity is advised to contact the British Export Houses Association, the address of which is found in Appendix E.

9.8 FACTORING

The practice of exporters using factoring companies is very much on the increase. Their prime function is to administer the sales ledgers and collect payments once the goods have been shipped. Such factoring companies provide a complete range of services which cover those aspects of exporting and leave the manufacturer free to concentrate on export production and sales. For a small service charge of between 0.75% and 2% of turnover, they will provide multi-currency and multi-language sales accounting backed up by credit management which is exercised in the customer's country by the factor's own employees or agents. Also included in this service charge is 100% protection against losses due to the insolvency of the customer and, in some cases, protection against political risk and exchange rate fluctuations. Factoring cannot effectively meet the particular needs of every industry, and the most suitable companies are likely to have an expanding turnover in excess of £100 000 and to be selling consumer goods, light industrial products or services on short-term credit.

Basically, a factor buys invoiced debts from his client exporter and becomes responsible for sales accounting, collection and credit protection, usually guaranteeing payment on a specified maturity date. Additionally, the factor will, if required, make available up to 80% of the value of the goods invoiced immediately on shipment thus financing the credit taken by customers. This trading system is particularly popular in Europe, USA and Canada. Details of factoring companies are available from freight forwarders or major banks. A number of banks also offer factoring services.

9.9 GROUP SELLING

Group selling is the system employed when two or more manufacturers market their products jointly. Each principal continues their own individual activity as a manufacturer of the same merchandise or range of products, except that the goods may be modified or the range extended to meet the overseas requirements. Hence, the only continuity of interest between the various manufacturers is in connection with the marketing function. The various producers will not amalgamate or merge and there is no interchange of shareholding amongst the various constituent members of the group-selling organization.

For a group-selling organization to be established with any reasonable chance of success, it must have sufficient in prospective turnover to cover expenses and yield a modest profit. Moreover, the constituent manufacturers forming the organization must usually be well established with a good basic trade in the home market, but without a sufficient share or potential share in the export market to warrant operating alone, except on a token basis.

The products dealt in must either be from a cohesive group of manufacturers, normally handled by a specialist type of marketing channel, or they must represent a number of different types of similar merchandise of varying quality. Alternatively, the goods must be produced under conditions of competition but marketed by the group-selling organization on a basis which eliminates such competition.

The disadvantages of this type of organization are mainly concerned with the possible future dissolution of the group as a trading body. This type of venture is always prone to disagreements concerning the general conduct of business; the sharing of unforeseen expenses; failure to make the anticipated profits; turnover lost through delays in delivery; attempts to secure price ruling on date of delivery etc.

Furthermore, if the venture is a success, the more the turnover achieved by any one manufacturer, the more likely he is to want to break away from the group and work alone. If the venture is only a moderate success, there will always be overseas parties who will try to by-pass the group-selling organization and establish direct dealing with one or more of the constituent members.

9.10 LOCAL BUYING OFFICES

Many marketing organizations in foreign countries buy so much from UK sources that they find it financially advantageous to maintain buying offices in the UK (particularly in London) or a European office based in Paris/Brussels. In some instances, this office may be part of a chain of buying offices covering Europe. It is usual for the buying office to look after affreightment, insurance and finance. Local buying offices also represent overseas governments, especially those from Eastern Bloc or economies with serious hard currency or debt problems. Their objective is to obtain products at very competitive prices and despatch the goods using their national airline or shipping line, thereby saving hard currency. In some markets it is the only market entry option.

The advantages of a UK manufacturer dealing with the local buying office are: prompt acceptance of orders; saving time and cost in visiting the markets; avoiding outlay on publicity; and avoiding excessive correspondence with foreign markets. Against all this it must be reconciled that the buyers 'shop around' so keenly that their prices are highly competitive, leaving little or no margin of profit for the manufacturer. Moreover, the UK manufacturer has no details of the end user and no access to market research data on consumer needs/behaviour. Neither has he any control over where the product is sold overseas. The sales could even be competing with another sales outlet such as an agent or distributor. The local buying office usually appoints a freight forwarder to look after/coordinate all the distribution arrangements often under Ex Works of FOB terms.

9.11   MOBILE EXHIBITIONS

In many countries there is an increasing tendency to use a mobile exhibition as a means of promoting and retailing a product. It is usually less costly than the static stand unit as the mobile unit can be used on numerous occasions and has a greater sales potential in the market place. The design and style of the vehicle should conform to the image of the company fleet and thereby enhance the reputation of the product being demonstrated – a feature more difficult to realize through a static stand unit.

It is feasible to arrange demonstrations at trade fairs and exhibitions, but the organization and timing must be efficient so that the product image achieves maximum impact on the largest number of viewers. It may be more harmful to participate in an exhibition in an inefficient manner than not to participate at all.

Some manufacturers have achieved enhanced sales at times when potential buyers are visiting exhibitions, without taking a stand in the exhibition area; this is done where the cost of a stand is considered unduly high; where one is too late in applying; or where the facilities offered are not suitable for demonstrating the product. A mobile demonstration is then mounted beside the road into the exhibition along which the visitors travel; an alternative is to arrange a demonstration at the agent's showrooms and 'hand out' leaflets announcing it at the exit from the exhibition ground or building, or even to advertise in the exhibition catalogue.

9.12   MAIL SHOT ADVERTISING

Mail shot advertising is an ever-popular technique of attracting demand by post, and the criteria are basically the same as found in any other sales promotion aid. The mail shot must stand alone to attract the sale as it is usually impracticable for the product to accompany the advertising material.

The mail shot technique has a wide range of functions:

1 Increasing sales turnover by attracting a fresh demand.
2 Announcing a forthcoming sales promotion, possibly with the opportunity of a special pre-promotion price.
3 Introducing new products or improved versions of existing products.
4 Supplementing the effort of the salesman or distributor.
5 Reviving interest in former areas of demand which have lapsed.
6 By-passing the retailer and thus gaining a direct access and relationship with the buyer/end user.

The material despatched must be sufficiently comprehensive to explain the functions and merits of the product, but should ideally retain a touch of intrigue so that the addressee will feel compelled to investigate further. The basic contents of good direct mail literature are as follows:

1 An attractive but accurate description of the product or product range.
2 Full illustrative support – in colour where this will enhance the prospects of sale.
3 Concise details of the functions or use of the product, supported by diagrams where necessary.
4 A comprehensive list of size and colour ranges.
5 A detailed price list with full information about credit sale, or hire-purchase arrangements where applicable.
6 Facilities for ordering or obtaining the product, i.e. enclosure of an order form, reply-paid self-addressed envelope. If necessary, it can involve a visit by a representative in response to the order or potential order such as a demonstration of the product in the respondent's home. Alternatively, where the material is in support of distributors, there should be a list of local distributors stocking or handling the product.

Where the direct mail approach is used as a clear substitute for other forms of sales activity, the nature and content of the literature must reflect the image of the product and the company promoting it. Brand image may already be established through a successful sales record and other advertising media but it is nevertheless important that the same good impression be maintained, and careful use of existing, accepted slogans may do much to capture the confidence of the reader in respect of this new approach.

This emphasis, and the nature of the material, will differ according to the type of market and the order of priority of the factors which appeal in that particular area. In some cases the price may be paramount, while in others the emphasis may be on fashion, colour, size ranges, availability of spares, after-sales service, etc.

The details contained in the direct mail shot and the general treatment of the product will vary considerably according to the type of product. Consumer goods may appeal on grounds of price and novelty; consumer durables because of design and prestige; capital goods on account payment terms, delivery dates, and servicing agreement plus advanced technology; and finally services by virtue of their individuality and originality. The production of the direct mail letter is a most important consideration, for the impression it creates upon the reader will probably determine the degree of attention that is paid to the remaining material.

The most effective production method is the individually typed letter, but it is also the most expensive, and few companies are able to afford this method. However, computer technology has overcome this high cost factor and an increasing number of companies are adopting the computerized personal mail shot. Attention should be given to the envelope containing the direct mail material since this creates the first impression upon the client, the layout and personal approach, as well as the quality of the envelope itself, may determine whether the contents are examined or the whole package discarded into a wastepaper basket as 'just another circular'. Care must also be taken to avoid infringing any trade description act by the terms or contents of the brochure. The brochure should be compiled in the language of the market and this should be checked to ensure it is absolutely correct and conforms to local dialect when relevant. A poorly translated mail shot will only cause offence or humour, and will fail to realize any satisfactory level of sales.

For direct mailing to succeed, it is essential that accurate records are maintained of all direct mail shots; the list of addresses; those who respond and those who do not; full details of resultant orders, indications of future sales, etc. Mailing lists should be checked regularly and changes made where necessary. Advertising agencies can usually provide useful mailing lists relevant to the product being promoted and the customer profile likely to be interested. Most such mailing lists are computer-operated and controlled by specialized mailing companies.

9.13   STORE PROMOTIONS

An increasingly popular and effective way of market entry and further consolidation of an overseas market is for the exporter to become involved in a stores promotion. Basically, this involves a major retail outlet situated in an overseas territory undertaking special promotions with a specifically British theme. Such events might include demonstrations, displays, entertainers and other attractions with a British flavour. The main aim is increased sales of British goods in the longer term. It applies both to consumer goods or service industries. Overall the theme promotion is a very big event indeed and well promoted.

Details of such events are found in the Trade Promotions' guide, published quarterly in *British Business*, trade associations, Chambers of Commerce, and the BOTB Export Intelligence Service.

The lead time is about one year and details of the methods of offering a company's products or services are found in the advance publicity. Access may be through a buying office in the UK or direct to the overseas store. When responding to such an enquiry it is important to bear in mind the following:

1 Reply in the buyer's language.
2 Give details of price and delivery.
3 Ensure that the goods supplied comply with the local regulations.
4 Send samples where possible.
5 Provide any information about the export company which will help the application and product/service promotion.
6 In the event of an exporter having a local agent or distributor, he should be contacted about the store promotion and asked to assist as appropriate.

The store promotion is especially popular in North America, Western Europe, Japan, and many other developed and developing markets. Most promotions take place in the Autumn, which means that stores will be looking for suppliers before the end of the previous year, although some products, such as food, will have a shorter lead time. Stores start buying up to a year before the event. Store buyers placing orders for the promotion are likely to be visiting Britain during the established buying season – generally late winter to early spring – and, if the promotion store knows in advance of an Exporter's products, the seller will have a better chance of being included in the store promotion.

It is an excellent way of market entry and for established exporters developing new lines in the overseas territory.

9.14 OVERSEAS SEMINARS

Seminars offer a direct and effective technique for an exporter to increase overseas awareness of a company's product or services. When arranged in a country where the market prospects are known to be good, seminars or conferences provide the opportunity to bring together many influential people in a specific sector of interest and to cover 'face to face' every aspect of product availability, supply and market suitability.

Participation at an overseas seminar involves the exporter presenting a paper, usually alongside a number of other companies in the same or related field, each dealing with varying aspects. It is likely to involve each company presenting a paper in the following cost areas, and, for UK participants, the BOTB will meet up to 50% of the participation fee:

1 Hire of auditorium, public address equipment, projectors, and possibly simultaneous translation equipment.
2 The translation and reproduction costs of one session paper.
3 The translation cost of film scripts associated with the paper.
4 Lecture interpreters, projectionists and, possibly, hostesses for the lecture rooms.
5 Preparation, printing and distribution of folders, programmes, and invitations.
6 Local publicity, including press conference and an appropriate reception.
7 Hire of any necessary additional local supporting staff.
8 Cost of graphics and display materials, for example at the entrance to the auditorium.
9 Participation by one or two invited speakers who are internationally known.

Sometimes, a seminar can benefit from an on-the-spot exhibition, usually on a modest scale, involving graphics, models or portable products. This can involve: rental of exhibition space (normally $10m^2$ per exhibitor); a panel scheme, and supply of services including floor covering, display table and chairs, fascias and storage space; and additional furnishings, telephones, and interpreters for exhibitors.

Overseas seminars are initiated, conducted and promoted by a sponsor, and can lead to effective market exposure of a company's product/service in a professional environment presented to an intrinsically interested audience. The role of the sponsor or conference manager is basically an organizing role, and he acts as a channel of communication with participating firms. The sponsor formulates the timetable in consultation with the participants, and co-ordinates travel, hotel accommodation, publicity, and the level of fees. The extent of the sponsor's involvement will vary by seminar. The sponsor promotes the overseas seminar.

9.15 MULTINATIONAL COMPANIES

During the past decade there has been substantial growth in the number of multinational companies, and this trend will continue, particularly as the number of trading communities increases as selling is made easier. The following are some points about multinational companies to consider:

1 The prime advantage is that the exporter has complete control over the product in terms of distribution, marketing and selling. This enables the manufacturer to control his product effectively and not rely on agents/distributors etc.

2 Emerging from item (1) is the major advantage of controlling cost and price. For example the manufacturer may be so established in the market in terms of sales volume that he has a number of distribution depots at key sites which feed local retail outlets using their own transport fleet.

3 A number of countries provide favourable financial assistance to multinational companies which want to set up their own plant and distribution arrangements, thereby providing local employment for the nationals and generating more wealth in the country. Such companies usually bring much professional expertise which aids the development of advanced technology in less industrial countries. Conversely, various regulations exist in many countries regarding such developments.

4 Multinational companies often gain substantial tax benefits from setting up overseas plants/distribution networks. These may be assembly plants, manufacturing units, or a combination of the two, to produce the most acceptable product in the market place at a competitive price.

5 A major drawback is that the government could take over the assets of a multinational company with little or no adequate compensation. This may be through a policy of state nationalization of a particular industry. Particular attention needs to be given to this point but it usually arises with an unstable political situation. It tends not to arise so extensively within trading communities.

6 Multinational companies, through manufacturing the goods in the buyer's country, bring much wealth to that country and develop an industrial workforce experienced in the latest technology. They engender customer loyalty, as the buyer regards the product as a local one, and thereby permit market research to be conducted on an on-going and product-development concept basis. It also provides an opportunity for the multinational to export the product to neighbouring markets at competitive prices and usually under more favourable terms when compared to the goods being manufactured and transported from the multinational's home country.

Overall, the advantages tend to much outweigh the disadvantages and the number of multinational companies' development is likely to continue to increase.

9.16   TRAINING OF SALES PERSONNEL

The training of sales personnel – both the general salesman and the technical sales engineer – is very important. In the past, company policy has tended, regretfully, to ignore this area to the detriment of the development of overseas markets. The training of sales personnel involves a certain amount of theory and a great deal of practice, controlled by the guiding hand of experience. The successful trainee will learn: how to make the successful contact; how to convince the client to place an order, and how gradually to win the customer's confidence and trust. The salesman must be committed to the product, that is to say, he must be completely convinced of the product's merits, and be able to give due emphasis to the major factors of appeal. The salesman must understand the basic composition of the product, the variations in size and colour that are available; the future plans for the product or for any similar new product that is in prospect. In particular, the salesman must be able to identify the strengths of the product, particularly in comparison with competitive products. (This technique is also used in advertising.)

Overall, the export salesman must be trained to be his company's representative and educated to be its ambassador. He must be a good linguist, have a strong personality, and be articulate and a good negotiator, tenacious, with an appetite for hard work.

The sales engineer or service technician has an important role to play in the company's promotional activity overseas. He will visit the customer to carry out the general servicing and maintaining of the product in accord with the export sales contract. Moreover, he could become involved in selling similar products to other clients. After-sales service may be of great significance when negotiating a deal and business can be secured on the strength of an impressive servicing/maintenance clause. If the servicing work is not satisfactory because of inefficient briefing of the technician, the company's reputation will suffer, and this will have repercussions on long-term prospects of repeat orders or similar orders being secured from other companies in the market place.

As well as carrying out repairs and servicing, the technician must be an ambassador and representative for the company. Accordingly the technician should be well informed about the customer, his business, the role of the equipment being serviced within the company plant structure, and the general policy of his company towards the customer. Briefly, the training/ education of the sales engineer or technician should equip him to be efficient, unobtrusive, helpful and courteous. Such attributes will convey an image of reliability and responsibility to the customer. This confidence must be continually fortified with fresh demonstrations and reminders of the true value of established opinions. For most products the work of 'educating' the customer is conducted by the sales engineer through convincing loyalty to the product and interest to the customer. The technician, however, through the knowledge imparted to the customer about the function and most effective use of the product, also builds up a good relationship.

Whilst the foregoing is true in regard to most products, and especially of consumer goods where the 'customer' is the party who buys the product retail, the same does not apply where capital goods are being sold abroad or where a service is exported, e.g. a constructional project is being supervised in the foreign country. Here the customer is a government or public authority, but it is still vitally important to educate. The essence of the agent's function might well be to persuade the customer to send civil servants or executive officers to the UK so that the firm can educate them here as part of the negotiations for the sale.

9.17   INTERNATIONAL 0800 TELEPHONE SYSTEM FACILITY

A recently-developed method to increase overseas sales has been the introduction of the 0800 international call, as promoted by British Telecom (International). This involves the exporter paying for the international 0800 calls, and gives the potential overseas buyer access to the seller. For the local buyer, it makes telephone communication easy through the use of a simply-coded number, with the added benefit that the caller does not pay for the connection except from some overseas countries, where charges up to the local rate may be applied.

To the seller/exporter, it makes customer contact more effective, efficient and controllable. The facility provides the following features:

1 Callers are connected without any operator involvement.
2 The service is available from most of the major world markets.
3 The 0800 calls are free of charge to callers from most countries, and are charged at only the local rate from others.

4 It is a simple service to use, from virtually any phone in any country at any time.

5 An 0800 number may also be connected to a modern data-transmitting device (e.g. a fax machine) for the instant transmission of hard copy.

6 It improves the customer service.

7 It stimulates sales.

8 It tests markets, especially when provided in conjunction with an overseas promotion.

9 It centralizes operations, concentrating all calls into one office.

10 It streamlines communications.

11 It reduces the cost of servicing the market through fewer visits, and develops a closer buyer/seller relationship. This is in part due to the fact that 0800 calls are cheaper than standard international calls.

12 The facility may be transferred to another number when the office is unmanned.

Overall, the system is cost-effective, and permits of the remote testing of overseas markets. Moreover, it provides valuable market information and sales leads without incurring expensive risks. It develops customer loyalty through the provision of added value to the product, and also enhances the company image. Furthermore, it increases the speed and scale of the customer response to advertising, enhancing the sales derived therefrom. Finally, it cuts out the middle man, improves communications, develops smoother operations, improves customer service and yields considerable financial savings.

10 *Organizations and resources which facilitate export marketing*

Our study of export marketing would not be complete without consideration of the numerous organizations and resources which exist to help both the UK exporter and overseas traders. It must be appreciated that export practice is a complex operation and numerous specialists operate in this field. Details of the more important marketing resources are found in this chapter, but the list should not be regarded as exhaustive. The reader should particularly Chapter 14 (Export Facilitation Organizations) in *Elements of Export Practice* (see Appendix A).

10.1 BRITISH OVERSEAS TRADE BOARD

The British Overseas Trade Board is the main organization of this type in the UK. In broad terms it is a government agency striving to support and stimulate the sale of UK products overseas (it receives an annual grant from the Department of Trade and Industry).

The BOTB is divided into four overseas trade divisions: the first, involving projects and export policy, is the focus of government support for firms and consortia chasing major project business overseas. It also includes export financing and the use of aid and general export policy; the next division embraces the markets, and their opportunities in North America, South East Asia and the Far East, and China and Hong Kong; the third overseas trade division encompasses the branches of export promotion policy, fairs and promotions, export promotions, exports to Europe, Eastern Europe, and export data; and, finally, the fourth division includes the Middle East, Latin America, the Caribbean and Australasia, and Sub-Saharan African markets. They are based in London, and are supported by regional offices in Newcastle, Manchester, Leeds, Nottingham, Birmingham, London, Bristol, Glasgow, Reading, Cardiff and Belfast: exporters are urged to approach their regional office initially to resolve their export enquiry.

The Department of Trade and Industry works through the BOTB in providing export services.

10.2   EXPORT INTELLIGENCE SERVICE

The Export Intelligence Service (EIS) is a computerized system designed primarily to give the potential exporter details of a specific trade opportunity/export order in an overseas market. It is run by the Department of Trade and Industry, and is available only to subscribers who specify the products/services in which they require details. The EIS gathers information provided by Diplomatic Service Posts and other sources worldwide. The computer data can access information received over the previous three years, thereby providing useful research data. The data are faxed or posted daily to the EIS subscriber as the data are received from overseas. EIS covers every country in the world, and has 10 000 products or services.

10.3   INWARD MISSION SCHEMES

Another way to promote an exporter's product is to participate in an inward mission scheme. Under such a project, groups of companies invite overseas businessmen and journalists who can influence exports to visit the UK. This is usually arranged through a trade association sponsorship or a Chamber of Commerce, and the number of delegates varies from ten to twenty persons. The arrangements usually have the following features:

1 The sponsor must ensure that the programme is well organized with a proper reception on arrival and opportunities to meet the media throughout the mission. Above all, adequate time must be given to meet and discuss the products with the UK businessmen and possibly include factory visits when relevant.
2 Companies and export salesmen participating in the mission must ensure that an adequate number of demonstration products are available and that they conform to the overseas market technical specification. Ideally company personnel must be multilingual, especially the sales and technical personnel. If this is not the case, interpreters should be available who are knowledgeable in the company products and especially in the technical areas. An adequate supply of brochures and technical manuals must be provided in the language of the overseas market. All sales personnel should be able to quote readily the sales price and delivery date and the export sales contract terms.
3 The programme should be well planned in consultation with all those involved to ensure that maximum benefit is gained from such a visit in terms of confirmed export orders. Adequate time must be given for relaxation and entertainment of the inwards mission personnel. Special attention needs to be given to the booking of comfortable hotels in a

congenial atmosphere, conducive to entertaining business clients. Overall a lead-time of six to nine months is recommended.

4 The UK organizer must liaise closely via the Department of Trade and Industry with the UK diplomatic post for useful guidance on personnel to be invited to form the inwards mission. In fact, the diplomatic post in the overseas market usually sends out the invitations on behalf of the organizer. It is usual to engage the services of the Overseas Visitors Bureau to formulate the programme, as they specialize in this area.

5 Great care must be taken in formulating the programme and the organizer should ideally contact the Department of Trade and Industry at a very early stage to take maximum advantage of their financial support available for such projects. Close liaison should be maintained with the Chamber of Commerce UK relevant to the overseas market and relevant trade associations. Also the ECGD should be consulted. The inwards mission should be sponsored by a non-profit making association to qualify for the Department of Trade and Industry financial assistance such as an export club, trade association, or local Chamber of Commerce.

The inwards mission scheme is an ideal way for the exporter at low cost to show off his shop window to would-be overseas importers and, in addition to make many useful social contacts.

10.4 MAJOR OVERSEAS CAPITAL PROJECTS

An area of major development in recent years is the provision of the overseas project: this has been particularly evident under the turnkey arrangements. This usually involves a group of companies, often operating on a consortium basis, in an attempt to win a large overseas contract. Considerable expense is incurred in formulating a tender for such a project and the BOTB offers financial assistance in the following circumstances with the appropriate conditions:

1 In the pre-contractual phases of package or turnkey projects: special consideration is given if the project is particularly significant in terms of the market or product development.
2 For a feasibility study likely to lead to the type of projects described in item (1).
3 For consultancy studies which are likely to lead to the type of project detailed in item (1).

Also available within the Department of Trade and Industry scheme is the Overseas Project Board – a body of senior businessmen and women with practical experience of overseas projects – which gives general advice on the formulation of policy in the major overseas project field. It also advises the Government on how best to support ventures in this area.

Another area of development is the provision of goods and services under the aid programmes administered by leading international agencies. This involves programmes from the World Bank; International Bank for Reconstruction and Development (BRD); the International Development Association (IDA); the Inter-American Development Bank (DB); the Asian Development Bank (ADB) and the European Development Fund (EDF). Such information is obtained by the commercial departments of British Embassies and High Commissions. The information is disseminated through the EIS.

The Department of Trade and Industry, through the Projects and Export Policy Division, also have similar details of projects from multilateral agencies including the African Development Bank/Fund, the Caribbean Development Bank (CBD), the European Investment Bank (EIB), the Middle East and United Nations' agencies.

10.5   OUTWARD MISSIONS

The prime purpose of an outward mission is to encourage UK exporters to visit overseas markets, either to explore and assess the prospects of selling their goods or services, or to reinforce their overseas market effort.

The Department of Trade and Industry, under prescribed conditions, offers generous financial assistance to exporters participating in such an outward mission which is sponsored by a non-profit making body such as a trade association, export club or Chamber of Commerce. The number of participants varies between ten and twenty, and the scheme involves products or services which have promise in a market, or to planned promotions, which have been selected for official support. The scheme is ideal for the smaller or medium-sized exporter who wishes to break into a new market at low cost or is considering revisiting a market which has been largely ignored in the recent past.

Planning an outwards mission for a group of exporters joining together to visit a particular area is undertaken by the sponsor (e.g. an export club) and the following features are relevant:

1 It is ideal to have equal participation by first-time visitors and those who are revisiting the market.
2 It is sensible to have an 'on the spot' briefing from the COI (Central Office of Information, section 10.9) diplomatic post on the first day in the market, coupled with some form of reception.
3 The diplomatic post should be made fully aware in advance of the purpose of the outward mission.
4 It is possible for a participant to combine the outward mission trip with a visit to other clients in the area. The participant would still be eligible for the Department of Trade and Industry financial support providing two thirds of his time was with the outwards mission.

5 A briefing meeting is held prior to departure and a secretary and leader appointed to the group. At such a discussion the itinerary will be agreed. The itinerary will feature a reception shortly after arrival which will be arranged by the diplomatic post. Usually the diplomatic post is happy to help construct a guest list for such a reception and also arrange for the media to be present. Such a start to a mission can allow the exporter to meet suitable clients and establish useful contacts. The briefing meeting will also discuss occasions during the visit at which the secretary and leader will meet the media. Again the diplomatic post can greatly facilitate such arrangements. The visit should also provide for relaxation and entertainment.

6 It is vital that every member in the outwards mission is thoroughly professional with regard to the price, delivery dates, specification, method of sale, cargo delivery terms, multilingual brochures/literature concerning the product, etc.

7 A report on the outward mission results should be compiled on completion of the overseas visit.

There is no doubt that the outward mission is a good marketing facility for exporters at modest cost, under the Department of Trade and Industry arrangements. It is one which should prove well worth while, particularly for new exporters.

10.6   TRADE FAIRS OVERSEAS

In recent years the overseas trade fair has become increasingly important. It is an excellent way of promoting one's product or range of products at modest cost to a very receptive audience of visitors to the trade fair, who usually come with the firm intention of placing orders. It may be operated by a trade association, Chamber of Commerce or the Department of Trade and Industry (the latter two are the most common operators). Many exporters are now using this facility as their first promotion in a specified overseas market, with resounding success as it is so professionally organized.

It is paramount the right event at the right time is chosen: the priority is the market and the segment the exporter wishes to target and not the exhibition. Exhibition organizers will be able to provide the exhibitor with facts and figures relating to visitors and categories from the last event and the kind of areas where the exhibition is being marketed. Contact your overseas agent to seek his advice and the profile the exhibitors stand should follow. It is essential the exhibition generates adequate interest of the exporter clients and the stand has a clear message to convey to its visitors. It may be a product launch; extension of the product range; improved design and reliability of existing product range; or simply the first experience at an exhibition. It is fundamental that the company has adequate stock available to meet the orders generated by the exhibition, otherwise the result will be counter-productive. Planning and research are essential ingredients to a successful exhibition participation. Planning embraces the complete profile of the exhibition involvement, embracing stand management, budget plan, personnel resources, products, stand layout, brochures/literature, etc. A project manager appointed at the outset and responsible for the stand involving in-house discussions and briefings is the most effective way to process the matter through an action plan. An area which requires particular attention is adequate research of the event/location. Ideally, the exhibition site should be visited by the exporter or his overseas agent to determine the best position and those to avoid. Also to determine the exhibition layout and the way traffic will be moving both in the aisles and on the stand. It is desirable to avoid the tiny corner stand between the cloakrooms and the outside door used by contractors. Early booking is desirable.

The BOTB provides space and a shell stand, or other appropriate display facilities, at attractive rates to firms taking part in group displays of UK products at overseas trade fairs. In addition, for events taking place outside Western Europe, the BOTB provides assistance towards each firm's travel costs under prescribed conditions.

Under the BOTB Joint Venture scheme, a number of firms in an industry participate in a collective presentation of UK goods or services at a specialized trade fair overseas under the sponsorship of an approved trade association, Chamber of Commerce, or other approved non-profit making body. To ensure suitable impact, the minimum number of firms acceptable in a joint venture is normally ten. For planning reasons, proposals for joint ventures should be made at the earliest possible date, and certainly no later than nine months before the opening of the event.

Exhibitors in joint ventures or UK pavilions in international trade fairs, and in all UK fairs overseas are normally provided, by the BOTB, with a single display shell consisting of floor covering, side and rear walls, a name panel, plus general lighting and the necessary basic internal fittings such as counters and display panels. Also provided are the essential subsidiary services such as electric power and, if available, compressed air, water and waste disposal facilities.

It is most important that the resources of the trade fair are fully professional in layout, operation and management to maximize the impact in the market place; the following guidelines should be adopted wherever possible:

1 A specialist display designer should be engaged. Many contractors maintain a design studio and will undertake the design and production of stand interiors often planned with a minimum of work on the site.

2 A unified group presentation at an overseas trade fair is often more powerful and effective than several smaller individual units. The fascia is part of the stand design and company names will be of a standard typeface and colour to ensure continuity of treatment of the UK area. This does not

prohibit the company featuring its own insignia or logo inside the stand. All graphic information must be prepared in good time for the display unit. Moreover, photographs, diagrams, illustrations and brochure text need particular attention. Captions should preferably be typeset (not sign-written) and reproduced to a size large enough to be comfortably read from a distance of two metres; headings should be larger and bolder. Photographs or enlargements should be wet- or dry-mounted on a card or panel. Pins and adhesive tape should be avoided.

3 The display stand should be well thought-out in terms of layout and visual presentation. It should not be overcrowded with furniture and displays, but be so designed to ensure it focuses the buyer's interest on the most important feature.

4 Particular attention should be given to a well-lit stand to aid good visual presentation. The skilful use of spotlights can be effective to highlight key exhibits at low cost.

5 The electrical current supply at some overseas exhibitions can fluctuate far more than in the UK, and remedial measures need to be taken. Such facilities must be resolved at an early stage at the exhibitors' meetings, otherwise the organizers of the trade fair may impose penalty charges.

6 Stand furniture should be selected carefully and ideally all exhibitors with the UK group should obtain their furniture from the same source. The use of spare furniture from local resources can ruin the effect of the stand.

7 The selection of personnel on the stand is a key factor in the successful outcome or otherwise of participating in a trade fair. It is essential that they are fluent in the appropriate languages (if English is not the predominant language) or a fully qualified interpreter should be provided. Basically, potential buyers are attracted to the stand by professional personnel who are well informed and courteous and authorized to make decisions on the spot. Ideally all the staff should arrive on site at least 24 hours before the fair opens, and earlier if the exhibits are difficult to display. Personnel should be provided with adequate funds to cover unforeseen minor but essential expenditures which can arise during an exhibition. If agency personnel are going to staff the stand, it is essential that they are fully aware of the exporter's company policy and the terms under which the stand is provided (e.g. under BOTB sponsorship). To conclude, the stand personnel must present the most favourable image possible and thereby ensure it makes the maximum impact in the market place. In particular, any queries or order opportunities are settled on the spot, and when this is not possible they are promptly followed up. Ideally they should be fluent in the buyer's language.

8 Most specialized trade fairs attract buyers from many countries and the staff should be able to quote delivery dates, and price in foreign currencies, under varying cargo delivery terms.

9 To maximize the benefit of exhibiting at a trade fair, it is desirable that

research be conducted first into the product potential in the markets concerned. Various commercial intelligence sources exist involving the COI, trade associations, Chambers of Commerce and Department of Trade and Industry.

10 It is desirable to have an agent to represent the exporter's interests in the market place, and in particular to contact local businessmen with a view to their visiting the stand during the exhibition. The appointment of an agent requires careful consideration to ensure the ideal one is chosen. Guidance can be given from a wide variety of sources including trade associations and chambers of commerce.

11 The exporter must check out all the technical and safety requirements of the product to be exhibited and advice can be sought from the THE as described in section 10.12. Product design should also be given attention (see section 4.10).

12 It is essential that trade literature and other copy for the exhibition, including exhibit captions, are produced in the language of the markets. This requires experienced and well qualified translators who are aware of local variations in language and colloquialisms. Ideally the local agents should see the text being printed or alternatively provide the translation themselves. The distribution of literature which is inaccurate, misleading and sometimes ridiculous can lead to the most unfavourable sales results. Moreover, all the literature should be on the stand from the day it opens.

13 The products should arrive at the trade fair in good time for installation before the opening. This requires special attention – late arrival of the exhibition merchandise can produce disastrous results. An experienced freight forwarder should be engaged to facilitate the programmed arrival of the goods.

14 Adequate publicity of the exporter's participation in the trade fair should be given, using all possible media. Again, the Chamber of Commerce, trade association or COI which is sponsoring the event can help. Equally, publicity should be sought on orders placed at the trade fair (see COI, section 10.1).

15 The stand will reflect the microcosm of the exporter's product/organization. Hence the need to be completely professional and reflect the company image adequately.

The following points are relevant to stand management techniques:

1 Avoid placing unnecessary obstructions on the stand – it impedes access and it discourages the visitor.

2 Stand personnel must not have a defiant guard-like stance on the edge of the stand.

3 Respond to traffic patterns and do not group personnel together: keep personnel well dispersed throughout the stand-contact areas.

4 Seating should not be occupied by brochures, exhibits or staff and personnel should avoid standing in a position which obscures exhibits or prevents access onto the stand.

5 All staff should wear badges and avoid pouncing on the visitor immediately. Moreover items must not be left on the floor which could be dangerous.

6 Personnel must display real enthusiasm/commitment to a product and ensure literature is attractively displayed and not in precise lines or geometric patterns.

7 Give the visitor time to focus on a particular item to generate interest, and do not neglect anyone: if the stand personnel are already busy, give an acknowledgement in the form of a wave, smile or nod.

8 When introducing a visitor to other members of the stand representatives, introduce them not only by name, area, and title but also recall the conversation that has already taken place. Avoid other personnel time by unnecessary introductions, and when discontinuing unproductive interviews, introduce the client to another member of the stand team.

The trade fair is an excellent market entry option and is especially ideal for the small exporter fresh to the market. It permits the exhibitor to display his products alongside his competitors.

Extensive planning is required by the exhibitor in regard to the participation at an international trade fair/exhibition. This involves appointing personnel to man it – usually the local representative should be part of the team, contact organizers to book sites and a supplier to provide/arrange stand layouts and equipment; draw up a list, in consultation with the local representative, to mail shot inviting visits to the stand; provide adequate publicity, with prices and in the appropriate languages, and take publicity space in the exhibitors' handbook.

Ideally a co-ordinator should be appointed with overall charge of planning and logistics. The co-ordinator should have the necessary authority to ensure that colleagues in other departments in the company make any deadlines set. It will include particularly the following:

1 Check that the facilities required to exhibit the products will be available on the exhibition site e.g. power, water, compressed air, waste disposal, adequate ceiling height, and floor loading.

2 Determine advertising needs, including compatibility with the market and timescale of translation and printing deadlines.

3 Determine stand exhibits and ensure they comply with local regulations.

4 Process shipping arrangements, including documentation and liaise with production department to ensure deadlines are met.

The export marketing manager, who is usually responsible for organizing the trade fair stand, will prepare an action plan with the co-ordinator which will be subject to the budget constraints. Company policy must decide at which trade fair(s) to exhibit and in so doing have regard to the cost and benefits which flow from each venue. It is regarded by many buyers as the exporters' shop window and failure to appear is interpreted as a lack of commitment to the market. Moreover, attendance gives the exporter the opportunity to meet existing customers and develop new ones in the most favourable environment with many products on display.

Although it may be regarded as expensive for the 3–5 day venue, the exporter is likely to see more clients in the period than compared with a visit to clients' premises. The stand should be equipped with a telephone, and the hotel at which the stand team reside equipped with all the secretarial resources including telex and fax machines. All enquiries received on the stand and unable to be processed at the time should be dealt with later in the day by communicating with the exporter's headquarters. Such enquiries should not build up to be dealt with when the stand personnel return home, as this will create a bad image with the client and market. Ideally, as few unresolved queries should remain when the trade fair team return home. Hence the need to ensure the stand personnel are competent and experienced in the product/service and the overseas market involved. All visitors to the stand displaying intrinsic interest in the product or service should be recorded to build up a portfolio of clients to develop a viable and effective mailing list.

The stand manager should produce a report on the effectiveness of the event/venue which may include numbers of visitors, orders secured, enquiries processed, new clients, competition analysis, market profile analysis, personnel/secretarial resources and their adequacy, future participation at the trade fair/exhibition; adequacy of stand, travel, hotel accommodation, etc., and, finally, an overview of the situation. It must be borne in mind that stand visitors will not only include those from the host country, but also from other nearby and distant overseas territories. A debriefing meeting should take place with relevant personnel/departments following the return of the stand personnel to the export office, and an action plan formulated.

10.7 MARKETING ROLE OF GERMAN, AMERICAN AND DUTCH CHAMBERS OF COMMERCE AND INDUSTRY IN THE UK

In the UK there are a number of chambers of commerce whose specific role is to develop trade between two specific countries or regions (see Appendix D). These form an important area in the development and marketing of overseas trade, and we will examine three such leading London-based organizations: the German Chamber of Commerce and Industry (UK), the American Chamber of Commerce (UK) and the Netherlands–British Chamber of Commerce.

10.7.1   German Chamber of Industry and Commerce in UK

The German Chamber of Industry and Commerce (UK) has 1315 members more or less equally divided between British and German members (if one regards German subsidiaries in the UK as German members). The German Chamber is founded on the principle of the indivisibility of international commerce and industry. Put in simpler terms, this means one's own prosperity is involved in the prosperity and well-being of one's trading partners. This policy is spelt out in the Chamber's Memorandum of Association, where the first of its objects is 'to study, promote, protect and extend the industrial and commercial relations between individuals, firms, companies, corporations, institutions and associations of Germany and the United Kingdom'. Since its inception the German Chamber has always stressed that it promotes two-way trade and investment, and its organization reflects this.

There are two market departments, one covering the German market and one the British market which offer advice, statistical information and even market reports. Sometimes these market reports are specifically commissioned and charged for accordingly. Others are general market sector reports which are published by the Chamber and may be bought (naturally at a preferential price for members). The legal department gives advice on commercial and industrial law in both countries as it affects businessmen. Whenever there is a general or recurring enquiry, then the legal department publishes a monograph on the subject concerned which is then available to the public at large.

The Co-operation and Agency Department acts as a form of 'marriage bureau' between German and British business interests. The simplest case is that of a firm (the principal) seeking a representative or agent in the partner's land. Often the search is initiated by the would-be representative. There are other variations on the co-operation theme, including joint ventures, licences, production rights, acquisitions and so on. Members of the Chamber may place their enquiries in the bulletin free of charge but non-members are charged a fee.

The Industrial and Social Affairs Department has special responsibility for liaison with the Federation of German Industries (BDI) and with the Confederation of British Industry (CBI). It also advises on industrial location and investment and organizes or co-operates in inward and outward investment missions. These services are given equally to both countries.

Finally, there is a Commercial Information Department which serves as the interface between the Chamber and the general public. These general enquiries are often answered by referring to the extensive library of reference books.

The Chamber also publishes a number of books. Additionally there are the quarterly Trade Enquiry Bulletins and the Chamber Journal called *British–German Trade*, which is published ten times per year. It is widely read in both partner countries and articles are extensively quoted because of the unique British–German dimension of the facts, statistics and conclusions contained in these articles. With the journal *British–German Trade* goes the *Chamber Newsletter* which spotlights other Chamber activities and events. These have included business luncheons open to members and their guests, and speakers include prominent industrialists and politicians. Export seminars with a panel of six or seven, including member companies as well as Chamber staff, are also held.

It is against this trading background that the German Chamber of Industry and Commerce offers its services to any businessperson wishing to enter or increase their share of this bilateral trade.

10.7.2 American Chamber of Commerce (UK)

The American Chamber of Commerce (UK) is the leading organization in the UK representing companies and individuals who share a direct and active interest in furthering and improving trade and investment between the USA and the UK. It was founded in 1916 and the Chamber is an independent non-profit-making organization which receives no government subsidy. It is sustained by the subscriptions of its members and by funds generated through its activities. The roles of the Chamber are detailed below:

1 To influence, persuade and inform governments, legislatures, regulatory agencies, the media and the public, of the problems and requirements of business enterprises conducting trade and investment between the USA and the UK.
2 To inform, educate and help its membership improve their performance in the current UK–USA business environment.
3 To act as a meeting place where executives from UK and USA companies can exchange ideas and created new opportunities for trade and investment. Also, to act as a conduit for closer relations between management, trade unions and government officials.

The Chamber has the following prime facilities and activities:

1 A research department which handles specific inquiries from members and is available to research and prepare reports and surveys on industrial and commercial matters.
2 A library for members' use. It includes a wide variety of UK and USA trade directories, telephone directories of principal USA cities, and up-to-date records of the firms representing major USA interests in the UK.
3 The Chamber's committee structure enables the organizations to keep the

membership informed on a wide variety of subject areas and issues of general interest. These specialist committees include legislation, taxation, industrial relations, international trade and direct investment; they monitor developments in their interest areas, help formulate the policies to be adopted by the Chamber and inform the Chamber as a whole on matters of concern. Whether the members actually take part in committee activities and, as a result, help formulate and implement policy, or simply gain from the information received, they derive immeasurable benefit from the existence of this committee structure.

4 Lobbying on both sides of the Atlantic on issues affecting its membership is becoming an increasingly important, and successful, part of the Chamber's activities.

5 The *Anglo-American Trade Directory* is published regularly by the Chamber, and is the most complete and up-to-date listing available of UK and USA companies with close transatlantic ties (e.g. parent companies, subsidiaries, affiliates, agents, distributors). This directory is unique in that it is a comprehensive listing of the UK and USA companies responsible for a very large proportion of USA/UK trade and investment. It is distributed free to members.

6 The Chamber's monthly magazine is called *Atlantic*, and features substantive articles and editorial comment on subjects of interest to the UK and USA business communities.

7 A directory of Chamber members, with complete details, together with a listing by business or professional groupings is supplied free to members on a regular basis.

8 The Chamber is well known for its regular monthly luncheons, to which are invited prominent speakers from business or public life on both sides of the Atlantic who address the Chamber members and their guests on an international topic of current interest.

9 Market place luncheons are designed to allow member companies to 'sell' their products and services to each other as well as provide an additional opportunity of getting together.

10 The Chamber holds regular informal functions with senior politicians, business leaders and government officials from the USA and the UK, at which members are invited to listen to a short presentation which is followed by informal 'off the record' discussion. These meetings are exceedingly informative and are of great value to the members.

11 Regular seminars and workshops are held on subjects of much interest to international trade and marketing.

Netherlands–British Chamber of Commerce

The role of the Netherlands–British Chamber of Commerce is to develop reciprocal trade between the Netherlands and the UK. It is organized in five divisions:

1 The General Division deals with group telex, continuous contracts, Anglo–Dutch trade bulletins, trade information, directories, exhibition information, mailing services, translations, membership matters and computers.

2 The marketing department is the most important of the Chamber, and deals with market research, market reports, agent's search, names and addresses, buyers' panels, periodicals, mini surveys, mail spot texts and trade announcements. The marketing department is bilingual, and offers a broad range of practical marketing facilities involving all aspects of Anglo–Dutch trade. It deals with market research, embracing market size, market structure, competition, distribution patterns, market preferences and trends, and advertising media. The Chamber also has extensive research staff resources and undertakes the selection of agents/distributors for clients/ members.

3 The management department deals with language training, a critique panel dealing with the differences in cultural and behavioural attitudes between the two countries, a clearing house scheme, mergers/joint ventures, licensing research, trade regulations, tariffs and customs, financial reports, debt recovery, taxation and investment.

4 The publicity department covers all aspects of trade between Holland the UK. It produces the Chamber magazine, monthly, which has a circulation of 10 000 monthly.

5 The regional department deals with matters emerging from the Regional Advisory Committee. This embraces the Scottish Advisory Committee, North West Advisory Committee, Anglia Advisory Committee, British Business Association, South West Advisory Committee and Netherlands Regional Committee.

There is no doubt that such Chambers, and others which are listed in Appendix E, are making an increasing contribution to international trade between the individual countries concerned.

10.8   LONDON CHAMBER OF COMMERCE AND INDUSTRY

The London Chamber of Commerce was founded in 1881 and is today the largest Chamber in the UK. It has two main functions: to protect the domestic trade interests of commerce and industry in London and the South East; and to develop the international trade of all UK companies. An examination will be made of the latter.

The Chamber has a membership of some 9000 firms covering all business sectors. Its operations are divided into departments: international, export services, home affairs, economic, press, administration, membership, finance and trade sections.

The London Chamber issues export documents, and these include primarily certificates of origin, ATA carnets (international customs documents to cover the temporary export of certain goods), national standard shipping notes, cocoa certificates and the certification of commercial invoices. The Chamber is the UK guarantor for ATA carnets. The Chamber deals with a wide range of enquiries concerning customs, regulations, and legislation, both in the UK and throughout the world. It also deals with tariffs and the general rules and conditions governing the movement and finance of exports and imports. A major function is the promotion of overseas trade, and this is a feature of all Chambers throughout the UK.

The London Chamber is one of the most active trade promotion organizations in the UK. These activities are the responsibility of the International Division and its 28 market sections. The sections, which are grouped together into six area divisions, bring together member firms with common interests in a specific geographical market. The five overseas divisions include Africa and the Middle East, Asia and the Pacific, Eastern Europe, Western Europe and the Western Hemisphere. The sixth division deals with requirements of overseas members. Each of the six area divisions has a separate membership. A fortnightly digest of commercial intelligence is prepared for each of the five overseas divisions, summarizing trade developments and acting as a link with members. A full programme of conferences, meetings, missions and other activities is organized, and advice and information on overseas markets and the UK is available – particularly market reports, market research, statistics, marketing techniques and marketing aids available from the Department of Trade and Industry.

The information department of the Chamber also gives details on: customs and regulations; openings for trade; translation bureau; members' library; telephone enquiry service; and special certification. Additionally, the Chamber offers extensive training facilities, and conducts its own examinations in many commercial subjects including international trade.

The exhibition department organizes UK participation in overseas trade fairs, as joint ventures with the Department of Trade and Industry. Special services for smaller companies going into export include: market feasibility studies; trade missions from small firms; and group market research schemes. A business travel service is also provided which aims to provide a comprehensive service of business travel schemes to all parts of the world.

In tracing the internationally orientated activities of the London Chamber of Commerce and Industry, it must be borne in mind that it is the largest in the UK. Most major cities and towns have a Chamber, but the extent of their services is limited compared to the London Chamber, although those found in the major cities such as Birmingham, Liverpool, Manchester,

Glasgow and Edinburgh offer comprehensive services. The exporter is well advised to contact his nearest Chamber if he is seeking advice on any aspect of international trade (see Appendix D).

10.9 CENTRAL OFFICE OF INFORMATION

The Central Office of Information (COI) provides publicity material to meet the requirements of other government departments, which are themselves responsible for determining policy. It is the government publicity agency, and supplies UK information services overseas with material which reaches people in most parts of the world. Acting on behalf of the Foreign and Commonwealth Office, and the BOTB, it deploys every medium of publicity except paid advertising to maintain and increase the industrial prestige of the UK abroad.

The main purpose of the publicity is to project UK industry overseas as a whole. However, the hard facts approach used by the COI also brings results for individual firms. Some have reported more than 200 overseas enquiries from a single story within a few weeks of its publication. The COI is particularly interested in news leads, pictures, publications or films about the launching of a new product, process, or service; a notable success in research or development; a large or unusual export order; membership of an outward trade mission; participation in overseas or UK exhibitions and other promotions; the newsworthy opening of a new factory in the UK or overseas; the anniversary of a notable invention or achievement; visits overseas of senior executives; important overseas visitors (and in some cases trainees from overseas); uses of imported raw materials, particularly from developing countries; good labour relations records; good productivity; consistency in meeting delivery dates, and finally evidence of customers' recognition of the high quality of a product.

If an importer is seeking to promote his newsworthy product overseas, he should contact the COI local regional staff office which will write the story, in consultation with the exporter. In due course, it will be sent to the COI headquarters in London (see Appendix E) for selective overseas distribution through the London Press Service. If the news is suitable for use in other media it will be passed for consideration to the media division concerned – photographs, television, radio, exhibitions, films or publications. Specialist staff edit, process or produce material and, as with the press stories, it is then sent overseas. Transmission can be worldwide or only in selected areas, including those specified by an individual firm.

Publicity material produced by the COI is sent to information officers at British Embassies, High Commissions and Consular posts in over 150 countries, who aim to place it with local newspapers, trade and technical magazines, and television and radio stations. From COI material, some overseas posts produce their own publications which reach potential buyers and other influential readers. Each year, the overseas information officers feed back to COI headquarters many thousands of press cuttings, as well as reports on usage. About 25 000 press cuttings a year are distributed to some 10 000 firms through the COI regional offices. From this publicity, UK industry receives thousands of enquiries from overseas companies.

Another aspect of the COI's role, under the sponsorship of the Foreign and Commonwealth Office, is to help brief foreign journalists resident in the UK, and to bring journalists, economists, industrialists and political figures from abroad on visits so that they get a positive picture of the UK as a stable, forward-looking trading partner with advanced technology. COI also mounts prestige exhibitions and displays abroad, many of which feature UK industrial design products.

There is no doubt that COI does much to develop the UK overseas trade market, and marketing and sales personnel are urged to take full advantage of the facilities provided at no cost to their company.

10.10   EXPORT CLUBS

Export clubs are informal associations in the UK which are usually formed on a regional basis by a number of local manufacturers, often with representatives of local freight forwarders, banks, insurance companies, container operators, etc. No rules are laid down as to how these clubs should operate, but in general they draw on the experience of member firms to give advice on overseas markets and export procedure, and in some cases practical help is given in selling through a market group or by organizing trade missions and exhibitions overseas.

Nearly 50 such clubs exist, and their addresses are found in Appendix E. They work very closely with the local chamber of commerce and local sectors of the Institute of Export and British International Freight Association. Such clubs hold regular meetings to which speakers are invited to give papers on various aspects of international trade, especially the marketing and trade opportunities. Field visits are often arranged to places of interest such as container depots, ICD (inland clearance depots), and the more distant venues in EC markets, and there are social functions. Overall, the number of such clubs is increasing, and they provide a useful forum for the development of overseas markets based on experience and professionalism.

10.11   THE INSTITUTE OF EXPORT

The Institute of Export is a professional body founded in 1924 as the British Export Society, and incorporated as the Institute of Export in 1935. The Institute's principal objective is to maintain a continuous supply of export executive staff to UK industry and commerce through its educational activities. Membership consists mainly of professional exporters employed in manufacturing companies, export merchant houses and other export organizations. It also extends to certain categories of brokers, civil servants,

insurance officials, lawyers, shipowners and other professional people concerned with export trade. The objectives of the Institute are detailed below:

1 To promote industry and commerce, and particularly international trade
in goods and services of all kinds.
2 To examine, research and analyse problems connected with industry and
commerce, particularly international trade in goods and services of all
kinds; to publish the results of such work, together with recommendations
and advice; and to make the same available to all persons, firms or
companies, whether or not they are members of the Institute.
3 To further public education with regard to commerce and industry, and
particularly the need for exports and the methods of realizing the same; and,
more so, to educate those who are or may become involved or interested in
international trade in all aspects of the same.

The Institute is very much in the lead regarding the development of
international trade. Since its foundation in 1935, it has emphasized that the
profit potential in exporting will be enhanced if export management is in
trained hands. It defines export marketing as the complete process of
discovering and providing the needs of overseas customers, at a profit. The
Institute, therefore, seeks in its educational programme to cover the whole
business activity from the drawing board to prompt delivery, payments,
establishing an after-sales service and, hopefully, gaining repeat orders.

There is no doubt that the Institute of Export will continue to take the
professional lead in the development of overseas markets. Its roles are very
extensive and it gives continuous advice on exporting techniques through
its member journal and area/regional sections. The Institute's address is
found in Appendix E, and the Author would be happy to give any advice
on membership benefits of the Institute. An education handbook is available.

10.12 TECHNICAL HELP FOR EXPORTERS

The British Standards Institution (BSI), embracing the Technical Help to
Exporters (THE), provides a range of services to exporters. It is operated
by the British Standards Institution and its staff of engineers and information
specialists. Its prime task is to give advice on mandatory technical standards
on products exported to overseas territories. Overall, the THE provides
advice on foreign requirements, including national laws, particularly in
relation to: safety and environmental protection; technical standards; and
certification processes in relation to customer needs. It also has a further
range of services which embrace: a technical enquiry service to answer day-
to-day problems; a consultancy service; technical research; major up-dating
services for particular industrial sectors, and a library of over 500 000
standards and regulations for over 160 countries, together with 10 000
English translations.

11 Hints to businesspersons on overseas visits

11.1 OBJECT OF THE OVERSEAS VISIT

Whenever a foreign trip is planned, it is imperative to establish a very clear picture of its objective(s) and to prepare a brief accordingly. The trip could be for one of the following purposes:

1 Field market research or initial market research to complement or complete market research started in the export office.
2 Continuing an existing market research or market intelligence campaign, involving up-dating of previous studies of the market or the pursuit of specific information about the current situation.
3 To appoint an agent from those shortlisted.
4 Finding a replacement agent following the retirement of the existing agent.
5 Discussing with an agent a differing market approach from that under which the agent is currently working, perhaps involving better cost elements in the price of the product, better distribution arrangements, improved documentation arrangements, etc.
6 Examining with agents the prospects of improved sales, better advertising, new opportunities within the market, improved sales training for staff, etc.
7 On the spot investigation with the agent into a customer complaint or query.
8 To examine the prospects of setting up a local company.
9 Participation at an overseas trade exhibition.
10 The running of an outwards trade mission, involving a local trade association or chamber of commerce.
11 An initial visit to determine market and culture structure prior to an extensive market research campaign being instigated.

11.2 PLANNING THE OVERSEAS VISIT

As a first stage in the planning of an overseas trip the following points should be borne in mind:

1 Contact in the UK the Trade Council/trade association or chamber of commerce of the country(ies) one is planning to visit to obtain details of prospective customers. This is especially important as it will maximize the benefit of the visit and ensure that time is well spent on visiting/discussing trade prospects with genuine clients and not with those who have only a cursory interest. This is particularly important on the first visit. Failing direct contact, the local agent can be relied upon to draw up a list of contacts.

2 Time the visit to ensure one does not arrive during any holiday period during which most businesspersons are likely to be away. Check out the normal working hours. In Yugoslavia, for example, the working hours are 0700 to 1430, so an early start is necessary.

3 Plan the itinerary allowing adequate time for travel and for seeing the various people with whom contact has to be made. Allow a modest amount of time for any journey delays. All necessary visas must be obtained before leaving, including 'transit visas' when merely stopping en route. If in doubt about the requirements for visas, seek advice from the Passport Office, Clive House, Petty France, London SW14 9HD or the local Trade Council or Chamber of Commerce. All journeys should be booked in advance through an airline, ship operator or accredited travel agency. Ensure onward flight reservations between countries are concluded as many carriers are often fully booked days before departure date. Allow for the traffic congestion in travelling to appointments.

4 Ensure that you have an adequate supply of samples in the requisite languages (see section 11.9). Also, determine ATA carnet requirements.

5 Be prepared to quote CIF prices and a realistic delivery time. In some countries it may be ex works or FOB. Check out the requirement before you go. Essential brochures/manuals available in buyer's language.

6 Ensure adequate personal insurance is arranged in all relevant areas. Baggage should be of modest proportions and clothes should be compatible with the climate and circumstances. Always appear smartly dressed when on business. If you cannot speak the language competently, an interpreter should be present at meetings. The visit should allow adequate time for relaxation and the usual health precautions should be adopted including any vaccinations prior to departure.

7 Ensure all the clients on your itinerary are aware of your visit and its purpose so that they are adequately prepared and the senior personnel are available. It is desirable that all clients be contactable by telex. Visits should on no account be terminated early because an inflexible timescale leaves the salesperson rushing to catch a flight.

8 Visits should ideally be concentrated in manageable areas each day. This permits the most effective use of the salesperson's time.

9 It is frequently a good idea to notify the Regional Export Directors office of the Department of Trade before leaving the UK. British commercial diplomatic officers can then be advised of the visit at the same time as the exporter tells his agent. Additionally, the British Commercial Diplomatic Office can thus provide (if required) a wide range of assistance to help the exporter achieve the purpose of his visit. This usually includes the provision of local economic and commercial information, and the introduction to prospective customers or representatives. Such overseas posts are not usually able to provide secretarial, translation, or interpreting facilities, although they will be able to advise on local commercial services and their cost. Moreover, exporters cannot expect such personnel to meet them at airports, provide transport or make hotel bookings, etc. However, if during the visit serious illness, an accident, or any other unforeseen personal difficulty should arise and help is required, the local British Embassy or Consulate-General should be contacted.

If any guidance or help is required by the exporter, it is usually available by contacting the local Export Director of the Department of Trade and Industry, or secretary of the nearest Chamber of Commerce.

To emphasize the benefits of the overseas business visit, let us briefly examine the USA market.

Overall, it is a volatile market and a supplier has to work very quickly to take advantage of any niche that may occur. Communication is easy within the market and as a whole it is easily accessible. Hence market research should take the form of a major visit to the USA.

The quickest way of getting a feel for doing business in the US and gathering information is to visit the market. Inexpensive air travel makes it possible for exporters to visit different parts of the US to see for themselves what is on sale. The primary reasons for visiting the market are:

1 To observe comparative prices and mark-up of competing products.
2 To decide on the most suitable channel of distribution: agent, distributor, wholesaler – importer, warehouse, own sales office, licensing, joint venture, marketing company, or direct to mail order house, department store, speciality store, discount store.
3 To discuss any health and safety requirements with appropriate US Government departments, standards enforcement agencies, or State Government agencies as necessary.
4 To gain knowledge of warehousing and transportation facilities plus the timescales and costs involved.
5 To look at US style of presentation and evaluate any changes which may have to be made.
6 To gather information on how to prepare the catalogues and other trade literature for the US market, size equivalents, technical specifications, use of American terminology, the way a product is displayed on the page. Too many products are photographed on a plinth or with the inevitable white coated laboratory technician looking on. Think of something else!

7 To meet potential representatives or buyers and note any specific requirements or commercial factors, such as how much profit the US side expects to make, and how much advertising and marketing support finance will be needed. What is the minimum size of orders likely to be? What are the payment terms?

8 To discuss progress with or seek introductions from consular commercial officials. One meeting with a locally engaged commercial officer with years of experience in a specific product sector can save an exporter weeks of work.

9 To arrange banking facilities using one's own bank or a US bank. Your customers may insist on paying through a small local independent bank and this, in turn, may involve at least one other US bank before your own bank becomes involved, thus increasing banking costs and the time it takes to clear funds.

10 To assess the impact of US product liability legislation on insurance costs. Everyone down the supply line is liable.

11.3   GENERAL INFORMATION

The following factors should be researched prior to any overseas trip:

1 An appraisal of the geography of the country or regions to be visited. This involves: demographical data, its make up by nationality, age, groups, and languages; and climatic conditions.

2 The type of clothing required to suit the prevailing climatic and social conditions.

3 There is a need to ascertain what health precautions (if any) are necessary. Are vaccinations required? Is the water supply safe to drink?

4 The weight and measures system in use. More and more countries are using the metric system whilst the imperial system is much on the decline. It is important that quotations are based on the system operative in the importer's country, and clearly understood by both the buyer and the seller.

5 The electricity supply voltage and frequency should be checked.

6 Details of the public holiday dates should be obtained, together with the normal hours of business. Such data is important when planning the businessman's schedule as, in some countries, business can only be conducted in the morning; the remainder of the day can be devoted to travelling to the next destination. Local time should also be established.

7 The location and hours of opening of the British High Commission, the Embassy or Consulate-General should be established. Details of what they have to offer should be obtained. Some Embassies, for example, have 35mm slide projectors and 16mm film projectors with optical and magnetic sound tracks available for loan. These are suitable for technical studies and films to be shown to invited audiences. The commercial section of the

Embassy can also give advice on many aspects of business opportunities and development in the area, including membership of trade associations and businessmen's clubs.

8 The Technical Help for Exporters (THE) organizations should be contacted regarding any assistance needed in the code of safety and technical specification operative in any of the countries to be visited, together with the issue of approval certificates. Such data should be obtained well in advance of the visit, and should form part of the desk research. Study section 10.12 on the role of THE.

9 An appraisal should be provided of the overseas territory method of doing business in terms of: currency; import controls; channels of distribution; physical distribution – services available/rates/frequency; terminals; and documentation.

11.4 'IN HOUSE' PREPARATION

The export sales person/team involved in the overseas trip will need to have an adequate brief before the visit, and its extent/depth will depend on the nature of the visit, especially whether it is the first visit or one of a series of visits. The following points are relevant:

1 The lead time of the 'in house' discussions can vary from six weeks to a matter of days prior to the departure date. Much will depend on the object of the visit.

2 Ideally, an annual strategy plan should be devised featuring the dates of each overseas visit, the countries involved, the projects/commodities concerned, the nature of each visit and company/personnel to be seen, an action plan for each project/commodity, and identity with the annual budget/sales/marketing plan. It should feature especially new launches and promotional initiatives.

3 Gifts should be taken as a token of friendship and mutual understanding between the seller and buyer (see section 10.5).

4 The sales person should devise a check list and action plan reflecting company strategy and objectives for each visit/client/company. This should have regard to the short term and long term prospects in the market.

5 A series of 'in house' meetings should be held prior to the departure date. This is likely to involve the production department, research and development, finance and personnel with the sales and marketing department. A brief is required on each part of the business trip on an individual client/company basis, thereby producing a customer portfolio. Aspects to be covered include customer portfolio, dates and outcome of previous visits, appraisal of items to be discussed including price, product specification, cost analysis, terms of sale, delivery timescale, channels of distribution, physical distribution, strengths/weaknesses of product/service, non-price items such

as after-sales service, warranty, and so on; identity of problems/risk areas and strategy to be adopted; market intelligence data embracing competition, market position of the buyer, market trends, market risks, market forecasts, strengths/weaknesses of competitive products; any special/additional items to be covered on the visit, especially the resolution of business details from previous visit; position within the company of the person(s) to be seen, buyer behaviour and attitude to seller's products emerging from previous experience/visits; outcome of market research findings; remit/objective of visit; items in dispute; and any contingency plan.

6 A cultural briefing may be required to ensure sales person(s) are adequately familiar with the overseas territory to be visited, especially in regard to etiquette, language, customs, etc. Emerging from such a briefing, intensive language courses may be required.

7 Adequate publicity material should be available in the buyer's language. This may involve videos, brochures, manuals, etc. The company's policy may be to simply insert a price list with the brochure, which may be multi-lingual. This is an on-going need for the overseas market (see section 11.7).

8 Provision of any samples, with the requisite documentation for importation and brief on the product.

9 The production department must specify the timescale of the product at varying volume levels and timescale/cost analysis. For example, the sales executive may require such data at 1000, 2000 and 5000 units.

Further full details are required of the product specification which are particularly relevant to technical items, such as a compressor. Usually, such products are best promoted in the overseas market by employing a qualified, experienced sales engineer with foreign language competence. It is likely the product will reflect local specification needs. Areas which may arise in the seller/buyer discussion include product modification, spares availability, proven product performance, maintenance arrangements, technical training needs by the buyer, commission arrangements and so on. Technical plans may be available to the buyer. A thorough 'in house' brief is required.

10 Adequate briefing is required in regard to the negotiation of the sales contract, and particularly the method of payment, terms and options, the legal aspects, and any contractual obligations.

The foregoing list should not be regarded as exhaustive. One must stress the briefing meeting conducted 'in house' prior to the sales executive departure should be well thought out/prepared to ensure all the likely areas of discussion are covered. Moreover, the company image presented by the sales person must be completely professional and display commitment to the client and market. Regular visits are desirable, as are plans for future discussions, which may include the possibility of any reciprocal visits to the seller's manufacturing base. The sales person should be equipped with the latest sales bulletin from the company which may interest the buyer, and other would-be clients, and establish the buyer's interest on specific areas of product development.

11.5 TRAVEL NEEDS

Knowing the most suitable arrangements for a trip comes with experience. It is desirable to have an itinerary plan, which must be flexible enough to cater for business opportunities which may occur during the stay. Experience and advice obtained from an agent or distributor will dictate the degree of flexibility required.

Business travel overseas now forms an important passenger market for airlines, and many of them offer special facilities, including hotel accommodation, car hire facilities, cheap rates for accompanying spouses, special 'in flight' facilities for the businessperson, and executive transport to and from the airport. It is a very competitive business with many fringe benefits available which vary by airline. One can obtain such details from the airline direct or from an accredited travel agent – many of which have business houses. With regard to the UK businessperson visiting Europe, an increasing number are taking their cars and are thereby able to convey much greater range/quantity of samples and become more flexible and independent relative to their travel arrangements. Overall, motorist travel cost can be much cheaper in certain circumstances, especially when two or more people are involved in the business trip.

Given below are details of other factors concerned in the travel arrangements:

1 Obviously, a valid passport is required together with, in some countries, a visa. Advice can be sought from the Passport Office (Clive House, Petty France, London, SW14 9ED; telephone 01 213 3344).

2 Many countries require vaccination certificates for specified diseases.

3 Business visitors should consult their banks for the current rate of exchange and currency regulations. Restrictions may exist on the amount of local or foreign exchange which may be brought into or taken from a country. Foreign exchange and traveller's cheques may be exchanged at banks, bureaux de change and exchange offices. International credit cards are tending to become increasingly popular and acceptable in many countries for a wider variety of products especially in hotels, restaurants and travel agents. If using currency the businessperson should budget generously, especially for entertaining clients. Traveller's cheques are ideal.

4 In many countries, no income tax regulations exist for the short term business visitor.

5 In addition to personal luggage which accompanies a traveller, visitors

may, according to the Convention and Customs Facilities in Tourism to which the UK are signatories, take in free of duty, various articles including personal jewellery, a camera with films, a personal stereo, a small cine camera and two reels, a tape recorder, a radio receiver, a portable typewriter, a pair of binoculars, sports goods, 200 cigarettes or 50 cigars or 250 grammes of tobacco, one litre of wine, a quarter of a litre of spirits, a quarter of a litre of eau de cologne, and 25 grammes of perfume, all in open, unsealed bottles. Any of the above items and any other goods apart from used personal effects must be declared on entry or there may be difficulties on departure. Not all countries are signatories to the Convention on Customs Facilities in Tourism, and the visitor should check the permitted customs allowance with the travel agent or national tourist office before travelling.

6 Travel arrangements to and from the destination countries can be obtained through a travel agent, national tourist office, airline or shipping company. Travel facilities within the country can be obtained from the national tourist office and include car hire, taxis, rail travel, road network and air travel.

11.6 HOTELS, RESTAURANTS AND COMMUNICATION FACILITIES

It is the usual practice to book one's accommodation in advance. In most countries, rates vary according to the time of year, particularly in tourist areas. Visitors attending trade fairs or major conferences are advised to obtain confirmed bookings months in advance, but latecomers can sometimes get private accommodation arranged for them through travel agencies. Tourist centres, especially resorts, tend to close many of their hotels out of season.

An increasing number of countries include a service charge in their tariff, and governments are tending to discourage hotel tipping as a result. The larger hotels are able to provide facilities for small displays or exhibitions. Bookings should be made in advance. It is desirable to choose a hotel with telex, fax machine, adequate security provision for personal effects and essential documents and (ideally) secretarial facilities.

Prior to leaving the country, the visitor should leave details of the proposed itinerary with the export sales department and/or his/her secretary with addresses and telephone or telex numbers. Appropriate details should be given to the next of kin. In many countries business visitors or their agents can make arrangements to communicate urgently with their company office in the UK by telegram, with the cost being charged to their company in the UK. Details of the scheme are available from the International Credit Card Service (Cable & Wireless Ltd, Mercury House, Theobalds Road, London WC1X 8RX; telephone 01 242 4433) who arrange international transferred account facilities on behalf of the Post Office.

One can now dial direct from most countries to the UK, business visitors may make arrangements whereby the cost of telephone calls made by them or their agents may be charged to their company in the UK. A leaflet giving details of credit card facilities may be obtained from British Telecom. Full use should be made of telex and fax facilities.

11.7   DEBRIEFING MEETING

The sales person must produce a sales report on each visit undertaken, covering the salient points including an action plan on points/aspects emerging from the visit. The report should include: date of visit and person(s) seen; matters discussed and their outcome; orders secured; price, terms and delivery timescale; future developments; and a general overview of the meeting. Important matters should be communicated to the exporter sales office by telex or telephone to ensure prompt action is taken on the day of the meeting and not left until the sales executive returns. As few items as possible should be unresolved prior to the sales executive returning home – an exchange of telexes may be able to clarify any outstanding points.

On arrival home, the sales executive should produce a comprehensive report of his/her visit for the senior management, and conduct debriefing meeting(s) with the departments/persons involved. Again, an action plan should be devised, and performance monitored to ensure of its prompt execution. The content of the report should be cross-checked with individual sales reports of the companies visited. Overall, debriefing meetings and accompanying reports form essential market intelligence data which, effectively monitored, should contribute to overseas marketing strategy.

Strategic aspects emerging from debriefing meetings include: pricing policy; product specification; appointment of agents/distributors; physical distribution policy; market research; budget review; marketing plan; promotion; political and legal aspects and future development. An appraisal of orders not secured should be given.

11.8   ECONOMIC FACTORS

The economic factors of the country should be ascertained, and the market analysis techniques detailed in Chapter 2 should be put into progress. The following items require evaluation relative to the product the business sales person is promoting. (Sources from which such data can be obtained are contained in Chapter 10, but in general terms the BOTB Export Intelligence Service or the local Chamber of Commerce can give guidance.)

1 The general economic situation in the country and especially attitudes towards imported products. Does the country follow a policy of protectionism to support a number of its home industries or adopt any quota system? Further details of such techniques can be found in Chapter 3 of *Economics of Shipping Practice and Management* (see Appendix A). Furthermore, does the country actively encourage foreign private investors by offering tax and other incentives and free repatriation of profits and capital? An analysis should be obtained of the country's natural resources and the level of industrialization.

2 Details of the agricultural element of the economy.

3 A broad assessment of the pattern of new investment and the reliance if any – on foreign investment, together with any fiscal incentives.

4 The purchasing power details (judged from the gross domestic product). Further details such as total population related to number of televisions, radios, cars and telephone subscribers are useful indicators. An analysis of the exchange rate during recent years and projection to the future would be helpful. This may, for example, involve the Asian dollar and gold markets for oriental countries such as Singapore.

5 Details of public utilities such as electricity, gas and water provision.

6 An analysis of the principal imports and exports by country of origin during the past three years.

7 Commercial banks in the visitor's country. The major international banks of the UK are usually found in leading industrial countries. They can give good guidance on trade prospects.

8 Details of any major industrialization programmes which are likely to effect the future level of imports.

9 Details of current local competition and the dominance of home-produced products. Also, consumer/buyer behaviour towards imported goods.

The following is a checklist, and is not compiled in any particular order of importance:

1 GDP and GDP per head including the distribution of income.

2 Levels of consumer and personal taxes, and what is taxed.

3 Household ownership of goods (cars and consumer goods). This is a good indicator of wealth. High saturation levels, as measured by the percentage of households who possess certain durables, is not necessarily a bad thing. There is a chance of further market growth through multiple ownership (cars) and product improvements (stereo and TVs).

4 Levels of inflation and interest rates.

5 Militancy level of unions, and unionization by sector.

6 Balance of payments and external debt levels.

7 Pattern and stability of exchange rate (look at its trade-weighted value as well as its value against important currencies).

8 Economic growth–manufacturing and consumer. Examine the volume trends and bear in mind that turnover is a monetary measure, and therefore subject to distortion through inflation.

9 Protection–tariffs and non-tariff barriers. If possible, consult existing exporters who may be able to tell of more imaginative protection methods e.g. each video imported into France undergoes two days of tests.

10 Organization of retailing – the influence of multiples, and the existence of out-of-town sites.

11 Population – its age, sex, size and geographical location.

12 Tastes and preferences, evaluated by regions.

13 Advertising media – cost and relative popularity.

14 Use of credit cards.

15 Level and type of competition – home and foreign.

16 Government aid packages for new and existing business – regional and inner city.

17 Attitude to foreign business.

18 Quality and service currently available to the consumer – there may be opportunities for developing a niche.

11.9   IMPORT AND EXCHANGE CONTROLS

The latest available information about import duties, import control regulations, taxes and any other legislation affecting UK exports should be sought. It is available from the Overseas Trade Division, Department of Trade and Industry, Victoria Street, London SW1H 0ET. The following information, where relevant, should be sought.

1 Exchange control. Some countries impose restrictions on transfer payments to the UK for goods or services of British origin. This could involve restrictions on allocation of foreign exchange.

2 Import licensing is common practice in countries which are not free trade areas and where the importer is outside a free trade area. This usually applies to specific items, and excludes samples.

3 Customs duty. The tariff will be based on the Harmonized Commodity Description and Coding System. Preferential rates may exist for British goods with no customs duty in free trade markets (see section 12.6). The basis of the valuation for customs duty may be CIF, *ad valorem*, or FOB at the British port or importer's frontier point.

4 In some countries taxes are imposed in addition to the customs duty. Usually they are based on the CIF value of the goods.

5 Documentation relevant to processing the imported consignment is complex and differs widely in different countries. Study closely Chapters 12 and 13 of *Elements of Export Practice.*

6 Samples are usually imported free of any duty but subject to the appropriate documentation completion. This usually involves an ATA carnet (see *Elements of Export Practice*, pages 343–4. Any sample attracting customs duty is refunded on re-exportation, within a period of up to six months.

7 The names and addresses of forwarding agents in most countries are available from the Export Services and Promotions Division of the Department of Trade.

8 Marking and packing of imported merchandise is a specialized subject area. Full details are found in Chapter 6 of *Elements of Export Practice* pages 82–117.

11.10   CONCLUSION

It must be stressed that the value of this chapter to the businessperson will vary greatly according to individual circumstances. Experience has suggested that too few export salesmen are conversant with the techniques of processing the export order. This includes especially the role of Incoterms and funding the export sales contract – all of which have been dealt with in earlier chapters. Overseas visitors are particularly recommended to obtain a copy of the booklet *Hints to Exporters* from the BOTB for the relevant country involved.

The businessman is well advised not to be too ambitious in his itinerary, especially on his early trips. Concentrate on a few items which are most likely to succeed and yield a profit with the prospect of long-term development. Always give adequate preparation to the trip with adequate time for relaxation and time to allow appointments to over-run their allotted time scale. Experience will provide the best guide.

Finally, one must bear in mind that although good preparation for the business trip is very important, successful overseas business is dependent primarily upon complete professionalism and dedication/commitment. This requires many skills in sales negotiation (see section 9.2).

12 *Distribution, political factors and the future*

As most export salespersons quickly realize, the subject of export marketing tends to become much broader when negotiating an export sales contract; in particular, the areas of finance, cargo delivery terms, distribution and the interplay of politics within the international trade scene. We have already dealt very extensively with cargo delivery terms and touched on exchange rates. It is now appropriate to consider distribution very briefly, but the reader should study the companion volume *Elements of Export Practice* which deals with the subject in much greater depth.

12.1 FACTORS TO CONSIDER IN EVALUATING THE SUITABILITY OF TRANSPORT MODES FOR AN INTERNATIONAL CONSIGNMENT

The overseas salesperson negotiating the terms of his/her export sales contract must give particular attention to the distribution arrangements of the consignment. This will depend on many factors. The ideal technique to use is called transport distribution analysis or, as it is sometimes called, physical distribution management. Basically, it is a system by which alternative methods of distribution are analysed and the optimum pattern of transportation selected.

The ultimate selection of transport mode can vary seasonally and by quantity of goods. Some services vary considerably from summer to winter due to market demand and climatic conditions. Moreover, the despatch of a small quantity urgently required may be ideal for air freight, but larger consignments which are less urgent may be suitable for a deep sea container schedule under consolidation arrangements.

As the overseas salesperson will quickly discover, particularly in Eastern Bloc, Latin American and Third World Countries, the increasing tendency is for the importer to decide on the cargo delivery arrangements, and, if the exporter demurs, the buyer will go to another client. In so doing, countries are trying to improve their overall trade balance, and many are insisting on shipment by their own national airline or shipping service irrespective of the commercial or economic advantages that may be derived from using competitive services. This is a difficult situation to combat, but the salesperson must strive to sell his goods under CIF terms involving a UK national airline or shipping service plus cargo insurance cover to maximize payment to the UK balance of payment account.

Today, more and more exporters are setting up their own shipping office. The cost of running such a department should more than offset the savings realized through international distribution costs by selecting the best transport and insurance arrangements. The seller may use a freight forwarder to take care of all the transportation/documentation arrangements (the role of the freight forwarder is explained in Chapter 16 of *Elements of Export Practice*).

It cannot be stressed too strongly that the overseas salesman should liaise closely with the export office about the cargo delivery arrangements. The discussions should take place regularly, and any problems relative to an overseas customer's account should be quickly resolved. This could involve: damaged goods; inadequate packing; poor transit time resulting in late arrival of the consignment; payment problems, including those arising from inadequacies in certain documentation. At the same time, the salesman can seek advice regarding the most suitable transportation arrangements for the commodities involved. Regretfully, the distribution arrangements do not always feature strongly enough in the salesperson's mind, and it is most desirable that he/she becomes well informed to ensure that the best arrangements are secured.

We will now examine the factors involved in the choice of transport mode for an international consignment:

1 The customer's choice is the prime consideration, and this is usually found in the export sales contract which we will examine later in this chapter. It is inter-related to the cargo delivery terms. The practice of the importer insisting on the goods being conveyed on his country's national shipping line or airline to save hard currency is called 'cargo preference law'.

2 The nature of the commodity, its dimensions, weight and whether any special facilities are required for it during transit; for example, livestock needs special facilities, gold requires special security or a strong room, and meat requires refrigerated accommodation. These are major considerations and one must establish, through research and enquiry, whether the actual dimensions are ideal for maximizing the use of the available container capacity and lessening the risk of broken stowage (broken stowage usually results in additional freight payments).

3 The degree of packing and the cost thereof. Packing cost can form a very significant proportion of the overall expense of distribution. For example, a consignment sent under 'tween deck tonnage arrangements usually requires very extensive packing (possibly involving a wooden case), whereas cargoes despatched by train ferry wagon, containerization (less

than container load) or (full container load), trailer–international road haulage, palletization and air-freight require less (particularly the latter four). In the case of air-freight, packing needs are very much reduced and numerous consignments are conveyed affixed to a pallet, with the cargo enveloped in a plastic cover to protect it from scratching, dust, moisture, etc. Likewise, an examination of the type and quality of the packing used can often produce favourable results for the exporter/shipper. One must endeavour to ensure that packing is not over-generous so that unnecessary packing costs are not incurred; numerous specialized packing companies exist, and the exporter new to the business is strongly advised to consult them. For example, the dimensions of the consignment must be kept down to the minimum practicable, as the larger the package the more expensive the freight rate.

4 The ease of handling the consignment. For example, palletized cargo is easy to handle by fork lift truck, whilst cartons are ideal for containers etc. Conversely, an awkwardly shaped cargo may require special facilities/handling arrangements, and may be subject to a freight surcharge; such consignments encourage broken stowage, which increases their insurance premium level. Ideally, the consignment should be easy to handle from the time it leaves the factory until it reaches the retailer. Accordingly, much progress has been made to develop a code of standardized international package sizes which will aid distribution and optimize use of containers and other forms of unit distribution (stillage, pallets, etc). There is a growing tendency to stack cargo to make the best use of warehouse space; the consignment needs to be able to withstand this treatment. Of course, the more often the goods are handled in transit, the more prone they are to damage. Hence, the product retailed through a distributor network involving poor quality local transport calls for more robust packing than the one conveyed in a road trailer from the factory direct to the consumer's premises. Experience will guide the salesman and export office to the best specification.

5 Any statutory regulations concerning transit. Certain products need special facilities, both in the transport mode and at the terminal. This in itself restricts choice of route/service and transport mode. For example, the movement of meat requires special facilities of the transport operator, and inspection facilities at the import terminal. Additionally, most countries have weight and length restrictions on road vehicles. This is particularly relevant to containerization. Likewise, there are restrictions on the hours that road haulage drivers work and some EEC countries rules restrict the movement of lorries at weekends. Statutory regulations involving quarantine also influence the type of packing (see page 84 of *Elements of Export Practice*); for example, the use of straw and marking of cargo in Australia. The sales person can consult the Trade Association or his own export office regarding such restrictions.

6 Dangerous cargo. Again regulations are stringent regarding its packing, stowage, marking, and mixture with other cargoes during stowage. This can restrict service/routing/schedules. International distribution of dangerous cargoes requires the most careful evaluation both by air (IATA regulations), by ADR (road) and by sea (IMO code). Overall, regulations are tending to become more stringent.

7 Suitability of available transport services. For example, air transport has limited capacity/weight/dimensions and the cargo may require extensive collection and delivery arrangements. Conversely, it offers fast transits and reduced packing needs. In contrast, the deep sea container service will have a much slower transit, probably less collection and delivery expense (if it is a consolidated consignment), slightly more packing expense, less frequent service, but lower freight rate. The roll on/roll off (Ro/Ro) operation will have similar features to the containerized consignment, except that in the UK/Continental trade the transit time is likely to be more competitive with air transport. An increasing number of exporters are now using their own vehicles to distribute their products in UK/Continental trade. In exceptional circumstances the shipper may resort to chartering an aircraft or vessel if sufficient cargo is available. One must bear in mind that some services are so popular that bookings should be made well in advance.

8 The transit time and related urgency of consignment. To determine the overall transit time, one must bear in mind the periods of collection and delivery of the cargo. Moreover, one must not discount any likely delays in customs clearance, which are commonplace in some countries. Air-freight services offer the fastest schedules and are particularly suited to the urgent consignment.

9 Quantity of cargo and period over which the shipment is to be made. In broad terms, the greater the quantity available for shipment, the lower the distribution cost per unit weight. For example, if the exporter can fill a container or trailer, the freight will be much cheaper to despatch than under consolidation arrangements. Furthermore, a guaranteed substantial quantity of cargo conveyed over a period of time could attract a concessionary tariff (this is particularly relevant to sea transport). Again, if circumstances are favourable, it may be advantageous to charter an aircraft or ship. A fundamental point for the overseas salesperson to bear in mind is that volume sales lower unit distribution cost, which permits more competitive pricing and hence improves the manufacturer's market share (see sections 2.3/14.2).

10 Insurance of cargo. The premium is determined by numerous factors, but the main ones are: nature of the cargo; mode of transport; likely risk and type of packaging. Air-freight insurance, with quick transits and low risk of damage and pilferage, tends to offer competitive insurance premiums. Container shipments are also competitive, bearing in mind the longer transit time.

11 Terms of export contract. The most common quotations in exporting are EWX/CIF/CFR/FOB. The overseas salesperson should strive to obtain CIF terms to maximize the income to the UK balance of payments through the insurance and freight being undertaken by UK-based companies.

12 Freight and documentation. In broad terms, the cost of seafreight tends to be very much lower than air-freight but it is not practical to consider such cost in isolation as one must bear in mind the total distribution which embraces elements such as packing and insurance. Air-freight tariffs are also high when compared with road and rail costs, but the margin lessens significantly the longer the transit. Documentation costs between various transport modes do not vary a great deal, but with the development of the combined transport concept in recent years (see *Economics of Shipping Practice and Management*), involving particularly road transport by ISO container and the long-established train ferry, the process has become easier because of through rates/consignment notes with no intermediate customs examination in transit countries.

The four most decisive factors in choosing transport are: terms of the export sales contract, commodity specification, freight, and overall transit time (including reliability and delivering the consignment undamaged). Other factors include cost of packing (very significant in air freight); convenience/reliability of service; and benefits derived from the more frequent service, including less warehouse accommodation with earlier commissioning of the product, reduced risk of product obsolescence and less working capital. The latter facilitates smoother production flow and better customer relations and service quality, and reduces the risk of damage and pilferage.

The foregoing factors will vary in importance according to individual circumstances; nevertheless, together with the transport distribution analysis technique (see section 12.3), this should prove a useful code of evaluation.

12.2   CRITERIA OF PHYSICAL DISTRIBUTION SELECTION

The mode(s) of transport used by the exporter to convey the goods to the market is a critical area of evaluation in export marketing terms. At the outset, one must view it in total cost terms and have special regard to the impact it will have on the market development of the product. Too few exporters view physical distribution in isolation, and many fail to realize that a study of the options available can yield valuable benefits in cost reduction and quality of service. For example, by centralizing the distribution resources on country/warehouse serving a cluster of markets can yield lower distribution cost, through volume cargo movements. Hitherto, the commodities were distributed by individual routes/carriers to serve each country market within the cluster, generating low volume movement but high cost per tonne shipped.

A further point to bear in mind is the constantly changing pattern of international physical distribution systems and the new opportunities open to the exporter to develop existing markets or enter new ones. It may be that the further extension of containerization, the introduction of the high cube container or the provision of the sea/air or air/sea combined transport operation are significant developments. Today, more and more international trade is being conveyed under the combined transport arrangements involving air freight, international road haulage with Ro/Ro, and containerization. To the UK exporter, Ro/Ro is ideal for the European market, containerization for the distance and deep sea markets, and air freight for commodities of high value and low cube density or those of a perishable nature. A development in the next few years will be the direct trailer shipment to the Middle East and other trade areas, with a voyage time of 2/4 hours and a road infrastructure to/from EC/Middle East markets. Overall, there are five factors to consider as physical distribution criteria, as listed below:

1 The frequency of the service. Overall, the more frequent the service, the greater the capacity available and the more established the route in the market. This in itself generates the market development and permits a 'just in time' management technique of warehouse management. In addition, it results in warehouse stacks being pitched at a low level in the knowledge that the goods can be replaced quickly through a reduced lead time as the service is frequent. A service which is frequent is particularly ideal in a fast-moving product market or one influenced by fashion trends where replenishment of stock is the key to high turnover and profitability. Overall, the frequent service aids cash flow, maintains working capital at a low level, and enables the exporter to respond quickly to market opportunities. Finally, a market which has a frequent transport service usually has a buoyant economy.

2 Reliability of the transport service is a major consideration in the physical distribution selection code. This is especially important when despatching goods against specific delivery dates and letter of credit terms. Penalties incurred through late delivery are severe and can result in the importer refusing acceptance of the goods. Moreover, it undermines confidence with the importer and does not generate goodwill between the seller and buyer. It can result in the buyer losing substantial sums when market dates are missed or the goods arrive too late for an exhibition etc. A transport service which is unreliable tends to be cheaper than its competitors and lacks quality management. Reliability of transport is especially important for exporters who despatch commodities against a production schedule.

3 Speed of transport is paramount when the goods are urgently required, are of a perishable nature or are needed against a tight schedule. Speed is costly to the carrier and likewise to the shipper. The quicker the service, the less capital tied up in transport. Moreover, the sooner the goods arrive, the quicker they can be sold or commissioned – an example being computer equipment. Furthermore, fast schedules reduce the risk of the goods deteriorating in transit, and enables earlier payment of the goods. Quick transits may also open up new markets, and this is especially true of the air-freight market. The development of combined transport services involving road/sea/road, sea/air, rail/sea/rail and other combinations have resulted in quicker transits and the development of unitized cargo involving the through transport consignment, unimpeded at transhipment points. As combined transport develops, more emphasis is being placed on quicker schedules and more reliable services, both of which considerations aid the development of trade between nations. Exporters are urged to examine the transit times of the transport services available in the market and the benefits they offer to the shipper in the areas of reduction in the amount of capital tied up in transit, less risk of commodity deterioration, earlier payment, more end-user satisfaction, reduced stockpiling with consequent reduced amount of capital tied up in the warehouse, and overall fast services generate a high profile in the market both to the exporter and importer.

4 The cost of transport to the shipper is of paramount importance. It represents an 'on cost' to the product manufactured to enable it to reach the exporter in the overseas territory. The more distant the market, the higher the 'on cost'. Exporters should well research the market to determine a low-cost transport service within the criteria of the buyer/consumer profile/market needs.

5 Quality of service represents all the foregoing four factors of speed, reliability, cost and frequency. The quality service generates a high profile, and is indicative of high calibre management with a modern transport infrastructure. It is competitively priced and should aid market development to the benefit of both the exporter and importer.

12.3   TRANSPORT DISTRIBUTION ANALYSIS

It is important that the overseas salesperson is aware of the transport distribution analysis technique. In broad terms, this is an analysis of alternative methods of distribution with a view to selecting the optimum pattern of transportation for a particular consignment.

In the home market, it is possible to retain overall control of sales outlets and related distribution arrangements. However, where exports are involved, problems of greater complexity arise. Sales made on a FOB basis are bound by the philosophy of 'lowest freight cost', often lead to a reduction of control over marketing efficiency overseas: distribution costs built up at home and abroad, and with the distribution function being far-reaching, several managers will have a direct interest in one or more aspects of distribution efficiency. Production, cash flow, release of capital and the level of sales can be substantially improved if the ideal pattern of transportation is selected.

Details of the factors involved are briefly dealt with as follows:

1 Quantity and type of packages.

2 Total weight of consignment.

3 Total volume of the shipment.

4 Value of goods ex works.

5 Packaging cost.

6 Inland charges at port of origin. This includes all the costs incurred in conveying the consignment from, for example, the factory to the nominated airport or seaport for despatch overseas (embracing cartage, handling charges, etc).

7 Freight. This includes the air- and sea-freight comparisons.

8 Inland charges at overseas point of arrival incorporates (customs clearance, agency expenses, etc.); and transportation costs from the airport or seaport to ultimate destination.

9 Duty and taxes. This includes VAT, or its equivalent, and import duties. Air distribution may be the most advantageous method if duties are based on FOB value (value at the place of exportation). This arises from reduced packing costs and reduced cost to the airport of departure. Duties, for example, are assessed on FOB value in Canada, USA and South Africa. Conversely, it may be a disadvantage to transport by air if the duties are based on CIF value (value at place of importation/destination), as the pure air-freight is likewise subject to duty. Similar advantages/disadvantages arise relative to sea transport. Some customs duties are assessed on gross weight which is particularly advantageous to air-freight tare weight.

10 Insurance premium.

11 Unpacking/refurbishing. Less packing will obviously make unpacking less expensive. Moreover, any special refurbishing process for the goods before use is not necessary such as degreasing of machinery/apparatus, ironing of textiles, etc.

12 Cost of capital tied up in transit. During transportation from door to door, either the exporter or importer has invested money into the merchandise without receiving an equivalent interest or deriving profit from it. The longer the transit and the higher the merchandise value, the greater the investment involved. This factor may be of minor importance for a single shipment, but will assume greater significance for many consignments over a specified period. This reinforces the need to use relatively fast deep sea container services or, for suitable consignments, air transport. The methods are becoming increasingly popular for spares distribution for after-sales service.

13 Inventory and storage costs. The cost of keeping stocks at the place of production or consumption involves four basic elements:

(a) cost of capital tied up in inventories;
(b) obsolescence, deterioration, insurance, taxes, etc;
(c) administration and handling;
(d) warehouse and other storage facilities.

The percentage of cost on the average stock value may be as high as 25% per year, but much depends on the location of the warehouse and on the size and type of commodity. The specific advantages of air freight (speed, safety, reliability and frequency) may result in a reduced lead time for the importer and enable him to increase the shipping frequency for the fast moving items. Instead of shipping quantities which cover the demand for several months, it might be more economical to air-freight smaller consignments more frequently. This produces a lower working stock, less warehouse accommodation cost, and reduced risk of stock deterioration/obsolescence.

14 Many export companies have great difficulty in achieving market objectives because insufficient consideration is given to distribution. Sales and communication combine to stimulate demand for a product but, unless (by planned distribution) the product is actually available at a point of sale when the consumer decides to purchase, a sale is often lost. Even if the sale is not lost, customer service standards fall and while the demand may be so strong that the delay is tolerated, the likelihood of a repeat purchase at a later date is reduced. A similar situation applies to goods for 'after-sales-service' such as spare parts. The speed at which the customer can obtain a replacement part for a machine strongly influences his opinion of the supplier, and therefore the likelihood of a repeat purchase of the product.

Quick delivery is often vital in providing a high level of customer service which would otherwise be achieved by holding a high level of stock at a prohibitive cost.

15 A high speed mode of transport reduces stock levels – both static and in transit – and the financial implications of this are apparent. In effect, the average lead time between manufacture and sale is shortened, and this must mean a saving in financial resources. Overall, this improves a company's cash flow or liquidity.

16 Other cost and revenue factors. In addition to the transportation and distribution costs already mentioned, the performance of a mode of transport has an influence on other cost and revenue factors, e.g. ordering, production and administration. These hidden advantages are difficult to evaluate, but they should be taken into consideration.

12.4   THE EXPORT SALES CONTRACT

The export sales contract is often the conclusion of some difficult negotiations and, accordingly, particular care should be taken in formulating its terms. It must be borne in mind that an exporter's primary task is to sell his products at a profit and, therefore, the contract should be capable of being executed under reasonable circumstances to achieve this aim. Of course, in the initial stages of developing a new market overseas, a loss may be incurred, but the long-term objective of the marketing plan is to increase the market share and should ultimately be to reach a favourable profit level. A further point to bear in mind is that the export sales contract also embraces the delivery terms which may be CIF, ex-works, FOB, etc.

Details of a typical UK export contract are given below, but it must be stressed that this will differ in individual countries and companies. Legal advice should be sought where necessary.

1 The exporter's/seller's registered name and address.

2 The importer's/buyer's registered name and address.

3 A short title of each party quoted in items (1) and (2).

4 Purpose of the contract. For example, it should confirm that the specified merchandise is sold by the party detailed in item (1) to the addresses quoted in item (2), and that the latter has bought according to the terms and conditions laid down in the contract.

5 The number and quantity of goods should be described precisely and fully to avoid any misunderstanding or dispute in the future. In particular, one must mention details of any batches, and reconcile goods description with custom tariff specification.

6 Price. This may be quoted in sterling (depending on its general stability) or some other currency (see section 14.3) which is not likely to vary in value significantly throughout the contract duration (such as US dollars or Deutsche-marks). To counter inflation, particularly in a long-term contract, it is usual to incorporate an escalation clause therein and, to reduce the risks of losses due to fluctuations in sterling, the tendency is to invoice in foreign currencies.

7 Terms of delivery, e.g. CIF New York, FOB Felixstowe, ex-works Luton. It is important that both parties to the contract fully understand their obligations, as the interpretation of the terms of delivery can sometimes vary by individual country. The ideal solution is to quote Incoterms 1990 which are recognized almost worldwide.

8 Terms of payment, e.g. open account, cash with order, sight bills or term bills. Many importers today require extended credit, and the exporter's local bank manager should be able to give guidance on this matter.

9 Delivery date/shipment date or period. The exporter should check with his production department that the delivery date quoted is realistic, and that the shipping or air-freight space will be available on the date or period specified. The exporter's obligations regarding the latter will depend on the terms of delivery.

10 Methods of shipment, e.g. container, trailer, Ro/Ro and air-freight.

11 Method of packing. It is desirable that both parties are fully aware of, and agree to, the packing specification to ensure no dispute arises later.

12 Insurance — policy or cover note terms.

13 Import or export licence details or other instructions. The period of their validity must be reconciled with the terms of payment and delivery date/shipment date or period.

14 Shipping, freight or documentary requirements and/or instructions. This includes marking of cargo.

15 Contract conditions, e.g. sale, delivery, performance (quality) of goods, arbitration, etc. Arbitration tends to speed settlement of any disputes without costly litigation.

16 Signature. Both parties to sign the contract, each by a responsible person (director or manager), and the date to be recorded. A copy of the contract should be retained by each party.

Concluding the export sales contract is an important part of the sales-person's job. The foregoing commentary gives a broad outline of the main clauses found in such a document, but readers who wish to consider the legal aspect should refer to Professor Schmitoff's book *The Export Trade* (see Appendix A).

The tendency in some overseas markets, especially those with debt/hard currency problems, is of the protracted period from the time the order is confirmed to the date the letter of credit confirmation is received by the exporter confirming the availability of funds and the timescale of the goods' despatch etc. It is important at the time of the negotiation that specific agreement be reached to allow adequate time for the exporter to produce and despatch the goods following receipt of the letter of credit. For example, an order for a piece of machinery secured on an overseas visit in January and providing for a delivery in late May involving a voyage time of 15 days gives little time for manufacture, if the letter of credit arrives three weeks before sailing date. Advice should be sought from the bank as to how best resolve such problems, as exporters are very reluctant to manufacture goods in high risk markets until they have confirmation that the funds are available, and do not wish to have to resort to air freight – at their expense – to meet the time schedule of the letter of credit. The procedure is for the exporter to despatch the *pro forma* invoice to the bank when the order confirmation is received, and not to proceed with manufac-ture of the goods until the letter of credit has been received from the bank.

Finally, sales are concluded without a sales contract with all conditions of sale, particularly cargo delivery terms, being recorded on the *pro forma* invoice. This invoice, together with export documentation, is fully described in Chapter 12 of *Elements of Export Practice*.

12.5 SALIENT DIFFERENCES BETWEEN EXPORT AND HOME MARKETING

The areas of differences between export and home marketing are considerable, and the more important ones are now examined.

1 The product specification is likely to be different in the overseas market (reflecting a different customer profile), and there may be differing technical specifications which are enforceable by statute.

2 The code of advertising principles and regulations equivalent to the UK *Trade Descriptions Act* are likely to be different overseas. Particular attention needs to be given regarding obligations of after-sales service.

3 Customer profile is almost certain to be different in every country, taking into account income level, culture, living standards, fashion, religion, politics and general attitude towards imported products (market research will establish the profile).

4 Communications in many under-developed countries are poor, which restrict promotional outlets. Such countries rely on poster sites and radio for product promotion. In other circumstances press advertising may be confined to newspapers circulating in cities and towns; many people in country areas are illiterate and have low living standards. Industrial countries tend to have the same promotional outlets as found in the UK.

5 The cargo delivery terms, as fully explained in Chapter 8, do not feature in pricing a product for the home market. Studying the factors to consider in pricing an export product (see section 6.3, Figure 6.1) will show that that there are many elements which contribute to the price. Moreover, the payment arrangements, distribution, insurance and the role of documentation are all rather different. Particular attention has to be given to exchange rates and customs, and other regulations governing the import of such products into overseas markets. Product packaging requires particular attention in the overseas market to ensure that it meets the customer needs and trading regulations governing product description, content, weight, date of sale deadline, etc., and does not cause offence in terms of colour or overall presentation.

6 The distribution facilities mentioned in item (5) require special attention to ensure that the optimum arrangements are devised to enable the goods to arrive on time in a good condition.

7 Language barrier is an area which requires particular attention to ensure the brochures/posters/general merchandise meet local requirements and are correctly presented. Any slogan must be properly researched to ensure it does not cause offence or opposition in the market place.

8 The method of retailing in the overseas market needs particular attention, as does the most acceptable customary role/use of the product in the overseas market. This involves product research, product design and training of sales personnel.

9 Trading regulations at the retail point of sale, and non-price areas such as after-sales, warranty, etc.

10 Approval certificates to ensure the products comply with local technical specification.

11 Import tariffs and distribution cost which enhance the price.

12 Variation in the product, promotional and price mix/constituents.

13 More costly to serve in terms of visits to the market, product launch, and increased expense in general in conducting business in an overseas market.

14 More complex to monitor and manage.

To conclude, one must bear in mind that the overseas marketing technique tends to be rather more complex and challenging, but the use of a good advertising agency in such a market tends to resolve most problems. Again, the chamber of commerce or trade association can give guidance.

12.6 POLITICAL FACTORS

Politics is becoming a more prominent factor in the conduct of international trade. This applies to all its areas, but especially finance and distribution. More and more countries are looking for an export-based economic expansion. Additionally, an increasing number are conducting their import trade on a minimum cost basis, particularly those with state-run economies as found in Eastern Bloc countries. Government legislation and other state-inspired techniques are tending, in some countries, to take much of the commercial interplay out of the decision-making process of international trade. A policy of protectionism and nationalism prevails. Protectionism acts to shield the home-based industries from the imported product through a quota system or by imposing a very onerous technical specification so that it is very difficult to enter the market at a competitive price. Nationalism shows itself through the development of state airlines and shipping lines and in the movement of imported/exported cargoes on such services. It shows the tight fiscal and monetary policies of most industrial countries.

We will now examine the various circumstances in which politics enters the scene of international trade:

1 The technique of flag discrimination is exercised in a variety of ways. Broadly, flag discrimination means the wide variety of acts and pressures exerted by governments to direct cargoes to ships flying the national flag, regardless of the commercial considerations which normally govern the routeing of cargoes. Examples are given below:

(a) Import licences. Some countries have used the licensing system to ensure that cargo is carried in ships flying their national flag. This tends to encourage reciprocal action which further hinders the growth of trade and can delay the shipment of goods if the relevant services are irregular.

(b) Discriminatory customs dues and other charges such as harbour, lighthouse, pilotage, and tonnage dues, consular fees and taxes on freight revenue. Such practices are particularly prevalent in countries where the ports are state owned.

(c) Administrative pressures. In some countries, official cargo (imports/ exports) is automatically conveyed on vessels flying the national flag. This applies particularly to state- or municipally-controlled organizations.

(d) Routeing of gifts and other non-commercial cargoes. Under certain foreign aid programmes half of the goods are carried in ships of the donor country, with complete disregard to commercial considerations.

(e) Exchange control. The manipulation of exchange control offers countless ways of making shipment in national vessels either obligatory or so commercially attractive that it has the same effect. Such fiscal measures are much on the increase and are complementary to other fiscal measures.

(f) Bilateral trade treaties. Many countries have entered into bilateral trade treaties which include shipping clauses where all or most of the trade between the two countries is carried on ships of the two nations.

2 Quota systems. An increasing number of countries, particularly those with balance of payments problems, impose a quota system on the volume or value of imported products. This is usually introduced to protect the home industry product, but it may be included as a result of an imbalance of trade with a particular country or it may form part of a bilateral trade treaty.

3 Fiscal measures over a wide range of techniques. This includes granting credit facilities to fund imports on a restricted range of products, applicable to specified importing countries.

4 Import controls. Many countries impose some form of import control, some of which have already been identified, such as through the import licence and/or quota systems. Others include onerous technical specifications for a particular product to conform with the home market standard or, often, to discourage imports to protect the home market, and/or the issue of a consular invoice to regulate the flow of imported products.

5 Credit availability. The successful negotiation of the larger export sales contract is not only linked to quality product specification, price, delivery date, after-sales service, etc., but also to credit availability. The exporter who can muster a favourable credit package is in a strong negotiating position.

6 International organizations such as UNCTAD, IMF, OECD, OPEC and ICC are playing a more prominent role in the development and facilitation of international trade. The ICC particularly have done much to establish an acceptable code of trading terms and conditions which are adopted almost worldwide. Governments become very closely involved in such organizations and it is inevitable that this trend will grow as national economies become more and more reliant on developing their overseas markets.

7 Allied to the previous item, organizations such as trade associations and national shipper's councils are tending to take a more dominant role in the development of trade and its facilitation as seen in the various national equivalents of the SITPRO organization. These tend to have some government allegiance.

8 Cargo preference laws in some countries now stipulate that all goods are exported CIF or CFR whilst all imported products are conveyed on an FOB basis. In each instance it ensures that the country maximizes its income from such international trade both by conveying the goods on their national shipping or airline, and by insurance cover provisions.

9 The development of free trade areas is much on the increase. This tends to facilitate greatly trading within the member states and also extends to unified policies in many areas (particularly fiscal and economic).

10 The greater participation of Third World countries in international trade will continue in the next decade. It will be encouraged by the improved availability of international funds to develop their national economies, together with an improved contribution from industrial nations by various means.

11 Political factors also extend to a number of the other government areas. These include general stability of a government which may be stable or unstable; friendly or hostile; efficient, or inefficient and bureaucratic. The currency may be strong and convertible, or weak, unstable, overvalued, and restricted. It could be a floating currency or one of fixed exchange values.

12 An area of increasing activity in recent years is the number of conferences held for major industrial nations at which discussions are held on world economic problems, particularly trade. In particular, the subject of trade facilitation is discussed and the role of the major industrial powers in helping to expand the economies of Third World countries to secure their future economic well-being. Finance is an area of much discussion together with the means by which greater technology can be injected into such Third World countries to make their products more competitive for overseas markets. Japan, USA, UK, West Germany and France, feature prominently in such discussions.

13 Free Trade Zones – usually located near a seaport or airport.

An unstable government tends to have import controls, quota systems and high import tariffs. The salesman must, in such circumstances, endeavour to ensure that the export sales contract gives adequate safeguards to the seller, particularly in terms of payment. Weak and unstable currencies often stem from weak governments and make marketing difficult and sometimes impossible. If in doubt, the exporter should consult his local bank, chamber of commerce or the BOTB for guidance. Circumstances may be such that the currency is of limited value in the money market, difficult to convert, or prone to early devaluation.

Countries which are engaged in hostilities make market penetration almost impossible and are best avoided. Moreover, if the exporter is already in such a situation and hostilities commence, it is often best to cut one's losses and pull out of the market.

Governments which are bureaucratic and inefficient, no matter how well intentioned, tend to cause expensive delays and difficulties in financial settlements. Their establishments tend to be overstaffed, with poorly trained and badly paid officials who often need to make 'extras' from the importers.

An area of increasing development is the Free Trade Zone. It is a specified area where trade is based upon the unrestricted international exchange of goods with customs tariffs used only as a source of revenue and not as an impediment to trade development. Free ports are thus onshore enclaves treated as customs-free zones – or technically as foreign territory for tax purposes. They are designed to attract overseas traders and manufacturers to set up businesses. Duty is payable only when goods move into the host country (see Elements of Port Operation and Management – Chapter 6).

To conclude, the exporter must continuously study the role of politics within the international trade scene, particularly the government's attitude towards buying goods and services from overseas. Advice is readily available from a wide variety of sources and should be sought at an early date.

13   1992 – The Single Market Entity

13.1   MARKETING CONSIDERATIONS AND STRATEGY

Our study of export marketing with special emphasis on developing overseas markets would not be complete without consideration of the 1992 Single Entity market which will arise from the European Community.

The objective of creating a single 'common' market in the European Community relates to the EEC Treaty (the Treaty of Rome) which established the Community in 1957. In 1985, EC Heads of Government committed themselves to completing the single market progressively by 31st December, 1992. It incorporates the countries of Netherlands, Belgium, Luxembourg, Federal Republic of Germany, France, Italy, Denmark, Irish Republic, United Kingdom, Greece, Spain and Portugal. Overall, the twelve states have a population of 320 million people.

The Single European Act came into operation on 1st July, 1987 and commits the EC to the aim of progressively establishing a single market over a period expiring on 31st December, 1992. It defines the single market as 'an area' without internal frontiers in which the free movement of goods, persons, services, and capital is ensured in accordance with this 'Treaty'.

Progress towards completing the single market has taken as its starting point the Commission's White Paper, submitted to EC Heads of Government at the Milan European Council in June, 1985. This outlined the Commission's programme for action to remove the remaining obstacles and distortions in trade between Member States by the end of 1992. The single market means a process of liberalization which allows market forces to work.

13.2   ORGANIZATION OF THE EUROPEAN COMMUNITY

There are four main Community institutions: the Commission, the Council, the Parliament and the Court of Justice.

The Commission has its headquarters in Brussels and Luxembourg, and has the following functions:

1 It proposes Community policy and legislation. It is then for the Council to discuss and, if appropriate, adopt or amend the proposals.
2 It executes the decisions taken by the Council of Ministers, and supervises the day-to-day running of Community policies.
3 It is the guardian of the Treaties, and can initiate action against any Member States which do not comply with EC rules.

The Commission has 17 members chosen by agreement of the Community governments. Each Commissioner is in charge of an area of Community policy, which embrace: external relations; internal market and industrial affairs; competition; agriculture; transport; science; research and development; financial institutions and company law; energy; and customs union and indirect taxation. Each Commissioner formulates proposals within his/her area of responsibility, aimed at implementing the Treaties.

The Council is the Community's decision-making body. It agrees/adopts legislation on the basis of proposals from the Commission, and has its headquarters in Brussels. The term Council not only embraces Ministerial Meetings (the Council of Ministers) but also working groups (Council Working Groups) of officials from the member states and the Committee of Permanent Representatives of the Member States in Brussels.

The European Parliament is a directly-elected body of 518 members. Under the EC Treaties, its formal opinion is required on many proposals before they can be adopted by the Council. Members are elected for a period of 5 years. The secretariat of the Parliament is in Luxembourg.

The European Court of Justice rules on the interpretation and application of Community Laws. It has 13 judges and judgements of the Court are binding on each member country.

13.3 SINGLE MARKET CONSTITUENTS

The creation of the single market will involve radical changes in nine areas summarized below:

1 European standards involving the development of the Euro brand product acceptable in all twelve States.
2 Liberalization of public purchasing, with contracts being awarded on merit and not on nationalistic prejudices.
3 Liberalization of open markets in information technology and telecommunications.
4 Liberalization of financial services embracing insurance, banking and investment, securities, etc., thereby permitting freedom of capital transfer through the Community.
5 Liberalization of transport services, involving deregulation of shipping, air transport and road haulage.
6 Acceptance of professional qualifications gained in one state and recognized

in the remaining eleven states, thereby permitting freedom of labour mobility amongst the professions.

7 Abolition of state subsidies, unfair competition, and restrictive agreements and abuses amongst companies within the market.

8 Adoption of one trade patent throughout the Community, and one patent law, instead of ten pieces of legislation at the moment, leading to greater access to intellectual property.

9 Elimination of physical barriers to trade, thereby permitting freedom of movement of goods and people across frontier points for inter-community transits.

A commentary on each of the areas now follows:

13.3.1 European standards
The provision of a Euro brand product specification acceptable in all twelve States.

Currently, member states have their own standards and laws which are important in setting quality and safety requirements for goods sold in their national home market. The standards are drawn up by national standards bodies such as the BSI.

National standards can be a serious barrier to trade when different standards apply in other member states, or a bigger obstacle when member states do not recognize each other's arrangements for testing and certifying products to ensure that they meet national or European standards. These 'technical' barriers fragment the market and add to cost by forcing producers to modify their products, or by subjecting them to different national testing and certification procedures if they wish to sell them in other member states. All too often, the effect is to discourage firms from seeking orders in other parts of the Community.

The single market entity will permit any product which can be sold in the member state in which it is produced to be freely marketable in all other parts of the EC, unimpeded by different national standards and testing and certification practices. It will incorporate the following relative to individual products:

1 Adopt a unified level of quality and safety which products must meet within EC.
2 Adopt common standards and specification.
3 Accept other member states' tests and certificates relative to products manufactured within the EC.

Overall, the Euro brand product will especially affect the following range:

1 Machinery, personal protective equipment, construction products and toys.

2 High technology products.
3 Medicinal products.
4 Food covering labelling, additives, foods for special dietary uses and materials, and articles in contact with food.

The implication of the Euro brand product can be summarized as follows:

1 It will enable the manufacturer to produce a product in one state and sell it throughout the remaining eleven states without any mandatory modification. It is likely that some products will be modified to meet consumer needs or to reflect culture tastes and territorial/climatic needs.
2 The opportunity to manufacture a product of one specification for a market of 320 million people enables the entrepreneur to exploit the economies of scale in production, distribution, and servicing the market.
3 Economies of scale realized through high production/sales volume lowers unit cost which allows flexibility in pricing strategy to aid market penetration. Companies which fail to extend their product sales to other states are likely to be less competitive in their home market than imported goods from other states at lower prices.

13.3.2   Public purchasing
The second area is the liberalization of public purchasing by governments and other public bodies.

Currently, purchases by governments and other public bodies account for some 15% of the Community's gross domestic product. Examples of the barriers are given below:

1 The tendency to buy home-produced materials, leading to outright refusal by public authorities in many areas to consider bids from suppliers outside their own country.
2 Lack of information about contracts, perhaps through failure to advertise them properly – if at all.
3 Discriminatory specifications.
4 Complex tendering procedures.

By 1989, a number of liberalization measures had been introduced, with the residue to be operative by 1992. The single market will result in public bodies buying on the basis of fair competition and not national identity and will have particular regard to the following:

1 Procedures will be made more open: for example, through clear requirements to give information on future contracts, to stop using specifications which keep out foreign suppliers and to publish details of contracts awarded.
2 Enforcement of procedures will be strengthened so that complaints about

discrimination can be pursued effectively and action taken against those who violate the rules.

Exporters, both large and small, have good opportunites to enter such markets. It is likely that the competition will be keen but the market-profile benefit will be high. Moreover, the financial risks are low and successful tenders/executed contracts can lead to offer contracts in other states and markets outside the EC. A close monitoring service should be devised to ensure the potential exporter is able to tender. Details of such contracts are available in the Trade journals and international press. Further details are available from the trade associations, Chambers of Commerce, and Department of Trade and Industry – British Overseas Trade Board.

13.3.3   Open Markets in information technology telecommunications

The next area is the liberalization of the information technology and telecommunication markets.

The markets for many information technology products and services are global. The absence of a European single market has resulted in manufacturers having a small home base in a fragmented European market. Achieving a single competitive information and technology market in EC will give users a wider choice, and manufacturers a larger home base from which to tackle world markets.

Currently, each major information technology manufacturer makes equipment which operates in a particular way. No two systems are alike. The result is that users are locked into the system of a particular manufacturer from whom they must buy extra equipment to ensure that it is compatible with existing equipment and software.

Moreover, in the past, member states have tended to favour a particular national information technology supplier. This has perpetuated a multiplicity of standards in the public sector so that in practice, most national public sector markets are far from open.

Additionally, users need to know that the equipment which they are buying conforms to agreed standards. This requires recognized testing and certification procedures.

Likewise information is of increasing importance in the modern economy, and the EC market for information services is one of the fastest growing sectors. Crucial to this is the technology which allows information to be stored in electronic form enabling it to be accessed easily and speedily, and the existence of a modern telecommunications network which allows information to be transmitted swiftly and accurately, thus doing away with traditional paper-based systems. These new services will enable suppliers and customers to exchange orders and process documentation directly and automatically via their computers, and will allow business to provide new services direct to consumers through telephone links in areas such as information services or teleshopping.

Television broadcasting is a significant economic activity and, with the development of new cable and satellite technologies, it has effectively become an international medium.

In the area of telecommunications, the market is currently dominated by state-owned monopoly postal and telecommunications authorities.

The foregoing areas are subject to a liberalization of attitudes and criteria, with a view to creating a single market in services and equipment. It will strive to adopt common equipment standards developed in a competitive environment. Users of information technology need to choose the most efficient system. Systems must be able to work properly with other equipment. These two targets will be met through: the development of open systems; interconnection standards for computers and communication; and open purchasing with public sector purchases conforming to OSI standards.

The objectives of the single market entity are contained in the Commission green paper on telecommunications services and equipment which included: full liberalization of the market for terminal equipment; accelerated work on common standards, complete separation of PTT's regulatory and operational functions; full application of the competition provisions of EEC treaty to telecommunications; greater emphasis on the development of Europe-wide services, and a liberalized environment for point-to-point satellite telecommunications.

13.3.4   Financial services

The liberalization of financial services is an important area in the realization of a single market concept.

The creation of a single market, however, goes beyond rights or establishment and assumes the right to do business throughout the Community across national frontiers without the necessity of physically locating in all member states. Developments in new technology and systems of electronic transfer will increase the opportunities of doing business in this way, and the concern is that national restrictions should not prevent companies from taking advantage of them.

The Commission has put forward proposals relative to the complete liberalization of capital movements by 1992 for the creation of a European Financial Area, which comprises the following:

1 To extend liberalization to all capital movements, subject to a safeguard clause permitting temporary controls to be reimposed in certain specified circumstances.

2 A requirement that monetary authorities in member states be permitted

to put certain controls into operation immediately, without enabling measures.

3 The establishment of a single facility providing medium-term financial support for any member state's balance of payments.

The foregoing measures will permit a French resident to open a bank account in the UK, or a Greek resident to borrow from a UK bank.

In the area of securities, common requirements are being established for the authorization of collective investment schemes, such as unit trusts.

With regard to insurance, EC insurers will be able to cover the risk of potential policy holders in any member state irrespective of where the insurer is established. It provides a more liberal regime for large commercial and industrial risk including all marine, aviation and transport business.

To conclude, freedom to transfer capital throughout the Community is essential for a single market in financial services. The objective is to remove restrictions on the movement of capital by 1992. It will result in no restrictions on raising finance in other countries or on the cross-border transfer of funds.

13.3.5 Transport services

The deregulation of shipping, road, and air transport will improve transport utilization and, in so doing, reduce cost to the user.

In the area of road haulage some member states require hauliers to have permits which limit the total number of journeys they can operate in a year. Moreover, the number of permits issued is limited. Such restrictions will be lifted by 1992 thereby permitting a freedom of movement amongst road hauliers on journeys within the twelve states and relaxation of cabotage involving the collection and deposit of goods within a state.

With regard to road passenger transport, it is proposed to liberalize and simplify the rules governing international road passenger transport and permit cabotage.

In the area of shipping, liberalization will operate on competition and unfair pricing practices, phase out unilateral cargo reservation, and deregulate coastal services.

The completion of the Channel Tunnel, scheduled for May 1993, will provide opportunities through quicker travel by rail, to open up extensive tourist and trade markets. Overland rail freight services will provide quick, cheap and reliable services between the UK and major industrial and commercial centres in Europe.

Civil aviation will also benefit from liberalization, which in this instance will embrace the following:

1 Introduction of a cheaper and less restrictive fares structure in off-peak periods.

2 Provision of more competitive economy and business fares which may run counter to other airlines on the route.

3 Permit airlines to offer increased route capacity to meet market needs.

4 All major air routes to be opened up to direct competition between airlines.

5 Traffic rights will be made available on as many as 60 new routes out of the UK.

6 To facilitate a more economic operation by combining two or more routes into a single multi-stop service.

7 To establish a mechanism for scrutinizing potentially inter-competitive inter-line agreements.

The liberalization of the EC transport system will facilitate a cheaper and more extensive transport infrastructure to meet consumer demand. Exporters, as they develop their business throughout EC, must review: their distribution systems; location of warehouse/distribution centres; and the ideal location manufacture centres, and plan for the most effective distribution system compatible with market needs in a very competitive environment.

13.3.6   The professions

The freedom of establishment for the professions is established in the EEC Treaty. It recognizes the freedom of movement for people to work throughout the EC. At present, someone qualified to practice a profession in one member state often has to requalify.

The current proposal would operate through a system of mutual recognition of 'higher education diplomas' – professional qualifications. Everyone would then be able to practice their profession throughout the Community.

The outcome of such recognition of professional qualification throughout the EC will stimulate labour mobility, especially amongst people in the age bracket 20–35 years and with good linguistic ability. Moreover, it will facilitate the development of multi-national workforces throughout the Community in all the professions.

13.3.7   Competition and state subsidies

The abolition of state subsidies, unfair competiton and restrictive practices and abuses.

The EC competition policy is designed to ensure that trade between member states takes place on the basis of free and fair competition, and that the barriers of trade between member states, when dismantled, are not replaced by private barriers which fragment the single market. One of the basic principles in the EEC Treaty is that the EC should set up a system ensuring that competiton in the common market is not distorted. Powers and procedures enabling the Commission to enforce these rules in all areas except transport were laid down in 1962. These were extended to cover inland transport in 1968, to maritime transport in 1986, and to intra-EC air services in 1987.

13.3.8 Intellectual property

The laws governing intellectual property (patents, industrial designs, trade marks and copyright) are in one sense a derogation from the operation of the free market, intended to stimulate innovation. Firms can recoup their investment in technical or design improvements by having the right, for a limited time, to prevent imitation by others who have made no such investment. Firms can also protect the reputation and goodwill which they have built up by registering their trade or service marks, so obtaining the right to prevent others from using them.

While the EEC Treaty prohibits restrictions on imports and exports between member states, restrictions are allowable where they are justified 'for the protection of industrial or commercial property'. For example, the proprietor of a UK patent can use the rights which it gives him to prevent goods produced elsewhere in the EC from being imported or sold in UK.

None of this, however, allows the owners of intellectual property rights to use them to divide up the market. Once the goods have been put on the market in the EC by the owner, or with his consent, he cannot prevent them from being re-imported or resold. In other words, intellectual property rights cannot be used to reinforce a policy of differential pricing within the EC.

Twelve years ago, complete patent protection across the whole Community could be obtained only by applying separately in each member state. The procedures involved, and the tests to establish what was patentable, differed between member states.

The European Patent Convention which came into operation in 1978 made it possible to obtain a European patent by applying to the European Patent Office in Munich. Although it originated in a Community initiative, the European Patent Office is not a Community body (its membership includes Austria, Switzerland and Sweden, but not Denmark, Ireland or Portugal). The Convention has made it possible to obtain patent protection in the contracting states through a single application. EC member states have also undertaken to bring their national patent laws into conformity with the rules applicable to European patents.

Although a European patent is granted in a single application, once granted it is in effect a collection of independent national patents, the enforcement and validity of which are determined by national laws and courts. Any litigation must be carried out separately in each country, and results need not be consistent between countries. In principle, a patent can be found to be valid and infringed in one country, valid but not infringed in another, and invalid in a third.

EC member states have therefore attempted to conclude a Community

Patent Convention under which a European patent having effect in the EC would be treated as a single EC patent and not as a collection of independent national patents. The Convention would at the same time establish a common body of law governing litigation on such matters as validity and infringement. Each member state would designate some of its courts as Community Patent Courts, and it would be possible to obtain a judgement from one of them having effect throughout the EC. There would also be a Common Appeal Court to ensure consistency between the decisions of the different courts.

Virtually all the provisions of the Community Patent Convention have been agreed. However, because of difficulties in certain member states, there is as yet no agreement as to when and how the Convention is to be brought into force. Ratification of the Community Convention is included in the single market programme, and there will be a determined effort to bring it into operation by the end of 1992.

Trade marks are in much the same position now as patents were twelve years ago. In the EC there are ten separate systems for registering trade marks – the three Benelux countries (Belgium, Netherlands and Luxembourg) have a common system, but other member states each have their own arrangements.

This means that anyone wishing to protect his trade mark throughout the EC must apply separately under each of the separate systems. This is obviously inconvenient for industry. Moreover, each system has its own tests as to what can be registered and for dealing with conflicts between trade marks. The rights conferred by a registered trademark vary between the system. A trade mark owner who seeks registration in several member states may find that he is able in one to prevent his mark being used on a wide range of goods, in another to obtain only a narrower protection, and in a third is unable to register his mark at all.

This has an inevitably restrictive effect on the free movement of goods. The Commission has therefore proposed that there should be a Community trade mark. This would enable businesses to secure Community-wide protection through a single application to a Community Trade Marks Office set up for this purpose. There would then be a single set of standards governing what may be registered and for resolving conflicts with other marks. A Community trade mark would confer the same rights in all member states. And (as proposed for patents), member states would designate some of their courts as Community Trade Marks Courts. A Community trade mark owner who considers that another business is infringing his trade mark in other member states would be able to go to one of the courts and obtain judgement valid for the whole of the EC.

The Community trade mark will not replace national trade mark systems – there will continue to be a demand for national trade marks from firms interested only in the home market. Nor will it always be possible to obtain a valid Community mark – for example, two businesses in different parts of the EC may, quite independently, be using the same mark; each would then be a barrier to the other's obtaining a valid Community mark, and they would have to continue with their respective national systems.

National trade marks systems will therefore continue to exist in parallel with the EC system. To reduce some of the existing problems caused by differences between these systems, the Commission has proposed a separate directive on trade marks. This would require member states to harmonize their laws on a number of significant points, such as the rights conferred by a registered trade mark, and the tests of what may be registered.

A number of issues are still to be resolved on the EC trade marks system, in particular the procedure for resolving conflicts, and the location of the Community Trade Marks Office and its working language. Agreement on the directive is close, but adoption is being held up because some member states consider that it should await agreement on the Community trade mark. The aim, which the UK strongly supports, is to ensure that the regulation and directive should be in operation by the end of 1992.

To conclude our examination of intellectual property, it is important that the exporter focuses attention on the subject continuously with a view to maximizing market penetration.

13.3.9 Physical barriers to trade

Physical barriers to trade involve the imposition of cross-frontier controls relative to persons and goods undertaken by immigration and customs.

Many steps have been taken already to make trade easier across EC frontiers. The elimination of customs duties between member states has been one of the foundations of the common market. Less obvious, but nevertheless important, has been the continuing process of administrative harmonization and simplification which is bringing member states' arrangements gradually into line.

Many of these steps are technical in nature and deal with matters of detail. Individually, their effect can therefore be small, but over time their cumulative impact has been substantial.

An EC Customs Code currently under discussion will be another important step in providing a comprehensive framework for EC customs law, and promoting procedural harmonization.

Much remains to be done, and major questions remains to be settled. For example, if customs documentation were to disappear altogether, there would be implications for VAT and excise duties on imports, monetary compensation amounts on agricultural products, and statistics.

13.4 CONCLUSION

To conclude our review of the 1992 Single Market Entity, the exporter must consider the following aspects:

1 Examine current market strategy and develop policies which will increase volume sales and thereby lower unit costs, improve market dominance and aid profitability.

2 Analyse closely the market throughout the twelve states, and identify major competitors and endeavour to determine their strategy in the 1992 situation.

3 Undertake a SWOT (strengths, weaknesses, opportunities and threats) analysis of the exporter's company (product(s) and service(s)).

4 Review the option of a merger and acquisition policy. Enter negotiations with a merchant bank who can give guidance in this area. Merger and acquisition will increase company's size and market dominance, increase cash flow and competitiveness, lower unit cost, develop market penetration, enlarge customer portfolio, increase skills and so on. The option may exist to merge with or acquire a company with an identical product/service, or something complementary, and of the same market profile. This may be, for example, a greenhouse manufacturer merging with a garden furniture company, or developing a working collaborative relationship.

5 Critically review personnel resources and their adequacy. This may involve retraining, recruitment, etc.

6 Review the distribution arrangements. This should be geared to a five-year marketing plan.

7 Critically review the product mix and its adequacy in the market. Ensure it features modern technology, and adequately research the market to ensure the product is consumer-led.

8 Formulate an action plan and identify one person at least in the company to co-ordinate and develop 1992 strategy. Such position should be at senior level.

9 Undertake a product life-cycle analysis, having regard to computers, technology advancements, product range, consumer needs, cost/price strategy, distribution, and so on.

Additional impacts of the 1992 Single Market Entity will include increased competition (with lower unit cost), higher standards, greater labour mobility, more job opportunities, new markets through previously closed procurement areas, more technology and cheaper distribution.

Thus 1992 will present a new era of opportunity and threat but will be geared especially for the enterprising entrepreneur who is both professional and multi-lingual.

14   *Export marketing stragegy*

Our study of export marketing management would not be complete without consideration of export marketing strategy. It is an area which tends to be neglected by numerous companies and merits more attention at the most senior level. In essence it involves the optimization of a company's resources in the manufacturer and sale of products, both at home and overseas. In particular, it embraces market selection criteria, market entry mode evaluation, pricing strategy, transfer of marketing mix and planning.

14.1   EXPORT MARKET SELECTION AND ENTRY MODE

Market selection criteria is an area of export management which requires continuous study and evaluation. This will ensure that the company and its products/services operate in the most advantageous markets both short- and long-term, and thereby maximize profitability and market dominance. This will result in adequate positive cash flow to devote, in part, to research and development and production of the next generation of products. Accordingly, one can define market selection as the process of a company/ entity to identify/evaluate and ultimately participate in a particular market or cluster of markets on a profitable basis. Overall, it is one of the most important decisions taken by the export management team.

14.1.1   Factors determining the number of markets

The tendency is for exporters to strive to sell their products in as many overseas markets as practicable and thereby enhance their international market exposure. Such a policy is often fraught with problems, and is not cost-effective. It encourages a 70:30 concept whereby 70% of the export resources of a company result in only 30% of the income. There may be sound commercial reasons for having a presence in so many markets, but the results must be put in perspective both in the short and long term. Management must ask the question in which markets they should best operate and compare the answer with the present market list. Additionally, resources allocated to unremunerative markets should be identified and redirected to more favourable outlets. An analytical review is required.

Given below are criteria which serve to determine the number of overseas markets in which a company may elect to participate:

1 The company size and resources, including: finance – capital availability and cash flow; personnel, embracing calibre, experience, expertise, professionalism, linguistic ability; and the production resources to cope with increased sales volume.

2 The servicing of the market. This embraces: product specification; merchandise; visits; promotion/selling; general administration, including documentation and invoicing; market research; after-sales service, including spares/warranties; product development budgets and planning; and the overall management of the market.

3 The compatibility of the market with the home market and/or existing overseas territories. For example, selling in one's own free trade area presents fewer problems than exporting outside it (see section 12.5). Moreover, selecting markets of a similar culture, market profile and consumer behaviour presents key benefits. These are enhanced if the market is of high volume with growth potential, with a stable economy/political system and is easy to serve.

4 The development of key markets. Such markets offer: high growth, ease of market entry; economic and political stability; low financial risk; a non-nationalistic consumer/buyer cultural behaviour favourable to imported products; and are easy markets to serve. A major advantage of entering a free trade area is that by selling in one country one has the option of promoting the goods in neighbouring free trade territories. This is very cost-effective as product modification is minimum, physical distribution and channels of distribution can be easily extended, company resources can be concentrated on one area thereby lowering administration costs; market profile, financial risk, and the infrastructure tend to be similar; and the company already has a presence in the market which is very advantageous in competitive marketing terms.

5 A further and similar criterion is that of cluster market development. This involves targeting a group or cluster of markets contiguous to each other, and centralizing the servicing of such markets. Each individual market would tend to have a small-volume sales potential, but collectively the group of markets could present a viable proposition. It offers a centralized system of servicing the market which has many competitive advantages.

6 Fragmented market effort often arises through a historical build-up of an export customer's portfolio within a company, with no company policy or objectives towards overseas business. Much of the custom is unsolicited and is not the result of any target marketing policy.

Overall market concentration would produce the following benefits:

(a) Develops in-depth market knowledge and close customer relations with the end user. This helps the exporter to become more competitive, and compete more effectively in non-price areas. It develops increased sales.

(b) Product unit costs are at an optimum level through economies of scale and developing volume sales markets.

(c) It aids the development of effective marketing plans, with commitment to objectives from all those associated with it.

(d) The exporter becomes more competitive overall.

(e) Market concentration tends to develop market segmentation techniques with the end-user and consumer-led product specification. This develops high margins, and maximizes market share and sales volume coupled with brand and customer loyalty. It is largely uneconomic to develop such a marketing strategy on a fragmented market basis as the volume is too low.

An alternative strategy to follow is global marketing (see section 9.15). In broad terms, this results in product-led marketing policies on a high volume but profitable basis. Here, the manufacturer imposes the product on the market place and leaves it to any intermediaries, such as distributors, to modify the product to meet the end-user's needs. The exporter's production costs are at optimum levels, which are maintained through the distribution network. These reduce market entry and servicing costs to a minimum level, and enable the product to be priced at a low but competitive level on a volume-sales basis. The single specification of the product, and its resultant competitive price in the market place with no value-added benefit to the specification, are the two key reasons why such a product can penetrate markets on a volume basis. Hence the global marketeer can operate in numerous overseas territories, which can number from 25 to 60 depending on the product and company size/profile.

Niche marketing is another area to examine. This is the process of finding a gap in an overseas market territory and developing the market. Often it emerges through visits to the market and market research.

It is appropriate further to develop the following aspects regarding the number of markets in which a company should operate.

1 Company size is a dominant factor. The larger the company, the more resources available and higher is the market profile. Moreover, the larger company tends to have more experience and expertise available as its salary and career structure can attract better calibre personnel. The ultimate is the multi-national company. Larger companies can obtain usually more favourable terms in maufacturing/distribution arrangements than the smaller company. Moreover, the larger company has more resources available to enter and develop a market.

2 Product specification is a major consideration. It will determine: import tariffs; documentation; import controls/restrictions such as are found on

defence equipment and computer technology; size and quantity will determine physical distribution arrangements and the resources required in the
overseas territory to handle the trade within the transport network; the
degree of technology, involving installation, servicing and training, specialized warehouse storage needed to house such goods as perishable/fragile/
bulk liquid commodities; and channels of distribution.

The importance of the foregoing points will vary by circumstance, but
it is stressed that the company should feature export objectives in the
business plan, its export strategy and overseas markets participation thereby
displaying commitment and professionalism.

14.1.2   Factors determining market selection

The factors determining market selection will vary by importance in
individual companies, but the ultimate consideration must be the profit
level both short- and long-term. Given below are the salient points
involved:

1 The market potential relative to the company's product(s). This will
involve extensive research, especially if the product/service is fresh to the
market: test marketing would be desirable. Market potential, translated into
sales forecast, is likely to be spread over a five-year period. Factors
influencing such forecasts would include size of the market, level of
competition, market trends, the stage of development of the market,
stability both economically and politically, government controls, and
factors determining consumer choice of price/quality, non-price areas,
brand image and so on.

The market profile is an important factor, and requires in-depth evaluation
especially in the area of legal constraints and government attitude towards
imported products.

2 The overall marketing/promotion factors. These embrace a range of
factors particularly in the areas of product, promotion, price and distribution
mixes. Mention has been made of all these factors earlier, but emphasis
must be placed on the need to have product acceptance in the market by
the consumer at a competitive price, quality, design and so on. Market
research will aid the decision-making process. Cultural attitudes and
effective communication through advertising and other options are essential
to develop a market. Full use should be made of market research/
advertising agencies.

3 Market accessibility is an important factor: it may be a near or distant
market; or its infrastructure may be poor, resulting in poor distribution
arrangements etc. Distant markets are costly to visit and more difficult to
manage unless one has a resident company representative. Some markets
have few data on their economy and commercial/industrial activities which

makes it difficult to make reasoned statistical analysis. The exporter must reconcile the market location with other overseas territories served and establish whether it fits in with the company strategy and objectives. Near markets are relatively easy to serve and manage and are ideal for the company entering exports for the first time.

4 Emerging from the previous factors is the need to produce a financial statement to determine the stage when the market will be in profit relative to the sales forecast and the investment return. It can also be compared with other markets in which the company operates, including servicing costs, method/costs of physical distribution and so on.

14.2   CRITERIA IN CHANNELS OF DISTRIBUTION SELECTION

Channels of distribution involve the options available to the exporter to reach the consumer/end user. It may be via a distributor, agent, joint venture, export house, local buying office, piggy back arrangement, etc. The choice commits the exporter to a type of marketing strategy and involves substantial resource obligations to the company in terms of finance, production, personnel and so on. One cannot stress too strongly that this is a major decision in the export marketing strategy evaluation and it is likely the option adopted in one market will be different to the channel of distribution followed in another overseas territory. Each market or cluster of markets must be considered independently. A major consideration, in the short and long term, is the sales volume in the market and the consequent level of profitability.

Given below are the more salient criteria involved in the channel of distribution selection:

1 The resources and size of the company. A multi-national company tends to have considerable resources available in terms of production, finance, calibre of personnel, and so on. Moreover, such a company usually has considerable experience in overseas trading and has a high market profile which aids selling and facilitates market entry. It can raise capital easily for a joint venture and switch personnel from one market to another.

Conversely the smaller company may be completely new to export trading and have limited product resources, problems in raising capital, and absence of high-calibre personnel in export trading. It may decide to join forces with another company experienced in the overseas territory and sell compatible goods.

The export director must examine closely his/her company's resources to decide which channel of distribution is best. This involves: total production capacity available, and capacity reconciled with the overseas sales territory forecast; investment needs in plant and product modifications to reflect the end-user market research findings and legal obligations;

personnel requirements to serve the market and manufacture the goods in the factory; and the financial results of these activities overall, which should be reflected in the business plan for the market.

2 The company's objectives as found in the business plan. This will reflect the timescale, nature of markets, financial results, marketing strategy, product strategy, manufacturing strategy, etc. In regard to the last, the company may be keen to manufacture overseas to gain price advantage, increase profit, accelerate market share/growth/penetration, and establish/encourage a higher market profile. The plan may be short- or long-term, with various options. The channel of distribution may be changed after three to five years as the market builds up and new options arise. Likewise, the product range may be extended, and this could reflect changes in the market environment in the areas of competition, political stability, currency levels, consumer/industrial profile, promotion opportunities and so on.

The smaller company is likely to develop a manufacturing base in the home market and rely on effective physical distribution methods to serve the overseas market. A similar policy could be followed by the larger company. In both situations, much depends on the economics of the situation and the financial results, both short- and long-term. The critical area is the market profile and this must be thoroughly researched to obtain the requisite data on which the decision can be based, especially with regard to identifying risk, growth and opportunities.

3 The scale of competition in the overseas market. This must be broken down by company profile/resources and home and imported manufacture. Home-produced goods have market advantage in terms of consumer support through nationalistic tendencies and the absence of import tariffs, protectionism or trade quota barriers. An analysis should be made of the competition, market trends and future predictions, together with the reason for such developments. Government attitudes towards imported products and subsidized production/protection should be established.

4 The exporter's product range and the degree of technical complexity and its user market – consumer or industrial – must be determined. The more technical the product, the more specialized is the channel of distribution required. This involves provision of literature and possibly the training of personnel. It can also involve provision of specialized servicing equipment to the requisite standard as prescribed for the distributor by the exporter.

It is usual to select the channel of distribution which has field experience of the product/service and reflects the profile of the exporter. This results in the exporter having the benefit of an established distributor with a good cumstomer portfolio. It is unlikely that the exporter would select a distributor who already is selling products which are competitive to the exporter.

5 The method of market entry may be direct, as through an agent, or indirect, through an export house.

Indirect market entry is virtually the same as selling to the home market in many respects. It may be that a local buying office situated in the exporter's country is buying on behalf of an overseas territory. Other examples include: an export house/merchant; a confirming house; a finance house; factoring or a consortium (see section 6.1). In all such situations, the goods are bought on local conditions, often at a discount/low mark-up price on a volume basis. All the requisite export documentation and physical distribution arrangements are undertaken by the buyer. No market research data are available to the seller/exporter on the end-user needs. In fact, the exporter usually has little data on the consumer profile or needs. The product could be specially packaged by the buyer and compete with the exporter's product in the overseas territory from another supply source. The exporter, when dealing with the indirect market entry system, usually has no financial risk and payment is prompt. It is ideal for the small exporter keen to enter the overseas market. A major drawback is that the exporter has no control over the price, distribution, packaging, etc. It is unwise to permit branded goods to be sold in this manner as the risk of losing control of the quality and brand image is serious. Usually, profits levels per unit sold are lower. However, costs are less to the exporter as no market servicing is required; nor is the provision of a shipping office.

Direct market entry involves the goods reaching the consumer/end user through an overseas channel of distribution system. It may be that goods manufactured in the home market are sold overseas through an agent, distributor, marketing subsidiary or overseas sales office set up by the exporter. Alternatively, it may involve the exporter producing the goods in the importer's own country under licensing, assembly, joint venture, full manufacture or contract manufacture agreements (see sections 4.11 and 4.13). It can also involve the merger and acquisiton option whereby two companies merge or one buys out the other and continues manufacture and marketing in both territories (see section 4.14).

Direct market entry has the following features in favour of the exporter: the facility to develop the consumer portfolio needs through market research; control over the distribution of the product to the consumer, and often the price; usually a higher 'mark up' on each product; opportunity to research and develop the market and product/service; and the opportunity to promote the product in the exporter's profile/brand image/packaging and so on. Conversely, factors not so favourable in the direct entry system are: the high market entry cost; high cost of servicing the market through the export marketing office or shipping office; risk in the variaton of exchange control regulations and import tariffs; and often, high financial risk. The foregoing applies especially to the home-manufactured product distributed overseas. Further general factors in setting up a manufacturing base/involvement in the overseas territory such as a joint venture include: high level of investment; political risk in some markets *viz* nationalization of assets and curtailment of repatriation of funds; risk of losing control of the venture; and the usually favourable market support of a home-manufactured product without any import controls.

6 Further aspects include: market experience of the particular channel of distribution, degree of market feedback to aid product development and consumer profile; control over price, promotion, product; level of profitability; sales volume and overall market prospects; associated financial, political and legal risk; the degree of flexibility in all areas of the channel of distribution selected, such as corporate goals, company resources, market environment; and finally the overall cost and creditability.

The foregoing aspects must not be regarded as an exhaustive analysis but merely an overview of the situation. Each market needs to be considered carefully and reviewed regularly in a changing environment. It requires adequate planning, finance and company commitment with a number of options being considered to arrive at a satisfactory conclusion including a risk analysis evaluation.

14.2.1   The decision-making process

The process of making the decision relative to entering an overseas market will vary by circumstance. It will particularly involve export marketing planning, utilizing and developing management experience, and evaluating in-depth market research data. The last area is especially important, particularly in regard to having reliable and relevant/compatible data. Ultimately, it will require a judgement/management decision which must not be extensively delayed otherwise a competitor could enter the market.

Details are given below of a check list to be compiled as a criteria evaluation for entering a market overseas:

1 An evaluation of the export market in the following areas:

(a) Potential for sales and growth in the short and medium term.

(b) Compatibility of the product mix fit, which may require minor or major modification to comply with legal obligations and/or consumer needs.

(c) Market stability reflecting economic, political and social considerations.

(d) Short- and medium-term profitability.

(e) Relationship/compatibility of home market with the overseas territory in the critical areas of customer profile, market structure, etc. (Alternatively a comparison with an overseas market in which the exporter currently participates, and export market currently under review. Such comparisons can help to develop a viable export marketing strategy.)

(f) Whether it is a near or distant market, and the availability, suitability and cost of physical distribution.

(g) The commercial infrastructure in the overseas territory and the effectiveness of the market entry options/channels of distribution.
(h) Availability and experience of company resources in terms of personnel, finance, research and development and production, identifying cost factors on a short- and medium-term basis.
(i) Servicing the market including spares, non-price areas and visits.
(j) Availability/development of information technology, especially in the area of end-user/market feedback data.
(k) Payment arrangements and any currency exchange rate risk/restrictions.
(l) Competitive factors embracing profile of competitors and their products' salient features, pricing structure, advertising, channels of distribution, customer/brand loyalty, and so on.

The exporter should produce a grid or comprehensive tabulation relative to the foregoing points as a first stage in export market evaluation.

2 The next stage is to summarize the data of (1) with a view to reconciling them with the export company overseas marketing strategy. In so doing, countries which look feasible require further evaluation in the form of desk research. Such data would be available from chambers of commerce, international banks, consulates, embassies, trade associations, international agencies and so on. This can embrace in-house data and market research agencies. Only current and reliable data should be used. Consultation with export companies already in the market can result in a useful evaluation and comparison. There may be the opportunity of a piggy-back operation. Such contacts can be gained through an export club.

3 The next stage, after eliminating unsuitable markets, is to undertake an in-depth study of remaining markets. Such markets should conform to the company objective and criteria.

At this stage the exporter should have visited the market(s) and obtained adequate data and contacted agents/distributors. Market visits form an important part of market selection/evaluation process, and several visits may be necessary to produce a shortlist of possible markets.

4 The penultimate stage is to produce and submit the data in report form to the company directorate or senior management. This can involve the use of video displays and question-and-answer sessions. Other resources closely associated with the report may be present such as the market research agency.

The report will include: an overview of present situation in marketing and financial terms; justification for entry into new market(s); outline of company objectives in overseas markets; list of markets examined and conclusions, particularly analysing the product fit and transfer of marketing mix; shortlist of markets examined in depth, and conclusions reached; overview of the market selected, particularly in areas of sales forecast;

product specification, profit-and-loss account of market entry over three- to five-year period including product modification cost and unit cost based on annual sales volume; income; an evaluation of market risk areas and so on. The report will place strong emphasis on the financial implications on the market entry and the company resources, available and required, to handle such a situation.

5 The final stage is to devise an action plan to execute the decision to enter a new market. This must be controlled by the export director and have the full commitment of all the chief officers within a company. It will involve the setting up of the infrastructure in the overseas market and concluding arrangements regarding physical distribution and channels of distribution. Numerous visits to the market will be necessary. Planning will play a major role.

14.2.2 Market entry option criteria

The range of market entry options available are outlined in section 6.1. The basis of their selection depends on many factors, which are given below:

1 The sales forecast, both short- and long-term. A market with a low sales volume is more suitable to an agent, whilst the high volume market may be better entrusted to a distributor. Much depends on the political and market-profile situation.

2 The stability of the market, both in economic and political terms. Stable markets favour more commitment by the exporter, especially in investment terms.

3 Exporting to member states within a free trade area are low risk ventures with no trade barriers and constraints in trading practices. Usually, they are easy markets to serve and provide easy access of market profile data.

4 Legal and political constraints. This extends to agency agreements, channels of distribution, patent registration, licensing, joint ventures, franchises and repatriation of funds, etc.

5 The extent to which market research data are available from the end user. For example, such data are available from the agent and subsidiary, but not from the export house or distributor.

6 The degree of control in the areas of price, quality, marketing and distribution. Complete control is obtained by the wholly-owned subsidiary or local representative. This is not so with the distributor.

7 The profitability of the market entry options, both in the short and long term. It may prove advantageous to switch from one market entry option to another as the sales volume increases allowing exploitation of the economies of scale.

The options available, which will vary by market, should be examined closely and adequately researched. Legal advice should be sought regarding the market entry option formulation. A full marketing, distribution and financial appraisal should be made for both the short and long term. One must bear in mind that the adoption of one market entry option may prove costly to change and present difficult legal problems to resolve. This situation can be avoided by adequate research and legal advice.

14.3   PRICING STRATEGY

Export pricing is a complex area and involves many considerations in price formulation. The salient points are given below:

1 Products manufactured and sold in the home market tend to have a cost advantage. Transportation costs are low as the goods do not have to be despatched from overseas; the goods are less prone to exchange rate fluctuation, although it is recognized that many home-produced goods embrace raw materials/component parts which are imported; the home-produced goods are not subject to any import tariffs; market entry costs, product modification to reflect consumer needs and foreign government approval certificates (usually home-produced products represent product core) are all less expensive, payment by the buyer for the home-produced commodity is much quicker compared with the product imported some 5000 miles away with a transit time of several weeks. Overall, the home market pricing strategy is determined by: selecting market targets; choosing a brand image; compiling an optimum marketing mix; selecting a pricing policy; determining a pricing strategy; and arriving at a specific price.

2 The exporter serving some ten markets is likely to have a product core representing 80–90% of the specification, with the residue reflecting each individual market need having regard to government legislation, consumer/cultural needs, overall market/customer profile, competition, and the exporter company's objectives/aims in each of the ten markets. Each of these markets will have a different cost factor embracing physical distribution, channels of distribution, exchange rate, mark-up, packaging, promotion/selling, product design/modification costs, production costs which will vary by volume geared to sales forecast, and so on. Generally, the lower the volume sales to a market, the higher the unit cost, as the economies of scale cannot be realized. This applies in all the cost analysis areas of production, distribution, administration and servicing the market, promotion through trade fairs, exhibitions, sales conferences, and so on. Such costs can be reduced by working with another exporter on a piggy-back system.

The pricing strategy adopted in any one market will vary by circumstance, and it is very unlikely that an exporter will fix the same price in all the overseas territories. Such a policy is impracticable and will not aid profit-ability and market development. The following factors will influence price structure:

1 Level of competition and their pricing structure related to the product/service specification.

2 Government import tariffs and price controls.

3 The export company's aims in the market relative to volume, market share, and policy relative to physical distribution, channels of distribution, promotion/selling technique, servicing the market, payment terms and so on – a thorough cost analysis should be undertaken.

In regard to company aims in the market place, a series of options should be devised with differing volumes and price levels. For example, it may be prudent to target major cities in year one and rural areas later, rather than promote the product nationwide in year one.

4 The range of products promoted by the exporter. It may be prudent to limit the product range in the early years of the market entry, and expand them as the market dictates. Any such strategy must be geared to the outcome of market research findings.

5 The benefit of a thorough market analysis will reveal whether the market is still in the development stage or demand has approached saturation point. For example, washing machines in a market may be at a 20% level, rising to 70% some 10 years later as the GDP rises, consumer spending power increases in real terms, home ownership increases, and the working population increases especially of women.

Alternatively, niche marketing opportunities may arise through identify-ing a gap in the market for a particular product. This could permit premium pricing which would yield above-average 'mark up'.

6 Consumer/buyer behaviour should be studied closely: this will identify trends and establish to what extent price plays a part in product/brand selection. A further aspect is the degree to which the culture favours imported goods relative to the home-produced item.

Research may suggest that the younger population, as compared to an ageing population, may be more responsive to change, less nationalistic, more widely travelled, better educated, more geared to modern technology and more responsive to advertising. The other benefit of having a younger rather than older customer loyalty portfolio is that the customer-loyalty lifespan is much longer, thereby opening up pricing strategy options to develop market volume and market penetration.

7 The price/value dimension. This involves the utility/value of the product/service as viewed/perceived by the user in terms of the selling price. Ad-ditionally, it reflects the return on the capital investment as determined by price and the sales volume and sought by the exporter in pricing strategy.

8 Finally, a whole range of pricing strategies exist which arise to meet individual market needs based on the following:

(a) Competitor-orientated pricing.
(b) Cost-orientated pricing.
(c) Demand-orientated pricing.
(d) Market penetration pricing.
(e) Market skimming pricing.
(f) Early cash recovery.
(g) Satisfactory rate of return.
(h) Differential pricing.

Pricing strategy seeks ultimately to pitch the price at the level which produces the maximum level of profit. This tends to be the economist's approach. An example is given below of a company with a production run of 800 and a unit cost of £40 and a variable/production cost of £100 yielding a surplus of £32 000 over variable/production cost. On the basis of the variable cost remaining constant at £100, and varying the price bands at 5% intervals, it establishes that the maximum yield contribution to fixed cost is gained at the £154 price level, producing £34 560. The table is based on a 10% change in volume/sales which in turn affects the unit cost level and ultimately the price.

This approach to pricing strategy is ideal in terms of profit maximization/contribution, but does not take account of the impact on the market place. For example, if we produced 1040 the yield would be £19 760, but the market share would be higher. Conversely, a higher price at £161 would generate 560 sales with a yield of £34 160, but allow the competitor to gain market share growth advantage. Overall, such a strategy requires careful evaluation relative to profit/maximization/yield both in the short- and long-term situations in the market place. Table 14.1 illustrates an economist's approach but the exporter often needs to have a marketing approach.

Table 14.1   An example of pricing strategy

Price (£)	Percentage change in price	Variable/production cost (£)	Unit cost (£)	Volume production level	Percentage change in volume	Surplus/contribution (£)
161	+ 15	100	61	560	− 30	34 160
154	+ 10	100	54	640	− 20	34 560
147	+ 5	100	47	720	− 10	33 840
140	Current price	100	40	800	Current volume	32 000
133	− 5	100	33	880	+ 10	29 040
126	− 10	100	26	960	+ 20	24 960
119	− 15	100	19	1040	+ 30	19 760

Table 14.2 Absorption and marginal costing techniques in export pricing techniques

	Company 'A' – Single Shift Factory System – Production Volume 10 000 per Year	Company 'B' – Two Shift Factory System – Production Volume 20 000 per Year (50/50 Home/Export Markets)	Company 'C' – Two Shift Factory System – Production Volume 20 000 per Year (50/50 Home/Export Markets – Export Market Bearing all Fixed Cost	
	Product Unit Cost	Product Unit Cost	Product Unit Cost – Home Market	Product Unit Cost – Export Market
	£	£	£	£
Fixed Cost i.e. depreciation, core product, development, administration	5	2.50	5	–
Variable Cost – labour materials energy	5	5.50	5	6
Profit mark up 30%	3	2.40	3	1.80 to 7.0
Selling price at factory gate	13	10.40	13	7.80 to 13.0
Gross Profit	30 000	48 000	30 000 plus	18 000 to 70 000

It will be appreciated that an increasing number of exporters today base their pricing strategy on the cost of the product plus a contribution to overheads unit cost as demonstrated in Table 14.1. This policy improves cash flow through a business and can be regarded as the price–earning ratio technique. It enables a comparison to be made between the results in one market compared with another. However, the strategy must be viewed within the overall business plan policy of the company.

As indicated earlier, cost analysis is essential on a 'per market' basis to aid the pricing strategy formulation. Equally full use should be made of the absorption and marginal costing techniques as detailed below. It will be recalled that absorption costing embraces both the fixed and variable cost of the product unit, including manufacturing/component cost and a proportion of depreciation, administration, etc. based on unit cost, whereas marginal costing operates on the principle whereby variable costs are charged to cost units and fixed cost attributable to the relevant period is written off in full against the contribution for that period.

A simple example of pricing strategy development is found in Table 14.2, and has the following features.

1 Company A has a production base of 10 000 units annually which is sold exclusively to the home market. Hence all the costs are reflected in the make-up of the price structure, adopting the absorption costing technique. The factory works a one-shift system thereby being under-utilized in production volume. Overall, the profit level is £30 000.

2 Company B produces an identical product, but operates a two-shift system. It produces 20 000 units per annum. The fixed cost of £50 000 is spread over 20 000 units. Variable cost, at £5.50, is slightly higher than Company A because it reflects the enhanced labour cost of unsocial hours inherent in the two-shift system. The price is lower, at £10.40. The company serves both the home and export markets. The profit total is based on a minimum price level of £10.40 with a yield of £48 000.

The option does exist in Company B for the home market product of 10 000 units to be sold at £13 – as in Company A – and the residue of 10 000 units allocated to the export markets at a minimum selling price of £10.40. This will yield a profit of £54 000. The absorption costing technique is used.

3 Company C, producing the same product but with the absorption costing technique for the 10 000 units for the home market, and marginal costing for the 10 000 units for the export markets. It offers a home market revenue of £13 000, and an export price of £7.80, which could be increased to as much as £13.00 if the home market price was adopted. The profit margin ranges from £48 000 to £100 000. The significant factor with Company C is that the home market will bear all the fixed cost, secure in the knowledge that 10 000 units will be sold at £13. The remaining 10 000 units, earmarked for a variety of overseas markets, will not bear the fixed cost, but have the

option to sell at a price ranging from £7.80 to £13.00 or beyond, depending on overseas market pricing conditions. If there are four overseas markets, the selling prices ex works could be £7.80, £8.50, £12.00 and £13.50.

The foregoing examples of three companies unequivocally demonstrates some of the options available to the entrepreneur to develop a viable overseas pricing strategy. A salient factor is the need to utilize production resources to an optimum level to achieve low unit cost and provide pricing flexibility to facilitate market penetration and generate volume sales. Moreover, it will adequately fund the fixed costs and thereby have sufficient financial resources to allocate to research and development to produce the next generation of products.

To conclude our pricing strategy review, it must be stressed that each situation requires careful evaluation.

14.4 MARKETING MIX

The marketing mix involves the four P's: product (page 90); price (page 68); place (page 138); promotion (page 136). Export marketing involves the transfer of the constituents of the marketing mix from the home market to the overseas territory. The extent of the transfer of each constituent will vary by product/service and overseas market. Moreover, the situation will vary annually as the market changes reflecting the level of competition etc.

Details of the four constituents of the marketing mix are found in Figure 14.1.

14.4.1 Transfer of the marketing mix: strategy considerations

The transfer of the marketing mix involving product, price, promotion and place from the established home market to an overseas territory is a major strategy decision which should be taken at senior management level. It involves the following considerations:

1 The nature of the marketing mix is the home market and the extent to which it can be reconciled in an overseas territory, which may be a near market (such as Europe) or a distant market (like the Far East). The near market is easy to serve, both in terms of visits and distribution, with a short lead time from the factory site to the consumer. Conversely, the distant market is more costly to visit, generally provides fewer data on market profile, may have a widely different culture, and involves a long lead time from the factory site to the end user. The servicing of the distant market is usually more difficult unless the exporter shows total commitment by having a permanent representative in the overseas territory, which can prove costly.

2 The level and nature of the competition in the overseas territory and how it differs from the home market or another overseas market in which the company operates. If the company is already selling in an overseas territory and wishes to extend its market range to a neighbouring market, it is possible the benefit would accrue from the cluster market concept (see page 290).

3 The degree to which the product core remains unchanged and the extent to which product modifications are necessary to reflect consumer needs as revealed by market research and in compliance with the local legal obligations in order to obtain the necessary approval certificate. This involves a cost factor in terms of product design, plant modification and production programme including materials and labour cost. The THE can help UK exporters determine the extent of product modification in order to gain acceptance in the overseas territory (see section 10.12).

4 The market profile of the overseas territory. This involves market size, culture, potential market share/volume, demographical and topographical data, political situation, economic factors, GNP, and consumer behaviour. It would also reflect the government and social attitudes towards imports, and any trading agreements between the two countries.

5 The stage at which the market is developed, both in volume terms and technological aspects: this depends very much on the product. Less-developed countries are less geared up to the latest generation of technology compared with those which operate in a Westernized economy. Additionally, some markets are more capable of development than others for a variety of reasons. For example a market with a low car-ownership could be developed if the price was lower, the consumer buying power was strong and the transport infrastructure in terms of roads existed to take advantage of such a facility.

6 The financial options available and the credit risk involved. This involves: exchange rate levels; availability of funds for imported products, and any constraints imposed by government or through third parties such as the World Bank; credit insurance availability; and local government attitude towards repatriation of funds from joint ventures and inward investments. Banks can give advice in these areas.

7 Donor agencies, such as the World Bank, fund major projects in less-developed countries and invite tenders from suitable clients (see section 14.6). This may involve a seaport development or a new airport passenger terminal etc. The credit risk is slight, but the lead time from its inception extensive. However, it does provide a high profile to the exporter, and can generate further business.

8 The range of market entry options available, both for direct and indirect market entry. The latter involves the export house, through which the exporter has no control over the price to the end user, or the gathering of useful market research data of the consumer profile. The former concerns

the company representative selling in the overseas territory: this involves a high cost to set up and launch, but displays commitment to the market and provides useful market intelligence and research data (see section 6.1).

9 The level of profit margin. Costings may be undertaken on an absorption or marginal cost basis (see section 14.3) plus mark up to determine price. The ultimate consideration is the bottom line result. This will depend on the predicted sales volume as recorded in the budget. Hence a small volume market with little prospect of growth can produce a modest return compared with the higher volume market. The market prospects, its entry/launch costs, and servicing, together with sales volume, all require careful evaluation and research.

10 A major area of consideration is the company resources. This includes: availability of funds to invest in new plant/product launch, and for setting up the market entry; availability of personnel in product design and for servicing the market. This includes selling, and requires personnel of adequate professional qualifications, linguistic skills, and experience in the market. In the technical field, for example, an engineering qualification is required. Such resources are usually incorporated in the three- to five-year business plan of the company.

11 The stage which the commodity or service has reached in its product life cycle. Ideally, the exporter who may be selling in overseas territories up to five different models of a particular product such as a car, prefers to discontinue the production of one model throughout all the markets and subsequently launch a replacement. The exporter does not usually favour the production continuance of a model for one market and its replacement in another market as it proves, long-term, uneconomic. Such a replacement model would displace the product which has reached the end of the product life cycle. The remaining four models would remain in the market and ultimately would be phased out on a staged basis as their life cycle expired and replacement products emerged. The product launch may not be instantaneous in all markets, but progress in accordance with a plan as the old model is phased out and the new one introduced. It is desirable when entering a new market that the product life cycle of the commodity has a reasonable and viable period to run, and is not likely to be undermined by competition. Companies already in the export field have the experience quickly to develop new markets. Those fresh to the export scene should contact other exporters already in the market to obtain any useful guidance. This is available through export clubs.

To conclude our review of marketing mix strategy factors it is desirable to feature the subject in the company business plan, thereby obtaining a company and management commitment. It requires adequate market research, both desk and field, and an early decision on the market entry and product specification. This will enable the planning to be instituted at an early stage and costing and pricing strategy to be formulated. Adequacy of personnel and finance are critical areas of consideration.

The constituents of the marketing mix, embracing price, product, promotion and place include the following:

1 Market research, which will identify the market profile and its acceptance. In particular: the product specification reflecting culture and national legal needs; the market size and level of competition; economic factors; the stage which the market has reached (is it a developing market, or near saturation point?); political considerations; market entry options and so on. The export director may need to obtain board approval prior to entering a new market, and market research data should be used extensively. This may involve desk research to determine basic data, which could be followed by field research of a more specific and qualitative nature. Long-term, the exporter is likely to conduct an on-going market research analysis using sales invoices, agent reports, market visits, and official statistics.

2 Product planning, which takes the form of formulating the design and specification of the product for the specific market, including: costing it; devising a production plan having regard to market entry/launch date, sales volume forecast, physical distribution and transit time; channels of distribution; and overall cost and profit margins. Ideally, the design/specification should, if possible, retain the product core which may represent 85% of production cost; the residual should reflect modification of the basic model to meet the market needs. Each situation will have a varying market and the entrepreneur should strive for high volume sales with adequate margins thereby maximizing profit levels (see section 14.3).

3 Advertising is a key area on which to focus attention, as the exporter must devise the most effective advertising plan possible. Much will depend on the product/service and resources available in the market. Many exporters engage an advertising agency in the overseas territory who will be able to formulate the correct advertising strategy. It requires regard to: the cost, product/service specification, market profile/literacy, what the competitors use in promotion terms; target market area by location/social economic class; resources available from the exporter of promotional material used in other markets; channels of distribution; linguistic considerations; advertising standards and so on. The strategy requires to be well thought out, adequately monitored to judge sales performance and flexible enough to take advantage of changing circumstances.

4 Selling options will vary by market and primarily depend on the market entry option adopted. The strategy to follow must take account of long-term market developments. It may be appropriate to sell initially through agents on a commission basis or through a distributor. In the longer term, as the sales volume builds up, and with a favourable market share, it may prove prudent to develop a subsidiary in the market over which the exporter has complete control in all areas of production or assembly, distribution, selling and after-sales service. Factors determining method of selling include: resources available in the market place; cost-effectiveness; profit margins; sales forecast, short- and long-term sales market forecast; how the competitors operate; degree of control in terms of price; monitoring of performance; feedback in terms of market research company resources; repatriation of funds and so on. Situations do emerge wherein the exporter is selling direct to an export house who in turn exports the product, together with other commodities from other companies, to the overseas territory in which the exporter is retailing through a distributor. Hence the consumer may have the same product offered at differing prices from two sources but in different packaging. In such circumstances, it is difficult for the exporter to institute effective control.

5 The process of handling and physical distribution requires careful evaluation. The availability of transport modes serving the overseas territory, including their cost, transit time, reliability, service frequency and overall suitability require careful evaluation. Some exporters undertake a transport distribution analysis (*Elements of Export Practice*, Chapter 11). If the exporter is developing a cluster market concept, it could be advantageous to centralize distribution in one overseas territory which would serve neighbouring markets. Some exporters develop the 'just-in-time' distribution system thereby holding minimum stock levels and replenishing them as they are consumed. Containerization is ideal for the distant market (UK–Americas) and the trailer for the nearer market (UK–Continent). Air-freight is also ideal for many products of high value and low weight ratio.

6 The channels of distribution, involving the method adopted to transfer the goods from the exporter/seller to importer/buyer are numerous. It is an area which requires careful consideration and several visits to the market. Market research and the consulates/embassies in the overseas territory can aid the selection process. The chosen channel may be an agent, distributor, or working on a 'piggy back' arrangement in association with another exporter already established in the market with a compatible product and acceptable customer portfolio. The exporter should engage a lawyer in the overseas territory to advise on the terms of the agent's/distributor's agreement, having regard to the exporter's company objectives.

7 The merchandise and display resources must have regard to the recommendation of the advertising agency and the legal obligations obtaining in the buyer's country. This includes advertising and display material, which must reflect the cultural and linguistic needs of the market. Moreover, the form of display and range of merchandise used must be cost-effective.

8 The branding and packaging strategy should reflect the market research findings and the exporter's image to the consumer/buyer. A company with a strong brand image should portray this in the market place, especially in the areas of quality, competitiveness, price, after-sales service and so on.

The product/service should contain the exporter's logo. Packaging requires special attention to ensure it is culturally acceptable, competitive, attractive at the point of sale, conforms with the relevant legislation, colour acceptance of the culture and is multi-lingual. One cannot sress too strongly the need to have effective packaging of consumer commodities to maximize sales and develop market penetration: test marketing involving packaging should be adopted. Packaging is an important sales aid and can vary significantly by market and culture.

9 The pricing strategy requires extensive research of competitive products and their specification and terms of sale, especially in the non-price areas of after-sales service and guarantee/warranty. Above all, the price must be competitive to ensure it will achieve the sales forecast, and reflect an adequate 'mark up' (see section 14.3).

10 Servicing the market requires effective organization in the exporters company. It includes correlating production with sales, effective physical distribution, availability of spares, product maintenance/servicing, training of maintenance personnel in overseas territory, devising quality standard maintenance workshops, effective feedback from the consumer/market place to the exporter to reflect buyer behaviour, consumer profile, market trends, analysis of competitor's products, advertising/selling effectiveness, and so on. The exporter must visit the market regularly and despatch regular sales and technical bulletins to agents/distributors etc. to ensure that they are continuously informed of developments in the exporter's company. Full use should be made of modern technology to aid effective communication between the exporter and importer.

11 The foregoing ten points require the effective planning and co-ordination of all the exporter's resources to achieve the optimum performance in accord with the company's objectives. The exporter's marketing department is responsible for the formulation, co-ordination, execution of the marketing mix on an optimum basis to achieve the budgeted sales and profit levels. Overall, an action plan should be devised.

The marketing mix transfer requires many considerations. It involves particularly adequate research and the development of the appropriate strategies to market on a cost-effective basis.

14.5   EXPORT MARKETING PLANNING

Planning for export marketing involves the process whereby the company must decide on the strategy to adopt in relation to its markets, and the allocation of resources which will be needed in order to put the chosen strategy into effect. It is basically a corporate function involving the company's resources of personnel, production, investment and research and development with a view to devise the strategy which will optimize the company's results in the market place. Overall, it is a management decision-making process and involves, particularly, market intelligence systems to ensure that the management can keep in touch with changing patterns of demand in the overseas markets and adjust their strategy accordingly.

Overall, export planning involves seven basic steps embracing the following:

1 The present situation, its strengths and weaknesses and the opportunites which flow from it.
2 The way forward and the stated objectives.
3 The timescale and priorities.
4 The control methods to monitor the plan's execution, and contingency plans to counter problem areas and shortcomings.
5 The methodology arising from item (3), especially strategy and tactics.
6 The cost and method of funding, having regard to the options available.
7 Allocation of personnel, responsibilities, and commitment to the plan.

We will now consider the foregoing planning steps:

1 To execute the first stage it is usual to adopt the SWOT analysis technique whereby the exporter establishes the strengths, weaknesses, opportunities and threats of the present situation. This incorporates all the ingredients of product specification, price, competitiveness of present strategy, technology, profitability, product life cycle, distribution, channels of distribution, market profile, experience in the market, market trends, market share, and so on. It can be called 'situation analysis', and each of the seven stages can embrace the decision-making process of commitment, overseas territory or territories of selection, market entry mode, overall marketing strategy, and the adequacy and development of the exporter's personnel and organization resources. All such criteria would be considered/formulated against a market screening analysis, marketing plan with objectives, budgetary formulation/control and level of profitability involving a negative or positive cash flow. Such a criterion would involve a plan of three to five year's duration depending on the market situation analysis results and overall company strategy/resources. A further aspect is the decision-making process and how it will reflect any corporate policy inherent in a large multi-national company. For the smaller company with less resources in finance, personnel, production, etc., the planning procedure will be on a smaller scale but with the same objectives and disciplines.
2 This involves the way forward and its stated objectives. This embraces the correlation between the identified market opportunities and available company resources embracing finance, personnel, production, research and development and so on. The objectives must be realistic, and profit-motivated within a reasonable timescale. Contingency options must be evaluated and processed including a risk analysis evaluation.

3 The timescale and schedule require careful consideration. It is most important that the schedule is realistic and all departments/personnel are aware of their commitments. This involves a detailed market and financial analysis to decide on the best option. Salient areas include the finalization of the product specification, production resources, and the result of the discounted cash-flow analysis. This includes imposition of adequate control/monitoring techniques and establishment of priorities.

4 This embraces the cost of the plan, and requires detailed financial presentation incorporating all the elements of the plan. It involves operating resources utilization and a logistical appreciation. One must bear in mind that the export manager is responsible for the contents and strategy of the plan and the finance department will cost it.

Hence arising from the foregoing, the plan will particularly embrace the following constituents: formulating evaluation of strategy; general market research; market entry options/discussions; entry options finalized; specific market research; in-house discussions; marketing strategy formulated; progress report; further in-house discussions; and full implementation of the agreed plan.

5 The methodology is is an important area and especially involves: market analysis including reviewing existing markets and their strengths and weaknesses; new market selection and options (see section 2.1) which is likely to involve product modification and market entry options (see section 6.1). It involves the transfer of the marketing mix and includes review of product specification, promotional mix, channels of distribution, pricing strategy, and so on.

In considering the strategy and tactics to adopt, the exporter should adopt a diversification planning policy involving a structured approach to identify and exploit new product/market opportunities in line with the export company or corporate objectives, strengths and weaknesses based on systematic screening and evaluation of product/market options. Typical inputs comprise the following:

(a) Independent review and analysis of client aspirations and goals matched to technical, production, commercial/marketing, management and financial resources and capabilities.
(b) Screening of product/market options for 'best fit' conditions of size, growth, competitive, environment, cost and feasibility of entry.
(c) In-depth study of 'best fit' market to establish market entry route and strategy.

6 Finally, the person responsible for the plan and the members of the team actually executing it – usually representing various departments – must be determined.

It will be appreciated the plan will overlap in parts but will have especial regard to the company resources and prevailing circumstances.

It is appropriate to examine some of the planning areas arising in the export marketing situations:

1 Marketing and sales plan (see section 7.3).
2 Media or campaign plan (see section 4.4).
3 Overseas market selection (see section 14.1).
4 Production department. This involves unit cost, labour resources, costing analysis, production cycle/programme, plant and machinery adaptation, liaison with export marketing department on order execution, etc.
5 Finance department. This has a major input to the planning process, especially in the areas of cost analysis, evaluation of the financial results of the various options available in product design, costings of varying production levels, identity of the various investment options available to develop/launch a product and those most ideal for the company adoption, costing data as required, and liaison with the export marketing and production department as required. A further area under the aegis of sales negotiation is advice on pricing strategy, currency options, the financial risk, and the suitability of the method of payment as proposed by the importer.
6 Personnel department. This embraces adequacy of personnel resources to meet the plan's objectives, including personnel in the export department embracing sales, market research, shipping, product development and so on. Likewise in the production department, with an increase, perhaps, from two to three shifts, requiring additional skilled labour.
7 The export marketing department offers enormous scope for effective planning, ranging from every order obtained to developing the most effective strategy in product design, market research, market selection, market development/penetration, pricing policy geared to sales volume, etc. It also includes the marketing and sales plan, media plan, and planning the overseas visit. An important function is to establish priorities and objectives.
8 The research and development department is guided by the marketing department in regard to the priority accorded to their individual projects. Emphasis is given of their market potential, the payback of an individual project and timescale, and the degree of competition. Innovation and product development is an important area of a company strategy having regard to the fact that individual products have a limited product life cycle. The marketing department can provide valuable market analysis/intelligence of the market in which they operate and conduct feasibility studies.

The benefits of effective export planning can be summarized as listed below:

(a) it optimizes the use of resources available and thereby develops minimum unit cost criteria, facilitating the generation of a positive cash-flow budget;

(b) it facilitates the exporter's competitiveness in all areas of the business;

(c) it develops the concept of the best value for money as the options are examined and the most favourable adopted;

(d) It develops the concept of management by objective as personnel work towards an attainable goal, and aids the formulation of the business plan and budget;

(e) it develops timescale and work disciplines within a company which helps to measure accountability of individuals' performance, enhancing motivation at all levels within the company;

(f) it minimizes the risk of wrong decisions and negative attitudes/policies being devised;

(g) it balances the available resources within a company against the market opportunities and alternatives both at home and overseas;

(h) it co-ordinates the company's resources and thereby ensures all personnel who have a commitment to the plan realize its objectives and the implications of any variation and, in so doing, it develops communications within a company and an *esprit de corps*.

To conclude, export marketing planning requires many skills and these must be acquired/developed by management at all levels to ensure the efficient running of the department on a competitive basis.

14.6 EXPORTING TO DEVELOPING COUNTRIES THROUGH INTERNATIONAL AID

During the past decade there has been a growth in the financial aid dispensed to developing countries worldwide, and the level of competition for such contracts is tending to increase. Overall, it is an ideal market for both the large and small company, and is comparatively risk free. To enter the market requires complete dedication/commitment, professionalism at the highest level and perseverance. Basically, it is a sound market to enter and carries a high market profile.

International aid agencies annually disburse some $50 billion in grants and loans to developing countries worldwide. This aid supports new and on-going projects and technical assistance activity totalling some $100 billion at any one time.

The international aid agencies fall into two main categories: bilateral and multilateral. Bilateral agencies are those funded exclusively by a single donor government. Examples include: the Overseas Development Adminis- tration (ODA); West Germany's KFW; and the United States Agency for International Development (USAID). Multilateral Agencies are funded by more than one donor government and include the World Bank Group, incorporating the International Development Association (IDA), the Inter- national Bank for Reconstruction and Development (IBRD) and the

International Finance Corporation (IFC), and the Asian, African, Caribbean and Inter-American development Banks. Other multilateral agencies are supported by member countries of a particular economic, cultural, or regional grouping such as the EC's European Development Fund (EDF), the Islamic Development Bank, and the OPEC Fund.

In general, procurement of goods and services by the bilateral agencies is tied to suppliers whose nationality is the same as the donor. However, some agencies are more flexible than others in their adherence to this policy. Notable exceptions are such Arab Bilateral Agencies as the Saudi and Kuwaiti Funds as well as some Scandinavian aid agencies. Multilateral agencies tend to shop more widely, but still mainly confined to suppliers from countries whose governments support the agency concerned. Suppliers based in aid-beneficiary developing countries are also favoured, and, in some situations such as EDF, are given a price advantage.

Aid is applied to almost all sectors in developing countries, with emphasis on projects and initiatives which contribute most to economic and social development and the health, education, employment and welfare of the local population. Some sectors naturally predominate. Agriculture and rural development receive the highest priority. Energy, water supply and sewerage, transportation, industry, health, education, telecommunications and urban development also feature prominently.

Many agencies now emphasize complete sectoral programmes, rather than a succession of individual and often unrelated projects. Also, less money proportionately is being devoted to big, new capital projects, and more to making existing facilities work better through rehabilitation, upgrading and improvements in management, operations and maintenance. Vocational education and training are therefore of growing importance.

The project cycle involves a dialogue and evaluation between the beneficiary government and the donor agency to determine priority sectors and sub-sectors. Specific projects are subsequently identified, prepared and appraised prior to aid agency approval. This is followed by calls for tender, adjudication, contract award, implementation and (on a sampling basis) evaluation. The project gestation period ranges from one to five years.

Aid agencies endeavour to strike a balance between getting the best deal for the developing countries and appeasing commercial pressures exerted by the industrialized countries, which provide their funds. Agencies are suspicious and watchful of commercial interests trying to influence vulnerable developing countries' government officials into sponsoring dubious schemes, which may not be to the country's advantage.

The variety and scope of aid-funded business encompassing so many developing countries makes opportunity analysis and precise targeting prerequisites for success. This is particularly pertinent to new market entrants and those whose new business interests embrace many sectors.

Preparatory analysis is essential to determine how one's products/services match opportunities, and equally by what means and in what form they are processed. Some firms' offerings may rarely feature as a discrete tender, but will be a component of a wider requirement. In such a situation the best route is through sub-contracting or joint bidding with another company. Suppliers of certain materials, components and small equipment items tend to fall into this category. Overall, it requires market research taking into account the exporter's experiences, resources and capability including calibre of staff.

The next stage is regularly to scrutinize forthcoming projects and technical assistance programmes to select the most promising prospects. This embraces studying published information and registering with the aid agencies. It is not always easy to identify exactly which projects require one's particular expertise and capability. Large projects in particular may require a vast range of different products and services. Requirements pertinent to the particular firm are not always obvious from a brief description of the project. Hence a search for embedded or hidden components is advisable. For example, an agricultural sector tea project may contain a sizeable telecommunications requirements which will be let as a discrete tender.

It is also possible to anticipate opportunities through discussions with aid agency and beneficiary country officials together by studying country indicative programmes, development plans, tentative project lists, financing proposals, and project dossiers. The documents specify how and where aid funds will be spent.

The exporter wishing to enter the donor aid market requires total commitment and a discretionary marketing strategy targeting only those products/services which they are competent to undertake on a professional basis in a competitive environment. It requires total commitment and support from the top management, who must recognize that instant success may not be possible since many projects have a lengthy gestation period. It requires patience, perseverance and dedication/professionalism. It also takes time for an untried company to become recognized and established in aid environment. The most difficult hurdle is to secure the first contract.

External consultants tend to adopt a multi-client approach to aid business marketing and realize cost savings to allow their client firms to defer significant investment until the market's potential is manifest. In any event, firms uncertain of the potential are advised to commission an initial opportunity analysis rather than waste time and money on chasing ill-defined and unproven possibilities.

A wide range of publications exist which includes: *Development Business*, issued bi-monthly by the United Nations; the EC's monthly courier magazine; and the supplement to the EC's Official Journal published daily.

In regard to the smaller company, the EC's European Development

Fund (EDF) actively encourage small-firm participation and break down project requirements into small-scale lots, purposefully to help the smaller supplier or consultant.

To conclude, the aid market is worth pursuing both for the small and large company.

14.7   MARKETING IN RECESSION

Manufacturers frequently find themselves in an environment of economic recession. This may be in the home market which they serve primarily, or one or more of their major overseas markets. It may arise through an unexpected event/situation, or be predictable and build up over a period of time because of high inflation, worsening external trade balance, depreciating exchange rate, high unemployment, rising energy costs, etc. The net result to the manufacturer is falling sales, lower profits, higher fixed unit costs, lower production levels and a worsening cash-flow situation. A heavy responsibility rests with the marketeer to redress the situation. However, it is made easier with the company selling in several markets, as the tendency can arise for some markets to be in decline whilst others are in a growth situation. A further factor to bear in mind is that a market in decline presents a new market profile and can lead to new market opportunities. Hence there is a need to research continuously the market in which the exporter operates and to undertake regular visits. Futhermore, close liaison must be maintained with agents, distributors, etc.

Listed below are a number of options which the international marketeer should consider to redress the company sales performance in a depressed market situation:

1 Conduct early discussions with the agent/distributor to evaluate the current situation and formulate a future marketing strategy. This will be aided by market research.
2 Examine the product range and establish their product life-cycle situation. The product range analysis should feature current and future sales volume and their profitability.
3 Undertake market research to determine the future market profile and its constituents. In particular, total market volume; competitors and their product/service; pricing; consumer profile, import controls, political situation, exchange rates, economic trends, GDP, GNP, market share, advertising/promotion, etc.
4 Review the prospect of niche marketing in the light of the new situation and opportunities. A 'one off' edition of a product slightly modified from the standard range can generate useful extra business and gain useful market exposure.
5 The product range may require to be rationalized and likewise selling and distribution arrangements to operate in a lower annual sales volume situation.

6 The research and development department may be able to advance the date of a new product launch. This will generate a competitive advantage in the market place and potentially yield improved market share and permit premium pricing. Its lead time could vary from 12–24 months and substantial costs will be incurred to launch the product. This involves plant investment, revised physical distribution arrangements, promotional/advertising material, sales training, sales conferences, etc. It needs to be carefully costed and requires a launch plan. Overall, such a decision requires to be reconciled with the company's business plan.

7 It may be prudent to change the advertising agency in the overseas territories. This could lead to the generation of new ideas and a fresh approach to the situation.

8 A critical review of the pricing strategy and the cost factors should be adopted. The latter may lead to improved efficiency through better stowage/utilization of transport unit capacity, less stockpiling, and quicker transits.

9 The packaging arrangements should be reviewed. Improved packaging at the point of sales could generate more business and develop more market exposure of the product.

10 Pricing strategy should be reviewed. Discounted pricing is not advocated as it reduces profit margins and generates a price war. It can with advantage, however, improve market share and clear stockpiles.

11 Sponsorship and other market exposure ideas should be examined.

12 Distribution arrangements need to be reviewed and possibly rationalized to develop the just in time technique (see page 249).

The foregoing should not be regarded as an exhaustive list, as each situation differs. However, it is desirable an action plan be devised and the situation is reflected in the budget.

14.8   THE FUTURE

The role of marketing is becoming increasingly important in today's industrial society throughout the world. Unless a company has a strong marketing policy, its products are unlikely to succeed in the market place. Marketing is also closely geared to production, and a company with a successful rising sales record can expand production and lower commodity unit cost, thereby making the product less expensive and more competitive. This improves the company's market share in the areas in which it operates.

Export marketing involves the successful transfer of the marketing mix and the development of a viable overseas marketing strategy. It demands many skills and the entrepreneurial qualities of professionalism, commitment and perseverance. Moreover, it demands the fostering of good relationships between the seller/exporter and buyer/importer to ensure that

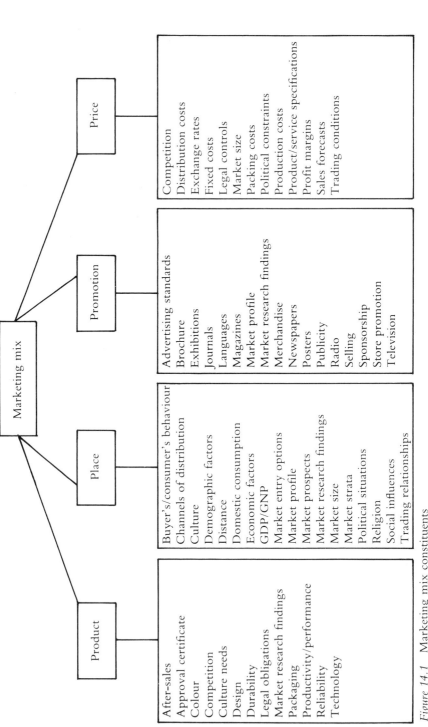

Figure 14.1 Marketing mix constituents

their joint development will result in favourable business results with the exporter supplying the product needed by the buyer for the end user.

As we progress through the 1990s, competition will become fiercer. It will result in higher professional standards in the conduct of international trade and more attention being focused on non-price areas of product quality, design, after-sales service, performance, technology and reliability.

The total ingredients of successful export marketing are contained in this book which, it is hoped, will contribute in a small way to the development of world trade. At the same time, it is hoped the reader may be persuaded to take one of the export courses available whether it be in the UK, Malaysia, Hong Kong, Middle East, the United States, etc. It could result in the further development of the reader's skills to develop trade overseas, to the benefit of his/her career and company expansion.

Appendix A

RECOMMENDED READING

Branch, A. E. (1984) *A Dictionary of Commercial Terms and Abbreviations* (6000 entries), Witherby & Co., London.
Branch, A. E. (1985) *Elements of Export Practice*, Second edition, Chapman and Hall, London.
Branch, A. E. (1986) *A Dictionary of Shipping/International Trade Terms and Abbreviations*, Third edition (9000 entries), Whitherby & Co., London.
Branch, A. E. (1986) *Economics of Shipping Practice and Management*, Second edition, Chapman and Hall, London.
Branch, A. E. (1986) *Elements of Port Operation and Management*, Chapman and Hall, London.
Branch, A. E. (1988) *Dictionary of English–Arabic Shipping/Commercial Terms* (4400 entries), Witherby & Co., London.
Branch, A. E. (1989) *Dictionary of Multi-lingual Commercial/International Trade/Shipping Terms in English–French–German–Spanish* (10 000 entries), Witherby & Co., London.
Branch, A. E. (1989) *Elements of Shipping*, Sixth edition, Chapman and Hall, London.
Branch, A. E. (1989) *Import/Export Documentation*, Chapman and Hall, London.
Mitchelhill, A. (1990) *Bills of Lading – Law and Practice*, Second edition, Chapman and Hall, London.
Schmitthoff, C. M. (1976) *The Export Trade*, Eighth edition, Sweet and Maxwell, London.
Watson, A. (1989) *Finance of International Trade*, Fourth edition, London Institute of Bankers, London.
International Code of Sales Promotion Practice, International Chamber of Commerce Publication No. 432A.
International Code of Advertising Practice, International Chamber of Commerce Publication No. 432B.
Rules for the ICC International Council on Marketing Practice, International Chamber of Commerce Publication No. 432C.
Incoterms 1990 Edition, International Chamber of Commerce Publication No. 350.
Guide to Incoterms, International Chamber of Commerce Publication No. 354.

Appendix B

Agent One who represents a principal, or buys or sells for another.

Aligned export documentation system Method whereby as much information as possible is entered on a 'master' document so that all or part of this information can be reproduced mechanically/electronically on to individual forms of a similar design.

Advertising agency Agency specializing in advertising/promotion techniques on behalf of a principal.

Balance of payments Financial statement of balance of a country's visible and invisible trade in exports and imports.

Balance of trade Financial statement of balance of a country's visible trade exports and imports.

Below the line A promotion technique whereby the expenditure does not feature in the paid advertising media plan, i.e. redeemable coupons, gifts, self-liquidating offers, etc.

Bill of exchange Written request from a creditor to a debtor ordering the debtor to pay a specified sum to a specified person or bearer at a certain date.

Bill of lading Receipt for goods shipped on board a ship signed by the person (or his agent) who contracts to carry them and stating the terms on which the goods are carried.

B/L Bill of lading.

Blue book Book issued by HM Government on recommendations for dangerous cargo packing/shipment by sea transport.

Broker A person who transacts the business of negotiating between merchants and shipowners about cargoes and clearances; or one who effects insurances with the underwriters.

Budgetary control A management technique whereby sponsoring officers within a company agree to a specified level of forecast expenditure, revenue and business volume throughout a given period, and strive to achieve it.

Budgets The process of formulating forecast and objectives of either expenditure and/or income during a specified future period for a particular trade or company.

Business plan A plan or programme covering a period (usually between three to five years) featuring the company's intentions/objectives/policy and identifying annually (by service/product/activity etc.) the predicted level of income, expenditure and capital investment.

Campaign plan A plan featuring a particular company's proposals relative to the promotion of a product(s) involving advertising – TV, press, radio, etc., product launch date, mail shots, etc. (see Figure 3.1, page 41).

CB Container base.

CBI Confederation of British Industry.

C & F Cost and freight (cargo delivery term).

Charterer Person who hires a vessel either on a voyage or time basis.

CIF Cost, insurance, freight (cargo delivery term).

CIF & E Cost, insurance, freight and exchange (cargo delivery term).

CIFCI Cost, insurance, freight, commission and interest.

Closing date Latest date cargo accepted for shipment by shipowner for a specified sailing.

Commission selling agency An agent who sells goods/merchandise on a commission basis for his principal.

Concessionaire Organization operating as a distributor for an export/seller/manufacturer with a special authority granted by the manufacturer in a particular market area, usually on an exclusive basis.

Confirming house An organization whose role is to assist the overseas buyer by confirming, as principal, orders already placed so that the exporter may receive payment from the confirming house as and when the goods are shipped.

Consortium A group of organizations operating as a group seller, or a group buyer whose role is to tender for a major export contract and if successful execute it on a consortium basis, sometimes under turnkey arrangements.

Consumer market A market which buys consumer type products, i.e. food, household appliances, general merchandise, etc. – usually through retail outlets.

Consumer profile The description of a consumer in a specified area for a particular product (age, income, fashion, spending habits, family composition, hobbies, etc.)

Consumer Research The process of researching/analysing the constituents of the consumer research market for a particular area and product(s).

CTO Combined Transport Operation.

Customs broker An agent specializing in inbound customs clearance.

Delivery at frontier Name, place of delivery at frontier (cargo delivery term).

Distributor An importer who buys goods direct from a manufacturer and distributes them in the market place to retailers.

Documentary letter of credit Document whereby at the buyer's request the importer's bank authorizes the exporter to draw a financial amount by a specified date for a particular shipment, subject to the detailed documents being forthcoming.

ECGD Export Credit Guarantee Department.

EIS Export Intelligence Service – a computerized information service provided by the BOTB which daily distributes to subscribers export intelligence embracing enquiries for products or services, calls for tender, agents seeking UK principals, early notification of projects, etc.

Evidence of shipment A confirmation that the cargo specified has been shipped on a specified sailing/date/vessel and usually evidenced in a consignment note, i.e. CMR/CIM or bill of lading.

Export agent Agent overseas responsible for promoting/selling his principals goods.

Export house Responsible as an export merchant for buying goods outright and selling them on their own account; acting as an export department or agent on behalf of a client; or acting for an overseas buyer.

Ex quay Cargo delivery term whereby importer (buyer) responsible for charges after delivery on quay in accord with destination specified in bill of lading; accepts all associated risk therefrom.

Ex ship Cargo delivery term whereby the exporter (seller) pays sea-freight and insurance, loading cost at port of despatch, and any other cost and risk up to port of discharge and the buyer (importer) meeting all such cost/risk thereafter.

Ex works Exports sold free of any insurance and freight (transport) charges.

FAK Freight all kinds – term used to indicate freight rate is applicable to all commodities.

Franco (French) Sender undertakes to pay all carriage charges and, in addition, all supplementary charges.

Free alongside ship Under this cargo delivery term the seller (exporter) undertakes to place the goods alongside the ship on the quay or in lighters at the specified port and bear all the resultant cost and risk up to this point.

FOB Free on board – under this cargo delivery term the seller places the goods on board a vessel at the specified port and bears all the resultant cost and risk up to this point.

Fuel surcharge A technique whereby a surcharge is raised by the shipowner on the basic freight to reflect increased bunker cost incurred due to the upward price of fuel, which may be attributed to currency variations or simply an increase in the basic bunker rate.

IATA International Air Transport Association.

ICC International Chamber of Commerce.

ILO International Labour Organization.

Incoterms 1990 Cargo delivery terms, i.e. CIF, FOB, Ex works, etc., as devised by ICC relative to the conduct of international trade.

IMF International Monetary Fund.

IMO International Maritime Organization.

Industrial research The process of conducting market research into industrial products such as turbines etc.

Investigator A person involved in market research conducting, for example, questionnaire interviews.

Inwards mission A number of businesspeople, journalists, etc., representing a group of companies from overseas, who visit (under a programmed arrangement) a particular overseas market.

Lead-time The preparation time required, for a specified product launch, for example.

Loco Price of goods includes cost of packing and conveyance to the place named.

Market Analysis The process of analysing the constituents of a particular market for a specified product(s) or service(s).

Marketing The process of promoting a product to meet a customer demand.

Marketing and sales plan The provision of a plan outlining the marketing/ selling techniques and the programme covering a specified period to promote a specified product(s).

Marketing manager Person responsible for promoting (marketing) his company's business or specified part of it.

Market price Price which commodity would reach if sold on the open market.

Market profile The description of a market.

Market report A comprehensive report featuring all relevant aspects of a specified market for a particular product and especially the market prospects and potential for the product involved.

Market research The process of conducting research into a specified market for a particular product.

Market share The volume/value of business enjoyed by a company for a specified product(s) in a particular market, or in various segments of the market.

Media plan A plan depicting a company's advertising campaign for a particular product, involving television, radio, press, etc.

PIRA Research Association for the Paper and Board, Printing and Packaging Industry.

Product range The range of products for sale in the market place.

Questionnaire A list of questions prepared to elicit data from respondents.

Random sampling A sampling technique whereby every item of a certain kind has an equal chance of being included in the sample.

Respondent A person who answers a questionnaire.

Response rate The overall number of respondents, in percentage terms, returning a completed questionnaire.

SITPRO Simpler Trade Procedures Board involved in the revisions of documentation and trade procedures to facilitate trade development.

TDA Transport Distribution Analysis.

THE Technical Help for Exporters.

Trade fair An exhibition held overseas featuring a particular product or range of products, to which overseas companies are invited to exhibit their goods and look at those of other companies.
UNCITRAL United Nations Committee of International Trade Law.
UNCTAD United Nations Conference on Trade and Development.

NB A very comprehensive range of marketing terms and abbreviations is contained in *A Dictionary of Shipping/International Trade Terms and Abbreviations*, Third edition (see Appendix A).

Appendix C

PUBLICATIONS AVAILABLE TO HELP THE UK EXPORTER

ABC Air Cargo Guide
British Business – weekly publication from the Department of Trade and Industry on export matters
Chambers of Commerce journals and newsletters
Croner's Reference Book for Exporters
Export and Forwarder – annual publication from the British International Freight Association
Export Daily Gazette
Export Director
Export Times
Export Today – journal of the Institute of Export
Freight Forwarding Journal – published by the British International Freight Association
Freight Management and Distribution Today – published by Fairplay Publications
Freight News
Handy Shipping Guide – published by Ship Press
Hints to the Exporter – BOTB publication for most countries of the world, designed to assist the exporter intending to visit overseas markets.
Kelly's Export Services – annual publication
Institute of Chartered Shipbrokers Journal – published by the Institute of Chartered Shipbrokers
Institute of Marketing Journal – published by the Institute of Marketing
International Freighting Weekly – published by Maclean Hunter Ltd, London
Lloyd's List and Shipping Gazette
Marketing Trends – published by Nielsen Marketing Research
Marketing Week – published by Centaur
Overseas Trade – published by the BOTB
Systematic Export Documentation Volumes I and II – published by SITPRO
The Economist
Various publications, trade briefs and handbooks on export practice and export finance available (usually free) from the major banks

Appendix D

ADDRESSES OF CHAMBERS OF COMMERCE IN THE UK

Aberdeen Chamber of Commerce
15 Union Terrace
Aberdeen AB9 1HF

Ayr Chamber of Commerce
12 Alloway Place
Ayr KA7 2AG

Barnsley & District Chamber of
   Commerce
12 Victoria Road
Barnsley S70 2BB

Birmingham Chamber of Industry
   & Commerce
PO Box 360
75 Harborne Road
Birmingham B15 3DH

Blackburn & District Incorporated
   Chamber of Industry &
   Commerce
14 Richmond Terrace
Blackburn BB1 7BH

Bolton Chamber of Commerce and
   Industry
Silverwell House
Silverwell Street
Bolton BL1 1PX

Boston & District Chamber of
   Commerce
31a Market Place
Boston PE21 6ET

Bradford Chamber of Commerce
Commerce House
Cheapside
Bradford BD1 4JZ

Bristol Chamber of Commerce and
   Industry
16 Clifton Park
Bristol BS8 3BY

Burnley & District Incorporated
   Chamber of Commerce &
   Industry
Keirley Walk
Burnley BB11 2DE

Burton upon Trent & District
   Chamber of Commerce &
   Industry
158 Derby Street
Burton upon Trent DE1 2NZ

Bury & District Chamber of
   Commerce
Lloyd's Bank Chambers
4 Bolton Street
Bury BL9 0LQ

Calderdale Chamber of Commerce
   & Industry
Op. 66 Dear Clough Office Park
Halifax HX3 5AY

Cambridge & District Chamber of
  Commerce & Industry
The Business Centre
Station Road
Histon
Cambridge CB4 4LF

Cardiff Chamber of Commerce &
  Industry
101–108 The Exchange
Mount Stuart Square
Cardiff CF1 6RD

Carlisle Chamber of Commerce
4 Brunswick Street
Carlisle CA1 1PD

Central & West Lancashire
  Chamber of Commerce &
  Industry
2–6 Camden Place
Preston PR1 8BE

Central Scotland Chamber of
  Commerce
Suite A Haypark
Marchmont Avenue
Polmont
Stirlingshire FH7 0NZ

Chester & North Wales Chamber of
  Commerce
6 Hunter Street
Chester CH1 2AU

Chesterfield & North Derbyshire
  Chamber of Commerce
Commerce Centre
Marsden Street
Chesterfield S40 1JY

Colchester & District Chamber of
  Commerce Ltd
1 High Street
Colchester CO1 1DA

Croydon Chamber of Commerce &
  Industry
Commerce House
21 Scarbrook Road
Croydon CR9 6HY

Derby & Derbyshire Chamber of
  Commerce & Industry
Enterprise House
4 Vernon Street
Derby DE1 1FR

Doncaster Chamber of Commerce
  (Incorporated)
50 Christchurch Road
Doncaster DN1 2QN

Dorset Chamber of Commerce &
  Industry (Incorporated)
Upton House
Upton Country Park
Poole BH7 7BJ

Dudley Chamber of Industry &
  Commerce
First floor Falcon House
The Minories
Dudley DY2 8PG

Dundee & Tayside Chamber of
  Commerce & Industry
Chamber of Commerce Buildings
Panmure Street
Dundee DD1 1ED

Edinburgh Chamber of Commerce
  & Manufacturers
3 Randolph Crescent
Edinburgh EH3 7UD

Exeter & District Chamber of
  Commerce & Trade
Equitable Life House
31 Southernhay East
Exeter EX1 1NS

Fareham Chamber of Commerce
75 High Street
Fareham PO16 7BB

Federation of Sussex Industries &
  Chamber of Commerce
Seven Dials
Brighton BN1 3JS

Glasgow Chamber of Commerce &
  Manufacturers
30 George Square
Glasgow G2 1EQ

Gloucester & County Chamber of
  Commerce
20 Cheltenham Road
Gloucester GL2 0LS

Goole Chamber of Commerce &
  Shipping (Incorporated)
46 Aire Street
Goole DN14 5QE

Grantham Chamber of Commerce
c/o Cole, Deckins and Hills
39 Westgate
Grantham NG31 6LY

Great Yarmouth Chamber of
  Commerce and Industry
Norwich Union Building
Hall Plain
Great Yarmouth NR30 2QP

Greenock Chamber of Commerce
14 Union Street
Greenock PA16 8JJ

Grimsby & Immingham Chamber
  of Commerce & Shipping
Yorkshire Bank Chambers
West St Mary's Gate
Grimsby DN31 1LA

Guernsey Chamber of Commerce
The State's Arcade
Market Street

St Peter Port
Guernsey Channel Islands

Guildford & District Chamber of
  Commerce
Friary Mews
28 Commercial Road
Guildford GU1 4SX

Halton Chamber of Commerce
57–61 Church Street
Runcorn WA7 1LG

Hertfordshire Chamber of
  Commerce
Andre House
Salisbury Square
Hatfield AL9 5BH

Hull Incorporated Chamber of
  Commerce & Shipping
Samman House
Bowlalley Lane
Hull HU1 1XT

Inverness & Highlands Chamber of
  Commerce
13a Island Bank Road
Inverness IV2 4QN

Ipswich & Suffolk Chamber of
  Commerce & Shipping
21 Museum Street
Ipswich IP1 1HE

Isle of Man Chamber of Commerce
  (including Trade & Shipping)
Royal Buildings
Parade Street
Douglas
Isle of Man

Isle of Wight Chamber of
  Commerce
16a High Street
Newport
Isle of Wight PO30 1SS

Jersey Chamber of Commerce &
  Industry (Incorporated)
19 Royal Square
St Helier
Jersey, Channel Islands

Kendal & District Incorporated
  Chamber of Commerce
PO Box 27
Exchange Chambers
10b Highgate
Kendal LA9 4SX

Kidderminster & District Chamber
  of Commerce
Slingfield Mill
Pitts Lane
Kidderminster DY11 6JR

Kirkcaldy & District Chamber of
  Commerce
17 Tolbooth Street
Kirkcaldy KY1 1RW

Kirklees & Wakefield Chamber of
  Commerce & Industry
Commerce House
New North Road
Huddersfield HD1 5PJ

Lancaster District Chamber of
  Commerce, Trade & Industry
St Leonard's House
St Leonardgate
Lancaster LA1 1NN

Leeds Chamber of Commerce &
  Industry
Commerce House
2 St Alban's Place, Wade Lane
Leeds LS2 8HZ

Leicester & County Chamber of
  Commerce & Industry
Fourth floor York House
91 Granby Street
Leicester LE1 6EA

Leith Chamber of Commerce
3 Randolph Crescent
Edinburgh EH3 7UD

Lincoln Incorporated Chamber of
  Commerce
15–16 St Mary's Street
Lincoln LN5 7EQ

London Chamber of Commerce &
  Industry
69 Cannon Street
London EC4N 5AB

Area offices (documentation only)
London Chamber Southern Area &
  Gatwick Airport Office
13a The Broadway
Crawley RH10 1DX

London Chamber SE Region
Ashford House
The Tufton Centre
Ashford TN23 1YB

London Chamber Barking &
  Dagenham Office
20 Cambridge Road
Barking IG11 8NW

London Chamber Cricklewood
  Office
1 Pond Row
Production Village
110 Cricklewood Lane
London NW2 2DS

London Chamber Greenford Area
Unit 21 Derby Road
Greenford UB6 8UJ

The London Chamber Commercial
  Education Schemes
Marlow House
109 Station Road
Sidcup DA15 7BJ

Londonderry Chamber of
  Commerce
c/o N. McKenna & Co.
1–3 Clarendon Street
Londonderry BT48 7EP

Lowestoft Incorporated Chamber of
  Commerce
The Waveney Business Centre
Gordon Road
Lowestoft NR32 1NL

Luton, Bedford & District Chamber
  of Commerce & Industry
Commerce House
Stuart Street
Luton LU1 5AU

Manchester Chamber of Commerce
  & Industry
56 Oxford Street
Manchester M60 7HJ

Medway & Gillingham Chamber of
  Commerce
149 New Road
Chatham ME4 4PT

Merseyside Chamber of Commerce
  & Industry
1 Old Hall Street
Liverpool L3 9HG

Milton Keynes & District Chamber
  of Commerce & Industry
Silbury Court
384 Silbury Boulevard
Central Milton Keynes MK9 2HY

Neath, Briton Ferry & District
  Chamber of Commerce
17 Elm Road
Briton Ferry
Neath SA11 2LP

Newark Chamber of Commerce
67 London Road
Newark NG24 1RZ

Newhaven & District Chamber of
  Commerce
24 Lee Way
Newhaven BN9 9SN

Newport & Gwent Chamber of
  Commerce (Incorporated)
Stelvio House
Basseleg Road
Newport NP9 3EB

Northamptonshire Chamber of
  Commerce & Industry
65 The Avenue
Cliftonville
Northampton NN1 5BG

Northern Ireland Chamber of
  Commerce & Industry
Chamber of Commerce House
22 Great Victoria Street
Belfast BT2 7BJ

North Staffordshire Chamber of
  Commerce & Industry
Commerce House
Festival Park
Stoke-on-Trent ST1 5BE

Norwich & Norfolk Chamber of
  Commerce & Industry
112 Barrack Street
Norwich NR3 1UB

Nottingham Chamber of
  Commerce & Industry
395 Mansfield Road
Nottingham NG5 2DL

Nottinghamshire County Office
60 Station Road
Sutton-in-Ashfield NG17 5GA

Oldham & District Incorporated
  Chamber of Commerce
8 Clydesdale Street
Oldham OL8 1BT

Oxford & District Chamber of
Commerce
30 Cornmarket Street
Oxford OX1 3EY

Paisley Chamber of Commerce and
Industry Ltd
c/o McFadyen and Semple
6 Gilmour Street
Paisley PA1 1BZ

Perthshire Chamber of Commerce
14–15 Tay Street
Perth PH1 5LQ

Peterborough Chamber of
Commerce & Industry
607 Lincoln Road
Peterborough PE1 3HA

Plymouth Chamber of Commerce
& Industry
29 Looe Street
Plymouth PL4 0EE

Port Talbot Incorporated Chamber
of Commerce & Shipping
Bryn Derw
141 Clasemont Road
Morriston
Swansea SA6 6AH

Preston – see Central & West Lancs

Reading Chamber of Commerce &
Trade
43 West Street
Reading RG1 1AT

Rochdale & District Chamber of
Commerce
County Court Building
Town Hall Square
Rochdale OL16 1NF

Rotherham Chamber of Commerce
and Industry Ltd
37 Moorgate Road
Rotherham S60 2AE

Royal Tunbridge Wells Chamber of
Commerce
10 Crescent Road
Royal Tunbridge Wells TN1 2PD

Rugby & District Chamber of
Commerce
9 Railway Terrace
Rugby CV21 3EN

St Helens Chambers of Commerce
& Industry
48 Barrow Street
St Helens WA10 1RY

Scunthorpe, Glanford &
Gainsborough Chamber of
Commerce
58 Oswald Road
Scunthorpe DN15 7PQ

Sheffield Chamber of Commerce &
Manufacture (Incorporated)
Commerce House
33 Earl Street
Sheffield S1 3FX

Shropshire Chamber of Commerce
& Industry Ltd
Industry House
Halesfield 16
Telford TF7 4TA

Southampton Chamber of
Commerce
Bugle House
53 Bugle Street
Southampton SO9 4WP

Southend-on-Sea & District
Chamber of Commerce, Trade &
Industry Ltd
845 London Road
Westcliffe-on-Sea SS0 9SZ

South-East Hampshire Chamber of
Commerce & Industry
27 Guildhall Walk
Portsmouth PO1 2RP

South of Scotland Chamber of
Commerce (Incorporated)
19 Buccleuch Street
Hawick TD9 0HL

Stockport Chamber of Commerce
& Industry
27 Higher Hillgate
Stockport SK1 3ET

Swansea Chamber of Commerce &
Shipping (Incorporated)
Rooms F4/F5
Burrows Chambers
East Burrows Road
Swansea SA1 1RF

Swindon Chamber of Commerce &
Industry
1 Commercial Road
Swindon SN1 5NE

Telford & Shropshire Chamber of
Industry & Commerce Ltd
Walker House
Telford Centre
Telford TF3 4HA

Thames–Chiltern Chamber of
Commerce & Industry
Commerce House
2–6 Bath Road
Slough SL1 3SB

Tynedale Chamber of Commerce
14 Gilesgate
Hexham NE46 3NJ

Tyne & Wear Chamber of
Commerce
65 Quayside
Newcastle upon Tyne NE1 3DS

Walsall Chamber of Commerce &
Industry
Chamber of Commerce House

Ward Street
Walsall WS1 2AG

Warrington Chamber of Commerce
& Industry
9 Springfield Street
Warrington WA1 1BB

Watford Chamber of Commerce &
Industry
Abbey House
26 The Parade
High Street
Watford WD1 2AA

Widnes – see Halton

Westminster Chamber of
Commerce
Mitre House
117 Regent Street
London W1R 8DJ

Wigan & District Incorporated
Chamber of Commerce
c/o 25 Bridgeman Terrace
Wigan WN1 1TD

Wolverhampton Chamber of
Commerce & Industry
Berrington Lodge
93 Tettenhall Road
Wolverhampton WV3 9PE

Worcester & Hereford Area
Chamber of Commerce &
Industry
Severn House
10 The Moors
Worcester WR1 3EE

York Chamber of Commerce,
Trade & Industry
c/o Joseph Terry and Sons
Bishopthorpe Road
York YO1 1YE

Appendix E

ADDRESSES OF ORGANIZATIONS AND INSTITUTES IN THE UK
INVOLVED IN AIDING EXPORT DEVELOPMENT, INCLUDING
EXPORT CLUBS

American Chamber of Commerce
(United Kingdom)
75 Brook Street
London W1Y 2EB

Anglo-Israeli Chamber of
Commerce
Information & Trade Centre
126–134 Baker Street
London W1M 1FH

Arab-British Chamber of
Commerce
26 Berkeley Square
London SW1X 8PH

Association of British Chambers of
Commerce
Sovereign House
212a Shaftesbury Avenue
London WC2 8EW

Association of International Courier
and Express Services (AICES)
PO Box 10
Leatherhead KT22 0HT

Australian-British Chamber of
Commerce
615 Linen Hall
Regent Street
London W1 5TB

Belgo-Luxembourg Chamber of
Commerce

36–37 Piccadilly
London W1V 0PL

Blackburn & District Export Club
Blackburn & District Incorporated
Chamber of Commerce &
Industry
14 Richmond Terrace
Blackburn BB1 7BH

Brazilian Chamber of Commerce
35 Dover Street
London W1X 3RA

British-American Chamber of
Commerce (UK)
2–5 Old Bond Street
London W1X 3TB

British Consultants Bureau
Westminster Palace Gardens
1–7 Artillery Row
London SW1P 1RJ

British Export Houses Association
16 Dartmouth Street
London SW1H 9BL

British Health Care Export Council
23–30 Market Place
London W1N 7AL

British Insurance Association
Aldermary House
Queen Street
London EC4

British Insurance Brokers
  Association
Fountain House
130 Fenchurch Street
London EC3M 5DJ

British Institute of Management
Management House
Cottingham Road
Corby NN17 1TT

British Laboratory Ware
  Association Export Club
S. Murray & Co. Ltd
Holburn House
Old Woking GU22 9LB

British Overseas Trade Board
1 Victoria Street
London SW1H 0ET

Bristol & West Exporters Club
Bristol Chamber of Commerce
16 Clifton Park
Bristol BS8 3BY

British-Soviet Chamber of
  Commerce
2 Lowndes Street
London SW1X 9ET

British Standards Institution
Technical Help to Exporters
Linford Wood
Milton Keynes MK14 6LE

Burnley & District Export Group
Burnley & District Incorporated
  Chamber of Commerce &
  Industry
16 Kierby Walk
Burnley BB11 2DE

Business and Technical Education
  Council
Berkshire House
168–173 High Holborn
London WC1V 7AG

Cambridge Exporters Club
c/o Transport Group Ltd
East Chackley Lane
Godmanchester
Cambridge PE18 8AU

Canada-United Kingdom
  Chamber of Commerce
British Columbia House
1–3 Lower Regent Street
London SW1Y 4NZ

CBI Central London Export Club
CBI
103 New Oxford Street
London WC1A 1DU

Central & West Lancashire Export
  Association
2 Camden Place
Preston PR1 8BE

Central Office of Information
  (COI)
Hercules Road
Westminster Bridge Road
London SE1 7DU

Confederation of British Industry
Centre Point
103 New Oxford Street
London WC1A 1DU

Cornwall Export Club
English China Clays Ltd
St Austell, Cornwall

Crawley & District Export Club
London Chamber of Commerce &
  Industry
Southern Area & Gatwick Airport
  Office
23 The Boulevard
Crawley RH10 1XD

Crown Agents
St Nicholas House
St Nicholas Road
Sutton SM1 1EL

Cumbria Export Club
c/o Albright & Wilson
PO Box 16
Whitehaven

Department of Trade and Industry
1 Victoria Street
London SW1H 0ET

Director of Marketing Services
Defence Export Services
   Organisation
Room 707
Stuart House
23–25 Soho Square
London W1V 5JF

Dyfed Business & Export Club
Avon Inflatables Ltd
Dafen
Llanelli SA14 8NA

East Anglian Exporter's Committee
The Ipswich & Suffolk Chamber of
   Commerce & Shipping (Inc)
21 Museum Street
Ipswich IP1 1HF

East Coast Export Group
Dale Electric International PLC
Electricity Building
Filey YO14 9PJ

Eastern Thames Valley Export Club
   (Slough Export Club)
Thames Chiltern Chamber of
   Commerce & Industry
Commerce House
2–6 Bath Road
Slough SL1 3SB

Essex Export Agency Ltd
Chelmer Court
Chelmsford CM1 1NH

Exeter Export Club
Exeter Chamber of Commerce

31 Southernhay Road
Exeter EX1 1NS

Export Association of Nottingham
c/o Sturmey Archer
Triumph Road
Nottingham

Export Buying Offices Association
Department of Trade and Industry
1 Victoria Street
London SW1H 0ET

Export Credit Guarantee
   Department
PO Box 272
Export House
50 Ludgate Hill
London EC4N 7AY

Export Licences
Export Licensing Unit
Kingsgate House
66–74 Victoria Street
London SW1E 6SW

Export Market Information Centre
1 Victoria Street
London SW1E 0ET

Export Marketing Research Scheme
The Association of British
   Chambers of Commerce
4 Westwood House
Westwood Business Park
Coventry CV4 8HS

Fairs and Promotions Branch
British Overseas Trade Board
Dean Bradley House
52 Horseferry Road
London SW1P 2AG

Federation of Sussex Industries and
   Chamber of Commerce
Seven Dials
Brighton BN1 3JS

Fife Export Club
c/o Glenrothes Development
Corporation
Balkirnee House
Glenrothes
Fife

Freight Transport Association
(British Shipper's Council)
Hermes House
157 St John's Road
Tunbridge Wells TN4 2QU

French Chamber of Commerce
197 Knightsbridge
London SW7 1RB

German Chamber of Industry &
Commerce
12–13 Suffolk Street
St James's
London SW1Y 4HG

Gloucestershire Overseas Trade
Club
Triple 'C' Export/Imports
83 Prestbury Road
Cheltenham

Guernsey Exporter's Group
S.O. Woodwood & Partners
Floor C
The Albany
South Esplanade
St Peter's Port
Guernsey, Channel Islands

Hertfordshire Export Club
Herts Chamber of Commerce
Andre House
Salisbury Square
Hatfield

High Wycombe & District Export
Society
Lucks Export Services
Wind Mill Lane
Haddesham

Indian Chamber of Commerce in
Great Britain
7 Artillery Lane
London E1 7LP

Institute of Export
Export House
64 Clifton Street
London EC2A 4HB

Institute of Freight Forwarders Ltd
(formerly the British
International Freight Association)
Redfern House
Browells Lane
Feltham TW13 7EP

Institute of Linguists
24a Highbury Grove
London N5

Institute of Marketing
Moor Hall
Cookham
Maidenhead SL6 9QH

Institute of Patent Agents
Staple Inn Buildings
London WC1V 7PZ

Institute of Practitioners in
Advertising
44 Belgrave Square
London SW1 8QS

Isle of Wight Exporter's Association
Isle of Wight Enterprise Agency
677 Town Lane
Newport

Italian Chamber of Commerce
71 Walmar House
296 Regent Street
London W1R 6AE

International Chamber of
Commerce (ICC)
Centre Point
103 New Oxford Street
London WC1A 1QB

Japanese Chamber of Commerce &
Industry in the UK
c/o Mitsui & Co. Ltd
Temple Court
Queen Victoria Street
London EC2

Kent & Sussex Exporter's Club
25 The Ridgeway
Tonbridge

Kent Export Association
LEP International Ltd
134–136 Snargate Street
Dover CT17 9DA

Leeds Export Club
Leeds Chamber of Commerce &
Industry
Commerce House
2 St Alban's Place
Wade Lane
Leeds LS2 8HZ

London Borough of Bexley Export
Club
Nat West Bank PLC
91 High Street
Tonbridge TN9 1DN

Luton & District Export Club
Wilimpex Ltd
27 Sun Street
Biggleswade

Mid Wales Export Association Ltd
Myrick House
Hendomen
Montgomery SY15 6EZ

Milton Keynes International Trade
Club
Standard Chartered Bank
PO Box 230
809 Silvery Boulevard
Milton Keynes MK9 3EZ

Netherlands-British Chamber of
Commerce
The Dutch House
307–308 High Holborn
London WC1V 7LS

New Zealand-UK Chamber of
Commerce
615 Liner Hall
Regent Street
London W1 5TB

Nigerian-British Chamber of
Commerce
75 Cannon Street
London EC4N 5AB

Norwich & Norfolk Exporter's
Club
Norwich Inc. Chamber of
Commerce
32 St David's Road
Hetherselt
Norwich NR9 3DH

Northamptonshire Chamber of
Commerce & Industry
The Cedars
4 Park View
Moulton NN3 1TW

North Derbyshire Export Club
Nat West Bank PLC
International Banking Centre
16 George Street
Sheffield S1 1NT

North East Export Club
Teeside & District Chamber of
Commerce & Industry
Commerce House
Exchange Square
Middlesborough TS1 1DW

North of Scotland Export Club
Osprey Electronics Ltd
E27 Wellheads Industrial Centre
Dyce
Aberdeen AB2 0GD

North Wales Exporter's Club
GER International Ltd
PO Box 7
Colwyn Bay LL2 4HP

North Western Export Club
W.M. Rawlinson Ltd
27 Kempston Street
Liverpool L3 8JS

Norwegian Chamber of
 Commerce, London, Inc.
Norway House
21–24 Cockspur Street
London SW1Y 5BN

Oldham & District Export Club
J. Crowther (Royton) Ltd
Eden Works
Belgrave Hill
Eden Road
Honeywell Lane
Oldham OL8 2JP

Overseas Press & Media
 Association
122 Shaftesbury Avenue
London W1V 8HA

Oxford & District International
 Trade Association
c/o Analysis Automation
Southfield House
Eynsham
Oxford OX8 1JN

Paper and Board Printing and
 Packaging Industries
Research Association (PIRA)
Randalls Road
Leatherhead KT22 7RU

Plymouth Export Club
Plymouth Chamber of Commerce
 & Industry
29 Looe Street
Plymouth PL4 0EE

Portuguese Chamber of Commerce
 & Industry
New Bond Street House
1–5 New Bond Street
London W1Y 9PE

Reading & District Export Club
Reading Chamber of Commerce &
 Trade
43 West Street
Reading RG1 1AT

Redditch Export Club
Heath Springs Ltd
Hewell Road
Enfield
Redditch B97 6BD

Road Haulage Association Ltd
Roadway House
104 New King's Road
London SW6 4LN

Scottish Thistle Export Group
Edinburgh Chamber of Commerce
 & Manufacturers
3 Randolph Crescent
Edinburgh EH3 7UD

Scunthorpe, Glanford &
 Gainsborough Export Club
Scunthorpe, Glanford &
 Gainsborough Chamber of
 Commerce
58 Oswald Road
Scunthorpe DN15 7UD

SE Essex Export Club
Trelawn Technical Services
837 London Road
Westcliff-on-Sea SS0 9SZ

Sheffield Export Club
Busk & Lloyd (Sheffield) Ltd
Bagshaw Hall
Bakewell DE4 1DL

Simpler Trade Procedures Board
(SITPRO)
Venture House
29 Glasshouse Street
London W1R 5RG

Southampton Chamber of
Commerce Export Group
Southampton Chamber of
Commerce
53 Bugle Street
Southampton SO9 4WP

South Wales Exporter's Club
John R. George Ltd
Caed Cae Lane
Portyclun, Mid Glamorgan

South West Export Association
2 Bracken Close
Aller Park
Newton Abbot TQ12 4NN

Spanish Chamber of Commerce
5 Cavendish Square
London W1M 0DP

Swansea Exporter's Club
Marean Optics
G.I. Burrows Chambers
East Burrows Road
Swansea POST CODE

Suffolk International Trade Group
Anderson Gardiner Ltd
Cliff House
Hamilton Gardens
Felixstowe IP11 7EY

Surrey & Hants Export Association
K.D. Associates
Thornhill
13 Orchard Gardens
Effingham

Swedish Trade Commissioner
73 Welbeck Street
London W1M 8AN

Thames Export Club
Cossor Electronics Ltd
The Pinnacles
Harlow CM19 5BB

Technical Help to Exporters (THE)
British Standards Institution
Linford Wood
Milton Keynes MK14 6LE

Watford International Business
Association
Watford Chamber of Commerce
Barclays Bank Chambers
1a King Street
Watford WD1 8B

Wessex Export Club
231 Sopwith Crescent
Merley
Wimborne BH21 1SU

West Anglia Exporter's Club
Barclays Bank PLC
Barclays Business Centre
Church Street
Peterborough PE1 1XE

West London Export Club
Fegabrook Group PLC
Hook Rise South
Surbiton KT6 7LD

West Midlands Export Club
Dijon
Oddingley
Nr Droitwich WR9 7NR

Wiltshire & Somerset Export Club
Cuprinol Ltd
Adderwell
Frome BA11 1NL

Worcester & Hereford Export Club
Morganite Crucible Ltd
Woodbury Lane
Worcester

Yugoslav Economic Chambers
Crown House
143–147 Regent Street
London W1R 7LB

Appendix F

WORLD CURRENCIES

Country	Currency
Afghanistan	One Afghani = 100 Puls
Albania	One Lek = 100 Qindarka
Algeria (Republic of)	One Algerian Dinar = 100 Centimes
Andorrra	Spanish Pesetas and French Francs
Angola	One Kwanza = 100 Lwei
Argentina	One Argentina Peso = 100 Centavos
Australia	One Australian Dollar = 100 Cents
Austria	One Schilling = 100 Groschen
Bahamas	One Bahamian Dollar = 100 Cents
Bahrain	One Bahrain Dinar = 100 Fils
Bangladesh	One Taka = 100 Paisa
Barbados	One Barbados Dollar = 100 Cents
Belgium	One Belgian Franc = 100 Centimes
Belize	One Belize Dollar = 100 Cents
Benin (Republic of)	Communauté Financière Africaine (CFA) Franc
Bermuda	One Bermuda Dollar = 100 Cents
Bolivia	One Bolivian Peso = 100 Centavos
Botswana	One Pula = 100 Thebe
Brazil	One Cruzeiro = 100 Centavos
Brunei	One Brunei Dollar = 100 Cents
Bulgaria	One Lev = 100 Stotinki
Burma (Socialist Republic of the Union of)	One Kyat = 100 Pyas
Burundi (Republic of)	One Burundi Franc = 100 Centimes
Cameroon (United Republic of)	Communauté Financière Africaine (CFA) Franc
Canada	One Canadian Dollar = 100 Cents
Cape Verde Islands	One Cape Verde Escudo = 100 Centavos
Cayman Islands	One Cayman Dollar = 100 Cents
Central African Republic	Communauté Financière Africaine (CFA) Franc

Country	Currency
Chad (Republic of)	Communauté Financière Africaine (CFA) Franc
Chile	One New Peso = 1000 Escudos
China (People's Republic of)	One Yuan (Renminbi) = 10 Jiao and 1 Jiao = 10 Fen
Colombia	One Peso = 100 Centavos
Comoros (Republic of the)	Communauté Financière Africaine (CFA) Franc
Congo (People's Republic of)	Communauté Financière Africaine (CFA) Franc
Costa Rica	One Costa Rica Colon = 100 Centimos
Cuba	One Cuban Peso = 100 Centavos
Cyprus (Republic of)	One Cyprus Pound = 1000 Mils
Czechoslovakia	One Czech Crown (Koruna) = 100 Hellers
Denmark (including the Faroe Islands and Greenland)	One Danish Crown (Krone) = 100 Oere
Djibouti (Republic of)	Djibouti Francs (related to the USA Dollar)
Dominican Republic	One Dominican Peso Oro = 100 Centavos
Ecuador	One Sucre = 100 Centavos
Egypt (Arab Republic of)	One Egyptian Pound = 100 Piastres = 1000 Millièmes
Equatorial Guinea (Rio Muni and Fernado Poo)	One Ekuele = 100 Centimos
Ethiopia	One Birr = 100 Cents
Falkland Islands and Dependencies	One Falkland Islands Pound = 100 Pence
Fiji Islands	One Fiji Dollar = 100 Cents
Finland	One Markka (Finnmark) = 100 Penniä (Pennies)
France (including Monaco)	One French Franc = 100 Centimes
French Guiana and French Antilles	French Franc
French Polynesia and New Caledonia and Dependencies	Communauté Française du Pacifique (CFP) Franc
Gabon (Republic of)	Communauté Financière Africaine (CFA) Franc
Gambia	One Dalasi = 100 Bututs
German Democratic Republic	One Mark (GDR Mark) = 100 Pfennig
Germany (Federal Republic of)	One Deutsche Mark = 100 Pfennig
Ghana (Republic of)	One Cedi = 100 Pesewas
Gibraltar	One Gibraltar Pound = 100 Pence

Country	Currency
Greece	One Drachma = 100 Lepta
Grenada	One East Caribbean Dollar = 100 Cents
Guatemala	One Quetzal = 100 Centavos
Guinea (Republic of)	One Syli = 100 Couris (Cauris, Cory)
Guinea Bissau	One Escudo = 100 Centavos
Guyana	One Guyanan Dollar = 100 Cents
Haiti	One Gourde = 100 Centimes
Honduras (Republic of)	One Lempira = 100 Centavos
Hong Kong	One Hong Kong Dollar = 100 Cents
Hungary	One Forint = 100 Fillér
Iceland	One Icelandic Crown (Krona) = 100 Aurar (Eyrir)
India	One Indian Rupee = 100 Paise (singular – Paisa)
Indonesia (Republic of)	One Rupiah = 100 Sen
Iran	One Rial = 100 Dinars
Iraq	One Dinar = 1000 Fils
Ireland (Republic of)	One Irish Pound = 100 Pence
Israel	One Shekel = 100 New Agorot (singular – Agora)
Italy	One Lira = 100 Centesimi
Ivory Coast (Republic of)	Communauté Financière Africaine (CFA) Franc
Jamaica	One Jamaican Dollar = 100 Cents
Japan	Yen
Jordan	One Jordan Dinar = 1000 Fils
Kampuchea (Democratic)	One Riel = 100 Sen
Kenya	One Kenya Shilling = 100 Cents
Kiribati (Republic of) (formerly Gilbert Islands)	Australian Dollar
Korea (Democratic People's Republic of)	One Won = 100 Chon
Korea (Republic of)	One Won = 100 Chon
Kuwait	One Kuwaiti Dinar = 1000 Fils
Laos (People's Democratic Republic of)	One Kip = 100 Ats
Lebanon	One Lebanese Pound = 100 Piastres
Lesotho	One Loti = 100 Lisente
Liberia (Republic of)	One Liberian Dollar = 100 Cents
Libya (Libyan Arab Republic)	One Libyan Dinar = 1000 Dirhams
Liechtenstein (Principality of)	One Swiss Franc = 100 Centimes (Rappen)
Luxembourg (Grand-Duchy of)	One Luxembourg Franc = 100 Centimes

Country	Currency
Macao	One Pataca = 100 Avos
Malagasy Republic (Madagascar)	Madagascar Francs (MG.Frs)
Malawi	One Kwacha = 100 Tambala
Malaysia	One Malaysian Ringgitt = 100 Sen
Maldives (Republic of)	One Maldivian Rupee = 100 Larees
Mali (Republic of)	Mali Franc (M.Frs)
Malta	One Maltese Pound = 1000 Mils
Mauritania (Islamic Republic of)	One Ouguiya = 5 Khoums
Mauritius	One Mauritius Rupee = 100 Cents
Mexico	One Mexican Peso = 100 Centavos
Mongolia (People's Republic of)	One Tugrik = 100 Mongo
Morocco (Kingdom of)	One Dirham = 100 Centimes
Mozambique	One Metical = 100 Centavos
Nauru (Republic of)	Australian Dollar
Nepal (Kingdom of)	One Nepalese Rupee = 100 Pice
Netherlands (Holland)	One Guilder (Florin) = 100 Cents
Netherlands Antilles (Netherlands West Indies)	One Antillian Guilder (Florin) or (Netherlands Antilles Florin – NAF) = 100 Cents
New Zealand (including Ross Dependency)	One New Zealand Dollar = 100 Cents
Nicaragua	One Cordoba = 100 Centavos
Niger (Republic of)	Communauté Financière Africaine (CFA) Franc
Nigeria (Federation of)	One Naira = 100 Kobo
Norway	One Krone = 100 Oere
Oman	One Rial Omani = 1000 Baiza
Pakistan	One Pakistan Rupee = 100 Paisa
Panama	One Balboa = 100 Centesimos
Papua New Guinea	One Kina = 100 Toea
Paraguay	One Guarani = 100 Centimos
Peru	One Sol = 100 Centavos
Philippines (Republic of)	One Philippine Peso = 100 Centavos
Poland	One Zloty = 100 Groszy
Portugal (including Azores and Madeira)	One Escudo = 100 Centavos
Puerto Rico (Commonwealth of)	US Dollar
Qatar	One Qatar Riyal = 100 Dirhams
Reunion Island	One French Franc = 100 Centimes
Romania	One Leu = 100 Bani
Rwanda (Republic of)	One Rwanda Franc = 100 Centimes
St Helena Island (including Ascension Island)	Currency rates issued by St Helena Currency Board (with Sterling parity)
El Salvador	One Colon = 100 Centavos

Country	Currency
Sao Tome and Principe	One Dobra = 100 Centimos
Saudi Arabia	One Riyal = 100 Halalas
Senegal (Republic of)	Communauté Financière Africaine (CFA) Franc
Seychelles	One Seychelles Rupee = 100 Cents
Sierra Leone	One Leone = 100 Cents
Singapore (Republic of)	One Singapore Dollar = 100 Cents
Solomon Islands	One Solomon Islands Dollar = 100 Cents
South Africa (Republic of)	One Rand = 100 Cents
Spain (including the Canary Islands, Ceuta and Melilla)	One Peseta = 100 Centimos
Sri Lanka	One Rupee = 100 Cents
Sudan (Republic of the)	One Sudanese Pound = 100 Piastres = 1000 Millièmes
Surinam	One Surinam Guilder (Florin) = 100 Cents
Swaziland	One Lilangeni = 100 Cents
Sweden	One Krona = 100 Oere
Switzerland	One Swiss Franc = 100 Centimes (Rappen)
Syria (Syrian Arab Republic)	One Syrian Pound = 100 Piastres
Taiwan (Republic of China)	One new Taiwan Dollar = 100 Cents
Tanzania (United Republic of Tanganyika, Zanzibar and Pemba)	One Tanzanian Shilling = 100 Cents
Thailand	One Baht = 100 Satang
Togo (Republic of)	Communauté Financière Africaine (CFA) Franc
Tonga (Kingdom of) (Friendly Islands)	One Tonga Dollar (Pa'anga) = 100 Seniti
Trinidad and Tobago	One Trinidad Dollar = 100 Cents
Tunisia (Republic of)	One Tunisian Dinar = 1000 Millimes
Turkey	One Turkish Pound (Lira) = 100 Kurus
Tuvalu	Australian Dollar
Uganda (Republic of)	One Uganda Shilling = 100 Cents
United Arab Emirates	One Dirham = 100 Fils
United Kingdom	One Pound (Sterling) = 100 Pence
United States of America (including Virgin Islands of the USA, Guam, American Samoa and Panama Canal Zone)	One US Dollar = 100 Cents

Country	Currency
Upper Volta (Voltaic Republic)	Communauté Financière Africaine (CFA) Franc
Uruguay	1000 Uruguayan Peso = One New Uruguayan Peso = 100 Centesimos
USSR	One Rouble = 100 Kopecks
Vanuatu (Republic of)	Vatu
Vatican City State	One Lira = 100 Centesimi
Venezuela	One Bolivar = 100 Centimos
Vietnam (Socialist Republic of)	One Dong = 100 Xu
Virgin Islands (British)	US Dollar
West Indies (East Caribbean area)	One East Caribbean Dollar = 100 Cents
Western Samoa	One Tala = 100 Senes
Yemen Arab Republic	One Riyal = 100 Fils
Yemen (People's Democratic Republic of	One South Yemen Dinar = 1000 Fils
Yugoslavia	One Dinar = 100 Paras
Zaire (Republic of)	One Zaire = 100 Makuta = 10 000 Sengi
Zambia	One Kwacha = 100 Ngwee
Zimbabwe	One Zimbabwe Dollar = 100 Cents

Index